Essays on Balance of Payments Constrained Growth

There are many theories of why output growth rates differ between countries. Mainstream, orthodox growth theory focuses on the supply side of the economy. An alternative approach is to consider factors of production and productivity growth as largely endogenous to demand, and to focus on demand constraints. In open economies, the balance of payments and foreign exchange are often a serious constraint.

The contributions in this book contain various theoretical papers which develop the model of balance of payments constrained growth, and then apply it to analyse the long-run growth performance of several developed and developing countries.

The book will be of interest to all economists and policy makers interested in the differential growth performance of nations, and the link between trade, the balance of payments and economic growth.

J. S. L. McCombie is a Fellow in Economics at Downing College, Cambridge, and the Director of the Centre for Economic and Public Policy at the Department of Land Economy, the University of Cambridge.

A. P. Thirlwall is Professor of Applied Economics at the University of Kent, UK. He has been an advisor to several government departments, and a consultant to many international development organisations.

Routledge studies in development economics

Essays on Balance of Payments Constrained Growth

Theory and evidence

**J. S. L. McCombie and
A. P. Thirlwall**

Routledge
Taylor & Francis Group

LONDON AND NEW YORK

First published 2004
by Routledge
11 New Fetter Lane, London EC4P 4EE

Simultaneously published in the USA and Canada
by Routledge
29 West 35th Street, New York, NY 10001

Routledge is an imprint of the Taylor & Francis Group

Typeset in Times by
Newgen Imaging Systems (P) Ltd, Chennai, India
Printed and bound in Great Britain by
Antony Rowe Ltd, Chippenham, Wiltshire

British Library Cataloguing in Publication Data
A catalogue record for this book is available from the British Library

Library of Congress Cataloging in Publication Data
A catalog record for this book has been requested

ISBN 0–415–32631–1

Contents

Figures

Tables

Contributors

José A. Alonso is Professor of Applied Economics at Universidad Complutense de Madrid, Spain.

P. S. Andersen was at the Bank for International Settlements, Basle, Switzerland.*

M. Ansari is Professor of Economics at Albany State University, USA.

Nelson H. Barbosa-Filho is at the Instituto do Economia, Universidade Federal do Rio de Janeiro, Brazil.

Robert A. Blecker is Professor of Economics at the American University, Washington, DC, USA.

Alberto Cruz B. is at the Universidad Nacional Autónoma de México, Mexico.

Carlos Garcimartín is at the Universidad de Salamanca, Spain.

N. Hashemzadeh is Professor of Economics at Radford University, Virginia, USA.

Miguel A. León-Ledesma is at the University of Kent at Canterbury, UK.

Julio López G. is Professor of Economics at the Universidad Nacional Autónoma de México, Mexico.

J. S. L. McCombie is a Fellow in Economics, Downing College, Cambridge, UK.

Juan Carlos Moreno-Brid is at the Economic Commission for Latin America and the Caribbean, Mexico.

Kevin Nell is at the Catholic University of Porto, Portugal.

M. Nureldin Hussain is at the African Development Bank, Tunisia.

Esteban Pérez is at the Economic Commission for Latin America and the Caribbean, Mexico.

Jonathan Perraton is at the University of Sheffield, UK.

Maurizio Pugno is Professor of Economics at the University of Trento, Italy.

---

* At the time of the original publication of the paper.

A. P. Thirlwall is Professor of Applied Economics at the University of Kent at Canterbury, UK.

Y. Xi is in the Office of Statistics and Programming, NCICP, Atlanta, USA.

Acknowledgements

The authors and publisher are grateful to the editors and publishers of: *Oxford Economic Papers*; *Journal of Post Keynesian Economics*; *International Review of Applied Economics*; *Banca Nazionale del Lavoro Quarterly Review*; *Applied Economics*; *African Development Review*, and *Applied Economics* for permission to reproduce the edited versions of articles previously published in their Journals.

1   Introduction

J. S. L. McCombie and A. P. Thirlwall

The orthodox, mainstream (classical and neoclassical) approach to the analysis of the growth performance of countries is to focus on resource availability and the supply of factor inputs, and to explain growth rate differences between countries in these terms. Heavy emphasis is placed on capital accumulation and technical progress. It should be obvious, however, that resource availability itself is not a sufficient condition for growth because resources may be unemployed or under-utilised. It should be equally apparent that most resources for growth are not fixed in supply, or exogenously given to an economic system, which conventional growth and trade theory tends to assume. Most resources for growth, such as the quantity and quality of labour inputs, capital accumulation and improved productivity through technical progress, are elastic in supply and endogenous to an economic system, dependent on the growth of output itself. This insight provides the starting point for the debate between those who believe that growth is supply driven (and analyse growth in this way) and those who believe that growth is demand driven, and that it is constraints on demand – be they economic or institutional – that explain growth rate differences between countries. One major economic constraint is the availability of foreign exchange. If a balance of payments deficit, or foreign exchange shortage, is not automatically eliminated through a change in the relative prices of domestic and foreign goods, it immediately becomes a constraint on demand if the deficit cannot be indefinitely financed at a constant rate of interest, and will therefore affect the growth process. This is the basic thesis of this book of essays, which elaborates theoretically, and supports empirically, the central proposition that it is impossible to understand differences in the long-run economic performance of nations without reference to the balance of payments. Before turning to the essays, however, the reasons why orthodoxy ignores the link between trade, the balance of payments and growth needs to be understood.

One reason is that mainstream economists have an abiding faith in the price system which leads them to believe that the balance of payments is self-equilibrating through internal or external relative price movements. In particular, if the exchange rate is endogenous to the current account, a balance of payments deficit can never be a constraint on output growth because currency depreciation will increase the value of exports and/or decrease the value of imports.

Second, it is argued that, in any case, most countries (and particularly developing countries) satisfy the 'small country' assumption of trade theory, and face infinitely elastic demand curves for their output in world markets, so they can sell any amount of goods at the going world price as long as they can supply. Growth performance, therefore, has nothing to do with the balance of payments. It is a supply problem, not a demand problem.

Third, many influential growth models, including the Harrod (1939) and Solow (1956) models, and much so-called 'new' growth theory, are closed economy models, where the balance of payments is not an issue. In models where trade features, it is the *real* effects that are considered, not the monetary effects. Trade brings dynamic supply-side benefits by stimulating domestic and foreign investment, which in turn generate internal and external economies of scale (Wacziarg, 2001).

Fourth, modern theories of the determination of the current account balance of payments focus on its role as a buffer against transitory disturbances to output and demand. In the small open economy version of the Ramsey model, for example (see Blanchard and Fischer, 1989), transitory disturbances affect savings rather than consumption, so that a current account deficit simply represents consumption smoothing, and has no real long-term effects on growth (Obstfeld and Rogoff, 1995).

Fifth, and related to the above, is the view that the current deficit is merely the mirror image of a surplus on the capital account, and therefore current deficits are a sign of economic strength rather than underlying weakness, otherwise capital would not flow into deficit countries.

Serious doubt can be cast on all of these propositions. It is not true, as the orthodoxy claims, that relative price, or exchange rate, movements are an efficient balance of payments adjustment weapon, or that demand curves facing countries in international trade are infinitely elastic. A whole variety of supply and demand conditions have to be met for exchange rate changes to rectify a balance of payments deficit, and most international trade is in differentiated goods with less than infinitely elastic demand curves facing them. Nor is it the case, for the most part, that deficits are simply temporary, reflecting consumption smoothing. At acceptable growth rates, to ensure rising living standards, deficits in many countries (and particularly developing countries) are persistent, relating to the structure of trade, with imports being more income elastic than exports. Finally, the argument that current account deficits are simply a reflection of capital inflows fails to distinguish between *autonomous*, long-term flows and *accommodating*, short-term flows. The latter, which predominate, pose severe problems for countries in terms of the interest rate that has to be paid to attract them, and their potential volatility and consequent disruption to the domestic economy.

The orthodox view of growth and trade

The neglect of the balance of payments and demand in the theory of growth goes back a long way in the history of economics. Classical growth theory, as epitomised by Ricardo, was a supply-oriented model. Profits determined investment, and investment determined growth. The pervasive classical belief in Say's Law that 'supply creates its own demand' implied that all output produced would be sold, and all resources would be fully employed. The fact that industry would have to sell ('exports') to agriculture to obtain wage (or consumption) goods ('imports') for workers was assumed to present no problems because any imbalance between the supply of, and demand for, 'exports' and 'imports' would be rectified by adjustment of the internal terms of trade.

Keynes (1936), in his *General Theory*, undermined Say's Law in the static closed economy and showed that output is not determined by supply but by effective demand, which may, within limits, generate its own supply. In the growing closed economy, Harrod (1939) then showed that there was no automatic mechanism which ensured that a country would necessarily grow at its assumed capacity rate, which he called the natural rate of growth. Plans to save may exceed the rate of *induced* investment at the natural rate, leading to secular stagnation. Not only the level of output, but also the growth of output, is determined by demand, not by available supplies. It is true that the natural rate of growth in the Harrod model sets the *upper* limit to growth (and in this sense, growth is supply determined), but there is nothing to say that the natural rate of growth is immutable and independent of demand (see Leon-Ledesma and Thirlwall, 2002). Neither Keynes in *The General Theory*, nor Harrod in his dynamic extension of Keynes's theory, explicitly addressed themselves to the open economy and the possibility that an imbalance between plans to export and import may present as much of a problem for demand as divergences between domestic plans to save and invest.[1]

Not only did classical growth theory ignore demand,[2] but classical trade theory also ignored the balance of payments. In classical economics, much emphasis is given to the importance of trade for growth, but it is all *real* theory, and again supply oriented. The monetary consequences of trade for growth are ignored. Ricardo invented the doctrine of comparative advantage which shows that countries specialising in what they are best at producing in an opportunity cost sense can increase total production and, by trading, improve the welfare of all. His was a very powerful and influential theorem, but it is based on several special and restrictive assumptions. One assumption is full employment; another is continuous balance of payments equilibrium. The full employment assumption is crucial to the predictions of the theorem, because if unemployment were to arise in the process of specialisation and resource reallocation, the resource gains from specialisation might be offset by resource losses from unemployment, and the mutual profitability of the free trade argument breaks down.

More important for the argument here, however, is the neglect of the effect of the structure and pattern of trade on the balance of payments of a country, because in classical theory the balance of payments is assumed to be self-equilibrating. If the balance of payments is not self-adjusting, however, this is another reason why unemployment may develop, and why trade and growth cannot be looked at simply from the point of view of the augmentation of the supply of resources. Early classical thinking was based on the price-specie flow mechanism outlined by David Hume (1752). Gold movements were the instrument by which payments balance was supposed to be achieved. Countries with a payments deficit would lose gold, causing an internal price deflation which would induce a rise in exports and a fall in imports, and the opposite for surplus countries. Continuous balance of payments equilibrium and full employment is maintained. More refined versions of the gold standard story were developed in the late nineteenth century when the operation of the system was at its zenith, recognising the fact that in practice no gold standard country operated a rigid 100 per cent reserve monetary system backed by gold. Fiduciary issues of currency were permitted. But a fixed relation between the monetary base and the total quantity of money was assumed so that the theory of balance of payments adjustment stayed essentially the same. The model was also extended to capital flows where gold moved in the same direction as the capital transfer, and the trade surplus in the country 'exporting' capital was the real counterpart of the capital transfer. Again, there was no adjustment of income or output. Monetary historians (e.g. Triffin, 1964; McClosky and Zecher 1976; Cooper 1982) have noted, however, that instead of the price levels of deficit and surplus countries moving in *opposite* directions, there was a tendency in the nineteenth century for countries' price levels to move together. In practice, it was not relative price changes that operated to achieve payments balance, but expenditure and output changes associated with interest rate differentials. Capital importing countries (in current account deficit) with high interest rates had expenditure damped relative to capital exporting countries (in current account surplus) with lower interest rates. Income adjustment is therefore implied. Even as late as the 1930s, however, very few economists were teaching this story. One notable exception was P. Barrett Whale at the London School of Economics (see Barrett Whale, 1932, 1937).

Notwithstanding the Keynesian revolution, and the manifest balance of payments difficulties experienced by many countries, the prevailing orthodoxy is still to analyse growth from the supply side. This is epitomised in the neoclassical approach to the analysis of growth and in the more recent 'new', or endogenous, growth theory. The neoclassical approach uses the aggregate production function and attempts to explain the growth of output in terms of the growth of factor inputs and their productivity. Differences in the growth of output between countries are thus accounted for in terms of differences in the rates of growth of labour inputs, capital accumulation and technical progress as the determinant of productivity growth. Major empirical studies that have used this approach include Denison (1967), Young (1995), and Senhadji (2000). Unfortunately, however, the approach does not answer the fundamental question of *why* factor supplies and productivity grow at different rates between countries. The approach treats factors of production and technical progress as essentially exogenous to an economic system, whereas in practice what is happening to the growth of the labour force, capital accumulation and technical progress is to a large extent endogenous to an economic system since their growth depends, at least in part, on the strength of demand. The response of labour supply to demand comes through higher participation rates; the absorption of surplus labour; longer hours worked, and immigration. Capital accumulation has a large induced element through the accelerator mechanism. We know also from studies of productivity growth that through the mechanism of static and dynamic returns to scale, productivity growth is induced by output growth itself – the so-called Verdoorn Law (see McCombie *et al.*, 2003). So we are back to the question of what determines output growth? In neoclassical growth analysis, demand constraints – either internal or external through the balance of payments – never enter the picture in an explicit manner. Long-run growth is determined by the rate of growth of the labour force in efficiency units, exogenously determined.

'New' growth theory, or endogenous growth theory, retains all the essential features of the neoclassical approach to growth except that the assumption of diminishing returns to capital is relaxed. The specification of the equations for testing neoclassical and 'new' growth theory also look suspiciously similar (Thirlwall, 2003). If the marginal product of capital does not decline as more investment takes place, the investment ratio becomes a determinant of long-run growth. In this sense, growth is said to be endogenous. The question then is: what are the forces that prevent the marginal product of capital from falling as countries get richer and invest more? Some models stress the role of research and development (Romer, 1986); others stress the role of human capital formation (Lucas, 1988). But it is clear from the definition of the capital–output ratio (which is equal to the capital–labour ratio divided by the productivity of labour) that anything which raises the productivity of labour in the same proportion as the capital–labour ratio will keep the capital–output ratio, or the productivity of capital, unchanged. Embodied technical progress of all kinds (including learning by doing) is sufficient, as Kaldor (1957) pointed out in his early growth model which included the innovation of the technical progress function to replace the neoclassical production function. None of the 'new' growth theory models address the issue of demand. Savings determine investment, and aggregate demand equals aggregate supply.

Most of the models of endogenous growth are also closed economy models. Where trade is included (see Grossman and Helpman, 1991) it is to capture the technological spillovers from trade which may also keep the marginal product of capital from falling as capital accumulation takes place. In the empirical studies to test 'new' growth theory, trade is usually measured as the ratio of trade to GDP as a measure of the openness of an economy. Sometimes the variable is statistically significant, but often it is fragile (Levine and Renelt, 1992). One statistical problem seems to be that investment performance is closely correlated with the measure of openness. From an economic viewpoint, however, the ratio of trade to GDP is a very static measure of the potential role of trade in the growth process. To capture the dynamic effects of trade from both the demand side and the supply side, the *growth of exports* would be a much more appropriate variable to take, and, indeed, it turns out to be highly significant (Thirlwall and Sanna, 1996). Exports are important from the demand side both directly and indirectly because they allow other components of demand to grow faster than otherwise would be the case in accordance with the Hicks supermultiplier (McCombie, 1985a: see chapter 5). Exports are the only component of demand that can pay for the import requirements associated with growth. Export growth is important from the supply side because it allows a faster growth of imports, and imports may be more productive than domestic resources, particularly if they allow a fuller use of resources by relaxing a balance of payments constraint on demand.

Challenges to orthodoxy

In the history of thought, the only school to have emphasised the importance of foreign exchange, and a strong balance of payments, for economic growth was the Mercantilists. The English Mercantilists of the sixteenth and seventeenth century (e.g. Misselden, 1623; Mun, 1664) recognised with great clarity and prescience that the strength of a country's balance of payments may affect its level of activity. Economies do not necessarily operate continuously at full employment, and money is not neutral. In particular, when the balance of payments is in surplus, and money is plentiful due to inflows of precious metals, the rate of interest will be low, which will be a stimulus to investment and enterprise. Contrariwise, when the balance of payments is in deficit, and a country is losing reserves, the rate of interest will tend to be high, discouraging the process of capital accumulation and depressing growth.

The mercantilist belief that countries can become rich by generating balance of trade surpluses and accumulating foreign exchange (gold) is supposed to have been first and decisively exposed as fallacious by David Hume's essays 'Of Money' and 'Of the Balance of Trade' which outlined the crude quantity theory of money that an increase in precious metals will simply raise the price level proportionately with no effects on the real economy. The neutrality of money argument, however, is premised on the assumptions that the rate of interest is a real phenomenon, not a monetary phenomenon, and that there is full employment so that no increase in output is possible. The Mercantilists recognised, by contrast, that the rate of interest is partly a monetary phenomenon, and that it may be too high to secure full employment. As Keynes put it in *The General Theory*, mercantilist thought never supposed, as later economists did, that there was a self-adjusting tendency by which the rate of interest would be established at the appropriate level (to equate savings and investment at full employment). It was, indeed, Keynes's view that throughout history the propensity to save has been greater than the propensity to invest, and that uncertainty, and the desire for liquidity, has in general made the rate of interest too high. In response to a comment by Harrod on drafts of *The General Theory* (see Moggridge, 1973), Keynes replied: 'What I want is to do justice to schools of thought which the classicals have treated as imbeciles for the last hundred years and, above all, to show that I am not really being so great an innovator, except as against the classical school, but have important predecessors and am returning to an age long tradition of common sense.' Keynes then concludes his partial defence of mercantilism in *The General Theory* by saying:

> the methods of the early pioneers of economic thinking in the 16th and 17th centuries may have attained the fragments of practical wisdom which the

unrealistic abstractions of Ricardo first forgot and then obliterated. There was wisdom in their intense preoccupation with keeping down the domestic rate of interest by means of usury laws – by maintaining the domestic stock of money and by discouraging rises in the wage unit; and in their readiness in the last resort to restore the stock of money by devaluation, if it had become plainly deficient through an unavoidable foreign drain, a rise in the wage unit or any other cause.

In more recent times, a handful of eminent economists has highlighted foreign exchange as a scarce resource which may not be easily substitutable by domestic savings, but their voices have not constituted a coherent school of thought. Raul Prebisch (1950), in thinking about the problems of developing countries, challenged the doctrine of the mutual profitability of free trade by arguing that the gains from specialisation in primary production may be offset by the balance of payments consequences of such specialisation, but his argument for viewing trade from a monetary standpoint, rather than from the viewpoint of real resource augmentation, was too unorthodox for the profession to grasp. Hollis Chenery and his collaborators (e.g. Chenery and Bruno, 1962; Chenery and Adelman, 1966) developed the concept of dual-gap analysis, also in a development context, which showed that if the foreign exchange gap to achieve a target rate of growth was greater than a domestic savings–investment gap, foreign flows would need to fill the larger of the two gaps, otherwise growth would be constrained by the most limiting resource (that is, foreign exchange), and domestic savings would go unutilised. This idea was also attacked by the neoclassical orthodoxy on the grounds that it ignores the substitution possibilities between imports of consumption and investment goods, and between domestic savings and foreign exchange. Excess domestic saving can be used to produce more exports. In the long run, a separate foreign exchange gap is impossible.

It was Harrod, however, who first introduced explicitly the idea of the foreign trade multiplier (i.e. income adjustment as opposed to relative price adjustment) as the mechanism by which a country's balance of payments is brought back into equilibrium in his book *International Economics*, published in 1933, which thus predates Keynes's savings–investment multiplier for the closed economy (although not its precursors, e.g. Kahn, 1931; Warming, 1932). Up to the First World War, balance of payments adjustment theory was dominated by the gold standard mechanism, and the idea that a country's balance of payments would adjust through relative price movements induced by gold flows (as described earlier). The underlying presumptions of the model were that economies somehow maintained a continuous state of full employment and that the aggregate price level was determined by the quantity of money. Harrod drew attention to the fact that classical theory assumed full employment, but the flow of gold clearly cannot automatically secure both a balance of trade and a full level of employment: 'Some determining force must have been left out of account.' He notes that 'it was not characteristic of classical thought to pay much attention to the level of activity', and that 'the failure of the classical theory is not due to any logical inadequacy, but only to the fact that its logic requires the postulate that full employment in any event is maintained'.

Harrod says he wants to consider the deeper question of the forces which tend to keep the balance of trade balanced in the long run. The exponents of traditional theory believed that if a country is in deficit, gold flows would proceed until rewards to factors of production are sufficiently reduced to restore equilibrium. By the workings of the foreign trade multiplier, Harrod shows that 'even if rewards in home industries are not reduced, a balance of trade will automatically be secured without the intervention of a gold flow'. Thus, the traditional theory is without foundation.

In the simple case with no government, and no saving and investment, income is produced by the production of home consumption goods (C) and exports (X), and income is disposed of by expenditure on home consumption goods (C) and imports (M). Thus, trade is always balanced ($X = M$). With no change in relative prices (or the real terms of trade), an autonomous change in exports or imports will change the level of income so as to bring exports and imports into line with each other again. This is the principle of the multiplier mechanism. In this simple case, the foreign trade multiplier is the reciprocal of the marginal propensity to import ($1/\mu$), analogous to Keynes's closed economy multiplier of $1/s$ which equilibrates saving and investment, where s is the marginal propensity to save.[3] Harrod recognises that his analysis relates only to a static equilibrium, whether of the short or the long period. He leaves to be developed the implications for output growth; what we now call the dynamic Harrod trade multiplier (see Thirlwall, 2001).

Even the concept of the static Harrod foreign trade multiplier lay dormant for over forty years until Kaldor revived it first in his controversial Harvard Lecture 'What is Wrong with Economy Theory' (Kaldor, 1975) and then, closer to home, in a letter to *The Times* in 1977 (12 September). Kaldor was responding to an article written by two economists in the UK Department of Trade and Industry (Wells and Imber, 1977) who questioned the seriousness of Britain's balance of payments problem by pointing out that although there had been a marked increase in import penetration in manufacturing industry, this had been matched by an equal rise in the ratio of exports to output. Kaldor accused the authors of being 'guilty of an economic howler which might have cost them dear if they had made it in a [Cambridge] Tripos examination'. Kaldor goes on:

> The fact that the rise in the proportion of exports in the national output fully matches the rise in the proportion of imports in home sales overall is an automatic consequence of the operation of the 'foreign trade multiplier'; and so far from providing a refutation of the case for import controls, it provides the strongest possible support for it. For it shows that the Harrod theory really works, and that any rise in the share of imports in total domestic expenditure causes a fall in demand for home output, which in turn leads to a reduction in both consumption and investment in successive steps until a sufficient contraction occurs in the gross domestic product relative to exports to make the spontaneous rise in the one ratio be matched by an induced increase in the other.

This is one of the most eloquent statements of the Harrod trade multiplier theory; and, of course, Kaldor is correct: it is impossible to measure the seriousness of a country's balance of payments situation independent of the level of employment and output (or a country's growth rate in a dynamic context).

Seven years earlier, Kaldor (1970) had put forward a 'cumulative' export-led growth model comprising four equations: (i) output growth as a function of export growth; (ii) export growth as a function of changes in relative prices (competitiveness) and world income growth; (iii) relative price changes as a function of wage growth and productivity growth; and (iv) productivity growth as a function of output growth (Verdoorn's Law). The model is 'circular and cumulative' (to use Myrdal's, 1957, terminology) because the faster export growth, the faster is the output growth, but the faster the output growth, the faster export growth because output growth improves competitiveness through Verdoorn's Law. Five years later, Dixon and Thirlwall (1975) formalised the model, but reasonable parameter variables for the model seriously overpredicted the growth rate of the UK economy for the period 1951–66. One explanation given was that the United Kingdom experienced a severe balance of payments constraint on growth, and the Kaldor model contained no balance of payments equilibrium requirement. It became clear, however, that if balance of payments equilibrium (however measured) is a long-run requirement, growth should be modelled within such a framework (Thirlwall 1979). Doing so, and using the same assumption as Harrod that the real terms of trade remain constant, gives the result that $g = x/\pi$, where g is the growth of output; x is the growth of export volume, and π is the income elasticity of demand for imports. This can be seen to be the dynamic analogue of the static Harrod trade multiplier result, $Y = X/\mu$,[4] where Y is the level of income; X is the level of export, and μ is the marginal propensity to import.

In this brief period 1977–79, the static Harrod trade multiplier was revived, and the dynamic Harrod trade multiplier was born. Paul Davidson (1990–91) has heralded the development of the dynamic Harrod trade multiplier as one of the most significant contributions to Post-Keynesian theory in its demonstration that 'international payments imbalances can have severe real growth consequences, i.e. money is not neutral in an open economy'.

Tests of the model

The test of the model is to see how closely the dynamic Harrod trade multiplier, or $g = x/\pi$, predicts the actual long-run growth rate of countries. There are at least four basic tests of the model.

The first is to do a rank correlation across countries between the actual growth rate and that predicted by the dynamic Harrod trade multiplier result. The rank correlation is typically over 0.7. In the original study by Thirlwall (1979) for eighteen developed countries over the two separate time periods 1951–73 and 1953–76, the rank correlations were 0.891 and 0.764, respectively. In a study of fifty-nine developing countries over the period 1970–84, Perraton (1990) obtains a Spearman rank correlation of 0.67, significant at the 99 per cent confidence level.

This is not a parametric test, however, and can be rightly criticised on the grounds that it does not show how close the model predicts the actual growth rate.

A second test, which overcomes the latter objection, is to take the average deviation of the actual growth rate from the predicted rate, ignoring sign. When this is done, the average deviation in most studies turns out to be less than one percentage point. In Thirlwall's original study, the average deviation was 0.63 percentage points (p.p.) for the period 1951–73 and 0.89 p.p. for the period 1953–76 (excluding Japan and South Africa). In a study by Bairam and Dempster (1991) for eleven Asian countries over the period 1961–85, the difference between the actual and predicted growth rate is less than one percentage point for seven of the countries. In a time series study for the US by Atesoglu (1993), taking overlapping 16-year periods from 1955–70 to 1975–90, the average deviation for 21 years is 0.38 p.p. In a similar study for Germany (Atesoglu, 1994), the average difference is 0.22 p.p. In a study by Andersen (1993) of sixteen developed countries over the period 1960–90, the average difference between actual and predicted growth is 0.7 p.p. (1960–73), 0.3 p.p. (1973–80), and 0.7 p.p. (1980–90). These are just some examples from a selection of the studies.

This test of the predictive power of the model, however, while impressive and persuasive, is not, a parametric test either. There are more precise statistical ways of answering the question of how close is close? There are basically two formal parametric tests of whether the dynamic Harrod trade multiplier result, or what is also called the balance of payments equilibrium growth rate (g_B), is a good predictor of the actual growth rate (g). The first is to regress g on g_B and to test whether the constant of the regression is significantly different from zero and the regression coefficient is significantly different from unity. If both tests are confirmed, g_B will be a good predictor of g. The test, however, has three drawbacks. First, there may be a bias if an incomplete sample of countries is taken, in which balance of payments surpluses and deficits do not cancel out (i.e. if there is a systematic tendency across the countries taken for $g_B > g$, or $g_B < g$). Second, if there are serious outliers where g does not equal g_B (such as Japan which, for most of the post-war years, has run large balance of payments surpluses with g_B considerably in excess of g), the inclusion of such countries in the sample may produce a regression coefficient significantly different from unity, erroneously leading to a rejection of the model for all countries. Third, the estimate of the income elasticity of demand for imports (π), which is used to calculate the predicted growth rate (g_B), has an associated standard error because it is estimated from a regression equation used to estimate the import demand function (which also includes relative prices as an independent variable, as well as domestic income). A better procedure would be to regress g_B on g, but this does not avoid the first two problems.

A second parametric test which avoids all these difficulties, originally suggested by McCombie (1989), is to take each country separately and to estimate the income elasticity of demand for imports that would make $g = g_B$, and to compare this estimate (π^*) with the estimated π from the time-series regression analysis for the country under consideration. If π^* does not differ significantly from π, then g

and g_B will not differ significantly either. When this test is performed on various samples of countries, the model is supported in the vast majority of cases, as we shall come to see in the various essays in the book.

Before proceeding to a brief description of the essays gathered in this book, it is important to reassure readers in advance that the dynamic Harrod trade multiplier result that growth will approximate to $g_B = x/\pi$ (or $g_B = \varepsilon z/\pi$, where z is the growth of world income and ε is the income elasticity of demand for exports) is not a tautology, arising from an identity, as has been sometimes suggested.[5] A typical example of such an erroneous argument is as follows: if the income elasticities of demand for imports and exports are defined as m/g and x/z, respectively, where m is the growth of imports, it follows that $g_B = xg/m$. If balance of payments equilibrium is a requirement so that $x = m$ (starting from equilibrium), then g and g_B must be equal.

The first point to make is that the estimates of π and ε are *not* definitionally derived as m/g and x/z, but are estimated from import and export demand functions specified as behavioural relationships which include variables other than income growth (including a measure of relative prices in international trade). If the neoclassical law of one price held, and demand curves facing countries were infinitely elastic, the coefficients on the domestic and world income variables should be statistically insignificant and the price elasticities should be (infinitely) large. In these circumstances, there would be no relationship between g and g_B.

Second, there is no reason a priori why the estimates of the income elasticities should be significantly different from zero, irrespective of whether a price term is included in the equations, bearing in mind they are estimated using time series data. Furthermore, it could be, even if relative prices were statistically insignificant, that the income elasticities, while statistically well-determined, showed little numerical variation between countries. If this was the case, their use could not explain disparities in growth rates between countries. In these circumstances, g_B would not differ between countries, and in most cases would not closely approximate g. This would occur, for example, if differences in non-price competitiveness were not being captured by the values of the two income elasticities.

Third, there would be no relationship between g_B and g if current account equilibrium was not a long-run requirement and international capital flows played a quantitatively significant role in the balance of payments adjustment process.

Bearing in mind all these points, the fact that g approximates to g_B in the majority of case studies that we shall be examining is evidence that we are not dealing with a tautology, but that the underlying assumptions of the model turn out to be verified; namely, that countries cannot continue to accumulate international debt (there is a limit to the deficit or debt to GDP ratio), and that relative price changes combined with the price elasticity of demand for imports (and exports if εz rather than x is the numerator of the equation) are not an efficient balance of payments adjustment weapon. It is income growth that adjusts to equilibrate the balance of payments. In our view, a country with g slightly above g_B for most of the time, with persistent deficits, that goes into payments crisis every time it tries to grow faster, when it has underutilised domestic resources, is *prima facie* balance of payments constrained in its growth performance. As long as there are big surplus countries such as (today) Japan, the European Union and some oil producers, this description would fit a large number of countries, particularly in the developing world.

The studies in this book

The essays are divided into three parts. The first part contains the original contributions to the theory of the dynamic Harrod trade multiplier made by the present authors, plus some of the important subsequent theoretical developments of the model. The second part contains empirical chapters that apply the model to developed countries, while the third section contains tests of the model relating to developing countries where capital flows and terms of trade (or real exchange rate) movements may be potentially more significant as determinants of growth performance.

The second chapter is Thirlwall's original (1979) derivation of 'the balance of payments equilibrium growth rate', or what is now known as the dynamic Harrod trade multiplier result. Growth is modelled within the constraint that, in the long run, current account equilibrium on the balance of payments is a requirement. Using standard (multiplicative, constant elasticity) import and export demand functions, and assuming relative prices measured in a common currency remain unchanged, yields the growth formula that output growth equals the growth of export volume (determined by income growth outside the country and the income elasticity of demand for exports) divided by the income elasticity of demand for imports.

In Chapter 3, Thirlwall and Hussain (1982) extend the model to allow for capital flows on the grounds that at least many developing countries seem to run payments deficits over considerable periods of time, so that the simple dynamic Harrod trade multiplier result may not be a good predictor of growth performance even in the long run. Also, real terms of trade (or real exchange rate) changes are more pervasive in developing countries than in developed countries. No limit to the debt to GDP ratio is imposed, however, which is a weakness of the model, subsequently remedied by McCombie and Thirlwall (1997a), Moreno-Brid (1998b) and Barbosa-Filho (2001).

McCombie shows in Chapter 4 that the dynamic Harrod trade multiplier result can be thought of as a reduced form model of the Hicks super-multiplier model because export growth allows all other components of demand to grow faster than otherwise would be the case because exports can pay for the import content of investment, consumption, government expenditure, and exports themselves. It is shown that exports are an important determinant of the growth of output even for those countries (such as the US) where exports constitute only a small proportion of GDP. On certain assumptions, it is possible to disaggregate the growth of output attributable to the different components of demand.

In Chapter 5, McCombie extends the basic model to allow for trade interlink-ages between countries, and it is shown how the economic performance of one group of countries may, through the workings of the balance of payments, con-strain the growth of other nations and limit the degree of control that the latter have over their economies. Attempts by any one country to relax its balance of pay-ments constraint by expenditure switching policies, such as devaluation or import controls, may lead to 'competitive' growth, that is, an increase in output at the expense of another country's production. This, in turn, may lead to retaliation. An implication of the model is that the most effective way to raise growth (and reduce unemployment) in the face of balance of payments constraints, is for countries to generate 'complementary' growth through co-ordinated action. Even in these cir-cumstances, however, certain countries may become resource constrained before others have reached their full employment growth rates.

Blecker in Chapter 6 is also concerned with adjustment mechanisms and devel-ops a model which combines the analysis of balance of payments constrained growth with the hypothesis of mark-up pricing (à la Kalecki) and partial exchange rate pass-through in order to make explicit the link between balance of payments equilibrium and changes in relative wages and living standards. It is shown that the dynamic Harrod trade multiplier result (with income adjusting) and the traditional neoclassical approach of price adjustment are two poles of a continuum of options available to a country in balance of payments disequilibrium. The model is used to analyse the circumstances under which different combinations of the exchange rate and income adjustment may be used to reconcile a country's balance of payments constrained growth rate with its capacity (natural) growth rate in order to avoid unemployment. Which type of adjustment is optimal in practice is an empirical question, but Blecker concludes that continuous real exchange rate adjustment is not feasible for most countries. The issue is also considered of whether real wage flexibility internally can simultaneously guarantee balanced trade and full employment, and it is concluded that it cannot in the absence of fiscal policy or other stimuli.

In Chapter 7, Pugno looks closely at the dynamics of the model and the under-lying structure necessary to explain dynamic stability. He correctly points out that the simple model predicts steady-state growth (with all variables growing at the same constant rate) disregarding both the size of the deficit or surplus on the balance of payments and the difference in the *level* of prices between countries. Pugno redefines the steady state as zero external balance (rather than any constant balance) and equality between export prices and foreign prices (rather than by a constant ratio between them) and shows that the growth path to equilibrium may be a cyclical one. The mechanisms through which a steady-state solution are arrived at in the long run include Phillips Curve behaviour in the labour market and some flexibility of the real exchange rate.

To complete the section on theory, in Chapter 8 Barbosa-Filho takes the extended model with capital flows and introduces two innovations. First, in the analysis of debt accumulation, he separates interest payments from imports of goods and non-factor services. Second, he allows for a 'sustainable' accumulation of foreign debt taking into account both the potential instability of capital flows and the impact of interest payments on debt accumulation. While the analysis is purely theoretical, the author says that he was inspired to write the chapter by the recent experience of Brazil where fluctuations in foreign lending are a major determinant of macroeconomic policy and growth, and where the trade balance adjusts residually by income adjustment to the maximum ratio of foreign debt to income that the international financial markets will allow before declaring the country uncreditworthy.

In the first essay (Chapter 9) in the empirical section on developed countries, McCombie starts by reviewing the robustness of the various methods that can be used to test how closely the growth rate of countries approximates to the dynamic Harrod multiplier result. He then discusses the most recent developments in time-series econometrics, and uses some of these new techniques, including cointegration, to re-examine the evidence for balance of payments constrained growth in the United States, the United Kingdom and Japan. He confirms that over much of the post-war period, the balance of payments equilibrium growth rate has been a good predictor of US and UK growth rates, but Japan has grown more slowly than its equilibrium rate, which is consistent with the accumulation of large balance of payments surpluses.

Andersen (in Chapter 10) tests the model for sixteen European countries over the period 1960–90, including different sub-periods, with and without Japan in the sample. Cointegration techniques are applied to estimate the export and import demand equations. The estimated income elasticities are similar to those found for other studies, but the price elasticities are very low, with the Marshall–Lerner condition satisfied for only a few of the countries. The one-to-one relationship (the 45°-rule) between the actual growth rate and the balance of payments equilibrium growth rate is confirmed for the long run when Japan (an outlier) is excluded from the sample.

Alonso and Garcimartín bring out clearly in Chapter 11 the fundamental difference between the neoclassical and Keynesian approach to the analysis of growth and the mechanism through which the balance of payments is assumed to adjust to equilibrium. In neoclassical theory it is relative price changes, and in Keynesian theory it is income. As an alternative approach to the analysis of balance of payments constrained growth, the authors therefore suggest testing a system of equations in which relative prices are endogenous compared with the alternative of income growth being endogenous. Tests are performed over a group of ten OECD countries for the period 1965–94 and show that the income adjustment parameter is significantly different from zero in eight of the ten countries, while there is no evidence of a relationship between relative prices and the balance of payments, not even in the two countries (the US and France) where there was no evidence of an income adjustment process. For all the countries in the sample, the price elasticities show a low absolute value.

León-Ledesma (in Chapter 12) applies the model to the Spanish economy using twenty overlapping time periods from 1965 to 1993. The results show that for the period analysed, Spain's growth rate was very close to the estimated balance of payments constrained growth rate, except for the period of monetary instability from the mid-1970s to early 1980s. Using the various non-parametric and parametric tests of the model, the correlation between the actual and predicted growth rate over the twenty periods is over 90 per cent; the regression of actual growth on predicted growth gives a regression coefficient of unity and a constant equal to zero, and the McCombie test is passed (i.e. the estimated income elasticity of demand for imports averaged over the whole period is not significantly different from the income elasticity that makes the actual and predicted growth rates equal).

In the first essay (Chapter 13) in the empirical section on developing countries, Perraton tests the model for a sample of fifty-one countries over the period 1973–95. Import and export demand functions are estimated using error correction techniques, from which long-run estimates of income and price elasticities are derived. It was only possible, however, to derive stable estimates of the income elasticity of demand for imports for twenty-seven of the countries. For these countries, the dynamic Harrod trade multiplier result is a good predictor of actual growth performance, particularly when the effect of terms of trade changes on import capacity are allowed for. The author also uses the estimates of income elasticities made by Senhadji (1998) to test the model, and finds even stronger results. In countries where the actual growth rate deviates from that predicted by the simple model, the deviations do not appear to be systematically related to capital flows, which is surprising, but the author warns of the poor quality of the data for developing countries which must be borne in mind in interpreting the empirical results.

Nureldin-Hussain (in Chapter 14) also uses a large data set of twenty-nine African countries and eleven Asian countries, and is interested in analysing to what extent the growth rate differences between African and Asian countries can be accounted for in terms of the balance of payments constrained growth model. He uses the 'full' model to calculate the contribution of export growth, terms of trade changes and capital flows to output growth for each of the countries in the sample, and to the average performance of Africa and Asia as a whole. The major cause of Africa's slower growth than Asia is the lower dynamic Harrod trade multiplier associated with Africa's dependence on primary commodities with a low income elasticity of demand in world markets. The contribution of terms of trade changes and capital flows to differences in growth performance between the two regions is minor compared with differences in export performance relative to the propensity to import.

Ansari, Hashemzadeh and Xi (in Chapter 15) examine the model in the context of four Southeast Asian countries – Indonesia, Malaysia, Philippines and Thailand – over the period 1970–96. After careful estimation of the income elasticity of demand for imports, the predicted growth rates from the balance of payments constrained growth model are derived. In the case of Indonesia, Malaysia and the Philippines the results indicate that the null hypothesis of no difference between the actual and predicted growth rates cannot be rejected at any reasonable level of significance. In the case of Thailand, however, the model considerably underpredicts the actual growth rate which the authors attributed to IMF support and currency devaluation.

Lopez and Cruz (in Chapter 16) apply the model to four Latin American countries over the period from the mid-1960s to the mid-1990s: Argentina, Brazil, Colombia and Mexico. They find support for the model in the sense that output growth closely tracks export growth in the long run, and higher exports tend to cause higher outputs. However, they give a lot of prominence to the real exchange rate as a determinant of the level of output at external equilibrium, but the association differs between countries according to whether the Marshall–Lerner condition is satisfied. It is not satisfied in the case of Brazil and Mexico, and even where it is met in Argentina there still appears to be a negative association between output and the exchange rate which the authors attribute to the harmful impact of a higher real exchange rate on domestic demand.

Moreno-Brid and Pérez (in Chapter 17) focus on the five Central American countries of Costa Rica, E1 Salvador, Guatemala, Honduras and Nicaragua over the period 1950–96. The empirical analysis, using cointegration techniques, strongly supports a long-run association between the growth of real GDP and of real exports and the terms of trade, with the growth of exports by far the most important explanatory variable. The countries with the fastest growth tended to be those with the fastest growth of exports and the lowest income elasticities of demand for imports. The balance of payments constrained growth model is confirmed for Costa Rica, Guatemala and Nicaragua, but for E1 Salvador and Honduras, the balance of payments equilibrium growth rate considerably underpredicts the actual growth rate which the authors attribute to private remittances and official aid, respectively. In these two cases, the extended version of the model with capital flows would seem to be more relevant for an understanding of growth performance.

Moreno-Brid (in Chapter 18) considers the case of Mexico and whether a tightening of the balance of payments constraint can explain the slow-down of Mexico's growth rate since 1982. Mexico's growth averaged nearly 7 per cent per annum from 1950 to 1981, but only 2.5 per cent from 1982–97. A limit to the current account deficit as a proportion of GDP is introduced into the model which yields a formula for sustainable growth equivalent to that derived by McCombie and Thirlwall (1997a) and Barbosa-Filho (2001). The model suggests that the grip of the balance of payments on Mexico's economic growth did tighten after the debt crisis and extensive trade liberalisation in the first half of the 1980s. Estimates of the income elasticity of demand for imports combined with export growth indicate that the sustainable growth rate up to 1981 was between 4.4 and 5.9 per cent. In contrast, from 1982 onwards, a persistent growth of GDP in excess of 2 per cent put pressure on the balance of payments because of a tripling of the income elasticity of demand for imports.

Nell (in Chapter 19) applies the model to South Africa and the rest of the Southern African Development Community (RSADC) and makes the interesting innovation of separating the sources of exogenous income growth between trading partners, with both 'countries' trading with each other and with the OECD. This extension of the basic model is very useful for considering neighbouring regions that are engaged in mutual trade arrangements, and especially where one of the 'countries' dominates the other in terms of economic size. It is found that South Africa's and RSADC's actual long-run growth rates closely match those predicted by the balance of payments equilibrium growth rate. However, South Africa is only balance of payments constrained with respect to the OECD, and RSADC is only balance of payments constrained with respect to South Africa. These differential findings have implications for the direction of policy in the two countries. South Africa needs to reduce dependence, or improve performance, with respect to the OECD, while RSADC needs to reduce dependence, or improve performance, with respect to South Africa. Other future studies could usefully use this 'generalisation' of the model and disaggregated approach.

Notes

1 Interestingly, however, Harrod (1933) had earlier addressed the open economy with his derivation of the foreign trade multiplier, and argued that on certain assumptions, output is determined by the level of exports divided by the marginal propensity to import (see later). He never turned the insight into a model of balance of payments constrained growth.

2 With the exception of Malthus; but as Keynes says in *The General Theory*: 'Ricardo conquered England as completely as the Holy Inquisition Conquered Spain' (p. 32).

3 Formally, if $X = M$ and $M = \overline{M} + \mu Y$, where $\overline{M}$ is autonomous imports, then $Y = (X - \overline{M})/\mu$. Therefore, $\Delta Y/\Delta X = \Delta Y/\Delta \overline{M} = |1/\mu|$, and any change in X or $\overline{M}$ will so change income as to preserve $X = M$.

4 To see this formally: $\Delta Y/\Delta X = \Delta Y/\Delta M$. Multiply the right-hand side by X/Y and the left-hand side by M/Y, and rearrange, which gives $\Delta Y/Y = (\Delta X/X)/[(\Delta M/M)/(\Delta Y/Y)]$ or $g = x/\pi$.

5 See, for example, the discussion and references in Bianchi (1994a). Williamson (1984) also seems to suggest that the law may be based on a tautology.

Part I
Theory

2 The balance of payments constraint as an explanation of international growth rate differences*

A. P. Thirlwall

The neo-classical approach to the question of why growth rates differ between countries, typified by the meticulous studies of Denison (1967), Denison and Chung (1976), and Maddison (1970, 1972) concentrates on the supply side of the economy using the concept of the production function. Having specified the functional form, the growth of output is apportioned between the growth of capital; the growth of labour, and the growth of total factor productivity obtained as a residual. By this approach, growth rate differences are 'explained' in terms of differences in the growth of factor supplies and productivity. While the approach is fruitful, interesting and mathematically precise, it does not tell us *why* the growth of factor supplies and productivity differs between countries. To answer this question, some would say that a more Keynesian approach is required which stresses demand. For the Keynesian, it is demand that 'drives' the economic system to which supply, within limits, adapts. Taking this approach, growth rates differ because the growth of demand differs between countries. The question then becomes why does demand grow at different rates between countries? One explanation may be the inability of economic agents, particularly governments, to expand demand. This explanation by itself, however, is not very satisfactory. The more probable explanation lies in constraints on demand. In an open economy, the dominant constraint is the balance of payments. In this chapter, it is shown how closely the growth experience of several developed countries approximates to the rate of growth of exports divided by the income elasticity of demand for imports, which, on certain assumptions, can be regarded as a measure of what I call the balance of payments equilibrium growth rate. In fact, the rate of growth of exports divided by the income elasticity of demand for imports gives such a good approximation to the actual growth experience of major developed countries since 1950 that a new economic law might almost be formulated.

The importance of a healthy balance of payments for growth can be stated quite succinctly. If a country gets into balance of payments difficulties as it expands demand before the short-term capacity growth rate is reached, then demand must be curtailed; supply is never fully utilised; investment is discouraged;

* First published in *Banca Nazionale del Lavoro Quarterly Review*, March 1979.

technological progress is slowed down, and a country's goods compared with foreign goods become less desirable so worsening the balance of payments still further, and so on. A vicious circle is started. By contrast, if a country is able to expand demand up to the level of existing productive capacity, without balance of payments difficulties arising, the pressure of demand upon capacity may well raise the capacity growth rate. There are a number of possible mechanisms through which this may happen: the encouragement to investment which would augment the capital stock and bring with it technological progress; the supply of labour may increase by the entry into the workforce of people previously outside or from abroad; the movement of factors of production from low productivity to high productivity sectors, and the ability to import more may increase capacity by making domestic resources more productive. It is this argument that lies behind the advocacy of export-led growth, because it is only through the expansion of exports that the growth rate can be raised without the balance of payments deteriorating at the same time. Believers in export-led growth are really postulating a balance of payments constraint theory of why growth rates differ. It should be stressed, however, that the same rate of export growth in different countries will not necessarily permit the same rate of growth of output because the import requirements associated with growth will differ between countries, and thus some countries will have to constrain demand sooner than others for balance of payments equilibrium. The relation between a country's growth rate and its rate of growth of imports is the income elasticity of demand for imports. The hypothesis we shall be testing, from the model to be outlined here, is that, if balance of payments equilibrium must be maintained, a country's long-run growth rate will be determined by the ratio of its rate of growth of exports to its income elasticity of demand for imports.

The determination of the balance of payments equilibrium growth rate

Balance of payments equilibrium on current account measured in units of the home currency may be expressed as

$$P_{dt}X_t = P_{ft}M_tE_t, \tag{2.1}$$

where X is the quantity of exports; P_d the price of exports in home currency; M the quantity of imports; P_f is the price of imports in foreign currency; E is the exchange rate (i.e. the home price of foreign currency), and t is time. In a growing economy, the condition for balance of payments equilibrium through time is that the rate of growth of the value of exports equals the rate of growth of the value of imports, that is

$$p_{dt} + x_t = p_{ft} + m_t + e_t, \tag{2.2}$$

where lower-case letters represent (continuous) rates of change of the variables. Using standard demand theory, the quantity of imports demanded may be specified as a multiplicative function of the price of imports (measured in units of the home currency in order to incorporate the effect of exchange rate changes), the price of import substitutes, and domestic income. Thus,

$$M_t = (P_{ft}E_t)^{\Psi} P_{dt}^{\Phi} Y_t^{\pi}, \tag{2.3}$$

where Ψ is the own price elasticity of demand for imports ($\Psi < 0$); Φ is the cross elasticity of demand for imports ($\Phi > 0$); Y is domestic income, and π is the income elasticity of demand for imports ($\pi > 0$). The rate of growth of imports may be written as

$$m_t = \Psi(p_{ft}) + \Psi(e_t) + \Phi(p_{dt}) + \pi(y_t), \tag{2.4}$$

where lower-case letters again represent continuous rates of change of the variables.

The quantity of exports demanded may also be expressed as a multiplicative function in which the arguments in the demand function are: the price of exports measured in foreign currency (to capture the effect of exchange rate changes), the price of goods competitive with exports, and the level of world income. Thus,

$$X_t = \left(\frac{P_{dt}}{E_t}\right)^{\eta} P_{ft}^{\delta} Z_t^{\varepsilon}, \tag{2.5}$$

where X_t is the quantity of exports; P_{dt} is the domestic price of exports; P_{ft} is the price of goods competitive with exports; Z is the level of world income; $1/E$ is the foreign price of home currency; η is the own price elasticity of demand for exports ($\eta < 0$); δ is the cross elasticity of demand for exports ($\delta > 0$); ε is the income elasticity of demand for exports ($\varepsilon > 0$), and t is time. The rate of growth of exports may be written as

$$x_t = \eta(p_{dt}) - \eta(e_t) + \delta(p_{ft}) + \varepsilon(z_t). \tag{2.6}$$

Substituting equations (2.4) and (2.6) into (2.2), we can solve for the rate of growth of domestic income consistent with balance of payments equilibrium which we shall call the balance of payments equilibrium growth rate, y_{Bt}.

$$y_{Bt} = \frac{p_{dt}(1 + \eta - \Phi) - p_{ft}(1 - \delta + \Psi) - e_t(1 + \eta + \Psi) + \varepsilon(z_t)}{\pi}. \tag{2.7}$$

Remembering the signs of the parameters ($\eta < 0$; $\Phi > 0$; $\delta > 0$; $\Psi < 0$; $\varepsilon > 0$, and $\pi > 0$), equation (2.7) expresses several familiar economic propositions:

(i) Inflation in the home country will lower the balance of payments equilibrium growth rate if the sum of the own price elasticity of demand for exports and the cross elasticity of demand for imports is greater than unity in absolute value (i.e. if $|\eta + \Phi| > 1$).

(ii) Inflation abroad will improve the home country's balance of payments equilibrium growth rate provided the sum of the own price elasticity of demand for imports and the cross elasticity of demand for exports is greater than unity in absolute value (i.e. if $|\delta + \Psi| > 1$).

(iii) Devaluation or currency depreciation, that is, a rise in the home price of foreign currency ($e_t > 0$), will improve the balance of payments equilibrium growth rate provided the sum of the own price elasticities of demand for imports and exports exceeds unity in absolute value, which is the so-called Marshall–Lerner condition (i.e. if $|\eta + \Psi| > 1$). Notice, however, the important point that a once-for-all depreciation of the currency cannot raise the balance of payments equilibrium growth rate permanently. After the initial depreciation, $e_t = 0$, the growth rate would revert to its former level. To raise the balance of payments equilibrium growth rate permanently would require continual depreciation, that is, $e_t > 0$ in successive periods.

(iv) A faster growth of world income will raise the balance of payments equilibrium growth rate.

(v) The higher the income elasticity of demand for imports (π), the lower the balance of payments equilibrium growth rate.

Empirical evidence

The interesting question is how well does the actual growth experience of countries approximate to the balance of payments equilibrium growth rate? There may, of course, be an asymmetry in the system. While a country cannot grow faster than its balance of payments equilibrium growth rate for very long, unless it can finance an ever-growing deficit, there is little to stop a country growing slower and accumulating large surpluses. This may, particularly, occur where the balance of payments equilibrium growth rate is so high that a country simply does not have the physical capacity to grow at that rate. This typifies many oil-producing countries and would also seem to typify the experience of Japan, as we shall see later.

To calculate the balance of payments equilibrium growth rate from equation (2.7) for a number of countries requires a substantial amount of data and estimates of parameters which are not readily available. If the usual assumption is made, however, that the own price elasticities of demand for imports and exports are equal to the cross elasticities ($\Psi = \Phi$ and $\eta = \delta$), equation (2.7) becomes

$$y_{Bt} = \frac{(1 + \eta + \Psi)(p_{dt} - p_{ft} - e_t) + \varepsilon(z_t)}{\pi}, \qquad (2.8)$$

which, if relative prices measured in a common currency do not change over the long run, reduces to

$$y_{Bt} = \frac{x_t}{\pi} \text{ (using equation (2.6)).} \qquad (2.9)$$

Many models (see Ball *et al.*, 1977), and the empirical evidence, suggest that over the long period there can be little movement in relative international prices measured in a common currency, either because of arbitrage (the law of one price) or because exchange depreciation forces up domestic prices equiproportionately so that in the long run ($p_{dt} - p_{ft} - e_t) \simeq 0$.

Applying equation (2.9) to international data gives a remarkable approximation to the growth experience of many countries over the last twenty years, and *ipso facto* provides an explanation of why growth rates differ. It might almost be stated as a fundamental law that, except where the balance of payments equilibrium growth rate exceeds the maximum feasible capacity growth rate, the rate of growth of a country will approximate to the ratio of its rate of growth of exports and its income elasticity of demand for imports. The approximation itself vindicates the assumptions used to arrive at the simple rule in equation (2.9). The hypothesis is tested on two sets of data on the growth of output and exports: one for the period from 1953 to 1976 (Kern, 1978), and the other from a different source (Cornwall, 1977) for the period from 1951 to 1973.[1] On the income elasticity of demand for imports, Houthakker and Magee's (1969) estimates have been taken as applying to the whole of these periods even though they were only estimated over the period from 1951 to 1966. They are the best consistently estimated international estimates available, but are probably now on the low side. The data, and the results of applying equation (2.9), are presented in Tables 2.1 and 2.2. In

Table 2.1 Calculations of the growth rate consistent with balance of payments equilibrium 1953–76

Country	% Growth of real GNP (y)	% Growth of export volume (x)	Income elasticity of demand for imports (π)	Balance of payments equilibrium growth rate from applying equation (2.9)
USA	3.23	5.88	1.51	3.89
Canada	4.81	6.02	1.20	5.02
West Germany	4.96	9.99	1.89	5.29
Netherlands	4.99	9.38	1.82	5.15
Sweden	3.67	7.16	1.76	4.07
France	4.95	8.78	1.62	5.42
Denmark	3.58	6.77	1.31	5.17
Australia	4.95	6.98	0.90	7.76
Italy	4.96	12.09	2.25	5.37
Switzerland	3.56	7.20	1.90	3.79
Norway	4.18	7.70	1.40	5.50
Belgium	4.07	9.24	1.94	4.76
Japan	8.55	16.18	1.23	13.15
Austria	5.17	11.12	n.a.	—
United Kingdom	2.71	4.46	1.51	2.95
South Africa	4.97	6.57	0.85	7.73
Spain	5.94	11.10	n.a.	—
Finland	4.55	6.63	n.a.	—

Sources: Kern (1978), and Houthakker and Magee (1969).

Table 2.2 Calculations of the growth rate consistent with balance of payments equilibrium 1951–73 using data given by Cornwall (1977)

Country	% Growth in GDP	% Growth of exports (χ)	Income elasticity of demand for imports (π)	Balance of payments equilibrium growth rate from applying equation (2.9)
Austria	5.1[a]	10.7	n.a.	—
Belgium	4.4[a]	9.4	1.94	4.84
Canada	4.6	6.9	1.20	5.75
Denmark	4.2[b]	6.1	1.31	4.65
France	5.0	8.1	1.62	5.00
Germany	5.7	10.8	1.89	5.71
Italy	5.1	11.7	2.25	5.20
Japan	9.5	15.4	1.23	12.52
Netherlands	5.0	10.1	1.82	5.55
Norway	4.2	7.2	1.40	5.14
United Kingdom	2.7	4.1	1.51	2.71
USA	3.7	5.1	1.51	3.38

Source: Cornwall (1977), p. 162.

Notes
a 1955–73.
b 1954–73.

both tables there is a general tendency for the estimates of the balance of payments equilibrium growth rate to be higher than the actual growth rate, which, if true, would produce a balance of payments surplus. For countries which have built up surpluses, the estimates are consistent with the empirical evidence. Japan is a striking example of a country where the gap between its actual growth rate and its balance of payments equilibrium growth rate has resulted in the build up of a huge payments surplus. Presumably Japan could not grow faster than it did because of an ultimate capacity ceiling. But Japan still grew considerably faster than other countries because demand was unconstrained and induced its own supply of factors of production. For countries which have moved into deficit over the period, the estimate of their balance of payments equilibrium growth rate must be too high. As suggested earlier, this may be because the assumed income elasticity of demand for imports is an underestimate for the period stretching into the late 1960s and 1970s. Also, adverse relative price movements combined with various price elasticity conditions cannot be entirely ruled out as determinants of the balance of payments even though they may be of minor significance compared to income movements and income elasticities of demand for imports and exports.

Despite the overestimation of the balance of payments equilibrium growth rate in some cases, and the fact that some countries may grow slower and build up payments surpluses, nonetheless the rank correlations between the predicted growth rates from applying our simple rule and the actual growth rates are very high for both sets of data. For the sample of countries in Table 2.1 the Spearman rank correlation is 0.764 and in Table 2.2 the Spearman rank correlation is 0.891.

Conclusion

The simple policy conclusion for most countries is that if they wish to grow faster they must first raise the balance of payments constraint on demand. To raise the rate of growth of productive capacity (e.g. by improving productivity) without being able to raise the rate of growth of demand because of the balance of payments will merely lead to unemployment. If the balance of payments equilibrium growth rate can be raised, however, by making exports more attractive and by reducing the income elasticity of demand for imports, demand can be expanded without producing balance of payments difficulties; and, within limits, demand can generate its own supply by encouraging investment, absorbing underemployment, raising productivity growth and so on. Thus, the explanation of growth rate differences must lie primarily in differences in the rate of growth of demand, and the major constraint on the rate of growth of demand in most countries is the balance of payments. Our model and the empirical evidence lends strong support to the advocates of export-led growth.

The deeper question lies in why the balance of payments equilibrium growth rate differs between countries. This must be primarily associated with the characteristics of goods produced which determines the income elasticity of demand for the country's exports and the country's propensity to import. For countries with a slow rate of growth of exports, combined with a relatively high income elasticity of demand for imports, the message is plain: the goods produced by the country are relatively unattractive at both home and abroad. We have concentrated in this study on growth rate differences between developed countries. The argument probably has even greater relevance for developing countries.

Note

1 I did not want to be accused of choosing the source to suit the argument!

3 The balance of payments constraint, capital flows and growth rate differences between developing countries*

A. P. Thirlwall and M. Nureldin Hussain

This chapter starts from the proposition that for most countries the major constraint on the rate of growth of output is likely to be the balance of payments position because this sets the limit to the growth of demand to which supply can adapt. Most countries, apart from the oil producing countries of the Middle East, can absorb foreign exchange without difficulty; and most cannot earn enough. It is true, of course, that the world as a whole cannot be balance of payments constrained, but it only requires one country or bloc of countries not to be constrained, for all the rest to be so. There cannot be many less-developed countries that could not utilise resources more fully given the greater availability of foreign exchange.

In a previous paper (Thirlwall, 1979) it was shown how closely the actual growth experience of several developed countries over the post-war period has approximated to the rate of growth of export volume (x) divided by the income elasticity of demand for imports (π). This ratio defines the balance of payments constrained growth rate on the assumptions that balance of payments equilibrium on current account is preserved and that the real terms of trade remain unchanged. The fact that the growth rate of so many advanced countries seemed to approximate to this simple rule suggested that for most countries capital flows are relatively unimportant in contributing to deviations of a country's growth rate from that consistent with current account equilibrium, and that relative price changes between countries measured in a common currency play only a minor role in balance of payments adjustment and in relaxing the balance of payments constraint on growth. It is largely real income (and employment) that adjusts to bring the value of imports and exports into line with one another to preserve balance of payments equilibrium.

The simple growth rule, that growth approximates to $y = x/\pi$ in the long run, is the dynamic analogue of the Harrod trade multiplier (Harrod, 1933), which has been recently revived by Kaldor (1975), and the workings of which have been explored by Kennedy and Thirlwall (1979). The empirical evidence suggests, therefore, that the Harrod trade multiplier works, at least for a range of advanced countries. The original Harrod trade multiplier assumes that the terms of trade

* First published in *Oxford Economic Papers*, November 1982.

are constant; that there is no saving and investment, and no government activity. Output or income is generated by the production of consumption goods (C) and exports (X), and all income is spent either on home consumption goods (C) or imports (M). On these assumptions trade is always balanced, and income adjusts to preserve equilibrium. We have

$$Y = C + X \tag{3.1}$$

and

$$Y = C + M. \tag{3.2}$$

Therefore

$$X = M. \tag{3.3}$$

Now let the import function be

$$M = \bar{M} + mY, \tag{3.4}$$

where $\bar{M}$ is the level of autonomous imports and m is the marginal propensity to import. We then have

$$X = \bar{M} + mY. \tag{3.5}$$

Therefore

$$Y = \frac{X - \bar{M}}{m}$$

and

$$\frac{\Delta Y}{\Delta X} = \frac{\Delta Y}{-\Delta \bar{M}} = \frac{1}{m}. \tag{3.6}$$

The multiplier, $1/m$, will always bring the balance of payments back into equilibrium through changes in income following a change in autonomous exports or imports.

The assumptions used by Harrod to derive his original result are clearly unrealistic, but it is easy to see (Thirlwall, 1982) that the Harrod result will still hold if (i) other induced expenditures and withdrawals from the circular flow of income balance each other in the aggregate or (ii) balance of payments equilibrium is, for one reason or another, a policy objective or requirement so that the level and growth of income must of necessity be constrained in the long run to preserve a balance between exports and imports.

Equation (3.6), when it is made 'dynamic', becomes the simple growth rule $y = x/\pi$. We have

$$\frac{\Delta Y}{Y} = \frac{\Delta X}{X} \Big/ \pi, \tag{3.7}$$

where $\Delta Y/Y$ is the rate of growth of income, and $\Delta X/X$ is the rate of growth of export volume. If the real terms of trade remain unchanged we can use the equilibrium condition under which the Harrod trade multiplier works and multiply the LHS of equation (3.6) by X/Y and the RHS by M/Y to give

$$\frac{\Delta Y}{\Delta X} \cdot \frac{X}{Y} = \frac{\Delta Y}{\Delta M} \cdot \frac{M}{Y} \tag{3.8}$$

or

$$\frac{\Delta Y}{Y} = \frac{\Delta X/X}{(\Delta M/M)/(\Delta Y/Y)} = \frac{\Delta X}{X} \Big/ \pi. \tag{3.9}$$

There are only two factors which may cause a country's growth rate to deviate from this rate: first, changes in the real terms of trade, and secondly capital flows allowing there to be a difference between domestic expenditure and income and a current account disequilibrium.[1] If equation (3.9) predicts well, the presumption must be either that these two factors are relatively unimportant, or that they are working in opposite directions, and by exactly the same amount to offset each other (which would seem to be highly coincidental).

The developing countries

The growth experience of the developing countries over the last thirty years has been even more diverse than that of the developed countries, and can hardly be explained by reference to differences in the autonomous rate of growth of factor supplies. Capital accumulation, labour supply and technical progress are partly, if not mainly, endogenous to an economic system and respond to variations in the pressure of demand. In this chapter, we attempt to see how well the Harrod trade multiplier model (which is a demand-orientated balance of payments constrained model) fits the growth experience of a sample of developing countries, wherein general foreign exchange is a more acute bottleneck than in the developed countries. It must be recognised, though, that developing countries are often able to build up ever-growing current account deficits financed by capital inflows (which are then written off!) which allow these countries to grow permanently faster than otherwise would be the case. If this is so, growth becomes constrained ultimately by the rate of growth of capital inflows, and, by itself, the simple growth rule enunciated would not be a good predictor of long-run growth performance. The model thus needs some amendment to allow for capital flows. What countries gain from capital inflows, however, they may lose by the adverse effects of relative price movements; indeed, the former may be partly in response to the latter. It is an interesting empirical question what the balance has been.

This chapter will proceed in two stages. First, the balance of payments constrained growth rate will be modelled, making allowance for the fact that the economy may both start off in balance of payments disequilibrium (with capital flows) and move further into disequilibrium over the time period under consideration. Second, both the simple and extended model will be applied to a range of developing countries where it has been possible to obtain from other studies, or to make ourselves, well-determined estimates of the income elasticity of demand for imports, which is the crucial parameter in the model. Again, we shall model under the assumption that relative prices measured in a common currency remain unchanged over the long period, so that any deviation of the actual growth rate from that predicted by the extended model with capital flows would be a measure of the invalidity of that assumption (barring errors in the measurement of variables and parameters).

The effect of capital flows on the balance of payments constrained growth rate

If the balance of payments is in initial current account disequilibrium, this may be expressed as

$$P_{dt}X_t + C_t = P_{ft}M_tE_t, \tag{3.10}$$

where X_t is the volume of exports; P_{dt} is the domestic price of exports; M_t is the volume of imports; P_{ft} is the foreign price of imports; E_t is the exchange rate (measured as the domestic price of foreign currency), and C_t is the value of capital flows measured in domestic currency. $C_t > 0$ measures capital inflows, and $C_t < 0$ measures capital outflows. Taking rates of change of the variables in equation (3.10) gives

$$\left(\frac{E}{R}\right)(p_{dt} + x_t) + \left(\frac{C}{R}\right)(c_t) = p_{ft} + m_t + e_t, \tag{3.11}^2$$

where the lower-case letters represent rates of growth of the variables, and E/R and C/R represent the shares of exports and capital flows as a proportion of total receipts (or the proportions of the import bill 'financed' by export earnings and by capital flows).

Now assume the normal multiplicative import and export demand functions with constant elasticities:

$$M_t = \left(\frac{P_{ft}E_t}{P_{dt}}\right)^{\psi} Y_t^{\pi} \tag{3.12}$$

and

$$X_t = \left(\frac{P_{dt}}{P_{ft}E_t}\right)^{\eta} Z_t^{\varepsilon}, \tag{3.13}$$

where ψ is the price elasticity of demand for imports ($\psi < 0$); η is the price elasticity of demand for exports ($\eta < 0$); Y_t is domestic income; Z_t is the level of 'world' income; π is the income elasticity of demand for imports, and ε is the income elasticity of demand for exports. From equations (3.12) and (3.13), taking rates of change of the variables, we have

$$m_t = \psi(p_{ft} + e_t - p_{dt}) + \pi(y_t) \tag{3.14}$$

and

$$x_t = \eta(p_{dt} - e_t - p_{ft}) + \varepsilon(z_t). \tag{3.15}$$

Substituting equations (3.14) and (3.15) into (3.11) gives the balance of payments constrained growth rate[3] starting from initial disequilibrium of

$$y_{Bt}$$
$$= \frac{((E/R)\eta + \psi)(p_{dt} - e_t - p_{ft}) + (p_{dt} - p_{ft} - e_t) + (E/R)(\varepsilon(z_t)) + (C/R)(c_t - p_{dt})}{\pi} \tag{3.16}$$

The first term on the RHS gives the volume effect of relative price changes on balance of payments constrained real income growth; the second term gives the terms of trade effect; the third term gives the effect of exogenous changes in income growth abroad, and the last term gives the effect of the rate of growth of real capital flows. If $p_{dt} = e_t + p_{ft}$ that is, if relative prices measured in a common currency were to remain unchanged over the long run, equation (3.16) would reduce to

$$y_{Bt}^* = \frac{(E/R)(\varepsilon(z_t)) + (C/R)(c_t - p_{dt})}{\pi}. \tag{3.17}$$

In other words, the balance of payments constrained growth rate starting from initial current account disequilibrium is the weighted sum of the growth of exports due to exogenous income growth outside the country, and the growth of real capital flows, divided by the income elasticity of demand for imports. Since by national income accounting (see note 1), equation (3.16) must hold, deviations of the actual growth rate from y_{Bt}^* will be a reflection of the two relative price terms in equation (3.16). Since we do not have information on $\varepsilon(z_t)$ for all countries we shall assume that $\varepsilon(z_t) = x_t$, thereby incorporating into the analysis from the start any volume changes in exports from relative price movements. The equation we focus on is thus

$$y_{Bt}^* = \frac{(E/R)(x_t) + (C/R)(c_t - p_{dt})}{\pi}. \tag{3.18}$$

The difference between the actual growth rate and that predicted by (3.18) will be a measure of the pure terms of trade effect on real income growth and of any import volume response from relative price changes relaxing or tightening the balance of payments constraint on growth according to the direction of movement in the terms of trade and whether the import volume response is normal or perverse.

This result may now be compared with the result of the simple model which starts from balance of payments equilibrium and assumes no growth of capital inflows. Three observations may be made which are as follows.

1   With no initial disequilibrium and no capital flows, $E/R = 1$ and $C/R = 0$, and equation (3.18) yields the old result

$$y_{Bt} = \frac{x_t}{\pi}. \tag{3.19}$$

2   If there is initial current account disequilibrium but the rate of growth of capital inflows is zero ($c_t = 0$), the balance of payments constrained growth rate will be lowered to

$$y_{Bt}^{**} = \frac{(E/R)(x_t) - (C/R)(p_{dt})}{\pi} \tag{3.20}$$

y_{Bt}^{**} is obviously less than y_{Bt}. The explanation of this result is that if export earnings are initially below the value of imports, an equal rate of growth of exports and imports would widen the disequilibrium absolutely, and if the difference is not filled by an increasing level of capital inflows, the growth of income must be lower in order to reduce the growth of imports below that of exports to keep the absolute gap between exports and imports (equal to the initial value of C_t) unchanged. Subtracting equation (3.20) from (3.19) we see that the absolute reduction in the level of the growth rate is equal to

$$\frac{(C/R)(p_{dt} + x_t)}{\pi}. \tag{3.21}$$

3   If there is an initial current account deficit financed by capital inflows and the growth rate is not to be lower than without an initial disequilibrium, there must be a positive rate of growth of capital inflows to compensate. We can find this rate by setting equation (3.18) equal to (3.21) and solving for c_t. This yields

$$c_t = p_{dt} + x_t. \tag{3.22}$$

This result should be apparent from equation (3.11) as we indicated in note 2. Without initial disequilibrium, the balance of payments constrained growth rate is defined where $p_{dt} + x_t = p_{ft} + m_t + e_t$, and for the weighted sum of $(p_{dt} + x_t)$ and c_t to equal $(p_{dt} + x_t)$, c_t must grow at the same rate as $(p_{dt} + x_t)$.

We end up therefore with a very simple guideline. If a country starts in balance of payments disequilibrium, the simple Harrod rule for predicting the growth rate will underpredict or overpredict according to whether $c_t \gtrless (p_{dt} + x_t)$, or, in other words, according to whether the growth of capital inflows is greater or less than the rate of growth of export earnings. The degree of underprediction or overprediction is given by subtracting equation (3.18) from (3.19) which gives

$$\frac{(C/R)(p_{dt} + x_t - c_t)}{\pi}. \tag{3.23}$$

In real terms, if $c_t - p_{dt} > x_t$, the dynamic Harrod trade multiplier result will underpredict; if $c_t - p_{dt} = x_t$, the prediction will be unaffected, and if $c_t - p_{dt} < x_t$, the Harrod trade multiplier rule will overpredict.

Empirical evidence

We are now in a position to fit the basic and extended Harrod trade multiplier models (equations (3.9) and (3.18)) to a sample of developing countries. Three samples of countries are taken. First, we use a sample of countries taken by M. Khan (1974), and his estimates of the income elasticity of demand for imports over the period from 1951 to 1969. Out of fifteen countries, seven yielded statistically significant equilibrium estimates. The countries (excluding Brazil) are listed in the first section of Table 3.1.[4] Secondly, we take the three developing countries for which Houthakker and Magee (1969) made estimates of the income elasticity of demand for imports over the period 1951 to 1966: Mexico, India, and Portugal. These are listed in Section II of Table 3.1. Finally we made estimates ourselves of the income elasticity of demand for imports for a selection of developing countries primarily chosen on the basis of data availability. The countries yielding statistically significant estimates in a traditionally specified import demand function are given in Section III of Table 3.1.

For all the countries, Table 3.1 gives data, over the relevant time period, on the actual growth rate (y); the growth of export volume (x); the income elasticity of demand for imports (π); the growth rate predicted by the simple dynamic Harrod trade multiplier ($y_B = x/\pi$); the growth of real capital imports (c_r); and the predicted balance of payments constrained growth rate with capital flows (y_B^*). We expect the extended model with capital flows to give a closer prediction of the actual growth rate than the simple Harrod multiplier result except to the extent that adverse or favourable effects of relative price movements may have worked in the opposite direction tending to push the actual growth rate back towards the prediction of the simple rule. The difference between the actual growth rate and that predicted by the extended model is a measure of the extent to which the balance of payments constrained growth rate has been affected by relative price movements

Table 3.1 The annual growth rate of output, exports and real capital flows; and growth rate predictions from the simple and extended Harrod trade multiplier model

Countries	Growth of income (y)	Growth of exports (x)	Income elasticity of demand for imports (π)	Simple Harrod trade multiplier prediction $y_B = x/\pi$	Growth of real capital imports $(c_t - p_{dt})$	Predicted growth rate from extended model including capital flows y_B^*
I. 1951–69[a]						
Costa Rica	0.040	0.080	2.046	0.039	0.350	0.053
Ecuador	0.048	0.064	0.555	0.120	−0.231	0.110
Pakistan	0.069	0.062	1.020	0.060	0.199	0.089
Sri Lanka	0.061	0.013	0.218	0.059	0.088	0.067
Phillippines	0.053	0.046	0.668	0.068	0.013	0.063
Colombia	0.050	0.025	0.290	0.086	−0.138	0.060
II. 1951–66[b]						
India	0.024	0.040	1.43	0.028	0.134	0.037
Portugal	0.051	0.080	1.39	0.057	0.039	0.050
Mexico	0.060	0.060	0.53	0.110	0.007	0.100
III. Various Dates[c]						
Tunisia	0.064	0.045	0.91	0.050	0.086	0.060
Cyprus	0.034	0.035	1.05	0.035	0.017	0.033
Kenya	0.081	0.085	0.99	0.086	0.017	0.060
Honduras	0.042	0.070	0.89	0.079	0.363	0.082
Jamaica	0.040	0.052	0.70	0.074	−0.022	0.058
Thailand	0.068	0.062	0.93	0.066	0.110	0.073
Sudan	0.054	0.053	0.64	0.083	0.070	0.085
Morocco	0.033	0.030	0.43	0.069	−0.004	0.062
Brazil	0.095	0.083	2.05	0.040	0.350	0.094
Zaire	0.060	0.037	0.53	0.069	−0.180	0.054
Turkey	0.058	0.056	0.92	0.061	0.053	0.059

Sources
a From Khan (1974).
b From Houthakker and Magee (1969).
c Own estimates.

in international trade. When we look at the prediction of the two models we find that the mean absolute error of the actual growth rate from that predicted by the extended model is in fact smaller than the error of prediction from the simple rule (1.55 percentage points compared to 2.01), so that complete offsetting movements of capital flows on the one hand and the effects of relative price changes on the other cannot have occurred.

To throw more light on the question of the relative importance of capital flows and relative price changes in accounting for deviations of growth from the Harrod trade multiplier result, it is interesting to divide the countries in Table 3.1 into two groups: those where growth has exceeded the predicted rate and those where it has fallen below. For those countries with $y > y_B$ we expect real capital inflows to have grown faster than the volume of exports, and for this to be the major explanation of the positive difference, unless relative price changes have been favourable to the relaxation of the balance of payments constraint on growth. Contrariwise for those countries with $y < y_B$, we expect real capital inflows to have grown slower than export volume unless the negative difference is wholly accounted for by the (adverse) effect of relative price changes. In Table 3.2 the countries are so divided. An interesting contrast between the two groups of countries is immediately apparent. In the six countries with $y > y_B$, the mean difference is 1.38. In all countries the rate of growth of real capital inflows was greater than the growth of exports which, according to the extended model, should have relaxed the balance of payments constraint on growth by an average of 2.03 percentage points. Since

Table 3.2 The 'explanation' of divergencies between the actual growth rate and the dynamic Harrod trade multiplier result

Country	Actual growth rate (y)	Harrod trade multiplier result $y_B = (x/\pi)$	Difference	Contribution to difference of	
				Real capital inflows growing faster (+) or slower (−) than exports	Effect of relative price movements
A. Countries with actual growth greater than Harrod trade multiplier result (% per annum)					
Brazil	9.5	4.0	+5.5	+5.4	+0.1
Tunisia	6.4	5.0	+1.4	+1.0	+0.4
Pakistan	6.9	6.0	+0.9	+2.9	−2.0
Thailand	6.8	6.6	+0.2	+0.7	−0.5
Sri Lanka	6.1	5.9	+0.2	+0.8	−0.6
Costa Rica	4.0	3.9	+0.1	+1.4	−1.3
Average deviations			+1.38	+2.03	−0.65
B. Countries with actual growth less than Harrod trade multiplier result					
Ecuador	4.8	12.0	−7.2	−1.0	−6.2
Mexico	6.0	11.0	−5.0	−1.0	−4.0
Honduras	4.2	7.9	−3.7	+0.3	−4.0
Colombia	5.0	8.6	−3.6	−2.6	−1.0
Morocco	3.3	6.9	−3.6	−0.7	−2.9
Jamaica	4.0	7.4	−3.4	−1.6	−1.8
Sudan	5.4	8.3	−2.9	+0.2	−3.1
Phillipines	5.3	6.8	−1.5	−0.5	−1.0
Zaire	6.0	6.9	−0.9	−1.5	+0.6
Portugal	5.1	5.7	−0.6	−0.7	+0.1
Kenya	8.1	8.6	−0.5	−2.6	+2.1
India	2.4	2.8	−0.4	+0.9	−1.3
Turkey	5.8	6.1	−0.3	−0.2	−0.1
Cyprus	3.4	3.5	−0.1	−0.2	+0.1
Average deviations			−2.41	−0.80	−1.61

the average deviation was only 1.38 percent, however, the conclusion must be that the effect of relative price changes was adverse, tightening the balance of payments constraint on growth in these countries by an average of 0.65 percentage points. In two of the countries out of the six, however, the effect of relative price movements was apparently favourable.

Turning to the countries with $y < y_B$, the explanation of the shortfall of growth appears to lie not so much in a shortfall of capital import growth below export growth but in the adverse effects of relative price movements. The average (negative) deviation of y from y_B is -2.41. In all countries but three, the growth of real capital inflows was lower than the growth of exports, but on average, according to the extended model, this would have contributed to a shortfall of y below y_B of only 0.08 percentage points leaving a residual of -1.61 which can only be explained by the adverse effects of relative price changes.

The effects of relative price changes on balance of payments constrained real income growth comprise two components in our model: one, a pure terms of trade effect, and the second, the effect of relative price changes on the volume of imports (both divided by the income elasticity of demand for imports). Where the effects of relative price changes have been apparently adverse on real income growth, this could be the result of a combination of an adverse terms of trade effect partly offset or reinforced by an import volume effect, depending on whether the price elasticity of demand for imports is 'normal' or perverse. Alternatively, the adverse effect could be the result of a favourable movement in the terms of trade but more than offset by the effect of a high price elasticity of demand for imports. Where the effect of relative price changes has apparently had a favourable effect on real income growth, the explanation would be the reverse of these arguments. In Table 3.3, the average annual percentage rate of change of the real terms of trade divided by the income elasticity of demand for imports is given for all the countries in the sample for comparison with the implied effect of relative price movements from the last column of Table 3.2. It can be seen that for most countries where the implied terms of trade effect has been adverse on real income growth, the actual real terms of trade has on average deteriorated over time, but in some cases the implied adverse effect is greater than the effect of the actual deterioration suggesting a perverse import volume response to adverse relative price movements. Where the implied terms of trade effect has been positive, however, the effect of the actual terms of trade improvement has generally been greater, which would be consistent with a normal import volume response. In three cases, a favourable pure terms of trade effect on real income growth is associated with an implied adverse relative price effect suggesting that the unfavourable effect of the import volume response has outweighed the favourable pure terms of trade effect. For the countries as a whole, the annual average deterioration in the real terms of trade has been approximately 0.075 per cent over the years taken for the different countries, which would amount to a deterioration of 1.6 per cent over, say, a twenty-year period. There is some variation in the experience of individual countries, but for most of them the evidence suggests that in the long run, relative prices measured in a common currency stay relatively stable.

Table 3.3 The actual and implied effect of relative price movements on real income growth

Country	Effect of relative price movements (% p. a.)	
	Implied effect (from Table 3.2)	Pure terms of trade effect[a]
A. Brazil	+0.1	+1.1
Tunisia	+0.4	+4.6
Pakistan	−2.0	−4.1
Thailand	−0.5	+1.1
Sri Lanka	−0.6	−12.4
Costa Rica	−1.3	−0.4
B. Ecuador	−6.2	−0.5
Mexico	−4.2	−0.4
Honduras	−4.0	−1.6
Colombia	−1.0	+1.4
Morocco	−2.9	−0.7
Jamaica	−1.8	+0.6
Sudan	−3.1	−1.7
Phillipines	−1.0	−3.1
Zaire	+0.6	+1.7
Portugal	+0.1	+0.8
Kenya	+2.1	−0.2
India	−1.3	−0.3
Turkey	−0.1	−0.9
Cyprus	+0.1	+2.7

Source: *International Financial Statistics Yearbooks.*

Note
a Calculated as the change in the terms of trade divided by π. The terms of trade is calculated as the ratio of the country's export price index to its import price index, where all prices are expressed in US dollars.

The conclusion of the analysis must be that the experience of countries is very mixed. On balance, changes in the real terms of trade seem to have constrained countries in their growth by about 0.6 per cent per annum, while capital inflows, on balance, have enabled the countries to grow slightly faster than the Harrod trade multiplier result, by about 0.05 per cent per annum. In some countries, however, the real terms of trade improved, while in many others the rate of growth of real capital imports did not keep pace with the growth of exports, thereby reducing the growth rate below that predicted by the Harrod trade multiplier result starting from initial deficit. Although the mean absolute error of the actual growth rate from the predicted Harrod multiplier result of 2.01 may be regarded as high, it is difficult to believe that the growth process, and constraints on it, can be understood properly in most countries without reference to the balance of payments, and the 'dynamic' Harrod trade multiplier provides a simple and useful starting point for analysis.

Notes

1 This important point can be appreciated by specifying the national income equation first in units of domestic currency and then in real terms. Measured in domestic currency we have

$$P_d Y = P_d \text{Con.} + P_d \text{Inv.} + P_d X - P_f EM,$$

where P_d is the domestic price of output; P_f is the foreign price of imports; E is the exchange rate measured as the domestic price of foreign currency; Con. is total domestic consumption, and Inv. is total domestic investment. Dividing through by P_d we have the equation for real income

$$Y = \text{Con.} + \text{Inv.} + X - (P_f E/P_d)M.$$

An excess of real expenditure over real income implies $X < (P_f E/P_d)M$, which must be filled by real capital inflows (C_r). Thus,

$$X - (P_f E/P_d)M + C_r = 0$$

is the equilibrium condition. Letting $M = mY$ we have

$$Y = \left(\frac{X + C_r}{m} \right)(P_d/P_f E).$$

What happens to real income depends on exports; capital flows, and relative price movements measured in a common currency (the real terms of trade). If imports and exports are related to relative price movements, the price effect will consist of a pure terms of trade effect, and a volume effect on imports and exports if the price elasticities of demand differ from zero.

   If accounting data are used to test the model, deviations from the trade multiplier result, due to a non-instantaneous multiplier process, are also ruled out.

2 To accommodate capital inflows into the model it is clearly not sufficient simply to add a term for the rate of growth of capital inflows to the export side of the equation since the terms on the left hand side of equation (3.10) are additive and a *given* rate of growth of capital inflows will not have the same import buying power as a *given* rate of growth of exports if the base *level* of capital inflows is lower than the value of exports. It is equally clear that for the model to give the same prediction as the model which starts from current account equilibrium, the rate of growth of capital inflows (c_t) must equal the rate of growth of export earnings ($p_{dt} + x_t$).

3 In the model with capital flows, balance of payments constrained growth must be interpreted to mean nothing more than the growth rate associated with the balance of payments balancing, that is, with all debits and credits summing to zero.

4 We made our own estimate for Brazil for a more recent time period.

4 Economic growth, the Harrod foreign trade multiplier and the Hicks super-multiplier*

J. S. L. McCombie

Introduction

The post-Keynesian view of economic growth denies that the performance of the advanced countries has been seriously constrained by the growth of factor supplies. Even during the expansionary period of 1950–73, when the average annual growth of output was double that achieved over the previous eighty years, labour shortages were never a limiting factor. There was either sufficient disguised unemployment in the non-manufacturing sectors or enough immigration to satisfy the demand for labour. The rate of capital accumulation is never a long-run constraint on economic growth as investment is as much a result of the expansion of output as its cause.[1]

If growth is indeed demand rather than supply-constrained, the question naturally arises as to why some countries have performed so much better than others. Furthermore, why has it not been possible to increase the rate of growth simply by the use of traditional demand-management policies? The answers to these questions have led to a consideration of the importance of the balance of payments constraint and a revival of interest in the Harrod foreign trade multiplier.[2]

In an open economy which is not fundamentally resource-constrained, the level of income is determined by the volume of exports. Exports represent the autonomous component of demand analogous to investment in the Keynesian closed economy model. Under fixed exchange rates, or in a situation where the volume of exports and imports are relatively insensitive to price changes, it is the level of output that adjusts to ensure equilibrium in the balance of payments. If, as Kaldor (1979) has noted, the average and marginal propensities to import are constant over time, investment is financed by retained profits, government expenditure is financed by taxation, and the other exogenous components of demand are ignored, then the level of income (Y) is simply determined by the level of exports (X):[3]

$$Y = \frac{1}{m}X, \tag{4.1}$$

where m is the marginal propensity to import.

* Revised version of a paper which first appeared in *Applied Economics*, February.

A logical consequence is that the growth of output will be primarily determined by the increase in exports through the foreign trade multiplier. Moreover, the latter is often taken to be equivalent to the Hicks super-multiplier.

It is useful to quote Kaldor's (1978c, p. 146) summary of the argument.

> From the point of view of any particular region,[4] the 'autonomous component of demand' is the demand emanating from *outside* the region; and Hicks' notion of the 'super-multiplier' can be applied so as to express the doctrine of the foreign trade multiplier in a dynamic setting. So expressed, the doctrine asserts that the rate of economic development of a region is fundamentally governed by the rate of growth of its exports. For the exports, via the 'accelerator', will govern the rate of growth of industrial capacity, as well as the growth of consumption; it will also serve to adjust (again under rather severe simplifying assumptions) both the level, and the rate of growth, of imports to that of exports.

Dixon and Thirlwall (1975) have likewise invoked the super-multiplier as an explanation of the relationship between output and export growth which forms an integral part of their cumulative causation model.

The purpose of this chapter is to examine and clarify the relationship between export-led growth, the Harrod foreign trade multiplier and Hicks's super-multiplier in the context of long-run economic growth. It is argued that the Keynesian model which has been traditionally used to examine short-run fluctuations also yields insights into the determination of the trend rate of growth. Consequently, the argument will be developed in terms of the orthodox Keynesian model and the New Cambridge variant (see Smith, 1976).

It will be shown that generally the workings of the Harrod foreign trade multiplier and Hicks' super-multiplier are not synonymous. It is also found that due to this there is no validity to the criticism that the growth of exports cannot be an important determinant of the growth of output for those countries (such as the US) where exports form only a small fraction of output.

We conclude with a discussion of Thirlwall's 'law of economic growth' and suggest the super-multiplier as a rationale for it. We also consider the relevance of the law for analysing the post-war growth of the advanced countries.

Export-led growth and the foreign trade multiplier

It is useful to begin the discussion with a consideration of the simple empirical relationship between the growth of GDP and exports that has been often held to confirm the importance of export-led growth. The relationship is usually estimated by regression analysis using cross-country data and growth rates over a decade or more. (Thirlwall, 1982, table 3; Batchelor *et al.*, 1980, table 7.4 provide a convenient summary of a number of other studies estimating this relationship.) A close fit is commonly found with a regression coefficient that is significantly less than one. Since the specification is so parsimonious, Occam's razor suggests it will be a powerful explanation of the disparate growth

Table 4.1 The relationship between the growth of GDP ($\overset{\circ}{Y}$) and
that of total exports ($\overset{\circ}{X}$)

1973–80[a]:	$\overset{\circ}{Y} = 1.549 + 0.209\ \overset{\circ}{X}$ (2.78) (2.10)	$\bar{R}^2 = 0.208$
1955[b]–73:	$\overset{\circ}{Y} = -0.052 + 0.600\ \overset{\circ}{X}$ (4.02) (4.92)	$\bar{R}^2 = 0.641$

Source: OECD National Accounts, 1950–79 and 1960–80.

Notes

Figures in parentheses are *t*-values. Sample consists of fifteen advanced countries.

a Terminal date is 1979 for three countries.

b The initial year is the peak of the trade cycle and varies from 1955 to
1957 depending upon the particular country.

rates of output, *provided it can be shown to have a satisfactory theoretical rationale.*[5]

For convenience, we estimated the relationship for the advanced countries for two periods, 1955–73 and 1973–80. The year 1973 represents the turning point when the advanced countries entered a period of prolonged recession from which they have yet to recover (notwithstanding a small upturn in 1979). The regression results are reported in Table 4.1. It transpires that there is a close relationship for the period 1955–73 between the growth of GDP and the export of goods and services. This immediately raises the question of the interpretation of the equation because correlation implies nothing about the direction of causality or indeed whether it exists at all. It is perfectly possible for those factors (such as entrepreneurial dynamism) that make for a fast rate of growth of GDP to be likewise responsible for a rapid export growth. Furthermore, it is possible that both growth rates may be exogenously determined by the growth of factor inputs.

However, it is beyond the scope of this chapter to assess the relative merits of the supply and demand-oriented explanations of economic growth. We are assuming here that there has generally been no long-run supply constraint in the growth of the advanced countries. (See Cornwall, 1977 and McCombie, 1982, for a discussion of these issues.) If this is accepted then the importance of the equation is that a failure to find such a relationship between output and export growth could be taken to be a refutation of the crucial role of the balance of payments in constraining the growth of output. Indeed, the weaker correlation that is found for 1973–80 indicates that the balance of payments may not have been a binding constraint as several countries pursued deflationary policies in order to restrict output with the supposed aim of combating inflation. In other words, the growth of output was often lower than the maximum which was made possible by the growth of exports.

If this relationship is supposed to reflect the foreign trade multiplier, then one objection, as mentioned in the introduction, is that its importance must vary considerably between the advanced countries, depending on the size of the export sector relative to GDP. This ratio varies from the US where it is 5 per cent (1956) to the Netherlands, 44 per cent (1956). Surely, the impact of an increase in exports of, for example, one percentage point will have considerably less impact in the case of the US than the Netherlands? This suggests that the relationship between $\mathring{Y}$ and $\mathring{X}$ estimated earlier is wrongly specified, *providing its theoretical rationale rests solely on the foreign trade multiplier.*[6]

Severn (1968) has pursued this argument by reasoning that an allowance ought to be made in the regression for the degree of openness of the economy. He suggested that the growth of exports should be weighted by an 'openness coefficient', namely the ratio of exports to total output. The regression to be estimated now becomes

$$\mathring{Y} = \alpha_1 + \beta_1 \left(\frac{X}{Y}\right) \mathring{X}. \tag{4.2}$$

The results are reported in Table 4.2.

It is sufficient to note that there is now no statistically significant relationship between the two variables. However, it will be shown later that this argument is in fact erroneous if the relationship between the growth of GDP and exports is representing the super-multiplier.

Ideally, in order to discuss the role of the two multipliers in the context of economic growth, we should use a full-scale econometric model of the economy. Nevertheless, the main arguments can be satisfactorily demonstrated with the use of simple Keynesian models. Clearly, the theoretical rationale must be Keynesian in nature since export-led growth has no meaning under the assumptions of global monetarism.

We further accept the argument that the money supply, broadly defined, is endogenous. By making this assumption we are presenting the strong or, no doubt some would say extreme, Keynesian interpretation of export-led growth. The differences in the growth of the advanced countries are seen to reflect ultimately real rather than monetary forces.

The orthodox Keynesian model may be described by the following equations ignoring, for expositional ease, indirect taxes:

$$Y = C + I + G + X - M, \tag{4.3a}$$

$$C = C_0 + b(Y - T), \tag{4.3b}$$

Table 4.2 The relationship between the growth of GDP ($\mathring{Y}$) and that of total exports weighted by the 'openness coefficient' ($\mathring{X}^*$)

1973–80	$\mathring{Y} = 1.905 + 0.526\ \mathring{X}^*$ (4.02)　(1.73)	$\bar{R}^2 = 0.134$
1955–73	$\mathring{Y} = 4.769 - 0.048\ \mathring{X}^*$ (4.69)　(-0.01)	$\bar{R}^2 = 0.009$

For notes and sources, see Table 4.1.

$$T = tY, \tag{4.3c}$$

$$I = I_0, \tag{4.3d}$$

$$G = G_0, \tag{4.3e}$$

$$X = X_0 + \gamma P, \tag{4.3f}$$

$$M = M_0 + mY - \rho P. \tag{4.3g}$$

Y, C, I, G, X, M and T denote GDP, consumption, investment, government expenditure, exports, imports and tax revenues. P is defined as an index of the ratio of foreign to domestic prices. The subscript 0 denotes autonomous expenditure.

The relationships of the model are well-known and hence need not be discussed here.

The level of income is given by

$$Y = \frac{1}{k}(C_0 + I + G + X_0 - M_0 + (\gamma + \rho)P), \tag{4.4}$$

where

$$k = (m + 1 - b + bt). \tag{4.5}$$

At this point it is worth digressing for a moment to discuss the cases of fixed and flexible exchange rates. P is a policy instrument and through exchange rate adjustment the government may be able to influence to some degree the level and growth of exports and imports. Prior to the breakdown of Bretton Woods in 1972, the predominant regime was one of fixed exchange rates. In this case P is constant and hence will not affect the growth of either exports or imports. (There were, of course, the notable exceptions of the French devaluation in the late 1950s and the British devaluation of 1967.) On the other hand, it might be thought that the introduction of flexible exchange rates in the 1970s effectively destroyed the notion of export-led growth. It is often argued that under flexible exchange rates, external equilibrium can be achieved at any desired level of economic activity.

Two points arise here. First, there is the problem of, for example, the translation of nominal devaluations into changes in the real exchange rate. The existence of 'real wage resistance' may mean that subsequent domestic price inflation will, after a lag, be sufficient to wipe out any initial advantage. Second, and more importantly for our purposes, even though there were substantial changes in real exchange rates throughout the 1970s, these were not sufficient to achieve anything but minor changes in the relative export performances of the advanced countries. In other words, the change in total exports was mainly due to changes in X_0 rather than in γP. (See Fetherston *et al.*, 1977 and Kaldor, 1978b, for the empirical evidence.)

Therefore, it is plausible to assume that the growth of exports can be regarded as exogenous. Under these circumstances, the growth of output is given by

$$\frac{\Delta Y}{Y} = \frac{1}{k}\left(a_{C_0}\frac{\Delta C_0}{C_0} + a_I\frac{\Delta I}{I} + a_G\frac{\Delta G}{G} + a_X\frac{\Delta X}{X} - a_{M_0}\frac{\Delta M_0}{M_0}\right), \qquad (4.6)$$

where a denotes the share of the relevant variable in total output.

If the only increase in the autonomous expenditure comes from exports, the rate of growth of output is given by $\Delta Y/Y = (1/k)(a_X)\Delta X/X$ which represents the impact caused by the foreign trade multiplier.

An alternative approach is to use the New Cambridge model of the economy which is similar to the orthodox Keynesian approach but with the important difference that, instead of two separate relationships for the determinants of consumption, there is only one for private expenditure (Smith, 1976).

This is given by

$$PE = d(Y - T) - NAFA. \qquad (4.7)$$

Private expenditure, PE, is a function of disposable income (in practice d is near unity) and the net acquisition of financial assets (*NAFA*). The latter was initially thought to be stable over time and small in relation to the level of GDP.[7] In the earliest version of the model the budget deficit ($D = G - T$) was taken to be exogenous so the rate of growth of output is, assuming $d = 1$, given by:

$$\frac{\Delta Y}{Y} = \frac{1}{m}\left(a_X\frac{\Delta X}{X} - a_{M_0}\frac{\Delta M_0}{M_0} + a_D\frac{\Delta D}{D}\right). \qquad (4.8)$$

since, by assumption, $\Delta NAFA = 0$.

However, it is clear that, since part of the government's spending and receipts is endogenous (such as payments for unemployment benefits and tax receipts), it is unlikely that the government could be totally successful in manipulating the exogenous components to obtain the desired budget surplus or deficit. Hence, it is more plausible to make tax receipts a function of income ($T = tY$). More recent models have also made *NAFA* a function of income (i.e. $NAFA = e(Y - T)$ although e is likely to be small). Under these circumstances

$$\frac{\Delta Y}{Y} = \frac{1}{(m + t - et + e)}\left(a_X\frac{\Delta X}{X} - a_{M_0}\frac{\Delta M_0}{M_0} + a_G\frac{\Delta G}{G}\right). \qquad (4.9)$$

Hence, the foreign trade multiplier is either $1/m$ or $1/(m + t - et + e)$. In either case it is larger than the orthodox Keynesian multiplier.

The direct impact of the foreign trade multiplier

In this section, we report the estimate of the increase in GDP induced, through the foreign trade multiplier, by an increase in the growth of exports of one percentage point per annum. In order to calculate this it is necessary to know the values of the multiplier for the various advanced countries, but unfortunately these are not always readily available. It was therefore necessary to first construct an estimate of each country's multiplier.

The multiplier used is defined as

$$k = \frac{1}{1 - b + bt_{\mathrm{d}} + t_{\mathrm{i}} + m}, \tag{4.10}$$

where b, t_{d}, t_{i} and m are the marginal propensities to consume, to tax directly, to tax indirectly and to import.[8] Direct taxation includes both social security contributions and imputed employee welfare contributions. The marginal propensities were calculated by estimating the ratios of the absolute changes in the relevant variables over the period and the data were taken from the OECD National Accounts. Since the marginal propensity to import is the propensity that varies the greatest between the countries, we also constructed an alternative estimate. The marginal propensity to import manufactures was taken to be double the average, while for raw materials and semi-processed goods the marginal propensity was taken to be equal to the average. (In practice it makes little difference as to which procedure is adopted.)

Since this approach was taken as a *pis aller*, the values of the multiplier are best regarded as orders of magnitude rather than being precise estimates. Nevertheless, the value obtained for the UK of 1.11 for the 1970s seems plausible, especially since Cuthbertson (1979) reports that the NIESR multiplier lies in the range 0.8–1.0, the Treasury Model gives a value of 1.1 and the CEPG's value is approximately 1.25. The value for the US of 1.37 also seems reasonable for what is virtually a closed economy.

The differences in the values of the multiplier (see Table 4.3, column 4) depend primarily on differences in the marginal propensities to import. For the pre-1973 period the average value of the other leakages, $(1 - b + bt_{\mathrm{d}} + t_{\mathrm{i}})$, is 0.55 with eight of the countries falling within ±0.05 of this figure. The extreme values are 0.65 for Norway and 0.47 for the US. For the period 1973–80, this stability of the marginal propensities of the other leakages is again observed, although the average value has fallen to 0.45.

The results of the calculations of the impact on GDP growth of a one percentage point increase in export growth are reported in Table 4.3, Column 5(a). It can be seen that there is a wide diversity of results across the countries. The US, although it has the largest multiplier, experiences the smallest increase in output through the foreign trade multiplier. Even Japan, often cited as the example *par excellence* of export-led growth, experiences only a small impact. In this case a one percentage point increase in total exports increases the growth of GDP by only 0.16 (1957) and 0.18 (1980) percentage points. Alternatively, the very open economies of Denmark, the Netherlands and Norway experienced an increase in their growth rates in the mid-1950s by over a third of a percentage point.

Table 4.3 The effect on the growth of GDP of an increase in the growth of total exports through the foreign trade multiplier and super-multiplier

Country	Ratio of total exports to GDP %	Marginal propensity to import	Value of the multiplier	Percentage point increase in GDP growth due to an increase of one percentage point in export growth		Ratio of values in 5a to 5b
				Foreign trade multiplier	Super-multiplier	
1	2	3	4	5a	5b	6
1980						
Austria	39.0	0.50	0.78	0.30	0.78	38
Belgium	59.7	0.82	0.66	0.39	0.73	54
Canada	29.3	0.31	1.05	0.30	0.94	33
Denmark	33.3	0.36	0.91	0.30	0.92	33
France	22.4	0.29	1.04	0.23	0.77	30
Germany	27.0	0.41	0.88	0.23	0.66	36
Ireland	53.9	0.82	0.73	0.39	0.66	59
Italy	25.2	0.31	1.02	0.25	0.81	32
Japan	14.0	0.19	1.26	0.18	0.74	24
Netherlands	53.0	0.73	0.67	0.36	0.73	49
Norway	47.6	0.38	0.76	0.36	1.25	30
United Kingdom	28.4	0.26	1.11	0.32	1.09	29
United States	10.0	0.15	1.37	0.14	0.66	21
Mid-1950s						
Austria	25.1	0.38	0.90	0.23	0.66	34
Belgium	33.7	0.52	0.81	0.27	0.65	42
Canada	20.0	0.25	1.07	0.21	0.80	26
Denmark	33.9	0.34	1.12	0.38	0.99	38
France	14.1	0.20	1.18	0.17	0.70	24
Germany	20.1	0.24	1.06	0.21	0.84	25
Ireland	31.0	0.46	0.99	0.31	0.67	46
Italy	10.9	0.21	1.27	0.14	0.52	27
Japan	11.5	0.16	1.43	0.16	0.72	22
Netherlands	43.9	0.60	0.94	0.41	0.73	56
Norway	43.8	0.46	0.76	0.33	0.95	35
United Kingdom	21.9	0.31	1.08	0.24	0.71	33
United States	5.0	0.08	1.42	0.07	0.62	11

Source: Author's own calculations.

Over time, the impact of the foreign trade multiplier has generally increased slightly as the increase of the size of the export sector has more than offset the decline in the value of the multiplier.[9]

The variation of the importance of the impact of the foreign trade multiplier across the countries would superficially seem to confirm the criticisms noted earlier.

A further objection to the fundamental role of the foreign trade multiplier in determining economic growth may be seen by considering equation (4.6) again. This may be written equivalently as

$$\frac{\Delta Y}{Y} = \frac{1}{k} \left(a_X \frac{\Delta X}{X} + a_E \frac{\Delta E}{E} \right), \tag{4.11}$$

where E is the sum of all other autonomous expenditures. It has been questioned as to why an increase in X should have any greater impact on the level of economic activity than an equal increase in E. The answer is, of course, that the growth of exports is the only element that simultaneously relaxes the balance of payments constraint. For example, the post-war history of the UK has been consumption-led expansion (1954, 1959, 1963, 1973) which resulted in an expansion of output above the trend rate of growth. This was brought to an abrupt end by the rapid increase in induced imports which led to the familiar balance of payments crises. It is therefore necessary to turn to an examination of the role of import growth in constraining growth, which leads to a consideration of the super-multiplier.

Export-led growth and the Hicks super-multiplier

The direct influence of an increase in exports through the foreign trade multiplier is only one mechanism by which output will be increased. A secondary route is that, by initially relaxing the balance of payments constraint, an increase in exports will allow other autonomous expenditures to be increased until income has risen by enough to induce an increase in imports equivalent to the initial increase in exports.

We have seen, in the short-run, that the absolute increase of output through the foreign trade multiplier is given by

$$\Delta Y = \frac{1}{k} \Delta X. \tag{4.12}$$

The increase in imports induced by the expansion of output is given by the marginal import–output ratio:

$$\Delta M = m \Delta Y, \tag{4.13}$$

$$\Delta M = \frac{m}{k} \Delta X. \tag{4.14}$$

Since $k > m$, the increase in imports will be less than the increase in exports and a balance of trade surplus will accrue, equal to

$$\left(\frac{k-m}{k}\right)\Delta X. \tag{4.15}$$

However, in the long-run the super-multiplier operates increasing the level of activity until the induced level of imports equals the increase in the volume of exports.

Consequently as $\Delta M = \Delta X$, it follows that

$$\frac{\Delta Y}{Y} = \frac{1}{m}\left(a_X \frac{\Delta X}{X}\right) \tag{4.16}$$

$$= \frac{1}{k}\left(a_X \frac{\Delta X}{X} + a_E \frac{\Delta E}{E}\right). \tag{4.17}$$

Equations (4.16) and (4.17) represent the working of the Hicks super-multiplier. Apart from the direct increase in output through the foreign trade multiplier $((1/k)(a_X)\Delta X/X)$, the initial relaxation of the balance of payments constraint permits (rather than automatically causes) an increase in 'autonomous' expenditure given by

$$\frac{\Delta E}{E} = k\left(\frac{1}{m} - \frac{1}{k}\right)\left(\frac{a_X}{a_E}\right)\left(\frac{\Delta X}{X}\right). \tag{4.18}$$

If autonomous expenditure is not expanded by the amount implied by equation (4.18), then the increase in output will be commensurately less and a balance of payments surplus will occur as outlined above.[10]

An idea of the magnitude of the impact of the super-multiplier may be seen again from Table 4.3 (column 5b) where the percentage point increase in GDP resulting from a one percentage point increase in exports is reported. It can be seen that the increase in GDP is greater, and shows less inter-country variation, than when the foreign trade multiplier operates. It is noticeable that the US and Japan now experience one of the greatest increases in GDP from a given increase in exports. Table 4.3 also reports the percentage of the increase in output resulting from the increase in exports that is attributable to the Harrod foreign trade multiplier (column 6). In the mid-1950s the percentage ranged from 11 (the US) to 56 (the Netherlands). The proportion has increased over time reflecting the increasing share of exports (and imports) in GDP leading to an increase in the impact of the foreign trade multiplier relative to the super-multiplier.

With these arguments in mind, we are now in a position to reconsider the relationship between the growth of output and exports, namely

$$\mathring{Y} = \alpha_2 + \beta_2 \mathring{X}. \tag{4.19}$$

It is clear that its most plausible rationale is as a reduced form equation reflecting the super-multiplier rather than as a mis-specified representation of the foreign trade multiplier, as was suggested in the second section. It is therefore erroneous to weight the growth of exports by an 'openness coefficient' in the manner suggested by Severn (1968).

While the coefficient β_2 is an estimate of the value of the super-multiplier, it is clear that the use of cross-country data is to a certain extent inappropriate as the value of β_2 shows some variation between the countries.[11] (The estimate of β_2 for 1955–73 of 0.6 compares with the average value of Table 4.3, column 5b, of 0.74.)

Thirlwall's law of economic growth

Thirlwall (1979, 1982a,b) has argued that the long-run growth of output is constrained by the balance of payments, and empirical confirmation is given by the rule

$$\left(\frac{\Delta Y}{Y}\right)_{\text{B}} = \left(\frac{1}{\pi}\right)\frac{\Delta X}{X}, \tag{4.20}$$

where $(\Delta Y/Y)_{\text{B}}$ is the rate of growth of output consistent with a balance of payments equilibrium and π is the income elasticity of demand for imports. Using values for π estimated by Houthakker and Magee (1969) and observed growth rates of exports, the equilibrium output growth may be calculated on the assumption that changes in the exchange rate do not greatly affect trade flows and that capital transfers are negligible. It is found that these values accord closely with the actual growth rates (see Table 4.5).

Equation (4.20) is not merely an identity, and the close fit suggests that the above assumptions are realistic. Equation (4.20) is similar to (4.19) although π varies between countries. (This may again explain the relatively large standard error of the regression coefficient when equation (4.19) is estimated using cross-country data for 1955–73, see Table 4.1).

Thirlwall (1982, p. 6) has argued that equation (4.20) is best interpreted as representing the Harrod foreign trade multiplier when made dynamic. However, this interpretation rests on certain simplifying assumptions. Thirlwall's simple Keynesian model (1982, pp. 5–6) yields the following solution for output:

$$Y = \frac{X - M_0 + E}{m + s + t - a - g}, \tag{4.21}$$

where E is the sum of autonomous expenditure excluding that on imports, s, t, a, g are the marginal propensities of saving, taxation, investment and government expenditure, respectively.

In the special case where either $s + t = a + g$ (or, in other words, all induced expenditure equals induced leakages) and there is no autonomous expenditure or

$M_0 = E$, equation (4.21) gives the foreign trade multiplier:

$$Y = \frac{X}{m}. \tag{4.22}$$

It follows that

$$\frac{\Delta Y}{Y} = \frac{1}{m}\left(a_X \frac{\Delta X}{X}\right). \tag{4.23}$$

Consequently, in equilibrium growth $a_X = a_M$, and so $a_X/m = a_M/m$, and a_m/m equals $(M/Y)/(\Delta Y/\Delta M) = 1/\pi$. It therefore follows that

$$\frac{\Delta Y}{Y} = \frac{1}{\pi}\frac{\Delta X}{X}. \tag{4.24}$$

However, the assumptions are not innocuous as implausibly high values are required for the static multiplier, which equals $1/m$. (In the case of the UK, the value would be over three.) Moreover, it is unlikely that there would be no autonomous expenditure. As Thirlwall (1982) has noted, if $E > 0$, there will always be a deficit on the current account regardless of the size of M_0. This is because $Y = (1/m)(X - M_0 + E)$ and $M = M_0 + mY$, so $M = X + E > X$, if E is positive.

These restrictions disappear if equation (4.24) is interpreted as the super-multiplier, so that

$$\frac{\Delta Y}{Y} = \frac{1}{k}\left(a_X \frac{\Delta X}{X} + a_E \frac{\Delta E}{E}\right) \tag{4.25}$$

$$= \frac{1}{m}a_X \frac{\Delta X}{X}. \tag{4.26}$$

and $1/m > 1/k$. As we have seen before, the growth of 'autonomous' expenditure will adjust to ensure the current account remains in equilibrium.

There is one further issue concerned with the interpretation of the law given by equation (4.26) as being a dynamic version of the traditional Harrod foreign trade multiplier. The Keynesian import demand function is given by

$$M = M_0 + mY. \tag{4.27}$$

However, empirical models generally use the power import demand function

$$M = Y^\pi. \tag{4.28}$$

Consequently, when the growth of imports equals the growth of exports, we may derive Thirlwall's Law from equation (4.28) as

$$\frac{\Delta M}{M} = \frac{\Delta X}{X} = \pi \frac{\Delta Y}{Y} \tag{4.29}$$

and it follows that

$$\frac{\Delta Y}{Y} = \frac{1}{\pi} \frac{\Delta X}{X}. \tag{4.30}$$

The equivalence between the two import demand functions may be derived as follows. From the linear import demand function, equation (4.27), holding M_0 constant, we may derive the result that $\Delta M / \Delta Y = m$ and

$$\frac{\Delta M}{\Delta Y} \frac{Y}{M} = m \frac{Y}{M} = \left(\frac{M - M_0}{Y} \right) \left(\frac{Y}{M} \right) = \pi. \tag{4.31}$$

However, it can be seen that as M_0 is positive (it is difficult to give an intuitive interpretation of a negative value of imports), π must be less than unity. Even if the volume of autonomous imports falls over time relative to total imports, the income elasticity of demand will only tend to unity. However, empirically for many countries, the income elasticity of demand for imports estimated from equation (4.28) (but including a relative price term) exceeds unity.

In order to avoid this inconsistency and to reconcile the models, it is useful to regard the linear import demand function, given by equation (4.27), as a short-run relationship, while the power function, equation (4.28), represents the long-run relationship derived from the shift of the short-run function over time as autonomous imports, M_0, and income increases.

This interpretation has the advantage that it is no longer necessary to enforce the equivalence of the values of the import elasticities derived from the linear import demand function and from the power import demand function. Consequently, it is possible for the elasticity of the power import demand function to exceed unity and, at the same time, for $M_0 > 0$, so that the elasticity derived from the linear function is less than unity.

Nevertheless, whatever is the exact relationship between the two import functions, the important point is that it is the external sector through the0 super-multiplier that determines the long-run growth of the advanced countries. In the next section we assess the relevance of the law in explaining the post-war growth of the advanced countries.

Economic growth in open economies

Given the assumptions underlying the super-multiplier and following Thirlwall's analysis, we have seen that the growth of output of a particular country, consistent with a balance of payments equilibrium, is given by the simple rule:[12]

$$\mathring{Y}_B = \frac{\mathring{X}}{\pi} \tag{4.32}$$

or, if exports are determined by world income ($X = Y_W^\varepsilon$),

$$\mathring{Y}_B = \frac{\varepsilon \mathring{Y}_W}{\pi}. \tag{4.33}$$

Table 4.4 Export and import income elasticities of the six largest advanced countries

Country	World income elasticity of demand for exports	Domestic income elasticity of demand for imports	
		(a)	(b)
Japan	3.55	1.23	n.a.
Italy	2.95	2.19	n.a.
West Germany	2.08	1.80	1.31
France	1.53	1.66	1.63
United States	0.99	1.51	n.a.
United Kingdom	0.86	1.66	1.82

Sources: Houthakker and Magee (1969) for export elasticities and the import elasticities in column (a); Panic (1976) for import elasticities in column (b).

Table 4.5 Observed and equilibrium growth rates of GDP, and growth of exports, six largest advanced countries

Country	1951–73			1973–80		
	Growth of		Equilibrium growth of GDP	Growth of		Equilibrium growth of GDP
	GDP (i)	Exports (ii)		GDP (i)	Exports (ii)	
Japan	9.79	12.67	10.30	3.68	10.64	8.65
Italy	5.22	11.13	5.08	2.75	6.54	2.91
West Germany	5.64	9.88	5.48(7.54)	2.30	5.03	2.66(3.83)
France	5.11	7.59	4.57(4.65)	2.80	6.21	3.83(3.81)
United States	3.58	5.04	3.33	2.22	5.58	3.70
United Kingdom	2.91	4.27	2.61(2.35)	0.91	3.30	2.19(1.81)

Source: OECD National Accounts.

Note
Equilibrium growth of GDP derived using import elasticities from Houthakker and Magee except those in parentheses which use Panic's estimates.

Table 4.4 reports the values of the world income elasticity of demand for the exports of the six largest countries, together with their income elasticities of demand for imports. Table 4.5 gives these countries, rates of growth of GDP, exports and the balance of payments equilibrium growth (calculated from equation (4.32)) for the years 1951–73 and 1973–80. The equilibrium growth of GDP is found to approximate the observed growth rates. (Using the standard errors of the estimates of the income elasticities by Houthakker and Magee, the difference between the equilibrium and actual growth rates is not statistically significant.) In the period 1973–80, two countries (Japan and the UK) have equilibrium growth rates significantly above their actual growth rates. This could be because demand was not expanded enough for fear of inflationary pressures or, as may well be the case in the UK, there was a marked increase in the propensity to import in the late 1970s.

In the context of long-term growth, it is readily apparent that the differing export elasticities are more important in explaining the different GDP growth rates than the import elasticities. For example, the countries with the fastest and the second fastest growth of GDP, Japan and Italy, had the lowest and highest import elasticities, respectively. To put the matter another way: if the UK had Japan's income elasticity of demand for imports then the equilibrium growth rate would increase by a little over 0.5 per cent per annum, *ceteris paribus*. If, on the other hand, the UK's exports were sufficiently competitive that her export elasticity matched even that of West Germany, the equilibrium growth rate would be double the actual equilibrium rate of 2.61 per cent per annum.[13]

This approach to economic growth is sometimes termed 'demand oriented' because of its emphasis on the role of the multiplier. Nevertheless, it places great emphasis on the importance of supply characteristics and provides no justification for the conventional Keynesian demand management policies as applied particularly to the post-war UK economy.

The key to the long-run growth of the economy is the rate of expansion of exports. This has more to do with such factors as quality, design and delivery dates than with price competitiveness (Connell, 1979). Thus attempts to increase the trend rate of growth of exports through macroeconomic policies, such as exchange rate adjustment, are unlikely to be very successful. The problem of the poor performance of UK exports is a structural problem requiring an industrial strategy at the microeconomic level. The fallacy of past UK policy has rested in the belief that if only growth generated by fiscal policies could be maintained for long enough (albeit at the expense of a 'temporary' balance of payments deficit) there should be no reason why the growth of the UK could not match that of the other European countries. However, this myth was finally exploded with the Barber boom of 1971–73. Even an 18 per cent devaluation could not prevent the occurrence of an untenable balance of payments deficit. An attempt to increase the growth rate by a consumption-led boom leads to an immediate increase in imports. It may be that increasing the trend rate of growth of output would eventually increase the growth of exports (through, for example, the Verdoorn effect) but such results are achievable only in the long term and would not have very much influence over a period of two or three years. It was hardly surprising that such attempts at demand management, based as they were on a theory essentially concerned with a closed economy, were bound to end in failure (Eltis, 1976).

Up to now, the analysis using the law has been based on a partial equilibrium model and neglects the interrelationships between the advanced countries. It explains how a given growth in world income (taken to be that of the combined OECD countries) and in world trade is distributed between the advanced countries, but it does not explain what determines the former. For example, the output of the advanced countries grew at about 5 per cent per annum during the period 1951–73 but in the subsequent decade it fell by about half. The reasons for the post-war rapid expansion of world trade prior to 1973 were based, *inter alia*, on the initial willingness of the US to run a trade deficit and to ensure sufficient international liquidity. This has been well documented and need not be repeated here (Cripps, 1978).

However, the interrelatedness of the advanced countries has had serious implications especially for the 1980s. The immediate cause of the 1979–85 world recession was undoubtedly due to the rise in oil prices, but the subsequent failure of the advanced countries to take sufficient measures to ensure a return to full employment must be due to an acceptance of the argument that this would inevitably lead to unacceptably high levels of inflation. The problem is that should one country disagree and try to obtain a return to full employment by reflating in isolation, then for the reasons outlined here, it would run into serious balance of payments problems. Even though there is widespread underutilization of resources throughout the western world, the multiplier effects will not be sufficient to generate a sufficient rise in world income to prevent the reflating country from running into a balance of payments deficit. This is, of course, a reflection of the $n-1$ 'redundancy problem'. If the other countries are content with their balance of payments position and assume the level of output is unalterable, then the nth country (such as France in the early 1980s) has no degrees of freedom within which to act.

The irony is that for any individual country the only satisfactory method of increasing its growth is by improving its export performance rather than by stimulating internal demand. But for the advanced countries as a whole, such measures as competitive devaluation and the imposition of 'beggar-my-neighbour' tariffs and quotas (in an attempt to reduce the growth of imports) will be self-defeating. The most effective solution is the one, advocated long ago by Keynes himself, of co-ordinated expansionary policies undertaken simultaneously in all the advanced countries. This would act to increase output in a manner analogous to the closed economy since there would be no deterioration of any country's balance of payments.

Concluding comments

The most satisfactory basis of the export-led growth theory is the operation of the Hicks super-multiplier. A corollary of this is that while some of the faster growing countries (most notably Japan and West Germany since the mid-1960s) may have experienced a labour supply constraint, the growth of factor inputs has never been the exogeneous determinant of growth. This role belongs to the growth of exports which, by relaxing the balance of payments constraint, determines the maximum growth of GDP even though this may not be sufficient to ensure the full utilization of the factors of production. The reason why the slower growing countries did not experience a marked acceleration in the rate of unemployment until the late 1960s was that the tertiary sector absorbed much of the labour supply even though it led to disguised unemployment.

Although the theory outlined in this chapter is post-Keynesian, in the sense that it is demand-oriented, in fact it emphasizes the importance of the supply side of the economy. The efficiency with which goods destined for the foreign market are produced ultimately determines the performance of the economy as a whole.

The export-led growth is also reflected in Thirlwall's 'law of growth'. It has been shown that the law (being based on a *power* import demand function) cannot be easily reconciled with the foreign trade multiplier (which is based on a *linear* import demand function) unless a distinction is made between short- and long-run relationships. Nevertheless the law, in spite of, or perhaps because of, its simplicity provides many insights into the post-war growth of the advanced countries. Of course, it is unlikely that the UK could ever have matched the economic performance of Japan, but if exports had grown at 7 per cent per annum over the post-war period the UK must surely have been capable of a growth of GDP between 4 and $4\frac{1}{2}$ per cent per annum.

Notes

1 See Cornwall (1977) for an exposition and survey of this approach.
2 Harrod's formulation of the foreign trade multiplier actually predated the Keynesian investment multiplier by three years, although it was subsequently overshadowed by the latter. The revival and reassessment of the foreign trade multiplier is largely due to Kaldor (1978a, 1979) and Thirlwall (1979, 1982, 1983).
3 These are very restrictive assumptions which we shall relax later.
4 Kaldor uses the term regions to denote different countries, groups of countries or different areas within the same country.
5 Some studies included other exogenous variables in the regression apart from export growth. These include the ratio of capital flows to output and the share of manufactured exports to total expenditure. However, the theoretical basis of these equations is often not made clear and only Thirlwall (1982) has explicitly interpreted the relationship as reflecting the (dynamic) foreign trade multiplier. We shall show later that the relationship is best regarded as a reduced-form equation derived from the operation of the super-multiplier. In this case, it is not a mis-specification to exclude the growth of other variables that are often held to be important determinants of growth (such as the level of investment). This is because these variables are in their turn determined by the balance of payments constraint and the rate of growth of exports. Strictly speaking, the rate of growth of capital flows (weighted by the share of the capital flows to total foreign exchange receipts) should also be included as a regressor in addition to the growth of exports (weighted by the value of exports in total receipts). In practice, the former is so small compared to the latter that for expositional purposes we can safely ignore it.
6 This criticism is based solely on the direct impact of export growth on that of output through the foreign trade multiplier and ignores the increase in output made possible through the relaxation of the balance of payments constraint. This point will be dealt with more fully later.
7 See the Cambridge Economic Policy Group (1981, p. 9).
8 The multiplier associated with the New Cambridge Model was also calculated but as it is not clear how applicable this approach is to the other advanced countries we only report the results of the orthodox Keynesian multiplier.
9 One exception that calls for comment is the case of the Netherlands which experienced a decline in the impact of the foreign trade multiplier from the mid-1950s to 1980. This occurred because, although there was an increase in both the marginal propensities to tax (both directly and indirectly) and to import, this was more than offset by a decrease in the marginal propensity to save. Indeed over the period 1973–80 the Netherlands' increase in consumption was greater than the increase in disposable income.
10 As we have seen, in the earliest New Cambridge model, the Harrod foreign trade multiplier and the Hicks super-multiplier are formally identical and equal to $1/m$. An increase in exports would increase income by exactly the amount required to induce an increase in imports equal to that of exports. In the more recent versions, the foreign trade multiplier is less than $1/m$ and so an increase in exports would generate a trade surplus

unless other 'autonomous' expenditures increase. In this last case, there is a distinction between the foreign trade multiplier and the super-multiplier along the lines discussed earlier.

11 It would be useful to estimate this relationship for each country separately using time-series data but this is outside the scope of this chapter.

12 We assume that the impact of changes in the terms of trade and net capital flows are not significant when compared with the influence of the growth of exports. Of course, this may not be such a satisfactory assumption when short-run deviation about a country's equilibrium growth rate are considered. Thirlwall (1983) has derived a more general expression for equation (4.32) incorporating these effects.

13 The differences in income elasticities to import can be largely explained by the differing composition of imports and, in particular, the share of manufactures imported. The income elasticity of demand for the import of manufactures is approximately 2 for most of the advanced countries (although for the UK it is nearer 3). The income elasticities for raw materials and fuels are generally less than unity. The low aggregate import elasticity of Japan may be explained by the fact that in 1973 the share of manufactures in Japan's merchandise import bill was 33 per cent whereas for the remaining five advanced countries the lowest was the UK with 57 per cent.

5 Economic growth, trade interlinkages, and the balance of payments constraint*

J. S. L. McCombie

The purpose of this chapter is to examine the determination of the long-term growth of the advanced countries and especially to consider how the growth of one country (or group of countries) may deleteriously affect the growth of another through the balance of payments constraint. The approach is Keynesian in nature since it is argued that the key to the understanding of the trend rate of income growth is the rate of expansion of effective demand. A necessary assumption for this approach is that the rate of growth of factor supplies, especially labor, has not been the autonomous determinant of the growth of output, as in the neoclassical approach. (See Kindleberger, 1967; Cornwall, 1977; Kaldor, 1978a; and Van der Wee, 1987, for evidence in support of this contention.) It will be shown, following the seminal work of Beckerman (1962), Kaldor (1970), Cripps (1978), and Thirlwall (1979), that the growth of an advanced country is primarily determined by its performance in overseas markets. In other words, growth is ultimately export-led. (A detailed discussion of this whole approach can be found in McCombie and Thirlwall, 1994.)

We begin with a consideration of Thirlwall's "law of economic growth" which states that the rate of growth of a country's income is determined, in the long run, by the ratio of its export growth to its income elasticity of demand for imports. This law reflects the operation, in a dynamic context, of the Harrod foreign trade multiplier or Hicks's supermultiplier (Kaldor, 1970, 1978a; Thirlwall, 1979; Thirlwall and Hussain, 1982). This approach provides an elaboration of the rationale for the export-led growth theory and also confirms the applicability of Keynesian principles to long-term economic growth. Nevertheless, it is essentially a partial equilibrium approach in that it argues that the fundamental determinant of the growth of any particular country lies in the growth of its exports and this, in turn, is determined primarily by the exogenously given growth of world income. (The model has been extended to allow for capital flows and changes in relative prices, but it is argued that, empirically, these are of secondary importance.)

In this chapter, we generalize Thirlwall's approach using the truism that one country's exports are the imports of another. Explicit allowance is made for trade interlinkages and it is shown how the economic performance of one group of

* First published in *Journal of Post Keynesian Economics*, Summer 1993.

countries may, through the workings of the balance of payments, constrain the growth of other nations and limit the degree of control the latter have over their economies.

Of particular importance, especially since 1973, is the "deflationary bias" that the asymmetry in the balance of payments adjustment process imparts into the international economy. This asymmetry results from the fact that a country is able to run a balance of payments surplus almost indefinitely, while there are strong pressures on a country to correct a deficit, normally through deflationary measures to reduce the growth of output and, hence, the growth of imports. The severe deflationary pressures that were introduced in the 1970s, putatively to reduce the rate of inflation generated by the commodity boom and oil price rises of 1973/74 and 1979, led to global recessions from which it became difficult for any one country to escape through the use of domestic demand management policies. It will be shown that when we consider the interlinkages between the advanced countries, the implications of the export-led growth theory have to be extended. Attempts by any one country to relax its balance of payments constraint by expenditure-switching policies (if, indeed, this is possible) may well lead to *competitive growth*, that is, an increase in output that is at the expense of another country's production. This is a situation that may eventually lead to a reciprocal devaluation and other protectionist measures to control trade that render such initial expenditure-switching policies ultimately self-defeating. An implication is that the most effective way to increase growth and reduce unemployment is to generate *complementary growth*, which involves the politically more difficult problem of coordinated reflation. Only by acting in concert in a manner analogous to a closed economy (which obviates the balance of payments constraint) can a faster rate of growth be generated.

To begin with, however, we shall first outline Thirlwall's explanation of "why growth rates differ."

The growth of an individual country and the balance of payments constraint

The assumptions underlying this approach are the usual Post Keynesian ones and, hence, need not detain us very long. Industrial markets in the advanced countries are oligopolistic and prices are determined by a markup on normalized unit costs. Fluctuations in demand are met primarily by output and income adjustments rather than by changes in prices. The determinant of the level of output is the level of effective demand, and in a closed economy reducing the real wage will not necessarily increase employment unless there is an increase, *pari passu*, in effective demand (McCombie, 1985–86).

The model, as a first approximation, concentrates on the real as opposed to the monetary aspects of the economy, and its emphasis is on the importance of real factors in determining the demand for exports and imports (and hence output). It is thus more reminiscent of the elasticity rather than the monetary approach to the balance of payments. The concept of export-led growth has, of course, no meaning under the usual neoclassical assumptions.[1] The formalization of the

Keynesian approach, at this stage, abstracts from the domestic financial sector, not because "money does not matter," but because it is thought to be of less importance than real factors in the context of explaining differences in long-term growth rates. It will be shown, however, that international monetary flows, as reflected in the balance of payments, are often a crucial factor in constraining the growth rate of an individual country to below its growth of potential GDP. International money certainly does matter.

Following Thirlwall and Hussain (1982), we begin with the balance of payments accounting identity:

$$P_d X + F \equiv E P_f M, \tag{5.1}$$

where P_d, P_f, and E are the price of exports in the domestic currency, the price of imports in the foreign currency, and the domestic price of foreign currency (the exchange rate); F is the value of nominal capital flows, measured in the domestic currency ($F > 0$ measures capital inflows and $F < 0$ measures capital outflows); and X and M are the volume of exports and imports.[2]

The demand functions for exports and imports are given by

$$X = k_1 Z^\varepsilon \left(\frac{P_d}{E P_f} \right)^\eta, \quad (\eta < 0), \tag{5.2}$$

and

$$M = k_2 Y^\pi \left(\frac{E P_f}{P_d} \right)^\psi, \quad (\psi < 0), \tag{5.3}$$

where Z is "world" income (excluding that of the country under consideration), Y is domestic income, ε and π are the income elasticities of demand for exports and imports, respectively, and η and ψ are the appropriate price elasticities. k_1 and k_2 are constants.

The following expression for the exponential growth of income may be obtained by taking the natural logarithms of equations (5.1)–(5.3), differentiating them with respect to time and substituting equations (5.2) and (5.3) into equation (5.1):

$$y = \frac{\varphi \varepsilon z + (1 - \varphi)(f - p_d) - (1 + \varphi \eta + \psi)(e + p_f - p_d)}{\pi}. \tag{5.4}$$

The lower-case letters of the several variables represent their exponential growth rates. φ is the proportion of total foreign receipts accounted for by sales of exports (i.e. $\varphi = P_d X / (P_d X + F)$).

It may be seen that the growth of a country's income is a function of three components divided by the income elasticity of demand for imports. The first term is the effect of the growth of world income on the country's growth rate; the second is the effect of the growth of real capital flows; and the third is the combined effect of the price elasticities and the rate of change of the terms of trade.

If we further assume that the growth of capital flows is negligible, that there is no initial balance of payments disequilibrium (i.e. $\varphi = 1$), and that there are no changes in the terms of trade, equation (5.4) reduces to

$$y_B = \frac{x}{\pi} \quad \text{or} \quad y_B = \frac{\varepsilon z}{\pi}. \tag{5.5}$$

Equation (5.5) shows that what may be termed the balance of payments equilibrium growth rate (y_B) is determined by the growth of exports divided by the income elasticity of demand for imports. It may also be seen from equation (5.5) that international differences in growth rates are fundamentally due to disparities among countries in the values of the world income elasticity of demand for their exports and their domestic income elasticity of the demand for imports (ε and π, respectively). Equation (5.5) may be interpreted as reflecting the working of the dynamic Harrod foreign trade multiplier (Thirlwall, 1979) or, more generally, the Hicks supermultiplier (McCombie and Thirlwall, 1994, ch. 6). The distinction will be clarified later.

Capital flows, price and nonprice competition in international trade

Thirlwall (1979) found, using Spearman's rank correlation coefficient, that there was a very close fit between the actual growth of income and that given by the expression $y_B = x/\pi$ for the period 1951–73 (and 1953–76). McCombie (1989) found, using a different statistical test, that over the period 1951–73 only five of fifteen advanced countries had differences that were statistically significant and even there the size of these differences was not large. Not surprisingly, one of those countries for which the rule failed to hold good was Japan, which over the postwar period had been accumulating large trade surpluses. Bairam (1988) has estimated the relationship for the European and North American countries for the period 1970–85 and also found support for Thirlwall's rule.[3] Comparison of equations (5.4) and (5.5) suggests that changes in relative prices and capital flows are either coincidentally offsetting or, more likely, as we shall show, both are small compared with the growth of exports.

If we turn first to capital flows, it seems that, in the words of an OECD paper, "some countries can be in current account deficit for many years, while others may be in persistent surplus. But for most a *change* in the current account position equivalent to 1 percent of GNP over one or two years would, depending on the starting point, be considered significant, and could well set in a train of adjustment" (Larsen *et al.*, 1983, p. 51). The train of adjustment is most likely to be caused by the deflation of domestic demand which reduces the growth rate. As Larsen *et al.* point out, the other alternative, a depreciation of the currency, is likely to be ineffective. First, the likely "J-curve" effect will initially worsen the current account in the short run and, indeed, a sustained depreciation may well induce a series of J-curve effects. Second, the resulting increase in inflation from the faster growth of import prices may be politically unacceptable, especially for the more open economies.

To these a third reason should be added, namely that, for reasons discussed later, even a large real exchange rate depreciation may have little impact on the growth of imports and exports.

While a ratio of the current account deficit to GDP of 1 percent as an indicator of an unsustainable current account deficit may be on the low side for some countries (especially the United States), even a current account deficit of, for example, 4 percent of GDP would be quickly reached by an increase in the actual growth rate above the balance of payments equilibrium growth rate. It should be emphasized that to increase the trend rate of growth requires a *sustained rate of increase* in capital flows. To stabilize the current account deficit at a certain level requires that the growth rate returns to the balance of payments equilibrium growth rate.[4] If, for example, the ratio of the trade deficit to GDP ratio is constant, the overseas debt to GDP may increase inexorably. The implications of this may be made clearer with the help of a simple example. After a decade of benefiting from the windfall gain of North Sea oil revenues, the United Kingdom was in the early 1990s experiencing a severe balance of payments deficit. Coutts *et al.* (1990, p. 20) have summarized the problem as follows:

> It would appear that countries enter the heavily indebted category (when borrowing only becomes possible on penal terms) when the debt to GDP reaches 30–40%. Assuming real interest rates of 6% and a growth rate of 2.75%, a trade deficit equal to 4% of GDP will generate debt equal to 30% of GDP after six years and 40% after eight years. To stabilise a debt ratio at 40% will require a permanent unrequited trade surplus of about 1.25% of GDP; and if the improvement in the balance of trade by 5.25% of GDP were achieved entirely by deflation, the GDP must be about 15.25% lower than would otherwise be required. In the latter case the total resource loss to the nation as a result of having a debt equal to 40% of GDP is thus equal to about 20.5% of GDP in perpetuity – equivalent to a permanent loss of seven years of normal growth.

It is important to make a distinction between long-term capital flows and short-run speculative capital flows. There is nothing wrong with a country experiencing substantial capital inflows over a long period if these are used for productive investment that will generate subsequent export earnings to cover both the interest and the eventual debt repayments. Indeed, an alternative definition of the balance of payments equilibrium growth rate would be one that includes the effect of such capital flows, that is, $y_B = [\varphi \varepsilon z + (1-\varphi)(f^* - p_d)]/\pi$, where f^* is the growth of net long-term nominal capital flows. In other words, balance of payments equilibrium growth requires "the basic balance" to be in equilibrium. However, Feldstein and Horioka (1980) suggest that there are considerable institutional barriers that greatly reduce the international mobility of long-term investment in response to disparities in yields: "While a small part of the total world capital stock is held in liquid form and is available to eliminate short-term interest rate differentials, most capital is apparently not available for such arbitrage-type activity among long-term investments" (p. 328). The growth of long-term capital flows is, however, likely to be an important factor for some less developed countries (Thirlwall and Hussain, 1982).

The problem with short-term capital flows is that they are highly volatile. They respond rapidly to small changes in international interest rate differentials and expected changes in the exchange rate that will lead to substantial capital gains or losses. The danger of a capital flight is that it will lead to a rapid depreciation of the currency and a vicious depreciation–inflation circle. With a current account deficit and the possibility of an exchange rate depreciation that will bring a capital loss to investors from overseas, the interest rate is likely to have to be increased in an attempt to prevent a capital flight. This in turn is likely to have an adverse effect on investment and, hence, reduce the growth rate. Moreover, there are limits to the extent to which interest rates can be raised to defend the currency. Whether or not there is a capital flight will also depend upon the sentiments of the world financial markets, which are not well-known for taking the long view. Lomax (1984, p. 5) argues that foreign lenders will scrutinize the creditworthiness of the particular country. One indicator is "the level of a country's reserves in relation to its borrowing needs in the market place." A second measure is the overseas debt service to foreign earnings ratio, which is calculated as the sum of interest paid and amortization of medium- and long-term debt as a percentage of the export receipts from goods and services (i.e. the debt–service ratio). Lomax states that "the international financial markets need firm criteria of creditworthiness . . . The criteria which we believe would be suitable, and on the evidence seem to be taken into account in the market place, are that a country should have enough reserves to cover six months' market borrowing and that its debt–service ratio on this measure should be no more than 20–25 percent."

Thus, the implication is that capital flows cannot permit an individual country to increase its growth rate above y_B by very much or for very long.

It is a central tenet of the approach of this chapter that changes in relative prices have very little impact on the growth of exports and of imports and it is nonprice competitiveness that dominates the performance of countries in overseas markets. As we have noted, differences between countries in their nonprice competitiveness are reflected in the international disparities in the income elasticities of demand for imports and exports. It is not argued that changes in relative prices, when measured in a common currency, have *no* effect on the balance of payments. Indeed, there are cases where a devaluation has improved the balance of payments, *for a given growth rate*, for example, the devaluations of the franc in 1957 and 1958 and sterling in 1967. What is denied is that it is feasible for the trend rate of growth of a country to be raised by a continuous depreciation of its currency. There are a number of reasons for this.

It may be difficult for a nominal depreciation to be converted into a real depreciation if there is an inflationary feedback from higher import prices to higher domestic costs. This may occur because of real wage resistance as workers increase their money wage claims to prevent a cut in the real wage caused by the higher import prices. If they are successful, domestic prices will increase to the same extent as import prices (Wilson, 1976).[5]

The 1980s, however, saw swings in effective exchange rates that have made the devaluations of the 1960s and early 1970s seem small by comparison. But as Krugman (1989b, p. 36) points out: "One of the most puzzling, and therefore one of the most important, aspects of floating exchange rates of the 1980s has been the huge swings in exchange rates that have had only muted effects on anything real." Consequently, even in the absence of any inflationary feedback, trade flows still appear unresponsive to changes in the real exchange rate.

One reason for this is that, with oligopolistic pricing, the prices of imported goods show little variation even in the face of large swings in the exchange rate. Exporters to the United States, for example, maintain their dollar prices constant even though there may be large fluctuations in their dollar costs caused by a volatile exchange rate.[6] A price leadership model could generate this result. Exporters to the United States try to ensure that their dollar prices move in line with those of similar domestically produced American goods, absorbing exchange rate changes as far as possible in their price margins, and rely on improving their nonprice competitiveness to increase their market share. Moreover, with a high degree of product differentiation, price elasticities are likely to be low so that even a large change in relative prices has little effect on the volume of imports and exports demanded. It should be noted that these do not require a rise in the overall domestic price level to vitiate the nominal exchange rate depreciation. It helps explain why a depreciation may not improve the balance of payments even for those countries like the United States that do not seem to experience a high degree of real wage resistance.

Firms are also unlikely to increase their exports if they believe that the depreciation of the currency is likely to be short-lived. Krugman suggests that the huge swings of the 1980s are more likely to have been interpreted as the temporary consequences of capital flows or speculative bubbles than earlier exchange rate changes. Krugman develops a model (based on the work of Dixit) to explain how uncertainty of the future exchange rate, "even when it is not regarded as resulting from some kind of process that quickly reverts to the mean, encourages firms to adopt a 'wait and see attitude'; they become reluctant both to enter new markets and to exit from old ones" (Krugman, 1989b, pp. 47–48).

Of course, there are areas where price competition is still important. These include, for example, the labor-intensive standardized manufactures where the newly industrializing countries, such as Korea and Taiwan, and more recently China, are rapidly gaining market share in the advanced countries. However, the volume of these exports is still quantitatively small, although they may pose severe problems for individual industries, such as textiles.

Evidence about the ineffectiveness of changes in the real exchange rate is to be found in Kaldor (1978b). Kaldor examined changes in the export shares for a number of advanced countries over the period 1963–75, together with changes in relative unit labor costs, and relative export prices. He found a paradox in that those countries that experienced the greatest decline in their manufacturing export shares (the United States and the United Kingdom) also experienced the greatest increase in their price competitiveness. Moreover, the converse also held true: those countries that had substantial increases in their shares also experienced large losses in price competitiveness. Only three countries satisfied the expected relationships of a fall in the trade share being accompanied by a decline in price competitiveness and vice versa. These were the Netherlands, Switzerland, and (marginally) Canada.

Kaldor (1978b, pp. 111–112) summarized the position as follows:

> The general picture which emerges from a study of the trade record of the last five or six years is that the comparative export performance of the main indus-trialised countries remained remarkably impervious to very large changes in effective exchange rates. The surplus countries tended to remain in surplus and the deficit countries to remain in deficit in much the same way as in the 1960s, when the complications caused by a fivefold increase in oil prices and their different impact on different countries are allowed for. The important thing is that Britain and America, who seemed to be losing out to the new industrial giants, Germany and Japan, continued to do so after the real exchange rates between them underwent drastic alterations.

This does not mean that relative costs have been acting perversely. Rather, as Fetherston *et al.* (1977, p. 66) point out: "The general picture to emerge, therefore, is of a trading system dominated by strong long-term trends in export shares whose effects were reduced but not reversed by effective devaluations. The result goes some way to explaining the 'Kaldor Paradox' that *ex post* the value of net exports appeared to respond peversely to effective devaluations. The reason is that relative cost changes, although moving in the right direction, have not been large enough or frequent enough to reverse the strong underlying trends in export shares."

These long-term trends are captured by the substantial differences in the income elasticity of demand for exports (ε) that exist between countries. Since these disparities in ε cannot be explained in terms of differing product mixes of the exports of the various countries (Cornwall, 1977, p. 161; Balassa, 1979), they must capture differences in nonprice competitiveness. The latter reflects such factors as quality, reliability, after-sales service, delivery times, and the emphasis placed on marketing and distribution. Under oligopolistic market structures, price competition is relatively unimportant compared with nonprice competition.

The findings of Fetherston *et al.* (1977) have been more recently confirmed by Fagerberg (1988), who attempted to explain the growth of GDP together with the growth of export and import shares by estimating a simultaneous equation model using cross-country data from fifteen advanced nations. He found that, *inter alia*, "the net effect of growth in relative unit labour costs on the growth of market shares measured in value terms turns out to be negligible" (Fagerberg, 1988, p. 376).

Posner and Steer (1979, p. 161), in their survey of competition in international trade, summarized their findings as follows: "Historically there is no doubt that non-price influences have dominated – the proportion of the total change they 'explain' is an order of magnitude greater than the explanatory power of price competitiveness."

This is echoed by Stout (1979, p. 181) who, generalizing from a number of studies, argued that for the United Kingdom:

> Given that, over a long period and using a variety of indicators of price competitiveness, exchange-rate changes have broadly compensated for the relative rise in sterling costs of production, and given that . . . the broad product composition of British exports and domestic output of manufactures is very similar to that of Germany and not very different from that of France, the differences between the British and the German or French income elasticities of demand for manufactured imports, as well as the differences in the elasticity of foreign demand for exports, support the now quite widespread evidence that non-price competitive disadvantages underlie Britain's industrial decline.

Ever since Posner's (1961) classic paper, it has been increasingly realized that such factors as product design, technical sophistication, quality, the adaptation of products for the requirements of specific overseas markets, and so on, are all of crucial importance in accounting for a country's success in international trade. Indeed, this has led to the development of a new theory of international trade that is progressively exposing the shortcomings of the traditional neoclassical theory (Dosi and Soete, 1988). Why countries differ in their nonprice competitiveness is a complex question and undoubtedly is related to the poorly understood reasons why firms differ in X-inefficiency.

Consequently, the values of the income elasticities of demand for exports and imports, compared with those of other countries, reflect such aspects of the microeconomic structure of the economy as "the innovative ability and adaptive capacity of a country's manufacturers in the field of product development" (Thirlwall, 1982, p. 12). It is these nonprice aspects of competition that determine the "strong long-term trends in export shares" identified by Fetherston *et al.* (1977). Nonprice competitiveness is difficult to improve even in the medium term as the experience of the United Kingdom over the postwar period has confirmed (Stout, 1979).

Furthermore, the evidence of Fetherston *et al.* (1977) and Connell (1979) has shown that in many cases very substantial changes in relative prices would be required to compensate for those deficiencies in nonprice competitiveness that are experienced by the slowest growing countries. To the extent that attempts to relax the balance of payments constraint through large exchange rate adjustments may be thwarted by "real wage resistance" and a resulting depreciation–inflation vicious circle, by competitive devaluations, or by the oligopolistic pricing policies of firms, there may be little scope for an individual country to improve its rate of growth relative to that of its major trading partners. This will be considered in more detail.

Resource-constrained, policy-constrained, and balance of payments constrained growth

In this section we discuss how the existence of international trade flows is an important factor in determining the maximum growth rate that a number of advanced countries are able to achieve. Notwithstanding the fact that the industrialized countries, in aggregate, are almost a closed economy, all that is necessary for the balance of payments to act as a factor constraining growth is for one country (or group of countries) to have an exogenously determined growth of output.

Prior to 1973, this condition was fulfilled by such countries as Japan and possibly West Germany, both of which achieved growth rates that were sufficiently fast to induce domestic factor supply shortages.[7] These countries may be termed "resource-constrained." It is difficult to argue convincingly that any country has been resource-constrained since the mid-1970s in the sense that the factor supplies have, in the long run, limited the growth of GDP. (There have been times, of course, when short-term capacity shortages may have restricted a country's rate of expansion.) Nevertheless, various countries have, at different times and to differing degrees, resorted to deflationary policies in the belief that therein lay the solution to the problem of inflation. From the point of view of the remainder of the advanced countries, the result is similar to the effect of resource-constrained economies – it restricts the degree of freedom possessed by these countries to pursue policies to raise their individual rates of growth.

For expositional purposes, it is convenient to divide the countries into two categories. "Group One" consists of those countries that are growing below their maximum potential and are constrained from growing faster by their balance of payments problems. "Group Two" are those countries that are either resource- or policy-constrained and hence are either unable or unwilling to increase their growth rate. Clearly, the composition of the two groups will vary from time to time. For example, the United Kingdom from 1945 to 1979 should be classified as balance of payments constrained (Group One), whereas for the period 1979–86 it was policy-constrained (Group Two). Since 1986, the United Kingdom is again encountering severe balance of payments problems, putting the country once more into Group One.

The level of real income of the two groups (measured in Group One's currency) may be expressed in terms of the familar Keynesian identity as

$$Y_1 = C_1 + I_1 + G_1 + X_1 - M_1 \left(\frac{EP_2}{P_1} \right), \tag{5.6}$$

and

$$Y_2 = C_2 + I_2 + G_2 + X_2 - M_2 \left(\frac{P_1}{EP_2} \right), \tag{5.7}$$

with the same notation as before and where C, I, and G denote consumption, investment, and government expenditure.

The following relationships are assumed to hold for each group:

$$C_i = \bar{C}_i + \delta(Y_i - T_i), \quad i = 1, 2; \tag{5.8}$$

$$T_i = \tau Y_i; \tag{5.9}$$

$$I_i = \bar{I}_i + \mu Y_i; \tag{5.10}$$

$$G_i = \bar{G}_i + \zeta Y_i, \tag{5.11}$$

where T is the amount of taxation. A bar over a variable denotes autonomous expenditure. Equations (5.8)–(5.11) are the consumption, taxation, investment, and government spending functions.

The level of aggregate autonomous expenditure, from equations (5.8), (5.10), and (5.11), is defined as

$$A_i = \bar{C}_i + \bar{I}_i + \bar{G}_i. \tag{5.12}$$

The sum of induced consumption, induced investment, and induced government spending may be determined from equations (5.8), (5.10), and (5.11) as

$$B_i = (\delta(1 - \tau) + \mu + \zeta)Y_i. \tag{5.13}$$

Substituting equations (5.12) and (5.13) into equation (5.6) and expressing the results in terms of exponential growth rates, we obtain:

$$y_i = \omega_{A_i} a_i + \omega_{B_i} b_i + \omega_{X_i} x_i - \omega_{M_i} m_i, \tag{5.14}$$

where ω_{A_i} is the share of autonomous expenditure in the total income of group, or country, i, etc. The lower-case letters denote the exponential growth rates of the variables with the usual notation. In deriving equation (5.14), we assume that the terms of trade do not alter in the long run, that is, $(e + p_2 - p_1) = 0$.

The growth of relative prices, therefore, is also absent from the (dynamic) import and export demand functions. The growth of imports is given by the import demand function, $m_i = \pi_i y_i$. Expressing equation (5.13) in growth rates gives $b_i = y_i$. Using these two results and the definition that the growth of the exports of one group equals the growth of imports of the other, the growth of income of the first group may be expressed in terms of the growth of its autonomous expenditure and the growth of income of the other group as

$$y_i = \alpha_i a_i + \beta_i \pi_j y_j, \quad i, j = 1, 2; \quad i \neq j, \tag{5.15}$$

where

$$\alpha_i = \frac{\omega_{A_i}}{(1 - \omega_{B_i} + \omega_{M_i} \pi_i)}$$

and

$$\beta_i = \frac{\omega_{X_i}}{(1 - \omega_{B_i} + \omega_{M_i}\pi_i)}.$$

α and β are the (dynamic) domestic expenditure and foreign trade multipliers, respectively.

The relationships for Groups One and Two are given by equation (5.15). These, for convenience, may be termed the "growth equations" and are shown diagrammatically in Figure 5.1(a) as the lines A and B, respectively.

The actual growth rates of the two groups are determined by the intersection of the two lines. (This is assumed to occur initially at point a in Figure 5.1(a) where the lines A_0 and B_0 intersect.)[8]

It may be seen that the growth of Group One is positively related to that of Group Two. This is because, as the growth of the latter increases, so does its growth of

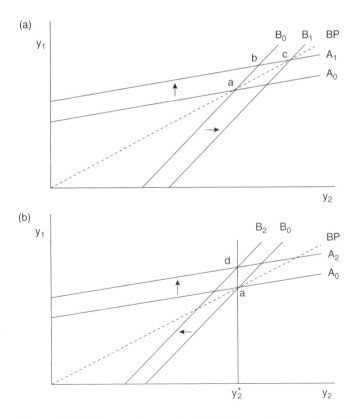

Figure 5.1 (a–b) Economic growth and the balance of payments constraint.

demand for Group One's exports and this will raise Group One's growth of output through the foreign trade multiplier.

The growth of Group One is thus a function not only of the growth of its own autonomous domestic expenditure (as in a closed economy), but also of the growth of comparable expenditure undertaken by Group Two. The growth of Group One is given by

$$y_1 = \rho(\alpha_1 a_1 + \beta_1 \pi_2 \alpha_2 a_2), \tag{5.16}$$

where $\rho = 1/(1 - \beta_1 \beta_2 \pi_1 \pi_2) > 0.$[9]

Given any value of a_2, the growth of Group Two's autonomous expenditure, equation (5.16) suggests that Group One could achieve any desired rate of growth by simply determining the appropriate rate of growth of its own autonomous expenditure and achieving this through domestic demand management policies. This may not be possible, however, because of the existence of a balance of payments constraint which it is now necessary to incorporate into the model.

The line BP in Figure 5.1(a) is the locus of points where the growth of the two groups is such that there is no change in the balance of payments. The equation of the BP line is derived from the import and export demand functions together with the balance of payments identity in a similar manner to equation (5.5). Assuming, for the moment, that there is no change in relative prices or in the exchange rate, and that Group One has an initial trade deficit, the equation of the BP locus is given by

$$y_1 = \frac{\varphi \pi_2}{\pi_1} y_2 + \frac{(1 - \varphi)}{\pi_1}(f - p_1), \tag{5.17}$$

where φ is Group One's share of exports in its total foreign exchange receipts; and f is the growth of long-term or autonomous net nominal capital flows from Group Two to Group One. The growth of these capital flows is assumed to be independent of the growth of Group One.[10]

For expositional ease, it is convenient to assume $\varphi = 1$, which means that there are no autonomous capital flows and that trade between the two groups is initially balanced. The equation of the BP locus is now given by

$$y_1 = \frac{\pi_2}{\pi_1} y_2, \tag{5.18}$$

which is formally equivalent to the result of equation (5.5).

In terms of Figure 5.1(a), the BP locus given by equation (5.18) passes through the origin, whereas if there is a growth of capital inflows to Group One as in equation (5.17), this will cause the BP line to shift upwards. Thus, a growth of long-term capital inflows enables the balance of payments equilibrium growth of Group One to be commensurately higher for any given growth of Group Two.

It may be seen from equations (5.17) and (5.18) that the greater the degree of nonprice competitiveness of Group Two compared with Group One (i.e. the smaller the ratio π_2/π_1), the lower will be the growth of Group One that is compatible with balance of payments equilibrium for a given growth of Group Two.

In Figure 5.1(a), both the groups are growing at their balance of payments equilibrium growth rates as the intersection of lines A_0 and B_0 is at point a, which is on the BP locus. If the intersection is above the BP line, Group One will be running an increasing balance of payments deficit that will have to be financed by a growth of short-term capital flows, or accommodating transfers, from Group Two. Conversely, if the intersection is below the BP line, Group One will be experiencing an increasing balance of payments surplus.

An increase in the growth of Group One's autonomous expenditure causes the line A_0 to shift upwards, through the domestic expenditure multiplier, to become, for example, the line A_1. For the moment, let us assume that Group Two is neither policy- nor resource-constrained. Consequently, the resulting increased growth of its exports to Group One will, through the dynamic foreign trade multiplier, lead to an increase in the growth of output of Group Two. The growth rates of the two groups are given by point b. Group One has a growing balance of payments deficit that has to be financed by a growth in short-term capital flows from Group Two. If, however, Group Two takes the opportunity of increasing its growth of domestic autonomous expenditure so that the output growth rates are given by point c, the balance of payments will be brought back into equilibrium. The overall movement from a to c represents the working of the Hicks supermultiplier. We have previously termed this type of economic growth as complementary and we shall return to its importance.

Figure 5.1(b) depicts the situation where Group Two is resource- or policy-constrained and has a constant growth rate of y_2^*. An expansion in the growth of Group One's autonomous expenditure now results in a movement from a to d. Once again, the growth of short-term capital flows from Group Two has to finance Group One's growing trade imbalance. In the short run, the growth of Group Two's autonomous domestic expenditure has to decrease to release resources for the increased growth of exports sold to Group One (i.e. the line B_0 shifts to B_2).

In the long run, however, the increasing balance of payments deficit becomes unsustainable as the ratio of international debt to GDP increases. In the absence of effective expenditure-switching policies to increase the growth of Group One's exports and reduce its import growth, the only remedy is to reduce its growth of output. Thus, in Figure 5.1(b), Group One's balance of payments constrained growth is that given by the point a. It would be purely fortuitous and highly unlikely if this rate of growth were such as to be associated with a full utilization (or a desired level of utilization) of Group One's factors of production. More likely, Group One's rate of growth would be below its full employment rate of growth, leading to rising unemployment (either overt or disguised) over time.

Since Group One is constrained by the balance of payments to grow below its maximum potential, if Group Two is policy-constrained but decides to raise its rate of growth, it is assumed that Group One will simultaneously increase its own rate of growth to the greatest extent compatible with balance of payments equilibrium. Hence, the growth of Group One is fundamentally determined by the growth of Group Two's autonomous expenditure (a_2^*):

$$y_1 = \frac{\pi_2 \alpha_2}{\pi_1 (1 - \beta_2 \pi_2)} a_2^*, \quad (1 - \beta_2 \pi_2) > 0. \tag{5.19}$$

If, on the other hand, Group Two is resource-constrained, then,

$$y_1 = \frac{\pi_2}{\pi_1} y_2^*, \tag{5.20}$$

where y_2^* is the growth of Group Two which is limited by its growth of factor inputs. (Equation (5.20) can also describe Group One's balance of payments equilibrium growth rate when Group Two is policy-constrained, except that y_2^* is now determined by a_2^*, rather than by the growth of factor inputs.)

While it has been argued that in the long run a depreciation of the exchange rate is unlikely to be effective in overcoming the balance of payments constraint, nevertheless, it may provide some amelioration in the short run. In the next section, the effect of a devaluation on the growth rates of the two groups is considered.

The impact of a devaluation

In order to analyze the effect of a devaluation or depreciation of Group One's currency, it is convenient to assume that trade is initially balanced and to commence again with the national income identities of the two groups expressed in real terms:

$$Y_1 = A_1 + B_1 + X_1 - \left(\frac{EP_2}{P_1}\right) M_1, \tag{5.21}$$

and

$$Y_2 = A_2 + B_2 + X_2 - \left(\frac{P_1}{EP_2}\right) M_2, \tag{5.22}$$

where, again, E is the exchange rate and P_1 and P_2 are the price levels of Groups One and Two. A and B, it will be recalled, are autonomous and induced expenditures.

The export and import demand functions (expressed in growth rate form) are given by

$$x_1 = m_2 = \pi_2 y_2 - \eta_1 (e + p_2 - p_1), \tag{5.23}$$

and

$$m_1 = x_2 = \pi_1 y_1 + \psi_1 (e + p_2 - p_1), \tag{5.24}$$

where, as we noted earlier, the price elasticties of demand, η_1 and ψ_1, are negative. (In the two-region model under consideration here, $\eta_1 = \psi_2; \eta_2 = \psi_1; \varepsilon_1 = \pi_2;$

and $\varepsilon_2 = \pi_1$, where $\eta_2, \psi_2, \varepsilon_1$, and ε_2 are the relevant elasticities of the other (redundant) export and import demand equations.)

The growth of the two groups may be determined by expressing equations (5.21) and (5.22) in growth rate form and substituting equations (5.23) and (5.24) into them. The resulting equations are given by (dropping, for notational convenience, the subscripts of η_1 and ψ_1):

$$y_1 = \alpha_1 a_1 + \beta_1 \pi_2 y_2 - \beta_1 (1 + \eta + \psi)(e + p_2 - p_1), \tag{5.25}$$

and

$$y_2 = \alpha_2 a_2 + \beta_2 \pi_1 y_1 + \beta_2 (1 + \eta + \psi)(e + p_2 - p_1). \tag{5.26}$$

The balance of payments equilibrium growth rate becomes

$$y_1 = \frac{\pi_2}{\pi_1} y_2 - \frac{(1 + \eta + \psi)(e + p_2 - p_1)}{\pi_1}. \tag{5.27}$$

It is important to note that in order to alter the growth rate of Group One, given the growth of Group Two, a *continuous* real depreciation is required rather than a once-and-for-all devaluation because of the multiplicative nature of the demand functions. (For convenience, we shall henceforth take the term "devaluation" as referring to a continuous depreciation of the currency.)

If the Marshall–Lerner condition just fails to be satisfied in the sense that the price elasticities sum to minus unity, it follows from equations (5.25)–(5.27) that a devaluation will have no effect upon the equilibrium growth rate of either group of countries. The growth equations and the balance of payments equilibrium locus are in this case given by equations (5.15) and (5.18). Empirical studies, however, suggest that the sum of the price elasticities for aggregate exports and imports falls within the range of -1.5 to -2.5, although the estimates are sometimes found to be statistically insignificant (Houthakker and Magee, 1969; Stern *et al.*, 1976).

In the circumstances where the Marshall–Lerner condition is satisfied, equation (5.25) demonstrates that, in terms of Figure 5.2, a devaluation will have the effect of shifting the BP locus upwards from BP_0 to BP_1. The devaluation also results in the line A_0 moving upwards to A_3. The shifts of the BP_0 locus and of the line A_0 are given by $-(1+\eta+\psi)(e+p_2-p_1)/\pi_1$, and $-\beta_1(1+\eta+\psi)(e+p_2-p_1)$, respectively.

Since β_1 is equal to $\omega_{x1}/(1 - \omega_{B_1} + \omega_{M_1}\pi_1)$, which is less than $1/\pi_1$, the shift of the BP line exceeds that of the line A_0. A corollary is that, from equation (5.26), the devaluation, *ceteris paribus*, shifts the line B_0 to the left to become line B_3.

The direct impact of the devaluation (i.e. the effect on the growth rates assuming no change in the growth of autonomous expenditure in either group) may be seen by considering the growth equations expressed in terms of a_1 and a_2 and the rates

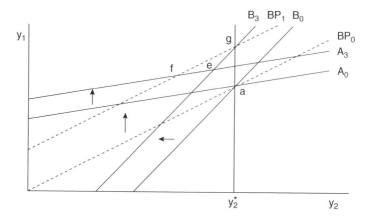

Figure 5.2 The effect of a devaluation.

of change of the terms of trade. These are given by

$$y_1 = \frac{(\alpha_1 a_1 + \beta_1 \pi_2 \alpha_2 a_2) - \beta_1(1 - \beta_2 \pi_2)(1 + \eta + \psi)(e + p_2 - p_1)}{(1 - \beta_1 \beta_2 \pi_1 \pi_2)},$$

(5.28)

and

$$y_2 = \frac{(\alpha_2 a_2 + \beta_2 \pi_1 \alpha_1 a_1) + \beta_2(1 - \beta_1 \pi_1)(1 + \eta + \psi)(e + p_2 - p_1)}{(1 - \beta_1 \beta_2 \pi_1 \pi_2)}.$$

(5.29)

The effect of a devaluation on the growth rates of the two groups may be determined by partially differentiating equations (5.28) and (5.29) with respect to e. Thus,

$$\frac{\partial y_1}{\partial e} = -\frac{\beta_1(1 - \beta_2 \pi_2)}{(1 - \beta_1 \beta_2 \pi_1 \pi_2)}(1 + \eta + \psi) > 0,$$

(5.30)

and

$$\frac{\partial y_2}{\partial e} = \frac{\beta_2(1 - \beta_1 \pi_1)}{(1 - \beta_1 \beta_2 \pi_1 \pi_2)}(1 + \eta + \psi) < 0.$$

(5.31)

It is apparent that the direct impact of a devaluation is to increase the growth of Group One at the expense of Group Two: growth is *competitive*. Group Two, seeing its growth rate being adversely affected by the devaluation, may engage in a retaliatory devaluation, thus rendering Group One's initial attempt to raise its rate of growth self-defeating. Moreover, Group One experiences an increasing surplus on the balance of payments whereas the other group suffers from a worsening deficit. With reference to Figure 5.2 again, the effect is that the growth rates move from the values given by point *a* to those designated by point *e*.

The eventual equilibrium position depends upon the reaction of both groups to the devaluation. To take one example: Group Two, in the face of an increasing balance of payments deficit, may consider that the most effective remedy is to engage in a competitive devaluation. If this was successful, it would return the economies to point *a*. Alternatively, Group Two might seek to improve its balance of payments by reducing its growth rate even further than the reduction induced by the initial devaluation. In this case, the line B_3 would shift to the left (not shown in Figure 5.2 for clarity) and the equilibrium solution would be given by point *f*.

If, on the other hand, the desired rate of growth of Group Two is its original rate, namely, y_2^* in Figure 5.2, and Group One simultaneously increases its rate of growth of autonomous expenditure thereby shifting the line A_3 upwards (not shown), the eventual equilibrium will be at point *g*. Thus, with a sufficiently fast rate of currency depreciation, Group One may be able to achieve its own resource- or policy-constrained rate of growth. Given this, the question arises why flexible exchange rates do not seem to have delinked the national economies and removed the balance of payments constraint.

In fact, the introduction of flexible exchange rates with the breakdown of Bretton Woods has not proved to be the panacea originally envisaged. As we have noted earlier, the existence of real wage resistance makes it difficult, if not impossible, to translate variations in the nominal exchange rate into long-run changes of the real exchange rate. Associated with this is the possibility of a vicious circle developing that comprises rising inflation, initially generated by the devaluation, and a depreciating exchange rate. Oligopolistic pricing and the effect of uncertainty induced by exchange rate changes also make trade flows unresponsive to changes in relative prices. The experience since the 1970s has shown that all these factors have effectively prevented flexible exchange rates from delinking the national economies. The failure of flexible exchange rates is perhaps best seen by the emergence of the European Monetary Union and the single European currency. There is, however, still exchange rate flexibility between countries in the European Monetary Union and the United States and Japan. Moreover, the evidence cited earlier in this chapter suggests that the magnitude of real exchange rate adjustments would have to be substantial to compensate for the differences in nonprice competitiveness between countries.

The imposition of import controls

The second method by which a country may attempt to relax the balance of payments constraint is through the imposition of import controls. These may take the form of tariffs or quotas.

The imposition of tariffs by, for example, Group One, would raise the price of imports in terms of domestic currency. (It should be noted that in order to reduce the rate of growth of imports the tariff must be increasing over time: once again the term "tariff" will be taken to refer to a continuously increasing tariff. A continuously increasing tariff, however, does seem implausible.) The effect of a tariff is thus analogous to that of a devaluation, with the exception, of course, that there is not the direct stimulus to export growth that a devaluation provides. As the case of a devaluation has been discussed in the last section, the impact of a tariff will not be dealt with separately here. (It is perhaps worth pointing out, though, that the effect of a retaliatory tariff imposed by Group Two may well vitiate any advantage provided to Group One by the original tariff.)

We assume that quotas are introduced to reduce the growth of imports. This may be viewed as a fall in the income elasticity of demand for imports. It is normally postulated that the licenses to import would be auctioned off, thus providing a source of revenue.

If Group One introduces a quota, its income elasticity of demand for imports will fall from π_1 to π_1' and hence the slope of the BP locus will increase from π_2/π_1 to π_2/π_1'. This is shown in Figure 5.3 where the BP locus will rotate from BP_0 to BP_2. The slope of the line A_0 will also increase from $\beta_1\pi_2$ to $\beta_1'\pi_2$ (where $\beta_1' = \omega_{X_1}/(1 - \omega_{B_1} + \omega_{M_1}\pi_1')$), but the increase is not so great as that of the BP locus.

That is to say, the size of the dynamic foreign trade multiplier increases as there is less leakage of the growth of expenditure into imports. There is also an increase in the contribution that autonomous expenditure growth makes to that of output, since $\partial\alpha_1/\partial\pi_1 < 0$ and, consequently, a fall in π_1 has the effect of increasing α_1, the dynamic domestic autonomous expenditure multiplier (see equation (5.15)).

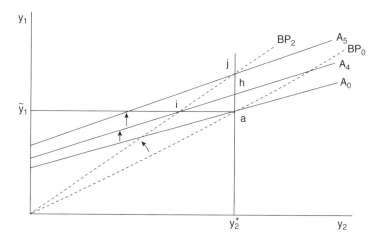

Figure 5.3 The effect of import quotas.

The post-import quota situation from Group One is given by the line A_4, where we assume that the growth of Group One's autonomous expenditure is the same as in the pre-quota case. (Note that the corresponding line B for Group Two is not shown in Figure 5.3 for clarity.)

Group Two now faces a decline in the rate of growth of demand due to a fall in the growth of its exports. Let us suppose it attempts to maintain its rate of growth at y_2^* by increasing its autonomous expenditure to compensate (Figure 5.3). In this case, the intersection of the line A_4 and the corresponding line for Group Two will occur at point h. In the long run, this is not sustainable, since Group Two is now running a growing balance of trade deficit. The reason for this is simple. The imposition of quotas by Group One has reduced the growth of its imports, which are, of course, the exports of Group Two, while the imports of Group Two remain at their pre-quota rate of growth. Unless Group Two is willing to finance an increasing inflow of capital, it will have to take measures to correct this disequilibrium.

There are fundamentally two choices open to Group Two. First (and more likely as the experience of the 1930s suggests), Group Two can retaliate by imposing its own import quotas in an attempt to return the ratio of the import elasticities to its original value. Even if this were successful, it should be noted that the growth of world trade would have fallen since the absolute values of π_1 and π_2 would have decreased. This would reduce both the benefits of international specialization of production and the welfare gains of the increased diversity of choice brought by trade. A likely outcome is a trade war with a progressive move toward autarky. Growth would again have become competitive.

Second, Group Two can pursue deflationary policies until the intersection of the two growth lines occur on the BP_2 locus. This occurs at point i in Figure 5.3, where Group One's growth rate is the same as that which it experienced before it introduced quotas. This may be shown as follows. The growth equation of Group One before the imposition of quotas is given by equation (5.15) as

$$y_1 = \alpha_1 a_1 + \beta_1 \pi_2 y_2. \tag{5.32}$$

Group Two is assumed to be intially either resource- or policy-constrained, and we assume that Group One is growing at its balance of payments equilibrium growth rate

$$\tilde{y}_1 = \frac{\pi_2}{\pi_1} y_2^*, \tag{5.33}$$

where $\tilde{y}_1$ is Group One's balance of payments constrained growth, given that Group Two is growing at y_2^*.

Substituting equation (5.33) into equation (5.32), we obtain the growth of Group One's autonomous expenditure, given the balance of payments constraint

$$\tilde{a}_1 = \frac{(1 - \beta_1 \pi_1)}{\alpha_1} \tilde{y}_1. \tag{5.34}$$

Initially, after the imposition of import quotas, and assuming that the growth of autonomous expenditure remains the same, the growth equation of Group One is

$$y_1 = \frac{\alpha_1'(1 - \beta_1 \pi_1)}{\alpha_1} \tilde{y}_1 + \beta_1' \pi_2 y_2, \qquad (5.35)$$

where α_1' and β_1' are the multipliers after the imposition of import quotas.

To preserve its balance of payments equilibrium, Group Two must reduce its growth to

$$y_2 = \frac{\pi_1'}{\pi_2} y_1. \qquad (5.36)$$

Substituting equation (5.36) into equation (5.35), we obtain Group One's new balance of payments equilibrium growth rate

$$y_1 = \frac{\alpha_1'(1 - \beta_1 \pi_1)}{\alpha_1(1 - \beta_1' \pi_1')} \tilde{y}_1. \qquad (5.37)$$

From the definitions of α_1 and β_1 (and, hence, α_1' and β_1') from equation (5.15) and the condition that in balance of payments equilibrium $\omega_{M_1} = \omega_{X_1}$, it can be simply shown that, at the initial shares,[11]

$$\frac{\alpha_1'(1 - \beta_1 \pi_1)}{\alpha_1(1 - \beta_1' \pi_1')} = 1. \qquad (5.38)$$

The outcome is thus that Group One obtains no immediate benefit from the imposition of quotas, while Group Two finds that its growth rate is reduced. The question then arises why Group One should ever introduce quotas. The answer is that, if at the same time that it introduces quotas Group One increases its growth of autonomous expenditure, then its balance of payments equilibrium growth rate will be higher than in the pre-quota situation, even though this is not true for Group Two.

However, the growth rate of Group Two need not fall if Group One, at the same time as imposing quotas, takes other measures to increase its growth of autonomous demand *and thereby ensures that its growth of imports remains at the previous rate.* (This was the policy prescription argued by the Cambridge Economic Policy Group. See, for example, Cripps and Godley, 1978.) This action will ensure that Group Two will no longer be faced with a trade deficit. In terms of Figure 5.3, Group One's growth line shifts up to A_5 and the post-import control growth rates are given by the point *j*. The outcome is that both countries are growing at their maximum or desired growth rates. The gains for Group One include a greater utilization of labor, a faster rate of capital accumulation, and an increase in the growth of income.

The Cambridge Economic Policy Group argued that the major advantage of import controls, compared with a devaluation, is that they are likely to be less inflationary. If Group One were to introduce reflationary measures to accompany a devaluation so that, assuming no retaliation, the end result would be a growth rate equivalent to that obtained with import controls, the former would be likely to set up larger inflationary pressures. The depreciation would, as we have mentioned before, lead to an increase in the growth of the prices of imported goods (in terms of the domestic currency) leading to an inflationary wage–price spiral. On the other hand, under import controls, all the tariff and quota revenues could be returned to the economy through tax reductions and so the effect would be likely to be less inflationary than with a devaluation.

The effectiveness, however, of import controls is controversial, not least because of the problem of retaliation. Even the advocates of import controls regard them as necessary only because of the lack of a better alternative. A devaluation would be preferable if it had a sufficiently large quantitative impact on trade flows, but, for the reasons already discussed, this is not seen as a feasible remedy. Import controls are, though, superior to the only other policy, which consists of restricting the growth of Group One to the rate determined by the value of its income elasticities of demand for imports and exports, together with the growth of Group Two. In the long term, it is possible that increased inefficiency induced by protectionism may eventually cause π_2 to fall and π_1 to rise, thus offsetting any short-run gains in the growth rate due to the imposition of the quotas.

The post-1973 slowdown in economic growth

The model outlined here may be used to illustrate the post-1973 recession and the slowdown from that date in the economic growth of the advanced countries. The oil crisis of 1973–74 exacerbated the "deflationary bias" inherent in the asymmetry of the adjustment pressures on deficit and surplus countries. Given the high savings propensities of the OPEC countries, the initial quadrupling of oil prices meant that to sustain growth, the OECD countries, collectively, would have to maintain a substantial current account deficit; indeed, this was appreciated by the policy makers at the time. Nevertheless, countries such as Japan and West Germany, accustomed to low inflation rates and annual surpluses on the balance of payments, introduced restrictive monetary and fiscal policies in order to curtail the rate of price increases (through a belief in some sort of short-run Phillips curve trade-off). The United States initially pursued expansionary policies, but this led to a marked deterioration of its current account between 1975 and 1978. The counterinflationary policies that were introduced in October 1978 were not sufficient to prevent a speculative run on the dollar, which necessitated the corrective action of a marked tightening of monetary policy. As Larsen *et al.* (1983, p. 56) commented: "This episode suggests that even the largest OECD country, with a relatively small share of trade in GNP, is not immune from the pressures of international linkages." The inevitable result of the Japanese, West German, and, later, United States policies was that deflationary pressures were transmitted to the advanced countries as a whole.

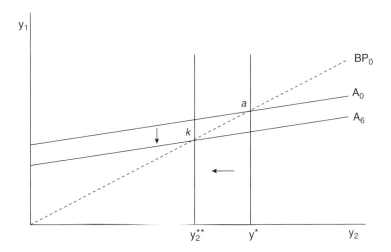

Figure 5.4 The international transmission of deflationary forces.

This is shown in Figure 5.4, where the policy-constrained rate of growth of Group Two falls from y_2^* to y_2^{**} in an attempt, for example, to restrain inflation. Given the ineffectiveness of expenditure-switching policies for the reasons outlined earlier, the growth of Group One has also to fall (regardless of whether or not this is a desired objective) to bring the balance of payments back into equilibrium. Thus, for the advanced countries as a whole, the balance of payments deficit fell as the growth of output declined.

This may have created the misleading impression that there was no longer a "balance of payments problem." Although, *ex post*, the balance of payments deficits were extinguished, this occurred at the cost of increasing underutilization of resources and the social cost of rising and prolonged unemployment. Nevertheless, there were some explicit balance of payments crises for countries that tried to expand faster than their balance of payments equilibrium growth rate permitted. These included the United Kingdom's sterling crisis of 1976 which led to IMF intervention and consequent deflationary policies, Italy in 1980–81, and France in 1982. During the 1980s there were still the large structural imbalances of the US deficit and the Japanese and West German surpluses. In the 1980s, the United States went from being the world's largest net creditor to the largest net debtor as a result of a growth rate that was faster relative to Japan and Europe than it had been in the past. However, there was increasing pressure from the world financial markets for the United States to undertake restrictive measures to reduce the external deficit. Once again, even the United States was not immune from the balance of payments constraint. (See Stewart, 1983, for a discussion of the problems facing the international management of demand subsequent to 1973.)

Financial interlinkages

The analysis so far has abstracted from considerations of the financial sector. A higher growth of output is assumed to be a function of a faster growth of autonomous expenditure, and this gives rise to a deterioration in the balance of payments. The exact method of the financing of this expansion (whether it is, for example, by bond issue or by an increase in the money supply) and whether exchange rates are fixed or floating will, of course, influence the magnitude of the changes in the several variables. Perhaps most importantly, no account has been taken of the interrelationship between changes (or expected changes) in both interest rates and exchange rates, and in the international flows of the substantial volume of short-term speculative capital that now exist.

Nevertheless, the fundamental determinant of the external constraint is the "basic" account of the balance of payments (i.e. the current account together with long-term capital flows); the working of the financial markets has merely served to reinforce this mechanism. Larsen *et al.* (1983) have summarized the experience of flexible exchange rates since the collapse of Bretton Woods as follows:

> Following the breakdown of the fixed rate system in 1973, it was hoped that floating would permit countries to pursue more independent domestic objectives than had hitherto been the case, insulating them from monetary policies of dominant partners. In part, this view rested on the assumption that capital movements would tend to offset temporary current account disequilibria and play a stabilizing role. These hopes proved too optimistic, however: *the exchange rate has remained a constraint and financial linkages have often compounded real linkages.* Moreover, exchange rates are, at times, affected by incipient capital movements induced by foreign financial disturbances or international political considerations. [Emphasis added]

Since the financial sector generally reinforces the effect of the balance of payments constraint, it would be desirable to include this formally in any subsequent development of the approach adopted here.

Conclusion

The close interlinkages that have developed between the advanced countries through the medium of trade have progressively circumscribed the latitude that individual countries have in implementing domestic policies. In particular, there is not much scope for a country to increase its rate of growth relative to that of its trading partners faster than in the past. This comparative economic performance is largely dependent upon the values of its export and import income elasticities of demand compared with those of its competitors. These primarily reflect differences in the nonprice aspects of competition that are supply characteristics not very amenable to change by macroeconomic policies. Attempts to raise the growth rate ignoring this balance of payments constraint have invariably resulted in large trade deficits (of over 2 percent of GDP) that could not be sustained for long in most countries. In this sense, Eltis (1976) is correct when he points out that British policy makers, brought up on the closed economy model of the *General Theory*, simply generated the familiar "stop–go" cycle by the use of Keynesian demand management policies. But it should be noted that the "failure of the Keynesian conventional wisdom," as Eltis entitled his critique, is not a failure of the theory, but one of drawing the appropriate policy prescriptions from that theory, *pace* Eltis. The approach we have adopted here is, of course, avowedly Keynesian in nature.

It has been shown that attempts by individual countries to overcome the balance of payments constraint through exchange rate adjustments and by the use of tariffs and quotas will be self-defeating if they generate a depreciation–inflation circle or competitive growth which involves retaliation. We have also argued that there are strong reasons for doubting the efficacy of these instruments in permanently raising a country's growth rate. From an individual country's point of view, the most effective solution is to improve the nonprice competitiveness of its exports through industrial policies that focus on research and development and training; but these are unlikely to achieve spectacular results in the short run.

This leaves the possibility of raising the growth rate of all the advanced countries through some form of coordinated reflation, thereby generating complementary growth. However, not only are there political problems in this approach, but the fact that countries are initially at differing levels of the pressure of demand also poses complications for the so-called "locomotive theory of expansion." If demand is simultaneously expanded, certain countries will become resource-constrained before others have reached their full employment growth rates. The balance of payments constraint will again operate in a manner similar to that pertaining to the pre-1973 period. Nevertheless, a return to the growth rates experienced during those years would be regarded as something of an achievement in itself.

Notes

1   See, for example, Corden (1985) for an essentially neoclassical approach to the problem of trade interlinkages.
2   Strictly speaking, the balance of payments accounting identity should include a category, "interest, profits and dividends" which forms part of the current account. This could easily be incorporated into the model, but, for simplicity, we have ignored it.
3   This approach has been unconvincingly criticized by McGregor and Swales (1985, 1986, 1991). See the rejoinder by Thirlwall (1986), the interchange between McCombie (1981) and Thirlwall (1981), and also McCombie (1989, 1992) for a more detailed discussion of the issues involved and a further rebuttal of McGregor–Swales's criticisms. Their critique essentially rests on three points. They claim correctly that lack of variation in relative prices cannot be justified by invoking the neoclassical "law of one price." But as neither they nor Thirlwall and McCombie subscribe to the "law of one price," this criticism is irrelevant. Second, they argue that testing by regression analysis refutes Thirlwall's rule as there is a statistically significant difference between y and y_B. Unfortunately, their regression procedure is misspecified and their conclusions do not stand up to scrutiny. Finally, they claim that differences in the income elasticities

of demand for imports and exports cannot explain changes in market shares and hence cannot capture the effects of disparities in nonprice competitiveness. In this, they are in error.

4   The balance of payments equilibrium growth rate will now be lower than originally. If initially the current account were in balance, the balance of payments equilibrium growth rate would be $y_B = \varepsilon z/\pi$. However, with a (constant) current account deficit the equilibrium growth would be at the lower rate $y_B = \varphi \varepsilon z/\pi$. The reason is that since the level of imports now exceeds that of exports, the former must grow more slowly than the latter to prevent the deficit increasing.

5   This mechanism should not be confused with the monetarist "law of one price" and the associated Purchasing Power Parity doctrine, which likewise predicts that the domestic price level will increase by the same amount as import prices. The monetarist explanation is that arbitrage will equalize the prices, measured in a common currency, of identical internationally traded goods, subject to transport costs and tariffs. The small open economy assumption implies an infinite price elasticity of demand for exports. As Ball *et al.* (1977, p. 2) put it: "Because the world market for manufactured goods is highly competitive each country must accept the world price for its tradeable goods and through competition in the labour market this will spread to non-tradeable products. Thus the failure of the devaluation to change the long-run relative prices is not the result of workers' refusal to accept a reduction in the real wage. Rather it stems from the assumption of high elasticities of substitution between domestic and foreign goods." In this approach, the concept of a balance of payments constraint has no meaning and the economy tends to its full employment level.

6   To model this phenomenon, the export demand function ideally should be specified in terms of the prices of exports and the domestic prices of the importing country, rather than import prices as in equation (5.2). This allows a distinction to be made between prices measured in a common currency of a domestically produced good destined for the home market and the same good that is exported. Likewise, the import demand function should be modeled in terms of import prices and the prices of home-produced goods (which may differ from the export prices) expressed in a common currency. However, this does not seriously alter the subsequent analysis and we shall not pursue this issue further, but follow Thirlwall's (1979) approach.

7   This does not mean that the neoclassical approach comes into its own. Rather, demand was constrained by the, admittedly fast, rate at which labor could be transferred from the nonmanufacturing to the manufacturing sector and, in the case of West Germany, by the rate of growth of immigration. It was not the *exogenous* growth of the labor force that determined the growth of output.

Through the cumulative causation nature of growth (the Verdoorn effect), these resource-constrained countries were also those whose competitiveness in overseas trade increased over the postwar period. They tended to run persistent balance of payments surpluses.

8   This analysis is a revised version of McCombie (1985b). See McCombie (1988) for an application and extension of the model and figure to explain the determination of regional growth rates.

9   The slope of the line A_0 is less than that of the BP locus so $0 < \beta_1 \pi_2 < \pi_2/\pi_1$. Consequently, $0 < \beta_1 \pi_1 < 1$ and it may be similarly shown that $0 < \beta_2 \pi_2 < 1$. Hence, $0 < (1 - \beta_1 \beta_2 \pi_1 \pi_2) < 1$ and $1/(1 - \beta_1 \beta_2 \pi_1 \pi_2) > 0$.

10 It should be noted that for the growth of net capital inflows to be defined, there must be an initial balance of payments disequilibrium with $0 < \varphi < 1$.

11 The shares, ω_{A_1} etc., will change slowly after the imposition of the quotas, but, for expositional ease, we ignore this complication here.

6 International competitiveness, relative wages, and the balance of payments constraint*

Robert A. Blecker

Several prominent neoclassical trade economists have recently launched attacks on popular notions that the US economy suffers from a loss of international competitiveness. Krugman (1994a, p. 44) proclaimed that "competitiveness is a meaningless word when applied to national economies. And the obsession with competitiveness is both wrong and dangerous." Corden (1994) dissected various definitions of competitiveness and concluded that what may appear to be losses of national competitiveness are really problems caused by rigid real wages or low saving rates at home. Krugman and Corden are certainly right in criticizing some loose notions of "competitiveness," as well as in pointing out that many competitive problems are really domestic in origin. But the significance of international constraints on economic growth and living standards should not be so quickly dismissed.

In fact, only a few years earlier, some mainstream neoclassical economists had conceded the existence of competitiveness problems and, curiously enough, Krugman was in the forefront of those who tried to define the phenomenon.[1] Hatsopoulos et al. (1988, p. 299) defined competitiveness as "the ability of a country to balance its trade . . . while achieving an acceptable rate of improvement in the standard of living."[2] Dornbusch et al. specified that:[3]

> The macroeconomic adjustment that the United States faces over the years ahead [in order to reduce the trade deficit] is *linked to the microeconomic issues of competitiveness* in particular products and the general performance of U.S. exports and import-competing industries. *How well we compete* will determine *how far the dollar needs to fall*, which in turn *makes a major difference to the costs in terms of our standard of living* of bringing our trade deficit down.
>
> (1989, p. 9, emphasis added)

These neoclassical definitions of competitiveness focus on the relative price changes (exchange rate and real wage adjustments) required to bring about

* First published in *Journal of Post Keynesian Economics*, Summer 1998.

balanced trade, taking the level of economic activity and the rate of growth as given.

In the Post Keynesian tradition, there is an alternative conception of competitiveness according to which a country is uncompetitive if it is compelled to reduce its income and employment in order to avoid chronic trade deficits. This approach has been most fully developed in the theory of "balance of payments constrained growth" (hereafter referred to as "BP-constrained growth"), also known as "Thirlwall's Law" (after Thirlwall, 1979).[4] According to this theory, assuming that real exchange rates are constant and that trade must be balanced in the long run,[5] a country's long-run growth rate cannot exceed the ratio of the income elasticity of its exports to the income elasticity of its imports,[6] multiplied by the growth rate of foreign income. The Post Keynesian approach thus focuses on the relative income (or growth rate) adjustments required to balance trade at given relative prices (real exchange rate) – the exact converse of the neoclassical approach. The Post Keynesian approach emphasizes the "non-price" or qualitative aspects of competitiveness that are reflected in income elasticities, rather than competition based on costs or prices.

The Post Keynesian approach also differs from the neoclassical in one other important respect. When Krugman argues that "it is simply not the case that the world's leading nations are to any important degree in competition with each other" (1994a, p. 30), he is implicitly assuming that nations can be treated as normally operating at resource-constrained or full-employment levels of production, at least in the "long run." In contrast, Post Keynesians believe that most countries are not generally resource-constrained in their long-run growth, which implies that aggregate demand matters in the long run as well as the short run. In a world in which resource constraints are not generally binding, all nations, large or small, are in competition in at least one important respect: they are in competition for shares of the global market.

This chapter makes three contributions to the debate over competitiveness. First, it shows that the neoclassical and Post Keynesian views of competitiveness can be treated as special cases of a more general model. This model is developed by combining Thirlwall's analysis of BP-constrained growth with the hypotheses of markup pricing and partial exchange-rate pass-through, in order to make explicit the link between balance of payments equilibrium and changes in relative wages and living standards. The general model reveals that the cases of Keynesian quantity adjustment (slower growth) and neoclassical price adjustment (real depreciation or wage decline) are two poles of a continuum of options available to an uncompetitive country for balancing its trade.[7] Which type of adjustment predominates in practice is thus shown to be an empirical question, and the crucial parameters that determine the extent of competitive problems are identified.

Second, the chapter considers whether real wage flexibility can cure national competitiveness problems, as implied by Corden. More precisely, does allowing the real wage to be flexible guarantee that a country can simultaneously achieve balanced trade with full employment? This issue is explored using a neo-Kaleckian or "structuralist" macro model in which aggregate demand is sensitive to the distribution of income between wages and profits. This model demonstrates that there is not necessarily any rate of relative wage decline (or real depreciation) that can achieve both full employment and balanced trade, in the absence of fiscal or other stimuli.

Third, this chapter addresses the empirical question of whether competitiveness problems are large enough to matter for the case of the United States. While the empirical estimates presented here are necessarily very tentative, they are sufficient to demonstrate that, under reasonable ranges of parameter estimates for the US economy: (i) the BP-constrained growth rate for the United States is below some plausible estimates of the long-term growth rate of potential (full-employment) output, and (ii) maintaining balanced trade with full employment would require a substantial, continuous real depreciation of the dollar, which in turn would imply continuous suppression of real wage increases below the growth rate of labor productivity.

A general model of competitiveness

A simple model of the trade balance can be used to illustrate the two alternative definitions of competitiveness.[8] Start with the equation for the trade balance T, measured in "real" terms (units of the domestic good), using standard constant-elasticity functions for export and import demand:

$$T = (P/EP^*)^{-\varepsilon_x} Y^{*\eta_x} - (EP^*/P)(EP^*/P)^{-\varepsilon_m} Y^{\eta_m}. \tag{6.1}$$

In equation (6.1), P is the price level, Y is real national income, E is the exchange rate (domestic currency price of foreign exchange), the $\varepsilon_i > 0$ $(i = x, m)$ are the price elasticities for exports and imports, the $\eta_i > 0$ $(i = x, m)$ are the corresponding income elasticities, and an asterisk denotes a foreign variable. Setting $T = 0$ in (6.1), taking natural logs, and then differentiating with respect to time yields the following condition for balanced trade to be maintained in terms of the exponential growth rates of prices and incomes:[9]

$$(\varepsilon_x + \varepsilon_m - 1)(p - p^* - e) = \eta_x y^* - \eta_m y, \tag{6.2}$$

where small letters indicate the growth rates of the corresponding variables. It is assumed that the Marshall–Lerner condition holds so that $(\varepsilon_x + \varepsilon_m - 1) > 0$.[10]

In order to relate this balanced trade condition to income distribution and the standard of living, it is convenient to adopt the hypothesis of markup pricing.[11] Let the price level in the "home" country be determined by

$$P = \Phi W / Q, \tag{6.3}$$

where $\Phi > 1$ equals one plus the markup rate, W is the nominal wage rate, and Q is labor productivity (the reciprocal of the labor coefficient). Again taking logarithmic derivatives with respect to time, price inflation equals the proportional change in the markup factor (ϕ) plus the rate of change in unit labor costs:

$$p = \phi + w - q, \tag{6.4}$$

where, for simplicity, the rate of labor productivity growth q is assumed to be exogenously given.[12]

In accordance with the literature on "profit squeeze" behavior or "partial exchange-rate pass-through" (also known as "pricing to market"),[13] it will be assumed that the markup rate is reduced when home production becomes more costly relative to foreign production (as measured by relative unit labor costs in a common currency). For mathematical convenience, this relationship is represented by the constant-elasticity function:

$$\Phi = Z\Omega^{-\theta}, \tag{6.5}$$

where $Z > 0$ is a positive constant, $\Omega = (W/Q)/(EW^*/Q^*)$ is relative unit labor cost (home/foreign), and $-\theta$ is the elasticity of the markup factor with respect to the relative wage, with $\theta > 0$ (a further, joint restriction on θ and θ^* for the foreign country will be noted below). Note that this formulation implies that (in growth rate form),

$$\phi = -\theta(\omega - q + q^*), \tag{6.6}$$

where $\omega = w - e - w^*$ is the relative rate of increase in home wages compared with foreign (thus $\hat{\Omega} = \omega - q + q^*$, where "^" indicates a proportional rate of change).

An analogous set of pricing equations is assumed to hold for the foreign country:

$$P^* = \Phi^* W^*/Q^* \tag{6.7}$$

is the equation for the foreign price level, which implies

$$p^* = \phi^* + w^* - q^* \tag{6.8}$$

in growth rates, with the markup factor determined by[14]

$$\Phi^* = Z^*\Omega^{\theta^*}, \tag{6.9}$$

or

$$\phi^* = \theta^*(\omega - q + q^*) \tag{6.10}$$

in growth rate form.

Making appropriate substitutions of equations (6.4), (6.6), (6.8), and (6.10) in equation (6.2), the following solution can be obtained for the relative change in home wages compared with foreign (ω):

$$\omega = (q - q^*) + \frac{\eta_x y^* - \eta_m y}{(\varepsilon_x + \varepsilon_m - 1)(1 - \theta - \theta^*)}, \tag{6.11}$$

where y and y^* are, respectively, the domestic and foreign growth rates. Note that the restriction $(1 - \theta - \theta^*) > 0$ must be assumed in order to rule out the (rather implausible) possibility that a real appreciation (or rise in relative home unit labor costs) could cause such extreme profit squeeze behavior as to make home products more price-competitive instead of less.

Equation (6.11) is essentially an external balance condition, showing the combinations of relative wage change (ω) and domestic growth (y) for which balanced trade can be maintained in the long run, given the foreign growth rate y^*. This locus is represented as the downward-sloping line $T = 0$ in Figure 6.1. Points above and to the right of the line are in the deficit region ($T < 0$), while points below and to the left of the line are in the surplus region ($T > 0$). When relative wages change at a rate equal to the difference between the home and foreign productivity growth rates, relative purchasing power parity (PPP) holds (the real exchange rate EP^*/P is constant). This level of ω is represented by the horizontal line $\omega_P = q - q^*$ in Figure 6.1, which is drawn on the assumption that $q < q^*$ (this is intended to be realistic for the United States, but is not essential to the argument). When $\omega = \omega_P$, balanced trade then requires $y = (\eta_x/\eta_m)y^*$, which is Thirlwall's BP-constrained growth rate (hereafter written as y_B). This is represented by point B in Figure 6.1.

Another important benchmark is the growth rate at which full employment of the labor force is maintained. For this purpose, the concept of the so-called "natural

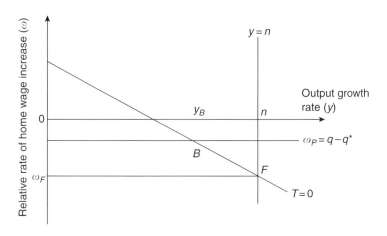

Figure 6.1 The BP constraint and relative wage changes.

rate of growth" may be invoked.[15] The natural rate of growth (n) is the growth rate of potential output, which is equal to the growth rate of the labor force (λ) plus the rate of labor-saving technical change (q): $n = \lambda + q$, all of which are taken here as exogenously given.[16] In spite of the difficulties with the notion of an externally given limit to growth, the natural rate concept is useful here as a device for representing the condition for full-employment or resource-constrained growth.[17] If n is substituted for y in (6.11), with the foreign growth rate y^* still taken as exogenously given, the solution yields the rate of change of the relative wage required to maintain balanced trade with full employment (ω_F, which is the level of ω at point F, where the $T = 0$ locus intersects the vertical line $y = n$ in Figure 6.1). Notice that there is no reason in general why the BP-constrained growth rate $y_B = (\eta_x/\eta_m)y^*$ should equal the natural growth rate $n = \lambda + q$. Figure 6.1 assumes that $y_B < n$, which is shown to be realistic for the US economy in the empirical discussion next.

The difference between points B and F in Figure 6.1 illustrates the conflicts facing an uncompetitive economy and allows us to represent the Post Keynesian and neoclassical definitions of competitiveness as special cases of the same equation. The fact that $y_B < n$ indicates that the country depicted is uncompetitive in the Post Keynesian sense that, at a given real exchange rate, it cannot balance its trade without a rising unemployment rate. The fact that point F is below the PPP line ($\omega_P = q - q^*$) indicates that the country is uncompetitive in the neoclassical sense that it cannot achieve full employment with balanced trade unless it accepts a continuous real depreciation of its currency (and a decline in the relative wage that is greater than the gap in rates of productivity growth).[18]

In between points B and F, there is a range of possible outcomes described by equation (6.11), which maps out a set of trade-offs between greater real currency depreciation (or declines in relative wages) and lower growth rates (implying higher unemployment). The degree to which such a trade-off exists depends on the slope and intercept of $T = 0$ and on the level of the "natural rate of growth" (growth rate of potential output). The slope and intercept in turn depend on the various parameters in equation (6.11). This trade-off is worsened by: a high income elasticity of import demand η_m, which implies a high slope (in absolute value); or by a low income elasticity of export demand η_x, slow foreign growth (low y^*), or high foreign productivity growth (q^*), any of which implies a low intercept.[19] The trade-off is also more severe if the sum of the price elasticities ($\varepsilon_x + \varepsilon_m$) is relatively low (i.e. not much greater than 1) or exchange-rate pass-through is very partial (i.e. θ and θ^* are relatively high).[20] Not surprisingly, these conditions for a severe trade-off correspond very closely to the beliefs of most Post Keynesian authors about the situations of the US and UK economies. By the same token, neoclassical optimism about how easily countries can avoid BP constraints must rest on opposite views about these key parameter values, along with a conservative view of the level of the "natural rate of growth" so that there is no significant trade-off between points B and F, and therefore PPP is not inconsistent with maintaining balanced trade with full employment in the long run.

Alternative policies for improving competitiveness

This section analyzes the policy alternatives facing a country that is uncompetitive in the sense just defined (i.e. cannot achieve balanced trade with full employment at a constant real exchange rate). The first set of alternatives consists of adjusting to the competitiveness constraint (i.e. line segment BF in Figure 6.1), while the second set consists of efforts to relax that constraint.

Much recent policy advice in both the United States and Europe essentially consists of recommending acceptance of point F as an inevitable outcome, and advocating dollar depreciation (for the United States) or greater wage flexibility (for Europe) as a strategy for getting there (see Bergsten, 1991, on the United States, and Corden, 1994, on Europe). There are two difficulties with this strategy. The first difficulty is one of feasibility; the other is one of desirability.

In order to reach point F, money wages in national currencies and/or exchange rates have to adjust over time at just the right speeds to maintain the equilibrium rate of relative wage decline. Note that, to stay at point F, there would have to be a continuous, long-run real depreciation, not just a one-time real depreciation. Either "real wage resistance" or rigidities in nominal wage setting can prevent the requisite relative wage adjustments from occurring. As for exchange rates, the flexible rates among the major hard currencies seem to be driven more by asset market events (capital account transactions) than by the conditions for trade (current account) balance. Even if a given country could cut its own wages and depreciate its currency fast enough to move toward point F, such a policy could still be nullified by competitive wage cuts or currency depreciation by other countries. Exchange-rate changes can also be destabilizing to both goods and asset markets, which can lead to efforts at exchange-rate management ranging from the European Monetary Union to US–European–Japanese "target zones" – all of which tend to prevent exchange rates from bearing the full burden of adjustment. Thus, we do not expect to find large, sustained, long-run changes in real exchange rates (as distinct from short-run fluctuations), regardless of whether strict relative PPP holds.[21]

For all these reasons (and others to be discussed in the following section), the neoclassical point of full employment with balanced trade F may be very hard to reach. But even if F could be reached, there is a question of whether it would be desirable to do so. Moving to point F might entail considerable reductions either in the growth rate of living standards or possibly in their absolute level. Such painful adjustments are bound to be resisted and to provoke popular opposition. Moreover, moving to point F does not really eliminate a competitiveness problem, as implied by Corden (1994); rather, the need for a continuous real depreciation and consequent reduction in relative living standards can be seen as a manifestation of competitive decline (as implied in some of the neoclassical definitions of competitiveness cited earlier).[22]

If the neoclassical adjustment proves unfeasible, an alternative is the adjustment implied by the theory of BP-constrained growth, which leaves a country at point B in Figure 6.1. Here, the real exchange rate is held constant and thus wage growth is kept equal to domestic productivity growth, but income growth is reduced and higher unemployment is likely to result. In fact, growth at the BP-constrained rate $y_B < n$ implies a chronically rising unemployment rate.[23] This unpleasant set of alternatives leads to a search for policies to relieve the competitiveness constraint at an acceptable social and economic cost. There are three basic ways in which such policies may operate (either singly or in combination).

First, the country can try to raise its productivity growth rate q. An increase in q to q' has the effects shown in Figure 6.2. First, both the PPP ($\omega_P = q - q^*$) and balanced trade ($T = 0$) lines shift up. Since the BP-constrained growth rate $y_B = (\eta_x/\eta_m)y^*$ is not affected, point B shifts up vertically to B'. At least, this means that a constant real exchange rate is now consistent with balanced trade at a slower rate of relative wage decline (or possibly even an increase in relative wages, if $q' - q^* > 0$).

However, ω_F (the rate of relative wage change corresponding to full employment with balanced trade) does not necessarily increase when q rises. This is because a rise in q also increases the natural rate of growth, and thus shifts the $y = n$ line to the right. As shown in Figure 6.2, point F shifts to the right to F', but whether F' is higher or lower than F (and thus whether ω_F rises or falls) is ambiguous a priori. Intuitively, this is because faster productivity growth requires a higher rate of output growth in order to maintain full employment (with a given rate of increase in the labor force), but a higher rate of output growth raises imports and thus fosters a trade deficit unless the currency depreciates (relative wages fall) sufficiently to offset this. Furthermore, more rapid productivity growth alone does not make y_B any closer to n, but rather increases the gap between these two growth rates.[24]

A second alternative, long favored by many British Keynesians and now accepted by some American industrial policy advocates (if not by many American

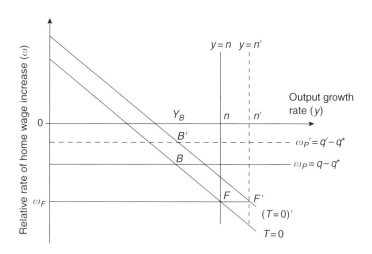

Figure 6.2 Increase in the rate of home productivity growth (from q to q').

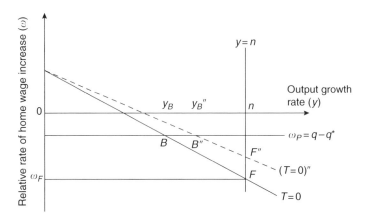

Figure 6.3 Reduction in the income elasticity of import demand (η_m).

economists) is to try to reduce the income elasticity of demand for imports, η_m.[25] This would essentially make the $T = 0$ line flatter in slope with the same intercept, thus making it rotate upward as shown in Figure 6.3. This has the effect of raising the BP-constrained growth rate, so that point B shifts horizontally along the $\omega_P = q - q^*$ line to B'', while point F moves vertically up the $y = n$ line to F''. Notice that a sufficiently large reduction in η_m could make B'' and F'' coincide at the point where the vertical $y = n$ line intersects the horizontal $\omega_P = q - q^*$ line, thus permitting balanced trade with full-employment growth at a constant real exchange rate. A reduction in η_m clearly improves the trade-off between keeping the relative wage from falling too fast and preventing rising unemployment. However, a decrease in η_m cannot by itself raise the rate of relative wage change consistent with a constant real exchange rate ($\omega_P = q - q^*$), nor can it increase real wage growth, *unless* there is a positive feedback from the relief of the BP constraint onto productivity growth.

The question then is how η_m can be reduced. If η_m is conceived as a weighted average of the income elasticities of imports for individual commodities, then it depends on (a) the non-price competitiveness of particular domestic goods relative to foreign goods, and (b) the composition of the domestic industrial structure (i.e. whether the country produces the goods that consumers and producers want more, as income expands). Thus, in order to reduce η_m, it is necessary to develop higher-quality, more "upscale" domestic products so that consumers with rising incomes spend an increasing fraction of their income on home goods and less on imports. This evidently requires domestic industrial policies rather than trade policies *per se*.

Nevertheless, some closing of the home market via import restrictions could also be used to lower η_m and may even be necessary to ensure the requisite transformation of the domestic industrial structure. Since a higher average tariff *rate* (but at a constant level) would not affect the *growth* of imports, and a continuously increasing tariff rate is implausible, quantitative restrictions such as quotas would have to be used for this purpose (although a different tariff *structure*, one that penalized imports of the products with high income elasticities, could help to reduce the weighted-average income elasticity of import demand). While such import restrictions may have static efficiency costs, the present model shows that they can have macroeconomic benefits in terms of allowing a country to grow faster without hitting a BP constraint.[26] It must also be emphasized that the purpose of lowering η_m is to reduce the *propensity* to import, not necessarily the *level* of imports; if faster growth is enabled, the actual level of imports need not be decreased.[27]

Finally, there is the option of increasing the growth rate of exports (which equals $\eta_x y^*$, at a given real exchange rate), either by raising the income elasticity of export demand (η_x) or by inducing foreign countries to accelerate their growth (y^*). Analytically, faster export growth shifts the $T=0$ line up in a parallel fashion (a higher intercept with the same slope), as shown in Figure 6.4. As in the previous case, this makes B shift to the right (to $\tilde{B}$) and F shift up (to $\tilde{F}$), and can potentially make these two points coincide. Once again, the BP constraint is relaxed, permitting more rapid growth with balanced trade at any given real exchange rate (or allowing full employment with balanced trade at a lower rate of relative wage decline).[28]

Here again the question of policies arises. One route is to urge expansionary policies upon one's trading partners so as to raise y^*. This is a classic Keynesian policy, insofar as it puts more of the burden of adjustment on the surplus countries and imparts an expansionary rather than a contractionary bias to the world economy (see Davidson, 1991; McCombie, 1993).[29] Also, domestic industrial policies of the same type that can lower the income elasticity of import demand η_m can, by the same logic, also raise the income elasticity of export demand η_x by making domestic goods more attractive to potential foreign customers. Foreign market-opening is another potential policy lever for raising η_x. However,

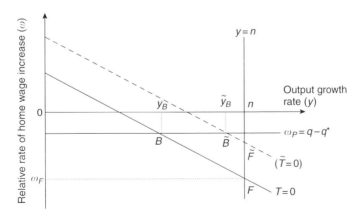

Figure 6.4 Increase in the growth rate of exports ($\eta_x y^*$).

since other countries are unlikely to make major market-opening moves without exacting some concessions in return, the market-opening strategy seems to offer at best only modest gains.[30]

Can cutting wages achieve balanced trade with full employment?

In the preceding sections, it was assumed for the sake of discussion that a national economy could move from the BP-constrained growth point B to the full-employment point F in Figure 6.1 by reducing its rate of relative wage change to ω_F, which requires a continuous real depreciation (terms of trade decline). But the line $T = 0$ is only a long-run equilibrium condition for maintaining balanced trade; it does not describe the actual movements of an economy in response to changes in ω. In fact, if an economy actually started at point B, lowering ω – even if feasible – would *not* generally move the economy toward F. Additional demand-side policies would be required to stimulate growth, and these would in most cases involve a domestic demand stimulus such as a fiscal expansion (or else an assist from foreign demand expansion).

To illustrate this point, this section develops a simple "structuralist" or neo-Kaleckian macro model, which emphasizes the dependence of aggregate demand on the "functional" (wage–profit) distribution of income.[31] Since the focus is on the open economy dimension, a very simple specification of the domestic economy is used.

Assuming for simplicity that all income is taxed at the uniform rate τ ($0 < \tau < 1$), all savings come out of (after-tax) profit income, and all (after-tax) wages are spent on consumption,[32] the consumption function is

$$C = (1 + s\pi)(1 - \tau)Y, \tag{6.12}$$

where s is the saving rate out of profit income and $\pi = (\Phi - 1)/\Phi$ is the profit share of national income. Assuming that investment depends positively on the level of profits (πY) and on aggregate demand or capacity utilization (represented by Y), the investment function is

$$I = a\pi Y + bY, \tag{6.13}$$

where $a > 0$ and $b > 0$. Total domestic expenditure or "absorption" ($A = C + I + G$, where G represents government expenditures) is then equal to

$$A = \{1 - [s(1 - \tau) - a]\pi + \tau - b\}Y + G. \tag{6.14}$$

For simplicity, constant terms have been omitted from the functions for C and I, and G is the only "autonomous expenditure." To complete the aggregate demand system, goods market equilibrium requires that

$$Y = A + T, \tag{6.15}$$

where T is defined by equation (6.1).

By making appropriate substitutions in (6.15), taking derivatives with respect to time, assuming that trade is initially balanced, and expressing the resulting equation in growth rate form (with lower-case letters representing exponential growth rates as before), the following solution for income growth is obtained:[33]

$$
\begin{aligned}
y = k^{-1}\{ &\alpha_g g + \alpha_x \eta_x y^* \\
&+ [(s(1-\tau) - a)(\Phi - 1)\theta\pi - \alpha_x(\varepsilon_x + \varepsilon_m - 1)(1 - \theta - \theta^*)] \\
&\times (\omega - q + q^*)\},
\end{aligned}
\tag{6.16}
$$

where $k = \{[s(1-\tau) - a]\pi + \tau - b + \alpha_m\eta_m\} > 0$ is the condition for goods market stability, and the α_i ($i = g, x, m$) are the shares of G, X, and M in GDP ($\alpha_g = G/Y, \alpha_x = X/Y, \alpha_m = (EP^*/P)(M/Y)$); note that $\alpha_x = \alpha_m$ on the assumption that $T = 0$ initially. Both the growth rate of government spending g and the foreign income growth rate y^* are assumed to be exogenously given.

For any given g and y^*, then, equation (6.16) describes another relationship – essentially a short-run "IS curve," although we shall call it "AD" for aggregate demand – between the domestic growth rate y and the rate of relative wage change ω, starting from a position of initially balanced trade. The effect of a change in ω on y, in the neighborhood of the locus $T = 0$, is given by

$$
\frac{\partial y}{\partial \omega} = k^{-1}\left\{ [s(1-\tau) - a](\Phi - 1)\theta\pi - \alpha_x(\varepsilon_x + \varepsilon_m - 1)(1 - \theta - \theta^*) \right\}.
\tag{6.17}
$$

The first term in brackets in equation (6.17) is positive if the saving rate out of pretax profits $s(1-\tau)$ exceeds the propensity to invest out of profits a, and negative in the opposite case.[34] The second term is negative as long as the Marshall–Lerner condition ($\varepsilon_x + \varepsilon_m > 1$) holds. The sign of equation (6.17) determines whether growth is "wage-led" (if $\partial y/\partial \omega > 0$) or "profit-led" (if $\partial y/\partial \omega < 0$). The former case has been referred to as "stagnationism" or "underconsumptionism," while the latter has been called "exhilarationism."[35]

This specification of aggregate demand permits an analysis of the effects of reducing ω on the actual growth rate of the economy. Consider, as a benchmark, the case where the economy is growing at the BP-constrained rate, $y_B = (\eta_x/\eta_m)y^*$, with balanced trade and a constant real exchange rate ($\omega = \omega_P = q - q^*$). This case could occur, for example, if the government had adjusted the growth rate of public expenditure g so as to keep trade balanced, given the foreign growth rate y^*. The question, then, is whether a reduction in ω will move the economy toward the neoclassical long-run equilibrium point F, at which there is full employment with balanced trade.

The aggregate demand relationship (equation (6.16)) is represented by the AD curves in Figure 6.5(a–c), which show the cases of stagnationism, mild exhilarationism, and extreme exhilarationism, respectively. In the stagnationist case

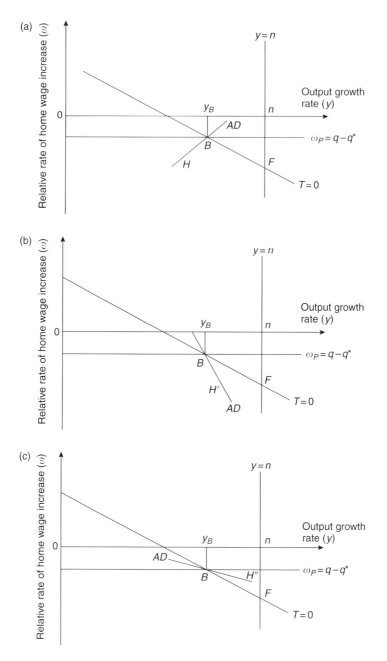

Figure 6.5 (a) Stagnationist aggregate demand. (b) Mildly exhilarationist aggregate demand. (c) Extremely exhilarationist aggregate demand.

(Figure 6.5(a)), the *AD* curve is upward-sloping, and a fall in ω moves the economy down and to the left to point *H* at which the growth rate is actually reduced. Since point *H* is in the trade surplus region (below $T = 0$), the faster real depreciation (or relative wage cut) is effective for improving the trade balance in this case. The trade balance improvement comes mainly from the contraction in growth, however, since the price elasticities of exports and imports must be relatively low for *AD* to be positively sloped.[36] In this case, reducing ω moves the actual growth rate *y* further from the full-employment growth rate *n*.

In the case of mild exhilarationism (Figure 6.5(b)), the *AD* curve is downward-sloping, but steeper than $T = 0$. In this situation, a fall in ω is expansionary, but still leads to a trade surplus (shift from *F* to *H'*). This outcome could result from relatively high price elasticities of export and import demand coupled with a high degree of exchange-rate pass-through (low θ and θ^*), which would tend to make $\partial y / \partial \omega > 0$. In this case, the improved price competitiveness from lower relative wages raises net exports by more than enough to outweigh the underconsumptionist effect of a higher profit share. The trade balance improvement is mitigated, however, by the induced increase in imports resulting from faster growth. In this case, reducing ω can get the economy to full employment, but only with a trade surplus (hence, expansionary demand policies are still required to reach point *F*).

Finally, in the case of extreme exhilarationism shown in Figure 6.5(c), the *AD* curve slopes down and is flatter than $T = 0$ at the initial point *B*. In this case, a decrease in ω moves the economy to a much higher growth rate at point *H''*, which is in the trade deficit region. As a result, a faster real depreciation of the currency (or decrease in the relative wage) is not only ineffective for improving the trade balance, but actually worsens it (although it does move the economy toward full employment). For this extreme case to occur, there would have to be a very high profitability effect on investment [$a > s(1 - \tau)$], coupled with a relatively high tax rate (τ), a relatively low utilization effect on investment (*b*), and a high income elasticity of import demand (η_m).[37] Essentially, the rising profit share would have to stimulate a large amount of additional domestic spending – enough to more than offset the effect of improved price competitiveness on the trade balance as well as the underconsumption effect.

These three cases show the range of possible effects of making the relative wage fall more or, equivalently, depreciating the currency faster in real terms. In the stagnationist case, the trade balance improves a lot but at the expense of slower growth; the economy actually moves further away from full employment. In the case of mild exhilarationism, growth increases, but the economy cannot get to full employment without a widening trade surplus. In the case of extreme exhilarationism, the growth rate rises so much that a trade deficit results in spite of a more rapidly depreciating currency; the economy cannot get to full employment without a widening trade deficit. Only in this last case would a contractionary fiscal policy be needed along with a fall in ω to achieve balanced trade with full employment, but this is an extreme case, and perhaps the least plausible of the three. Only by sheer accident would the parameters of the system make the *AD* curve follow the $T = 0$ line so that a decrease in ω would move the economy to the point of growth with full employment and balanced trade, F.

In a sense, the preceding analysis merely demonstrates the well–known proposition that, in general, it is not possible to achieve two economic targets (in this case, balanced trade and full employment) with only one instrument (the rate of change in the relative wage, ω). Yet this point seems to be forgotten in those policy discussions that advocate accelerated real currency depreciation (or a more rapidly falling relative wage) as the main policy response to declining competitiveness. In order to achieve those twin targets, accelerated depreciation (or faster relative wage decline) would have to be accompanied, in the two more realistic cases (stagnationism or mild exhilarationism), by fiscal expansion or some other demand-side stimulus (such as a foreign demand expansion, as emphasized by McCombie, 1993).

Empirical plausibility for the US case

It remains to be seen whether competitiveness problems, as defined above, are large enough to make a difference to aggregate economic outcomes for relative wages or growth rates. It would be beyond the scope of this chapter – and perhaps impossible in any case – to come up with a definitive set of estimates that would resolve the issue of how much competitiveness matters to growth and living standards. This section attempts something more modest, namely, to provide a range of estimates showing the plausible dimensions of the competitiveness problem for the United States. The calculations that follow are based on previously published studies that have estimated some of the key parameters in the general model of competitiveness presented earlier. All that is claimed is that these numbers show that competitiveness problems cannot be dismissed a priori as trivial in magnitude (as claimed by Krugman, 1994a,b).

The estimates are presented in Table 6.1. Three different sets of price and income elasticities are used from the estimates by Lawrence (1990), Blecker (1996), and Cline (1989).[38] For the profit squeeze parameters, I relied on several leading studies of exchange-rate pass-through for US imports and exports to come up with a range of low, medium, and high values for the sum of $\theta + \theta^*$ (which are 0.0, 0.3, and 0.6, respectively).[39] The data for GDP growth and productivity growth were taken from the Organisation for Economic Cooperation and Development (OECD, 1996), and are averaged for the period 1979–94 (productivity is measured by real GDP per person employed).[40] The foreign growth rate y^* is constructed as a weighted average of the growth rates for the other OECD countries ("OECD *less* US") and for developing countries (the latter computed from data in International Monetary Fund, 1996), with weights of 0.6 and 0.4, respectively (since the industrial countries account for about 60 percent of US exports). Foreign productivity growth was proxied by the series for "OECD *less* US" since comparable, reliable data on productivity growth in developing countries were not available.

Table 6.1 Alternative estimates of the BP-constrained growth rate (y_B) and rate of relative wage change consistent with balanced trade and full employment (ω_F) for the United States

Elasticity estimates	Lawrence (1990)			Blecker (1996)			Cline (1989)		
	Low	Med.	High	Low	Med.	High	Low	Med.	High
$\varepsilon_x + \varepsilon_m$	2.08	2.08	2.08	2.00	2.00	2.00	3.10	3.10	3.10
η_x	1.60	1.60	1.60	1.38	1.38	1.38	1.70	1.70	1.70
η_m	2.47	2.47	2.47	2.22	2.22	2.22	2.44	2.44	2.44
Profit squeeze/ pass-through coefficients $(\theta + \theta^*)^a$	0.0	0.3	0.6	0.0	0.3	0.6	0.0	0.3	0.6
Growth rates									
q	0.9	0.9	0.9	0.9	0.9	0.9	0.9	0.9	0.9
q^*	1.6	1.6	1.6	1.6	1.6	1.6	1.6	1.6	1.6
$\omega_P = q - q^*$	−0.6	−0.6	−0.6	−0.6	−0.6	−0.6	−0.6	−0.6	−0.6
y^*	3.1	3.1	3.1	3.1	3.1	3.1	3.1	3.1	3.1
Estimated BP-constrained growth rate									
$y_B = (\eta_x/\eta_m)y^*$	2.0	2.0	2.0	1.9	1.9	1.9	2.2	2.2	2.2
Relative wage change estimates assuming n = 2.1 (low)									
ω_F	−0.9	−0.9	−1.2	−1.0	−1.2	−1.6	−0.6	−0.5	−0.5
$\omega_F - \omega_P$	−0.2	−0.3	−0.5	−0.4	−0.6	−1.0	0.1	0.1	0.2
Relative wage change estimates assuming n = 2.8 (medium)									
ω_F	−2.5	−3.2	−5.2	−2.6	−3.4	−5.5	−1.4	−1.7	−2.5
$\omega_F - \omega_P$	−1.8	−2.6	−4.5	−1.9	−2.8	−4.9	−0.7	−1.1	−1.9
Relative wage change estimates assuming n = 3.5 (high)									
ω_F	−4.1	−5.5	−9.2	−4.1	−5.6	−9.4	−2.2	−2.9	−4.5
$\omega_F - \omega_P$	−3.4	−4.9	−8.6	−3.5	−5.0	−8.7	−1.6	−2.2	−3.9
Addenda									
y (actual)	2.4			2.4			2.4		
x (actual)	5.8			5.8			5.8		
$\tilde{y}_B = x/\eta_m$	2.4			2.6			2.4		

Notes
See text for variable definitions, data sources, and estimation methods. All growth rates are average annual rates for 1979–94. Individual items are rounded separately.
a The low, medium, and high values of $\theta + \theta^*$ imply full, medium, and low exchange rate pass-through, respectively.

Using equation (6.11), these inputs for elasticities, profit squeeze effects, and growth rates were used to calculate three alternative estimates for the BP-constrained growth rate (y_B, which depends only on the income elasticities and foreign growth rate) and nine alternative estimates of the rate of relative wage change corresponding to full employment with balanced trade (ω_F, which depends on all the parameters). Since ω_F is calculated by solving equation (6.11) on the assumption that $y = n$, estimation of ω_F also requires assumptions about the "natural rate of growth," n. I used the US Congressional Budget Office (1996)

estimate of the growth rate of potential output (defined as non-accelerating inflation output) of 2.1 percent per year (in the scenario with current fiscal policy)
as the low estimate of n. This is a very conservative estimate, which assumes
that the United States cannot grow even as fast as it did on average in the
1979–94 period (2.4 percent) – a period marked by three major recessions and
historically high real interest rates! While there is considerable uncertainty about
how much faster growth the United States could sustain in the long run, the
medium and high estimates of n used here (2.8 and 3.5 percent, respectively)
are well within the range of past historical growth performance in the postwar US
economy.[41]

The estimates of the BP-constrained growth rate $y_B = (\eta_x/\eta_m)y^*$ are very similar using all three sets of income elasticities, ranging between 1.9 and 2.2 percent
annually. These growth rates are very close to the low estimate of n, and considerably less than the medium and high estimates of n. Of course, the actual growth
of the US economy has been somewhat higher than this, averaging 2.4 percent per
year between 1979 and 1994, which does not seem unreasonable since the US trade
deficit generally rose during that time. Thus, these estimates can be interpreted
as showing how much slower the United States would have had to grow during
that period to avoid rising trade deficits, and also suggest that the CBO's notion
of "potential" output growth may be closer to a BP-constrained rate than to a truly
resource-constrained rate.

However, alternative estimates of BP-constrained growth based on actual US
export growth.[42] ($\tilde{y}_B = x/\eta_m$), shown at the bottom of Table 6.1, are somewhat
higher (in the range of 2.4–2.6 percent per year) and much closer to actual US
growth. If these alternative estimates are to be believed, then the BP constraint has
actually been approximately binding in the US case – assuming that the medium
or high estimates of n are closer to the true potential of the US economy than the
low estimate – in spite of rising trade deficits and an increased net debtor status.
This may not be as surprising as it seems, however, since the broadly defined US
trade balance (net exports of goods and services in the GDP accounts) fell only
slightly, from -0.9 percent of GDP in 1979 to -1.4 percent in 1994.[43] Exploring
the reasons for the discrepancy between these two estimates of the BP-constrained
growth rate is an important area for future research.[44]

The estimates of the full-employment, balanced-trade rate of relative wage
decline ω_F range from -0.5 to -9.4 percent per year. As expected, ω_F is generally
lower (i.e. more negative) when lower price elasticities and more partial exchange
rate pass-through (higher θ and θ^*) are assumed.[45] The estimates of ω_F are also
decreasing with respect to the assumptions made about the natural rate of growth n.
In fact, with the low (CBO) estimate of n, ω_F is generally estimated to be close
to (or only slightly below) the PPP rate of relative wage decline, $\omega_P = q - q^*$.
However, if one thinks that output could potentially grow at our medium or high
estimates of n, then ω_F is notably lower than ω_P, implying a need for a substantial,
continuous real depreciation (see the lines in Table 6.1 for $\omega_F - \omega_P$).

Thus, under reasonable ranges of parameter values, based on previous estimates
in the literature on US trade, and under a reasonable range of assumptions about

the potential output growth of the US economy, it is quite plausible that there is a significant trade-off between the degree to which growth would have to be cut in order to maintain balanced trade at a constant real exchange rate, and the degree to which the real exchange rate would have to fall (and relative living standards would have to decline) in order to achieve balanced trade with sustained full employment. However, the estimates presented here are evidently tentative, especially since the parameters are drawn from a number of different studies and are not based on a single, consistent model of US trade. More empirical work is needed to reach firmer conclusions in this area.

Conclusions

This chapter has presented an analytical framework for conceptualizing the issue of international competitiveness. This framework shows that an uncompetitive country faces a trade-off between faster real depreciation (relative wage decline) and a slower growth rate in order to maintain balanced trade in the long run. This analysis allows us to represent neoclassical and Post Keynesian concepts of competitiveness problems as different cases of the same basic model, with neoclassicals emphasizing the possibility for price adjustment (real depreciation) and Keynesians seeing a form of quantity adjustment (slower income growth) as the more likely outcome. Theoretically, this analytical framework shows that it is not generally possible for a country to achieve full-employment growth with balanced trade simultaneously while maintaining relative PPP (i.e. at a constant real exchange rate).

The model developed in this chapter also clarifies the key assumptions about parameter values that distinguish the neoclassical and Post Keynesian positions. Neoclassical faith in the ability of flexible wages and exchange rates to "solve" competitiveness problems at an acceptable social cost must rest on optimism about the values of certain key parameters, such as relatively high price-elasticities of export and import demand, relatively equal income elasticities, relatively full exchange rate pass-through, and a low "natural" rate of growth. If any of these assumptions does not hold, then competitiveness problems as defined here are likely to involve more severe trade-offs.

The purpose of this exercise is mainly to clarify thinking rather than to reach definitive policy recommendations. Nevertheless, some policy implications do follow from the analysis developed here. First, the chapter reveals a number of problems with the strategy of relying on wage "flexibility" to cure competitive problems. To succeed in the long run, this strategy requires continuous real depreciations that are unlikely to be observed in practice. Even if the requisite depreciations take place, actual growth may not be accelerated because of the potentially negative effects of lower wages on aggregate demand. Second, this analysis also suggests that there are alternatives to accepting the inevitability of a low-wage path to improved competitiveness. Three kinds of structural changes (faster productivity growth, a lower income elasticity of import demand, and a higher income elasticity of export demand) can enable a country to grow more rapidly and maintain higher employment with balanced trade and a lesser decline in (or greater increase in) the relative wage (standard of living). In addition, the analysis presented here highlights the need to *combine* policies to raise the growth rate of productivity with policies to raise the BP-constrained growth rate by increasing the ratio of income elasticities for exports and imports. Only such a combined effort can both increase the rate of relative wage change at a constant real exchange rate and lessen the conflict between keeping the real exchange rate constant and maintaining full employment with balanced trade.

Finally, it must be emphasized that acknowledging the existence of competitiveness problems in the sense defined here does *not* necessarily imply support for beggar-thy-neighbor policies. On the contrary, the BP-constraint framework emphasizes that competitive devaluations or wage cuts are unlikely to bring permanent gains, and stresses that international cooperation to ensure more expansionary macro policies can help to relieve BP constraints in most countries. Increased foreign income growth has exactly the same effects as a higher income elasticity of export demand in relaxing the BP constraint. Paradoxically, recognizing that countries can be in competition with each other in a world constrained by aggregate demand problems can lead to a search for more cooperative solutions.

Notes

1 Referring to his earlier heresy, Krugman later confessed that "many sensible people have imagined that they can appropriate the rhetoric of competitiveness on behalf of desirable economic policies. . . . It's tempting to pander to popular prejudices on behalf of a good cause, and I have myself succumbed to that temptation" (1994a, p. 44). Even in his later writings, Krugman (1994a,b) does not deny that competitiveness can be a problem in principle, only that it is an empirically significant problem for the US economy.

2 A similar definition is found in Tyson (1992, p. 1).

3 In a similar vein, Robert Z. Lawrence wrote that

> changes in the relative trade performance of American industries . . . will put downward pressure on U.S. wages and prices, and, more important, will tend to depress the exchange value of the dollar . . . to the point where the trade deficit turns around and moves back to an equilibrium determined by the country's fundamental spending–saving behavior.
>
> (1989, p. 29)

4 Later extensions of Thirlwall's approach include the work of Thirlwall and Hussain (1982), who modified the model to incorporate capital mobility, and McCombie (1993), who developed a two-country version of the model with repercussion effects. For more recent summaries and discussions of the literature, see McCombie and Thirlwall (1994, 1997) and McCombie (1997).

5 Although it has not been widely recognized, the Post Keynesian model of BP-constrained growth actually rests on two widely believed propositions in the mainstream international finance literature for the industrial countries: (1) long-run relative purchasing power parity (PPP), which implies that short-run fluctuations in real exchange rates do not lead to permanent deviations from mean levels, and (2) the close correlation of long-run, average national saving and investment rates, which implies that current

accounts tend to be balanced in the long run. The empirical evidence for each of these two propositions is somewhat mixed, however. Recent tests of PPP are surveyed by Froot and Rogoff (1995) and Rogoff (1996), who note that PPP holds well in very long-run data but performs poorly in the short and medium runs. The second proposition derives from the seminal article of Feldstein and Horioka (1980). For more recent analyses and surveys of the subsequent literature, see Frankel (1991) and Blecker (1997).

6 This view of income elasticities as exogenous parameters that constrain growth has been challenged by Krugman (1989a). See Thirlwall (1991) for a rejoinder. Bosworth (1993, pp. 164–165) reports some evidence that is consistent with endogeneity of income elasticities, but that also contradicts part of Krugman's argument.

7 Lawrence (1990, pp. 365–368) shows an awareness that unfavorable income elasticities can potentially constrain either the growth rate or the real exchange rate. Ajit Singh's definition of an "efficient" manufacturing sector also incorporates both the quantity and price dimensions of competitiveness:

> [G]iven the normal levels of the other components of the balance of payments, we may define an efficient manufacturing sector as one which . . . not only satisfies the demands of consumers at home, but is also able to sell enough of its products abroad to pay for the nation's import requirements. This is, however, subject to the important restriction that an "efficient" manufacturing sector must be able to achieve these objectives *at socially acceptable levels of output, employment, and the exchange rate.*
>
> (Singh, 1977, p. 128, some italics omitted)

8 This modeling effort grew out of a presentation that the author was invited to give at a panel discussion on international competitiveness at the Division of International Finance of the Board of Governors of the Federal Reserve System, Washington, DC, March 1993.

9 An alternate version of the model allowing for imbalanced trade with capital flows in the long run is developed by Thirlwall and Hussain (1982).

10 Some of the literature on BP-constrained growth considers the borderline case where the Marshall–Lerner condition holds as an equality ($\varepsilon_x + \varepsilon_m - 1 = 0$) as a serious possibility. The empirical literature suggests that, at least for the United States and other industrial countries, the evidence for the sum of these elasticities exceeding unity by a significant margin is overwhelming. (See Cline (1989), Lawrence (1990), Meade (1991), Blecker (1992, 1996), and Bosworth (1993)). Thirlwall (1997, p. 380) hints that $\varepsilon_x + \varepsilon_m - 1 = 0$ is only a reasonable approximation in less developed countries.

11 To the author's knowledge, this is the first time that the markup pricing hypothesis has been introduced explicitly into the BP-constrained growth model. However, markup pricing has been used in other, related types of open-economy macro models, such as by Dornbusch (1980, pp. 70–74), Blecker (1989), and Sarantis (1990–91).

12 The idea of endogenous productivity growth can be integrated into a BP-constrained growth model, as shown by Thirlwall and Dixon (1979). Given the other complexities considered in this chapter, however, the simpler specification of exogenous productivity growth is preferred for the formal modeling exercise conducted here.

13 The profit squeeze idea refers to the notion that higher domestic unit labor costs force firms to cut their profit margins in order to remain internationally competitive (Glyn and Sutcliffe, 1972). Partial exchange rate pass-through occurs when, in response to an appreciation of the home currency, a nation's firms cut the domestic currency prices of their goods (and thus reduce their profit margins) in order to keep their products more competitive and thus to preserve market shares (both at home and abroad). See Menon (1996) for a comprehensive survey of the theory and evidence on partial pass-through, and Milberg and Arestis (1993–94) for a Post Keynesian variant. To clarify terminology,

the greater is θ, the more profits are squeezed, but the *less* exchange-rate changes are "passed through" into foreign currency prices (i.e. the *more partial* is the pass-through).

14 At least one study (Hooper and Mann, 1989) has found that the pass-through of changes in exchange rates and foreign costs into US import prices is similar. The formulation in equations (6.5) and (6.9) further assumes that pass-through is symmetrical with respect to foreign or domestic costs, which may not be strictly realistic but greatly simplifies the mathematics.

15 The concept of the natural rate of growth was first used by Harrod (1939). It is fitting that this concept should be used in this chapter, since Thirlwall's BP-constrained growth rate is a dynamic version of another of Harrod's insights – namely, his trade multiplier for determining national income (Harrod, 1933; see also McCombie and Thirlwall, 1994).

16 Note that q should be measured at full utilization of capacity, and therefore may exceed the actual, observed rate of productivity growth in an economy operating with excess capacity. For further discussion of the measurement of q, see the empirical section given later.

17 Among other things, this concept ignores the endogeneity of the labor supply (due to changing patterns of labor-force participation, as well as both intersectoral and international labor migration) emphasized in neo-Marxian and structuralist approaches (Cornwall, 1977), and the endogeneity of technological progress emphasized in both the Post Keynesian literature (McCombie and Thirlwall, 1994) and the new neoclassical models of endogenous growth (Romer, 1990). Nevertheless, most Post Keynesians accept that resource constraints on growth can sometimes be reached. See, for example, the explanation of why Japan grows more slowly than its BP-constrained rate in McCombie and Thirlwall (1994, p. 241).

18 Note that this does not necessarily imply a falling real wage. To see this, suppose that workers spend the fraction $0 < \mu < 1$ of their wage income on imports; then, using a geometric-weighted consumer price index $P^{(1-\mu)}(EP^*)^\mu$, the real wage changes at the rate $q - \mu(e + p^* - p)$, which equals just q if PPP holds so that $e + p^* - p = 0$. Thus, the real wage changes at the same rate as domestic productivity grows if relative PPP holds (at B), or at a lower rate if the currency is depreciating (anywhere along $T = 0$ below B, including point F). Thus, the real wage could either be rising slowly or falling absolutely at point F.

19 The effects of lower home productivity growth (q) on the trade-off between points B and F are more complex, since they affect the location of the $y = n$ line as well as the $T = 0$ line. See the next section for an analysis of this issue.

20 The effects of these parameter values may seem ambiguous, since they tend to make both the slope and the intercept higher. However, it can be seen that these parameters have no impact on the location of the BP-constrained growth point B and therefore, as $(\varepsilon_x + \varepsilon_m)$ falls or $(\theta + \theta^*)$ rises, the $T = 0$ line pivots on point B (becoming steeper) and the distance between points B and F increases.

21 There is much ambiguity in the literature on whether PPP holds in the post-1973 period of floating exchange rates. Lindert and Pugel (1996, pp. 367–369) report descriptive data that appear to confirm relative PPP (at least approximately) in the 1975–93 period. Econometric tests using time-series methods have found that the hypothesis of unit roots in real exchange rates cannot generally be rejected for the post-1973 period, however. See Froot and Rogoff (1995) and Rogoff (1996), who suggest that the post-1973 period may be too short for identifying relatively slow rates of mean reversion in real exchange rates. Bleaney and Mizen (1996a) report evidence that post-1973 real exchange rates do exhibit mean-reversion around a (relatively wide) band, using a nonlinear model.

22 To some extent this is just a semantic difference, as Corden defines an industry (or, by implication, a country) as "internationally competitive if it produces tradables and is profitable" (1994, p. 267). Since reducing wages helps to restore profitability, Corden's

definition implies that wage cuts actually restore competitiveness. While this is true from a business vantage point, it is not true from the standpoint of national living standards as reflected in real wages, which is the benchmark used in the other definitions cited earlier.

23 The implication of a perpetually rising unemployment rate at point B may seem unrealistic, but results from some of the simplifying assumptions used in this model. First, while the productivity growth rate has been taken as exogenously given here, actual productivity growth would be expected to fall below the true potential rate of productivity growth under conditions of depressed aggregate demand and excess capacity, in which case such continuous increases in the unemployment rate might not be observed (only higher levels of the unemployment rate). Also, the present model assumes only one sector in each country producing tradeable goods. If there is also a nontradeables sector, employment could be expanded there to make up for the loss of jobs in tradeables, as has occurred in the United States since the 1980s. This is what Eatwell (1995) calls a form of "disguised unemployment."

24 More formally, to see how ω_F changes when q rises, consider equation (11) with $y = n = \lambda + q$. When q rises to q', ω_F will rise if $\varepsilon_x + \varepsilon_m - 1 > \eta_m$, and will fall if $\varepsilon_x + \varepsilon_m - 1 < \eta_m$. Since most conventional estimates of η_m for the United States are at least 2, and most estimates of $\varepsilon_x + \varepsilon_m$ are about 3 or less, it seems quite possible that ω_F would fall in the American case (see the elasticity estimates in Table 6.1).

25 See Cripps and Godley (1978) for an argument in favor of protection of the British economy, and Norman (1996) for a more general Post Keynesian theory of protection.

26 See Norman (1996) for an analysis of how protection can have positive quantity effects on domestic production that help to mitigate price effects (and therefore reduce efficiency losses). Of course, any policy of import restrictions would have to be designed in ways that would minimize problems such as rent seeking and maximize the potential for long-run productivity gains and quality improvements.

27 This point was suggested in remarks by Ajit Singh at a conference at the University of Notre Dame in March 1993. See also Cripps and Godley (1978).

28 There could also be a positive feedback to productivity growth, via scale economies and dynamic gains from producing for a wider market.

29 However, pessimism over the prospects for stimulative policies by surplus countries is one of the motives for the protectionist option advocated by Cripps and Godley (1978).

30 See Tyson (1992) and Bergsten and Noland (1993) for evaluations of US efforts to open up the Japanese market, especially in high-technology products.

31 This type of model is developed, for example, by Taylor (1983, 1991) and Dutt (1990), who give references to earlier antecedents. See also Bowles and Boyer (1995) for an empirical version.

32 The model could easily be generalized to accommodate positive saving out of wages, at a rate lower than the saving rate out of profit income, as well as tax rates that differ by source of income.

33 The method of obtaining equation (6.14) is similar to that used by Carlin and Soskice (1990) and by McCombie (1993), except that these previous authors used simpler Keynesian models that did not explicitly incorporate markup pricing and that did not make consumption or investment demand depend on income distribution. The derivation of (6.14) uses the fact that $\pi = (\Phi - 1)/\Phi = 1 - \Phi^{-1}$, and the fact that $\phi = \hat{\Phi} = -\theta(\omega - q - q^*)$, which together imply that $\hat{\pi} = -\theta(\Phi - 1)(\omega - q - q^*)$.

34 Note that $a > s(1 - \tau)$ does not necessarily violate the stability condition $k > 0$, if the positive terms in k are large enough.

35 For examples of stagnationist macro models, see Dutt (1990) and Taylor (1983). These models emphasize the depressing effect of a higher profit share on consumption. The term "exhilarationism" was coined by Marglin and Bhaduri (1990) and Bhaduri and Marglin (1990), who emphasized the possibility of a strong positive effect of profits on

investment. See also Blecker (1989), who showed the possibility of profit-led growth as a result of international competition. The model used in this chapter does not adopt the Marglin–Bhaduri investment function, but allows for an exhilarationist outcome through international competitive effects as well as the positive uniform tax rate (which implies a positive leakage out of wage income).

36 The fact that a devaluation could be contractionary due to the underconsumptionist effects of increased profit markups was first pointed out by Diaz-Alejandro (1963), and later developed by Krugman and Taylor (1978).

37 A high τ, a low b, and a high η_m are needed to ensure that the stability condition $k > 0$ still holds when $a > s(1 - \tau)$.

38 Similar results are obtained by using most other elasticity estimates for the United States, which generally find a higher income elasticity for imports than for exports (as originally found by Houthakker and Magee, 1969). Helkie and Hooper (1988) found that these income elasticities were nearly equal, in a model that included capital stock variables (which pick up the long-term trends that are otherwise reflected in the income elasticities). But Meade (1991) showed that Helkie and Hooper's result was sensitive to the measurement of computer prices and that the Houthakker–Magee result reappears when computers are excluded from the data.

39 Since θ and θ^* enter equation (6.11) symmetrically, only the *sum* of these two parameters matters. Note that the low estimate ($\theta + \theta^* = 0$) corresponds to *full* exchange-rate pass-through, while the higher values of $\theta + \theta^*$ indicate *more partial* pass-through. This range of estimates is based on several leading studies of pass-through. For example, Hooper and Mann (1989) found that pass-through into US import prices for manufactures ranged between 50 and 60 percent, which would correspond to a θ^* of about 0.4–0.5. Meade (1991) found a higher pass-through rate between 81 and 89 percent for US manufactured imports, using three different price indexes (implying θ^* ranges between 0.11 and 0.19). Both of these studies used time-series data for aggregate manufacturing. However, using more micro-level data (a panel of twenty-six four-digit SIC industries for the 1978–87 period), Feinberg (1996) found that pass-through into import prices was only between 36 and 51 percent, implying correspondingly higher estimates of θ^*. Most studies have found little effect of exchange rates on US export prices in dollars, implying that $\theta < \theta^*$ for the United States.

40 I used geometric-weighted averages of the growth rates reported for 1979–89 and 1989–94, assigning exponential weights of 2/3 and 1/3 to each period, respectively.

41 Since the US labor force grew at an average annual rate of 1.1 percent between 1989 and 1994 (OECD, 1996, p. 29), the CBO estimate implicitly assumes anemic productivity growth of about 1.0 percent per year as the maximum "potential" of the US economy. However, the labor force grew at a 1.7 percent rate as recently as the 1979–89 period, and with the entry of the baby boomers' children into the labor force and continued rapid immigration, labor-force growth can be expected to pick up again in the early 2000s. Moreover, productivity growth rates in the 2.0–2.5 percent range are well within the recent historical experience of the United States. Thus, our medium and high estimates of the potential growth rate of the US economy are certainly plausible.

42 Export growth was measured by the series for the real volume of exports of goods and services for the United States in OECD (1996, p. 61). This "alternative" calculation is the method that has actually been used in most empirical studies of the BP-constrained growth model (see McCombie and Thirlwall, 1994; McCombie, 1997), even though theoretically y_B is defined as $(\eta_x/\eta_m)y^*$.

43 Author's calculation, based on data in US Council of Economic Advisers (1997, pp. 300–301). According to Thirlwall and Hussain (1982), net capital inflows relax the BP constraint on growth if and only if those inflow grow more rapidly than export earnings. Somewhat surprisingly, US net capital inflows grew only slightly more rapidly

than export earnings between 1979 and 1994 (a 9.6 percent annual rate for net capital inflows, versus 7.9 percent for export earnings, based on the same data source), suggesting only very slight relief of the BP constraint.

44 There are several reasons why the alternative estimates might differ, including: violation of the assumption of a constant real exchange rate (so that actual export growth incorporates relative price effects); exaggeration of the growth of "real" exports in the US GDP accounts (due to the use of a hedonic price index for computers); and the omission of services (and even some types of goods) from most of the elasticity estimates.

45 An exception occurs using Cline's elasticities and the low estimate of n; since in this case $y_B > n$ (2.2 > 2.1), the sign reverses on the last term on the right-hand side of equation (6.11), and ω_F increases with $\theta + \theta^*$.

7   The stability of Thirlwall's model of economic growth and the balance of payments constraint*

Maurizio Pugno

Thirlwall (1979) proposes a model explaining that rates of economic growth differ between countries because of different balance of payments constraints, that is, because of the different income elasticities of exports and imports. In Thirlwall's world, the exports of one country are imperfect substitutes for the exports of another country, and the labor supply is not constraining, in the long run. Thus, relative prices and the adjustment in the exchange rate, that is, price competitiveness, become irrelevant to growth.

The solution of the model provides a formula of surprising simplicity and of appealing interpretive capacity. In fact, it has been extended in several directions (Cimoli and Soete, 1992; Fagerberg, 1988; Padoan, 1993), and it has been favorably tested to capture the stylized fact that relative growth rates differ in the same proportion as the export/import elasticity ratio.[1] The model has also been challenged both theoretically and empirically by McGregor and Swales (1985, 1986, 1991), while Krugman (1989a) suggests an alternative explanation for the same stylized fact. McCombie and Thirlwall (1994) collect contributions to the debate, together with their replies, and provide further material for discussion, while McCombie (1996) and McCombie and Thirlwall (1997a) refine the model.

However, neither the original model nor its subsequent developments spell out the underlying structure necessary to explain dynamic stability. Thirlwall's model in fact provides only a steady-state solution, where all the variables grow at the same constant rate. Most important, the model predicts a steady growth disregarding both the *size*, rather than the changes, in the deficit or surplus of the balance of payments, and the gap in the *levels*, rather than in the changes, of domestic and foreign competitive prices. Hence, the model fails to explain the working of the external constraint on economic growth.

Overcoming this failure is the main aim of the present chapter. It presents a substantial extension of the original model, by drawing on Thirlwall and McCombie's verbal arguments, discussions, and, sometimes, hints. In particular, treatment of the labor market becomes necessary, and the adoption of the short-run Phillips curve becomes difficult to avoid. As a consequence, a short-run case emerges

* First published in *Journal of Post Keynesian Economics*, Summer 1998.

where the Thirlwall growth formula does not apply, and where, for very slow adjustments, the growth path assumes a Goodwinian cyclical pattern. A further extension of Thirlwall's model concerns the possibility of a flexible exchange rate. This allows study of a further price-mechanism for the adjustment of the balance of payments.

Thirlwall's model and its shortcomings

Thirlwall's model, first, consists of a demand function for exports and one for imports, as follows:[2]

$$\hat{X} = x_0\hat{Z} - x_1\hat{R} \qquad \text{with } 0 < x_0 < \infty, \ 0 < x_1 < \infty$$

$$\hat{M} = m_0\hat{Y} + m_1\hat{R} \qquad \text{with } 0 < m_0 < \infty, \ 0 < m_1 < \infty.$$

The volumes of exports (X) and of imports (M) of goods and services are due to an income effect from abroad (Z) and from the domestic side (Y), respectively, and to a price effect (R). All the variables are in exponential growth rates (^), and R is thus defined:

$$\hat{R} = \hat{p} - \hat{p}_f - \hat{e},$$

that is, it is the reciprocal of the real exchange rate, where p, p_f, and e are the price of exports in domestic currency, the price of imports in foreign currency, and the nominal exchange rate, respectively.

Thirlwall then states the equilibrium condition in the external balance on current account, again in change rates:

$$\hat{X} + \hat{R} = \hat{M}.$$

Thirlwall argues that this condition actually prevails, because deflationary policies are usually pursued against deficits and permissive policies usually allow domestic expenditure to grow and to absorb surpluses. However, the argument must refer only to the worsening in the deficits and to the accumulating of the surpluses, but not to their sizes. Moreover, the recent easy access to international financial markets does not sensibly change this equilibrium condition in the long run, according to Thirlwall, because the accumulation of foreign debt is subject to a severe limit.[3] Thirlwall calls this condition the balance of payments constraint.

Therefore, the domestic growth rate is given by the following solution:

$$\hat{Y} = \frac{x_0\hat{Z} - \hat{R}(x_1 + m_1 - 1)}{m_0}.$$

However, this is not the long-run solution, according to Thirlwall, because the restriction $\hat{R} = 0$ would tend to emerge. McCombie and Thirlwall (1997) propose two arguments for this claim. The first is that real wages resist rising import prices. McCombie (1996) bases the argument on the following (simplified) two-equation submodel:

$$\hat{p} = \omega_\omega(\hat{w} - \hat{\pi}) + \omega_f(\hat{p}_f + \hat{e}) + \hat{q}$$
$$\text{with } 0 < \omega_\omega, \omega_f < 1 \quad \text{and } \omega_\omega + \omega_f = 1;$$
$$\hat{w} = b_1\hat{p} + b_2\hat{\pi} \quad \text{with } 0 < b_1 < \infty, \ 0 < b_2 < \infty,$$

where w denotes the money wage, π labor productivity, and q the monopolistic markup. The price equation states that export prices change according to changes in the costs of labor and of imported inputs per unit of output, and to changes in the markup. The wage equation states that changes in money wages are pushed by changes in prices and in productivity. McCombie recognizes that the degree of wage resistance (b_1) depends on "the level of employment, on the degree of trade union bargaining power, et cetera," but he assumes that in the long run $b_1 = 1$, and, moreover, that $b_2 = 1$ and $\hat{q} = 0$. He then is obviously able to conclude that $\hat{p} = \hat{p}_f + \hat{e}$, that is, that $\hat{R} = 0$. However, he does not explain how the level of employment, the degree of unionization, or some other factor makes wages (with some time) perfectly price-indexed, and (in any time) productivity-indexed.

The second reason for claiming the restriction $\hat{R} = 0$ is that the markup will be reduced by exporters when they see their market shares decline. A full adjustment in q would thus again imply $\hat{p} = \hat{p}_f + \hat{e}$. This second argument, according to McCombie and Thirlwall, tends to substitute for the first one, since wage resistance has diminished in the most recent period.[4] However, if this were true, income distribution would move where foreign prices and the exchange rates go. For example, a jump in foreign prices would inflate the markup and squeeze the wage share permanently, while the restriction $\hat{R} = 0$, and the steady state would promptly reappear unchanged.

Therefore, having argued for $\hat{R} = 0$, the balance of payments equilibrium growth rate becomes a simple formula:

$$\hat{Y} = \frac{x_0}{m_0}\hat{Z}. \tag{7.1}$$

The external constraint is given by the elasticity ratio, which reflects non-price competition, while the demand side aspect of the model is due to the fact that world demand (Z) does not encounter any other constraint. Finally, Thirlwall's observation that a once-for-all depreciation of the currency only temporarily raises the rate of growth is consistent with the model.[5]

However, to draw these conclusions, it is not sufficient to prove that the formula (7.1) is obtained by taking as a priori assumptions the equilibrium in the balance of payments and the equalization between growth in real wages and productivity, and between growth of relative prices. It is necessary to prove that the formula (7.1) emerges after adjustment processes that bring the balance of payments into equilibrium, cause real wages to grow at the same rate as productivity, and export prices to grow at the same rate as foreign prices.

An extended model for the stability of Thirlwall's solution

Since studying the stability of Thirlwall's solution for his simple algebraic model requires a substantial extension to five nonlinear differential equations, the analysis proceeds in steps. First, the equations for trade are extended to take account of the level of relative competitiveness as well. Then the stability of an extended submodel is examined where the balance of payments is initially not in equilibrium but can be adjusted, while the restriction on relative prices always holds. In a parallel extended submodel, the stability is studied when growth in real wages is not equal to growth in productivity, and relative prices do not grow at the same rate, while the balance of payments is not constraining. The integration of the two submodels, however, does not give Thirlwall's formula. This is obtained when we allow for a long-run flexibility of labor supply. Finally, the introduction of flexible exchange rates complicates matters, but with small changes in the conclusions.

A preliminary extension of Thirlwall's model concerns the export and import functions as follows:

$$\hat{X} = x_0 \hat{Z} - x_1 \hat{R} + x_2(1 - R) \qquad \text{with } 0 < x_0, x_1, x_2 < \infty; \qquad (7.2)$$

$$\hat{M} = m_0 \hat{Y} + m_1 \hat{R} - m_2(1 - R) \qquad \text{with } 0 < m_0, m_1, m_2 < \infty. \qquad (7.3)$$

In contrast to Thirlwall's model, the price effect on exports and imports is captured both by the *change rate* and by the *level* of relative prices.[6] This enables us to consider the adjustment of demand, through the coefficients x_2 and m_2, to the supply price, where it is more economically advantageous. The improvement or worsening in this advantage further encourages or discourages demand, through the coefficients x_1 and m_1. The restriction $R = 1$ would cancel out both components of the price effect, thus guaranteeing equilibrium in the export and import markets. But starting from $R \neq 1$, demand for exports and for imports shift toward foreign or domestic supply, thus changing the country's world ranking for growth in income and trade. However, this change will be temporary, and R will revert to 1. The hypothesis of a central equilibrium equal to 1, rather than to some positive constant, is assumed only for the sake of simplicity.

If the equilibrium condition in the balance of payments and the restriction on relative prices were imposed a priori, the formula (7.1) would obviously be obtained again. The only difference is that equations (7.2) and (7.3) require setting the real exchange rate in the level $(1/R)$, and consequently also the balance of payments equilibrium must be set: $XR = M$.

The adjustment of the balance of payments

For analysis of how the external constraint works, starting from a disequilibrium in the balance of payments ($XR \neq M$), it is necessary to study the relationship between export and income growth. Formula (7.1) states that

$$\hat{Y} = \frac{1}{m_0}\hat{X}.$$

But this is a particular case, since it gives the balance of payments equilibrium growth rate exactly. McCombie and Thirlwall (1994, ch. 6), however, show that implicit in this equilibrium relationship between the two variables is a more complicated relationship, namely

$$\hat{Y} = \omega_x\hat{X} + \omega_a\hat{A} \quad \text{with } 0 < \omega_x, \ \omega_a < 1. \tag{7.4}$$

The underlying assumption is that income growth is determined by the growth of both exports and of the other autonomous demand components (A). It is further assumed that, if export growth is excessive, with respect to the growth of A, for maintaining the balance of payments equilibrium, that is, if

$$\omega_x + \omega_a\frac{\hat{A}}{\hat{X}} < \frac{1}{m_0},$$

then A will be permitted to accelerate in order to meet the equilibrium condition. In the extended model, this acceleration is not assumed as instantaneous, but it reacts as follows:

$$\hat{\dot{A}} = a_0(XR/M - 1) + a_1(X\hat{R}/M), \tag{7.5}$$

where $0 < a_0, a_1 < \infty$ if $\hat{Z} > 0$, and $-\infty < a_0, a_1 < 0$ if $\hat{Z} < 0$. The balance of payments equilibrium appears as an argument both in the level, as equations (7.2) and (7.3) require, and in change rates, as Thirlwall might prefer.

The same specification (7.5) will be used here in the opposite case where export growth is insufficient to prevent an external deficit. McCombie and Thirlwall argue that in this case, deflationary policies are pursued, so that A decelerates ($\hat{\dot{A}} < 0$).[7] If these policies cannot be maintained, because of mounting unemployment, a stop-go pattern emerges, which is typical of what Kaldor (1971) calls consumption-led growth.

Having fixed the restriction $R = 1$, and having reduced equations (7.1)–(7.3) as follows:

$$(X\hat{/}M) = x_0\hat{Z}(1 - m_0\omega_x) - m_0\omega_a\hat{A}, \tag{7.6}$$

it can be proved that the subsystem of equations (7.6) and (7.5) is asymptotically stable around the singular point ($\hat{A}^*, X/M^*$) (Gandolfo 1996; and see the Appendix). At this point $(X/M)^* = 1$, and Thirlwall's formula (7.1) emerges by substituting equation (7.2) and the equation for A* into equation (7.4). Therefore, in this case the balance of payments is rigorously in equilibrium, and not just constant. For this more rigorous definition of steady state, it is necessary that $0 < a_0 < \infty$ (or $-\infty < a_0 < 0$ if $\hat{Z} < 0$), and for the stability it is necessary that $0 < a_1 < \infty$ (or $-\infty < a_1 < 0$ if $\hat{Z} < 0$).

The adjustment of the real exchange rate via prices and wages

To relax the restriction $R = 1$, it is necessary to specify the equations governing the dynamics $\hat{p}, \hat{p}_f$, and $\hat{e}$, since

$$\hat{R} = \hat{p} - \hat{p}_f - \hat{e}. \tag{7.7}$$

While the hypothesis that $\hat{e} = 0$ is only temporary (until we reach the case of flexible exchange rates), henceforth it is assumed that $\hat{p}_f$ is *exogenous* and constant, and that export prices are formed according to the monopolistic markup rule as seen earlier

$$\hat{p} = \omega_\omega(\hat{w} - \hat{\pi}) + \omega_f \hat{p}_f + \hat{q} \quad \text{with } 0 < \omega_\omega, \omega_f < 1 \text{ and } \omega_\omega + \omega_f = 1. \tag{7.8}$$

McCombie's (1996) argument to explain changes in wages and in the markup suggests the following extensions:

$$\hat{w} = b_1 \hat{p} + b_2 \hat{\pi} + h(l) \quad \text{with } 0 < b_1, b_2 < 1; \tag{7.9}$$

$$\hat{q} = c(1 - R) \qquad \text{with } 0 < c < \infty. \tag{7.10}$$

In equation (7.9), the Phillips curve implicit in his equation (see the section on Thirlwall's model) is made explicit by the function h of the employment rate l. A familiar specification is adopted, since wages have only limited downward flexibility (if $l = 0$, then $\hat{w}$ will diminish at a rate given by $-\hat{w}_{min}$), but they are upwardly highly flexible (if $l \rightarrow$, then $\hat{w} \rightarrow \infty$). Note that in this case the coefficients b_1 and b_2 are no longer exactly equal to one, as assumed by McCombie for the long run, but always smaller than 1, since the pressure applied by the employment stance is already considered. Equation (7.10) together with equation (7.2) states that, if the market share declines, exporters reduce their markup in order to improve competitiveness while, if the market share expands, the markup is allowed to grow.

From equations (7.7), (7.8), (7.9), and (7.10), one obtains

$$\hat{R} = -\alpha_0 + \alpha_1 h(l) + \alpha_2(1 - R), \tag{7.11}$$

where

$$\alpha_0 = \hat{\pi}(1 - b_2)\alpha_1 + \hat{p}_f(1 - b_1)\alpha_1 > 0;$$
$$\alpha_1 = \omega_\omega/(1 - \omega_\omega b_1) > 0;$$
$$\alpha_2 = c/(1 - \omega_\omega b_1) > 0.$$

The definition of the employment rate implies

$$\hat{l} = \hat{Y} - \hat{\pi} - \hat{N}, \tag{7.12}$$

where N is the labor supply.

Substituting equations (7.4) and (7.2) into equation (7.12) yields:

$$\hat{l} = (\beta_0 + \omega_a \hat{A} - \hat{N}) - \beta_1 l + \beta_2 (1 - R), \qquad (7.13)$$

where

$$\beta_0 = \omega_x (x_0 \hat{Z} + x_1 \alpha_0) - \hat{\pi};$$
$$\beta_1 = \omega_x x_1 \alpha_1 > 0;$$
$$\beta_2 = \omega_x (x_2 - x_1 \alpha_2).$$

It is worth dwelling on the subsystem of equations (7.11) and (7.13), assuming for the moment that $\hat{A}$ (and $\hat{N}$) are *exogenous* and fixed. This subsystem is thus independent of the system of equations (7.6) and (7.5) of the previous section. This subsystem explains the stability of the condition $\hat{R} = 0$, while that subsystem explained the stability of the balance of payments equilibrium.

As the phase diagram in (R, l) shows in Figure 7.1, the subsystem is stable at the relevant singular point (see the Appendix for proof), where

$$R^* = 1 + \frac{\omega_x x_0 \hat{Z} + \omega_a \hat{A} - \hat{\pi} - \hat{N}}{\omega_x x_2}.$$

Hence, Thirlwall's claim that a once-for-all depreciation of the currency has only temporary effects is proved. This is also true for any other shock in R or l.

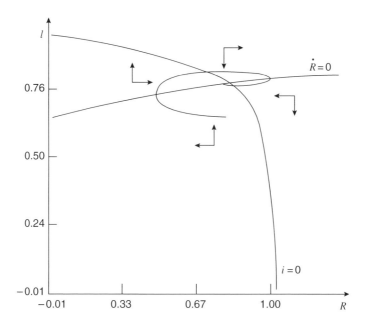

Figure 7.1 Phase portrait in *R*- and *l*-axis.

However, the steady-state growth rate is not that predicted by Thirlwall, since, by substituting R^* in equation (7.2), and then in equation (7.4), one obtains:

$$\hat{Y} = \hat{\pi} + \hat{N}.$$

In other words, the steady-state growth is the natural growth rate. This result is due to the fact that, in the system (7.11)–(7.13), labor is constraining, but not the balance of payments. Nor do real wages grow, in the steady state, at the same rate as productivity, because

$$\hat{w}^* - \hat{p}^* - \hat{\pi} = \frac{c(\omega_x x_0 \hat{Z} + \omega_a \hat{A} - \hat{\pi} - \hat{N})}{\omega_\omega \omega_x x_2} = -c(1 - R^*)/\omega_\omega.$$

This is because R^* is generally different from 1, though $\hat{R} = 0$, and hence, through equation (7.10), the markup rises or declines – that is, the labor share declines or rises.

If the coefficients c and x_1 are sufficiently small with respect to x_2, then the growth path is cyclical, though damped, around the steady state. This is the case of Figure 7.1, where an initial competitive advantage with high unemployment (small values of R and of l) first induces an acceleration of exports and of income. Then the labor constraint pushes wages up (smaller R and greater l), so that competitiveness worsens, thus decelerating exports and income (greater R and l). High unemployment reappears (l reduction), thus allowing competitiveness to be restored (R reduction).

In the extreme case where $c = x_1 = 0$, the cycle becomes persistent. In this case the subsystem (7.11)–(7.13) could be called an "open Goodwin model." The reference to the Goodwin (1967) model is evident, given that both models generate a persistent cycle *à la* Lotka-Volterra around the natural rate derived from conflict in the labor market. The open model, however, presents two novel features, besides the fact that Goodwin considers a closed economy: one is that conflict in the labor market affects inflation, and therefore the real exchange rate; the second, which imparts a more Keynesian flavor lacking in Goodwin's model, is that income is determined by exports and not by the productive capacity generated by saved profits.

The subsystem of equations (7.11)–(7.13) does not consider the external constraint. Not only is the balance of payments generally not in equilibrium, that is, $XR \neq M$, but it changes as well, that is, $\hat{X} + \hat{R} \neq \hat{M}$. The underlying reason for this is that generally $R^* \neq 1$. If it is greater (smaller) than 1, then export growth decelerates (accelerates) and import growth accelerates (decelerates).[8]

Let us again consider $\hat{A}$ as endogenously determined. In this case, the balance of payments equilibrium will be attained in steady state, but Thirlwall's formula does not yet emerge. In fact, the relevant singular point of the system composed of equation (7.6) for (XR/M), equation (7.5) for $\hat{A}$, equation (7.11) for $\hat{R}$, which enters the other three equations, and equation (7.13) for $\hat{l}$, gives the following results:

$$R^* = 1 + \frac{x_0\hat{Z} - m_0(\hat{\pi} + \hat{N})}{x_2 + m_2};$$

$$(X/M)^*R^* = 1;$$

$$\hat{Y} = \frac{x_0}{m_0}\hat{Z} + \frac{x_2 + m_2}{m_0}(1 - R^*) = \hat{\pi} + \hat{N};$$

$$\hat{w}^* - \hat{p}^* - \hat{\pi} = \frac{c(x_0\hat{Z}/m_0 - \hat{\pi} - \hat{N})}{\omega_\omega\omega_x x_2}.$$

Therefore, in this steady state, R, which does not obviously change, is fixed at a value greater or smaller than 1, so that Thirlwall's growth formula is conversely greater or smaller than the natural rate, and, moreover, real wages grow more or, respectively, less than productivity.

Long-run adjustment in the labor market

The result obtained in the previous section adapts the condition for obtaining a growth rate with balance of payments in equilibrium – which differs from Thirlwall's formula – to the labor constraint. But Thirlwall regards labor supply as elastic because of immigration or intersectoral transfer of labor. These are long-run phenomena that are distinct from a short-run labor shortage due to an accelerating income, which instead affects wages. This distinction can be maintained in the model, and Thirlwall's formula can be reestablished by introducing the following assumption: growth in the labor supply will rise or fall depending on a rise or fall in real wages with respect to productivity, in the long run. Formally

$$\hat{N} = \frac{dc(x_0\hat{Z}/m_0 - \hat{\pi} - \hat{N})}{\omega_\omega\omega_x x_2}, \tag{7.14}$$

where $0 < d < +\infty$ for $x_0\hat{Z}/m_0 > \hat{\pi}$ and $-\infty < d < 0$ for $x_0\hat{Z}/m_0 < \hat{\pi}$.

It is thus apparent that, in steady state

$$\hat{N}^* = \frac{x_0}{m_0}\hat{Z} - \hat{\pi},$$

and hence $R^* = 1$, and that

$$\hat{Y} = \frac{x_0}{m_0}\hat{Z} = \hat{\pi} + \hat{N},$$

although in this case it is the natural growth rate that adapts to Thirlwall's formula, since $\hat{N}$ is *endogenous*. Moreover, it becomes

$$\hat{w}^* - \hat{p}^* = \hat{\pi}.$$

Thus, income distribution is also in steady state.

The dynamic stability of the system of equations (7.2) through (7.14) – reducible to five equations: (7.6), (7.5), (7.11), (7.13), and (7.14) – can be shown in two complementary ways. First, two necessary conditions can be proved for the stability of the linearized system at the singular point $(\hat{A}^*, XR/M^*, R^*, l^*, \hat{N}^*)$: that the trace and the determinant of the Jacobian matrix are both negative (see the Appendix). It is interesting that the condition for stability of the balance of payments, of the equality between prices, and of the long-run equilibrium in the labor market can be singled out from the trace.

Second, the global stability of the original system, which is made up of nonlinear equations, can be shown by performing numerical simulations.[9] An example is given in Figure 7.2(a)–(c). Unfortunately, this is not a final proof. A sensitivity

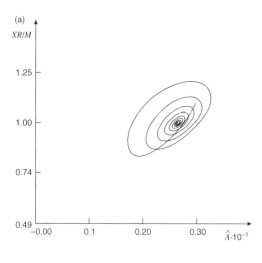

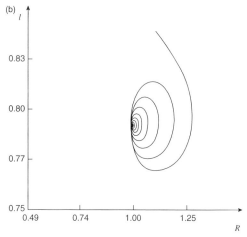

Figure 7.2 Phase portraits in (a) $\hat{A}$- and XR/M-axis; (b) R- and l-axis; (c) time profile of $\hat{N}$.

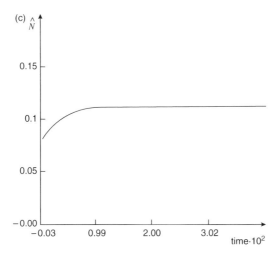

Figure 7.2 Continued.

Note: The phase portraits are obtained by simulating the following dynamical system:

$$\hat{A} = a_0(XR/M - 1) + a_1(XR\hat{/}M), \tag{7.5}$$

$$(X\hat{/}M) = x_0\hat{Z}(1 - m_0\omega_x) - m_0\omega_a\hat{A}$$
$$\qquad - [x_1(1 - m_0\omega_x) + m_1 - 1]\hat{R} + [x_2(1 - m_0\omega_x) + m_2](1 - R), \tag{7.6}$$

$$\hat{R} = \frac{\omega_\omega}{1 - \omega_\omega b_1}[(1 - b_2)\hat{\pi} + (1 - b_1)\hat{p}_f]$$
$$\qquad + \frac{\omega_\omega}{1 - \omega_\omega b_1}\left[\frac{h}{1-l} - 1 - \hat{w}_{min}\right] + \frac{c}{1 - \omega_\omega b_1}(1 - R), \tag{7.11}$$

$$\hat{l} = \omega_x[x_0\hat{Z} - x_1\hat{R} + x_2(1 - R)] + \omega_a\hat{A} - \hat{\pi} - \hat{N}, \tag{7.13}$$

$$\hat{N} = \frac{dc(x_0\hat{Z}/m_0 - \hat{\pi} - \hat{N})}{\omega_\omega\omega_x x_2}, \tag{7.14}$$

with $a_0 = 0.2$; $a_1 = 1$; $x_0\hat{Z} = 0.05$; $m_0 = 1.6$; $\omega = 0.2$; $\omega_a = 0.8$; $x_1 = 1.5$; $m_1 = 1.5$; $x_2 = 0.02$; $m_2 = 0.02$; $\omega_\omega = 0.8$; $b_1 = b_2 = 0.5$; $\hat{\pi} = 0.02$; $\hat{p}_f = 0.02$; $h = 0.025$; $\hat{w}_{min} = 0.1$; $c = 0.01$; $d = 1$. The steady-state solutions are: $\hat{A}^* = 0.0265625$, $XR/M^* = 1$, $R^* = 1$, $l^* = 0.826$, $\hat{N}^* = 0.01125$. The initial conditions are $\hat{A} = 0.03$; $XR/M = 1.1$; $R = 1.1$; $l = 0.84$; $\hat{N} = 0.008$.

analysis has been carried out by preliminarily giving reasonable values to the most familiar parameters, like the growth rates of world demand, of productivity, of foreign prices, of price and income elasticities, as the weights ωs. Then, by varying the adjustment coefficients, one can check that, in order to obtain asymptotic stability, m_2 and a_0 must take low values, while a_1 and c must take high ones. The coefficient d governs the speed of adjustment of the natural rate to Thirlwall's growth rate only.

The case of flexible exchange rates

McCombie and Thirlwall (1994, p. 382) observe that equation (7.1) also gives good results when applied to the most recent period, in which exchange rates are more flexible. However, they do not deal with this problem theoretically.

It is possible to conduct a theoretical study of the case of flexible exchange rates by using the extended model. This case is interesting because the exchange rate adjustment is a price mechanism, while in equation (7.1) this type of mechanism is irrelevant.

Let us adopt the familiar theory of purchasing power parity, that is, that nominal exchange rates move to approach a level of the real exchange rate. This level is unitary since the reference of the real exchange rate in the export and import functions is unitary, but a constant may be taken as a reference as well. The equation chosen is the following:

$$\hat{e} = k(R), \tag{7.15}$$

where k is an increasing function. More precisely, as Bleaney and Mizen (1996b) suggest on both theoretical and empirical grounds, the function is S-shaped, as depicted in Figure 7.3.

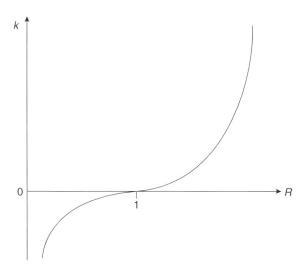

Figure 7.3 Exchange-rate function in a flexible exchange rate regime.

The addition of equation (7.15) to the model (7.2–7.14) thus extends the reduced equation for $\hat{R}$:

$$\hat{R} = -\alpha_0 + \alpha_1 h(l) + \alpha_2(1 - R) - k(R). \tag{7.16}$$

If this extended equation is taken in combination with equation (7.13) for $\hat{l}$, and if the restricted case of fixed $\hat{A}$ and $\hat{N}$ is temporarily assumed, then it can be proved that local stability at the singular point is accelerated (see the Appendix).

The acceleration of stability is confirmed in the case of the full system (7.2)–(7.15) by performing simulations for certain values of the parameters, as in Figure 7.4.

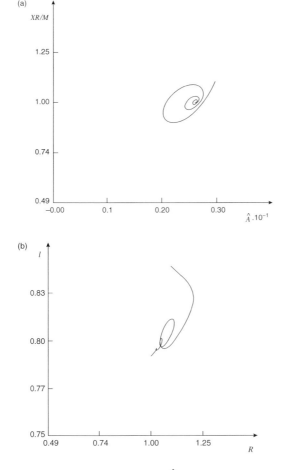

Figure 7.4 Phase portraits in (a) $\hat{A}$- and XR/M-axis; (b) R- and l-axis; (c) time profile of $\hat{N}$.

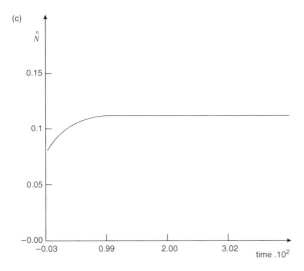

Figure 7.4 Continued.

Note: The phase portraits are obtained by simulating the dynamical system used in Figure 7.2(a)–(c), with the exception of equation (7.11), which is replaced by the following:

$$\hat{R} = -\frac{\omega_\omega}{1 - \omega_\omega b_1}[(1 - b_2)\hat{\pi} + (1 - b_1)\hat{p}_f]$$

$$+ \frac{\omega_\omega}{1 - \omega_\omega b_1}\left[\frac{h}{1 - I} - 1 - \hat{w}_{min}\right] + \frac{c}{1 - \omega_\omega b_1}(1 - R)$$

$$- k_1[1/(4 - R) - 1/3] + k_2(1/R), \tag{7.16}$$

with $k_1 = 0$ for $R < 1$, and $k_1 = 1$ for $R \geq 1$; $k_2 = 0$ for $R > 1$, and $k_2 = 1$ for $0 \leq R < 1$.

By more closely observing the paths for R and I in Figure 7.4(b), it is possible to discern a spiraling movement around a baricenter, and a movement of the baricenter pointing to the steady-state solution. The explanation of this emerges from observation of the path for N in Figure 7.4(c), which is not changed by the introduction of equation (7.15). Hence, flexible exchange rates accelerate stability both of the balance of payments equilibrium and of the condition $\hat{R} = 0$, but not of the condition $R = 1$.

Conclusions

With his 1979 model, Thirlwall suggests an explanation of economic growth in terms of the balance of payments constraint, that is, in terms of the capacity to export relative to the necessity to import. He provides a simple and handy steady-state solution. However, he also imposes external equilibrium *a priori* and a restriction that makes price competitiveness irrelevant to the solution. Recently, McCombie has replaced the restriction on prices with the restriction that real wages grow at the same rate as productivity. Moreover, exchange rates are always assumed to be fixed.

This chapter relaxes these assumptions by endogenizing both the emergence of the external equilibrium and the neutralization of price competitiveness through adjustment in the labor market. Technically speaking, the dynamic asymptotic stability of the model is analytically shown and numerically simulated, thus explaining the working of the model.

A substantial extension of the model has been necessary. Required in particular has been a more rigorous definition of the steady state, and a distinction between adjustments in the labor market. The steady state has been defined as characterized by zero external balance, rather than by any constant balance, and by equality between export prices and foreign prices, rather than by any constant ratio between them. A distinction has been drawn in the labor market between a short-run adjustment through the Phillips trade-off, and a long-run adjustment through a flexible labor supply.

Therefore, the assumptions and the working of the model now become clear. First, demand management policies bring the balance of payments into equilibrium; second, the Phillips curve, by capturing temporary bottlenecks in the labor market, induces real wages to grow at the same rate as productivity, and it brings export prices to the same level as foreign prices; third, this equalization is helped by markup changes; fourth, flexible exchange rates accelerate equalization even further; fifth, only a long-run flexibility in the labor supply makes the external constraint effective.

These adjustments thus explain the mechanisms by which Thirlwall's (and McCombie's) steady-state solution, once more rigorously defined, can be achieved in the long run. Moreover, the first four types of adjustment can explain how the cyclical dynamics arise, provided that some adjustments are sufficiently slow. As a particular case, a persistent cycle generated by the conflict in the labor market can be obtained exactly as it is in Goodwin's celebrated 1967 model for a closed economy.

To conclude, I cite what Krugman (1989a) calls the "international economists' schizophrenia," that is, the fact that they adopt the elasticity approach to the balance of payments in the short run, which implies changes in the real exchange rate, whereas they adopt the purchasing power parity approach to explain the constancy of the real exchange rate in the long run. It is now clear that this chapter offers a remedy for this schizophrenia.

Appendix

The stability of the subsystem (7.6) and (7.5) (the balance of payments equilibrium)

In the subsystem of equation (7.6) for X/M, and (7.5) for $\hat{A}$ the isocline $X/M = 0$ is a straight line perpendicular to the $\hat{A}$ axis at $\hat{A}^*$, while the isocline $\hat{A} = 0$ is a positively sloped straight line. The trace and the determinant of the Jacobian matrix of the system linearized in the nontrivial singular point (henceforth labeled respectively as T and D) are the following:

$$T = -a_1 x_0 \hat{Z}(1 - m_0 \omega_x);$$
$$D = a_0 x_0 (1 - m_0 \omega_x),$$

which are negative and positive, respectively, if $m_0 \omega_x < 1$. This restriction is not severe, since it implies that a rise (fall) in exports improves (deteriorates) external balance despite the induced rise (fall) in imports.

The system is globally stable since the linearized system is locally stable at $(\hat{A}^*, X/M^*)$ and the isoclines are straight lines.

As a_1/a_0 declines, the singular point passes from a stable node to a stable focus. For $a_1 = 0$, it becomes a center.

The stability of the subsystem (7.11)–(7.13) (the $\hat{R} = 0$ condition)

In the subsystem of equation (7.11) for $\hat{R}$ and (7.13) for $\hat{l}$, the isocline $R = 0$ is positively sloped, with $l = 1$ as the upper asymptote because of the h function (see Figure 7.1). The isocline $l = 0$ is negatively sloped if $x_2 > x_1 c/(1 - \omega_\omega b_1)$ (as in the figure). If the opposite condition were true, it would be positively sloped, with $l = 1$ as the upper asymptote, but anyway less sloped than the isocline $R = 0$. The T and the D are the following:

$$T = \alpha_2 R^* - \alpha_1 \omega_x x_1 h'(l^*) l^*;$$
$$D = \alpha_1 \omega_x x_2 h'(l^*) l^* R^*,$$

which are negative and positive, respectively.

The system is globally stable since the linearized system is locally stable at (R^*, l^*) and the isoclines are monotonic.

As c/x_2 and x_1/x_2 decline, the singular point passes from a stable node to a stable focus. For $c = x_1 = 0$, it becomes a center.

The stability of the full system (7.6), (7.5), (7.11), (7.13), and (7.14)

Two necessary conditions for the stability of the linearized system at the (nontrivial) singular point concern the trace (T) and the determinant (D). For the system (7.6), (7.5), (7.11), (7.13), they are

$$T = -[a_1 x_0 \hat{Z}(1 - m_0 \omega_x)] - [\alpha_2 + \alpha_1 \omega_x x_1 h'(l^*) l^*)] - \frac{dc(x_0 \hat{Z}/m_0 - \hat{\pi})}{\omega_\omega \omega_x x_2},$$

$$D = -a_0 x_0 \frac{\hat{Z}}{m_0}(1 - m_0 \omega_x)\alpha_1 h'(l^*) l^*(x_2 + m_2) \frac{dc(x_0 \hat{Z}/m_0 - \hat{\pi})}{\omega_\omega \omega_x x_2}.$$

Since both $(1 - m_0\omega_x)$ and $d(x_0\hat{Z}/m_0 - \hat{\pi})$ are already assumed to be positive, both the trace and the determinant are negative. Because the system consists of an odd number of equations, the conditions for stability are fulfilled.

Note that T includes the two traces of the subsystems (7.6)–(7.5) and (7.11)–(7.13) already studied.

The stability of the subsystem (7.16)–(7.13) (the $\hat{R} = 0$ condition with flexible exchange rates)

The T and the D at (R^*, l^*) are:

$$T = -[\alpha_2 + k'(R^*)]R^* - \alpha_1\omega_x x_1 h'(l^*)l^*;$$
$$D = \alpha_1\omega_x x_2 h'(l^*)l^* R^*.$$

Since they are, respectively, negative and positive, the original nonlinear system is locally stable.

Whereas the determinant remains unchanged with respect to the subsystem (7.16)–(7.13), where the exchange rates are fixed, the trace is increased in the negative, because of the term with $k(R)$.

The stability of the full system (7.6), (7.5), (7.11), (7.13), and (7.14) (flexible exchange rates)

The T at $(\hat{A}^*, XR/M^*, R^*, l^*, \hat{R}^*)$ is

$$T = -[a_1 x_0\hat{Z}(1 - m_0\omega_x)] - [\alpha_2 + k'(l) + \alpha_1\omega_x x_1 h'(l^*)l^*]$$
$$- \frac{dc(x_0\hat{Z}/m_0 - \hat{\pi})}{\omega_\omega\omega_x x_2},$$

which is negative. The D is exactly the same as in the case of the full system with fixed exchange rates. Note that T includes the term with $k(R)$ with the negative sign.

Notes

1 Besides Thirlwall (1979), see Bairam (1988), Asensio (1991), and Andersen (1993) for an updated sample of developed countries; Atesoglu (1993) and Hieke (1997) for the United States, Atesoglu (1994) for Germany; Bianchi (1994b) for Italy; Thirlwall and Hussain (1982) and Bairam and Dempster (1991) for a sample of developing countries; McCombie (1997) for a survey on the topic.

2 This chapter uses a different notation from that employed in Thirlwall's original article.

3 McCombie and Thirlwall (1997) explicitly consider international capital flows in the model, but they also estimate the effects as quantitatively small. The limit on foreign indebtness is also studied in a Solovian model of growth by Choen and Sachs (1986). For a recent evaluation of the external constraint as a policy objective, see Alogoskoufis *et al.* (1991).

4 A third argument points to the irrelevant effect of $\hat{R}$ on growth through negligible price elasticities (i.e. $x_1 = m_1 = 0$) since monopolistic competition would completely rely on product differentiation. However, in this case, the restriction $\hat{R} = 0$ would remain unexplained.

5 In support of this observation, Bahmani-Oskooee (1995) shows, using cointegration analysis, that there is no long-run relation between exchange rates and trade balance for a group of developed and developing countries. But Himarios (1989) finds that devaluation improves the trade balance over three years for a large group of countries.

6 The export function with just the level of relative prices was first proposed by Beckerman (1962). For a recent discussion, see Boggio (1988) and Pugno (1996).

7 The empirical literature in support of equation (7.4) is abundant (from Balassa, 1978 to Kugler and Dridi, 1993). In support of equation (7.5), Artis and Bayoumi (1991) find a significant estimate of a reaction function for some developed countries that relates monetary policies to current account balance.

8 Import growth may alternatively decelerate (accelerate) if the direct effect of R on imports is outweighed by the indirect effect of R through income on imports.

9 All simulations are run by using the DMC package written by G. Gallo (Medio, 1992).

8 The balance of payments constraint: from balanced trade to sustainable debt*

Nelson H. Barbosa-Filho

Introduction

The balance of payments (BP) constraint on growth is usually associated with Thirlwall's (1979) model, which imposes balanced trade as a necessary long-run constraint on open economies. According to Thirlwall's Law, international capital flows and interest payments balance out during long intervals of time so that, given a stable real exchange rate, the long-run growth rate of a small open economy is limited by the growth rate of its exports divided by the income elasticity of its imports. Independently of whether such an empirical law holds for some sufficiently long intervals of time, in practice open economies may take several years to show balanced trade and, in the meanwhile, capital flows and interest payments are an important part of the BP constraint.

To deal with capital flows, Thirlwall and Hussain (1982) extended Thirlwall's (1979) original model to allow trade deficits and showed how the growth rate of a small open economy may also be constrained by capital inflows in addition to trade factors. However, a particular characteristic of their extension is that

> although it allowed for nonzero capital inflows, it imposed no restriction whatsoever on their trajectory except for the balance-of-payments accounting principle, which forces debit and credit items to cancel out.
>
> (Moreno-Brid 1998b, p. 283)

In other words, Thirlwall and Hussain obtained a dynamic accounting identity that shows how capital inflows may tighten or relax the BP constraint on growth.

To impose a limit on capital inflows, Moreno-Brid (1998b) redefined the BP constraint in terms of a stable ratio of trade deficits to income on the assumption that this is a sufficient condition for a nonexplosive accumulation of foreign debt.[1] Notwithstanding its contribution to a better understanding of the BP constraint, Moreno-Brid's (1998b) extension has two important limitations of its own. First, its BP constrained growth rate is not necessarily stable and, second, its BP constraint

* First published in *Banca Nazionale del Lavoro Quarterly Review*, December 2001.

does not separate interest payments from imports of goods and nonfactor services in the analysis of debt accumulation.

With these points in mind, this chapter extends Thirlwall's (1979) model to allow for a "sustainable" accumulation of foreign debt taking into consideration both the potential instability of such a constraint and the impact of interest payments on debt accumulation. The analysis is purely theoretical but heavily inspired by the recent Brazilian experience.[2] The objective is to model a case where fluctuations in foreign lending are a major determinant of macroeconomic policy and growth, and where the trade balance adjusts residually to the maximum ratio of foreign debt to income allowed by international financial conditions. The underlying principle is that international financial markets are incomplete, so that a small open economy may be liquidity constrained.

The text is organized into four sections in addition to this introduction. The second section outlines Thirlwall's (1979) balanced-trade version of the BP constraint and analyzes its implications for growth and real exchange rates. The third section presents the unbalanced-trade version of the BP constraint of Moreno-Brid (1998b) and analyzes under which conditions such version is consistent with a stable growth rate. The next section presents the sustainable-debt version of the BP constraint and analyzes its implications for trade, growth and real exchange rates. The last section concludes the analysis with a summary of the main points of the chapter.

Balanced trade

Assume that the world economy consists of a large "foreign" country and a small "home" country. To simplify the exposition, assume further that both countries are one-sector economies and that there is imperfect substitution between the foreign and home goods. Finally, assume that the foreign currency is also the international currency, so that the foreign country can create money to finance its BP deficits. Since the home country cannot do the same, it may face a BP constraint when financial markets are incomplete.[3]

Following the post Keynesian approach of Thirlwall (1979), assume that the home and foreign goods are produced with constant labour productivity and priced through a stable markup rule over unit labor costs, meaning that the home and foreign supply curves are horizontal in the absence of changes in nominal wages.[4] In this context, Thirlwall (1979) represented the home exports and imports from the demand side, that is

$$Q_m = A \left(\frac{P_h}{EP_f} \right)^\alpha Q_h^\beta \tag{8.1}$$

and

$$Q_x = B \left(\frac{EP_f}{P_h} \right)^\gamma Q_f^\delta, \tag{8.2}$$

where Q_m and Q_x are the real imports and exports of the home country, respectively, E the home price of the foreign currency (the nominal exchange rate), P_f the price of the foreign good in foreign currency, P_h the price of the home good in home currency, Q_f the real foreign income, and Q_h the real home income. The nonnegative parameters α, β, γ, and δ are the price and income elasticity of home imports and exports, respectively, whereas the nonnegative parameters A and B control for other effects than price and income.[5]

If the BP constraint implies balanced trade as assumed by Thirlwall (1979), then $P_h Q_x = E P_f Q_m$ and, therefore,

$$p_h + q_x = e + p_f + q_m, \tag{8.3}$$

where the lower-case variables represent the exponential growth rates of the upper-case variables in (8.1) and (8.2).

From (8.1)–(8.3) we obtain Thirlwall's (1979) balanced-trade home growth rate, that is

$$q_h = \left(\frac{\delta}{\beta}\right) q_f - \left(\frac{1 - \alpha - \gamma}{\beta}\right) r, \tag{8.4}$$

where q_f is the exponential growth rate of foreign income and, to simplify notation, r is the exponential growth rate of the real exchange rate $R = E P_f / P_h$.

Given the foreign growth rate and the trade parameters, equation (8.4) implies an adjustment of q_h, r, or both. According to Thirlwall's Law the adjustment comes fully through the home growth rate because, in the long run, the real exchange rate does not change ($r = 0$) or does not matter ($\alpha + \gamma = 1$).[6]

Notwithstanding the debate over its empirical validity,[7] the theoretical implication of Thirlwall's Law is clear, namely, to rule out the mainstream alternative of a full adjustment via the real exchange rate. More specifically, according to neoclassical growth theory both the home and foreign growth rates are determined from the supply side. If (8.4) is a relevant long-run constraint, the adjustment has to come completely through relative prices. Building upon Harrod's (1933) trade multiplier, Thirlwall's (1979) post-Keynesian alternative is to close (8.4) completely from the demand side.[8]

The intermediary alternative is an adjustment of quantities and relative prices where, say, the home country uses its macroeconomic policy to control not only growth, but also the real exchange rate.[9] Since this "closure" implies active demand-management, it is perfectly consistent with Thirlwall's (1979) demand-led approach.

Unbalanced trade

If there is unbalanced trade between the home and foreign countries, then $P_h Q_x - E P_f Q_m = NX$, where naturally $NX \neq 0$ represents home net exports in home currency. From this accounting identity Thirlwall and Hussain (1982) derived an extended version of the BP constraint where the ratio of capital inflows to the sum of capital inflows and exports enters as an exogenous variable. Although correct from an accounting perspective, such an extension does not elaborate on the implications of limited capital inflows.[10]

Moreno-Brid's (1998b) alternative was to propose a stable ratio of net exports to income as the relevant BP constraint on small open economies on the assumption that this is a sufficient condition for a stable ratio of foreign debt to income. As we shall see in the next section, this is actually a necessary condition for a stable debt–income ratio if one separates interest payments from imports of goods and nonfactor services. For the moment, let us proceed under Moreno-Brid's (1998b) assumption that trade deficits or surpluses are not explosive.

Why should the home country stabilize its ratio of net exports to income? The answer involves a "proof by contradiction" since, if the home country has explosive trade surpluses in relation to its income, it will eventually produce all world output without consuming any of it. By analogy, if the home country has explosive trade deficits in relation to its income, it will eventually consume all world output without producing any of it. The history of capitalist economies indicates that these are mathematical possibilities without any economic sense, since even the most frugal of the countries would eventually want to use part of its international wealth to consume. In the same vein, even the least frugal of the countries would eventually have to adjust its current expenditures to the demands of foreign creditors. In fact, a stable ratio of net exports to income is nothing more than the "non-Ponzi" condition one finds in mainstream and non-mainstream models of international finance to rule out infinite borrowing.

Normalizing NX by the nominal home income, we have $x - m = nx$, where naturally $x = Q_x/Q_h$, $m = RQ_m/Q_h$, and $nx = NX/P_hQ_h$. If the BP constraint implies a stable ratio of net exports to income, then $dx/dt = dm/dt$ and the crucial question is what are the implications of this condition for growth and real exchange rates. To answer this, note that

$$\frac{dm}{dt} = m(r + q_m - q_h) \qquad (8.5)$$

and

$$\frac{dx}{dt} = x(q_x - q_h) \qquad (8.6)$$

by definition. So, after substituting these equations in $dx/dt = dm/dt$ and using (8.1) and (8.2) to solve the resulting expression for q_h, we obtain the unbalanced-trade home growth rate proposed by Moreno-Brid (1998b), that is

$$q_h = \left(\frac{z\delta}{\beta - 1 + z}\right) q_f - \left(\frac{1 - \alpha - z\gamma}{\beta - 1 + z}\right) r, \qquad (8.7)$$

where $z = x/m$ is the export–import ratio of the home country.

Equation (8.7) is a more general definition of the BP constraint to account for unbalanced trade and, not surprisingly, it encompasses (8.4) as a special case when trade is initially balanced. Despite this connection, there exists a crucial difference between the "balanced" and "unbalanced' versions of the BP constraint, namely, unlike in (8.4), causality runs in both directions in (8.7) because the home export–import ratio is itself a function of the home growth rate. More formally, since

$$\frac{dz}{dt} = z[\delta q_f - \beta q_h - (1 - \alpha - \gamma)r] \tag{8.8}$$

when (8.7) holds, we necessarily have

$$\frac{dz}{dt} = z\left[\frac{(\beta - 1)(1 - z)\delta}{\beta - 1 + z}q_f - \frac{(1 - \alpha - \gamma + \beta\gamma)(z - 1)}{\beta - 1 + z}r\right] \tag{8.9}$$

and, therefore, z is not necessarily stable unless trade is initially balanced. Moreover, even if one follows Moreno-Brid (1998b) and assumes that $r = 0$, z is still not necessarily stable unless trade is initially balanced or the income elasticity of home imports equals one.[11] Moreno-Brid's (1998b) model is thus one possible case of the unbalanced-trade BP constraint on growth.

To check all cases, let us follow Moreno-Brid's (1998b) approach and assume that $r = 0$. The simplest way to represent the dynamics of the BP constraint is to define the growth adjustment of the home country as

$$\frac{dq_h}{dt} = \chi\left[\left(\frac{z\delta}{\beta - 1 + z}\right)q_f - q_h\right], \tag{8.10}$$

where $\chi > 0$ measures how fast the home growth rate converges to the BP constraint given by (8.7). From (8.8)

$$\frac{dz}{dt} = z(\delta q_f - \beta q_h), \tag{8.11}$$

which, together with (8.10), form a 2×2 nonlinear dynamical system for the home growth rate and export–import ratio. The joint and nontrivial stationary solution of this system is $(q_h^*, z^*) = (\delta q_f/\beta, 1)$ and, to analyze local stability about this point, let $\tilde{q}_h = q_h - q_h^*$ and $\tilde{z}^* = z - z^*$. In matrix notation the linear version of (8.10) and (8.11) is

$$\begin{bmatrix} d\tilde{q}_h/dt \\ d\tilde{z}/dt \end{bmatrix} = \begin{bmatrix} -\chi & q_f\chi\delta(\beta - 1)\beta^{-2} \\ -\beta & 0 \end{bmatrix}\begin{bmatrix} \tilde{q}_h \\ \tilde{z} \end{bmatrix}. \tag{8.12}$$

Since $\chi > 0$ by assumption, it is straightforward that equation (8.12) is stable if and only if $\beta > 1$. In economic terms, given a constant real exchange rate, the home country tends to its BP-constrained growth rate with balanced trade when the

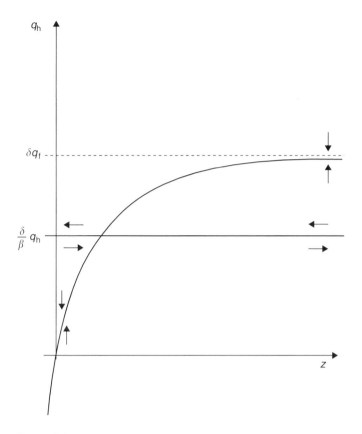

Figure 8.1

income elasticity of its imports is greater than one, as shown in Figure 8.1. If the income elasticity is smaller than one, the equilibrium point is a saddle point and, therefore, (8.12) is stable only under the strong assumption that exogenous shocks do not drive the state variables out of their stable path. The phase diagram of this case is shown in Figure 8.2. If the income elasticity equals one, the "equilibrium lines" of the home growth rate and export–import ratio coincide and, therefore, the home country tends to the BP-constrained growth rate with balanced or unbalanced trade. In short, equation (8.12) has multiple equilibrium points, as shown in Figure 8.3.

From the three cases given, we can conclude that if equation (8.7) holds and $r = 0$ as assumed by Moreno-Brid (1998b), then the only way to have stable and unbalanced trade in the long run is to impose the auxiliary assumption that the income elasticity of home imports equals one. Since small open economies usually have income-elastic imports, the case analyzed by Thirlwall (1979) is more likely to occur.

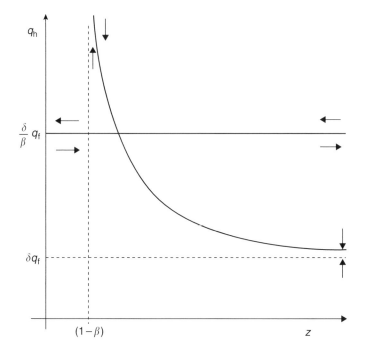

Figure 8.2

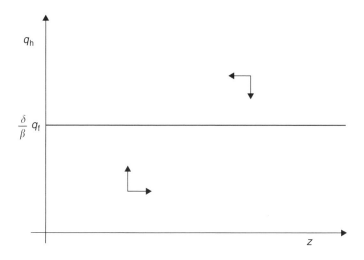

Figure 8.3

If one wants to preserve stable and unbalanced trade without restricting the income-elasticity of home imports, the natural solution is to include r in the problem and redefine the unbalanced-trade constraint as stable export-income and import-income ratios.[12] More formally, let $dm/dt = 0$ and use equation (8.1) to solve equation (8.5) for the home growth rate. The result is the loci of points (r, q_h) for which the home import ratio is stable, that is

$$q_h = [(1 - \alpha)/(1 - \beta)]r. \tag{8.13}$$

By analogy, the loci of points (r, q_h) for which the home export ratio is stable is given by

$$q_h = \gamma r + \delta q_f. \tag{8.14}$$

Solving these equations for q_h and r,

$$q_h = \left[\frac{(1 - \alpha)\delta}{1 - \alpha - \gamma + \beta\gamma} \right] q_f \tag{8.15}$$

and

$$r = \left[\frac{(1 - \beta)\delta}{1 - \alpha - \gamma + \beta\gamma} \right] q_f. \tag{8.16}$$

So, assuming for the moment that the home country can control growth and relative prices, equations (8.15) and (8.16) give us the policy rules consistent with stable import and export ratios.[13]

Focusing the analysis on the cases where both α and β are different from one,[14] equations (8.15) and (8.16) give us three qualitatively distinct cases, namely:

(i) when $\alpha > 1$ and $\beta < 1$ or $\alpha < 1$ and $\beta > 1$; income expansion in the foreign country implies income expansion in the home country and appreciation of the home good, as shown in Figure 8.4;

(ii) when $1 - \alpha - \gamma + \beta\gamma > 0$ and either $\alpha > 1$ and $\beta > 1$ or $\alpha < 1$ and $\beta < 1$: income expansion in the foreign country implies income expansion in the home country and depreciation of the home good, as shown in Figure 8.5; and

(iii) when $1 - \alpha - \gamma + \beta\gamma < 0$ and either $\alpha > 1$ and $\beta > 1$ or $\alpha < 1$ and $\beta < 1$: income expansion in the foreign country implies income contraction in the home country and appreciation of the home good as shown in Figure 8.6.

By analogy the implications of income contraction in the foreign country can also be grouped in the same three qualitatively distinct cases.

Since for almost any arbitrary division of the world economy one observes positive growth in the "foreign" and "home" blocks during, say, 10-year intervals of time, case (iii) tends to be a rare real-world phenomenon. Moreover, since small open economies usually have income-elastic imports ($\beta > 1$), the

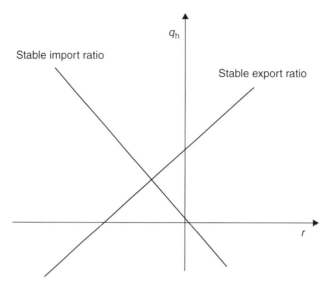

Figure 8.4

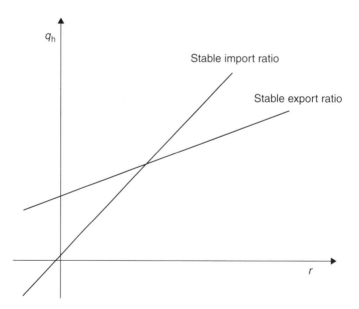

Figure 8.5

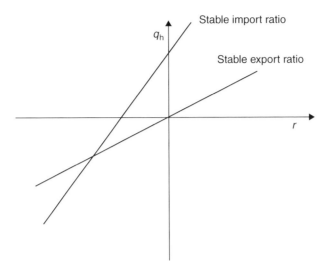

Figure 8.6

distinction between case (i) and (ii) tends to lie on the price elasticity of home imports.[15]

Now the crucial question: can the home country really control growth and real exchange rates? Theoretically, this can only happen if there is a stable "technological-institutional" structure connecting income, prices, and exchange rates in the home country where macroeconomic policy and foreign conditions enter as exogenous variables. In the jargon of Keynesian economics, if there exists a stable "Phillips curve" connecting growth and inflation in which macroeconomic policy enters as an exogenous variable, then it may be possible for the home government to achieve (8.15) and (8.16) with the aid of some exchange-rate parity condition. For instance, assume that the home growth rate is a function of monetary policy, fiscal policy, and the appreciation or depreciation of the home good, that is

$$q_h = \phi_0 + \phi_1(i_h - p_h) + \phi_2 g + \phi_3 r, \tag{8.17}$$

where i_h is the nominal interest rate in the home country, g an index that measures the demand impact of fiscal policy,[16] and $\phi \neq 0$ for $j = 0$, (8.1)–(8.3). If there is also a risk-adjusted parity between the home and foreign interest rates,

$$i_h = i_f + e + \sigma, \tag{8.18}$$

where i_f and σ are the nominal foreign interest rate and risk premium paid by home borrowers in the foreign financial market, respectively.

Since $e = r - p_f + p_h$, equation (8.18) can be used to obtain the home real interest rate consistent with the target growth rate of the real exchange rate. Then, substituting this result in (8.17), we obtain the fiscal-policy variable necessary to achieve the target income growth. Altogether, the risk-adjusted parity between nominal interest rates and the real-exchange rate target determine monetary policy, and then monetary policy and the income-growth target determine fiscal policy.

The stable institutional and technological structure implicit in (8.17) is obviously a very strong assumption for the long run but, on the other hand, it is a reasonable approximation of the reality of small open economies in the short run. Price rigidities, asymmetric information and fundamental uncertainty usually lead to a short-run relationship of the kind depicted in (8.17). The increasing integration of world financial markets tends to subordinate monetary policy to foreign conditions, as modeled in (8.18). The result is a short-run structure that allows the home government to control income and relative prices.

On the empirical side, the experience of some Latin American countries since the end of the Bretton Woods system indicates that stop-and-go policies may indeed be able to control income and relative prices during short intervals of time, at the cost of periodic currency crises.[17] In fact, the opportunities brought by cheap foreign credit and the inability to issue foreign currency during times of crisis are usually more convincing than the Lucas critique in the determination of macro policy in small open economies.

Overall, (8.15) and (8.16) should be interpreted as short-run targets for income and real-exchange rate growth rates when the home country is constrained to have a non-explosive trade pattern. Since these targets are consistent with balanced and unbalanced trade, they do not tell us at what level the home export and import ratios are stable. This is exactly where the concept of a sustainable accumulation of foreign debt closes the analysis.

Sustainable debt

So far we analyzed the impact of unbalanced trade on the BP constraint without mentioning interest payments and the dynamics of foreign debt. However, since the home country does not issue foreign currency, it can only have persistent trade deficits by receiving a continuous inflow of foreign capital. The counterpart of unbalanced trade is a change in the stock of foreign debt and, therefore, we have to check under which conditions the unbalanced-trade constraint given by (8.15) and (8.16) is consistent with a nonexplosive accumulation of foreign debt.

Following the approach of Moreno-Brid (1998b), let a stable ratio of foreign debt to income be the definition of a sustainable accumulation of foreign debt.[18] Assuming that the home country is a net debtor and that capital flows involve only interest-bearing bonds,

$$P_h Q_h - E P_f Q_m - (i_f + \sigma)ED + EF = 0 \qquad (8.19)$$

where D is the net foreign debt of the home country, and F the net inflow of foreign capital into the home country, both in foreign currency.[19] Normalizing (8.19) by home income

$$x - m - (i_f + \sigma)d + f = 0, \tag{8.20}$$

where $d = ED/P_h Q_h$ and $f = EF/P_h Q_h$.

Given a constant ratio of capital inflows to income, (8.20) implies not only that x and m should be stable as in the previous section, but also that the debt ratio d should be stable. In other words, given the availability of foreign finance (f), the BP constraint now implies stable trade (x and m) and debt ratios (d).

Using the fact that the net inflow of foreign capital equals the change in foreign debt ($F = dD/dt$),

$$\frac{dd}{dt} = m - x + (i_f + \sigma + e - p_h - q_h)d. \tag{8.21}$$

So, given x and m, it is straightforward that d is stable as long as the home growth rate exceeds the real cost of foreign debt in home currency. To insert the trade parameters into the analysis, note that from (8.15) and (8.16) we can rewrite (8.21) as

$$\frac{dd}{dt} = m - x + \left[i_f + \sigma - p_f - \left(\frac{\beta - \alpha}{1 - \alpha - \gamma + \beta\gamma} \right) \delta q_f \right] d \tag{8.22}$$

and, therefore, the stability condition for d is

$$\left(\frac{\beta - \alpha}{1 - \alpha - \gamma + \beta\gamma} \right) \delta > \frac{i_f + \sigma - p_f}{q_f}. \tag{8.23}$$

The economic intuition is that, given its trade parameters, the international financial stability of the home country depends on its risk premium and the growth and real interest rates in the foreign country.[20]

From the steady-state solution of (8.22) we also have

$$x - m = \left[i_f + \sigma - p_f - \left(\frac{\beta - \alpha}{1 - \alpha - \gamma + \beta\gamma} \right) \delta q_f \right] d, \tag{8.24}$$

which completes the home control problem by setting a target for the home net-export ratio in terms of the trade parameters and foreign conditions.

Altogether, the BP constraint implies managing q_h and r according to (8.15) and (8.16) to keep x and m stable at the level given by (8.24).[21] The economic intuition is that the trade parameters, the risk premium, and the debt ratio allowed by foreign financial conditions determine the net export ratio of the home country, which in its turn determine its income and real exchange rate growth rates.[22]

Recalling that we assumed earlier that the home country is a net debtor ($d > 0$), the target net export ratio in (8.24) is negative when (8.23) holds and positive otherwise. Thus, when the debt ratio shows stable dynamics, the BP constraint is consistent with trade deficits and vice versa. From (8.24) we can also see that, independent of the value of the trade parameters, an increase in the risk premium or the foreign real interest rate always increases the "trade burden" of sustainable debt ($x - m$).

The trade parameters are important to determine the impact of foreign growth on the target net export ratio. Considering the three cases analyzed in the previous section, an increase in the foreign growth rate always reduces the target net export ratio in case (i). In case (ii) this happens only if $\alpha < \beta$ and, in case (iii), only if $\alpha > \beta$.

Recalling that case (iii) is a rare phenomenon and that small open economies usually have income elastic imports, we can conclude that an increase in foreign growth tends to reduce the target net export ratio when the price-elasticity of home imports is smaller than its income elasticity ($\alpha < \beta$) and vice versa.

Conclusion

Thirlwall's (1979) original specification of the BP constraint can be extended to include unbalanced trade, interest payments, and a sustainable accumulation of foreign debt, provided that we expand its definition to include the real exchange rate and the trade balance.

In relation to the previous theoretical literature on the BP constraint, four points should be mentioned. First, similar to the models of Thirlwall and Hussain (1982), McCombie and Thirlwall (1997a) and Moreno-Brid (1998b), the model of this chapter allows persistent trade deficits or surpluses, encompassing Thirlwall's Law as a special short-run case or the long-run case. Second, unlike the model of Thirlwall and Hussain (1982), and similarly to the models of McCombie and Thirlwall (1997a) and Moreno-Brid (1998), the model of this chapter imposes nonexplosive trade deficits or surpluses on the country in question. Third, the model of this chapter gives us theoretical hypotheses about growth and real exchange rates and, differently from the models of McCombie and Thirlwall (1997a) and Moreno-Brid (1998b), it does not result in a potentially unstable BP-constrained growth rate. Fourth, unlike the models of Thirlwall and Hussain (1982), McCombie and Thirlwall (1997a), and Moreno-Brid (1998b), the model of this chapter separates interest payments from the imports of goods and nonfactor services.

Altogether, the model of this chapter shows the connection between trade parameters, foreign growth, foreign interest rates and trade ratios in the determination of a sustainable accumulation of foreign debt. Its main disadvantage in relation to the existing literature lies in the heroic assumption that the country in question can control business fluctuations and relative prices. Notwithstanding the fact that many developing economies have been trying to do exactly this since the end of the Bretton-Woods system, continuous and discontinuous changes in technology, preferences, and institutions restrict the analysis of this chapter to the short run.

During long intervals of time the trade parameters and foreign conditions change and, therefore, so do the targets for q_h, r, and $x - m$. Hence, if the trade parameters do not change, in the long run one of the countries may become infinitely large, one of the goods may become infinitely cheap, or both. Since one does not see this in the world economy, in the long run the BP-constraint equations become accounting identities of any country that does not display explosive trade and debt patterns.

Whether or not the BP constraint proposed in this chapter is an adequate description of the short-run operation of small open economies is a point to be investigated empirically. On a first approximation, the recurrent currency crises in developing countries and the autonomous or IMF-imposed adjustments to them indicate that such a constraint usually comes through quantities, relative prices, and debt ratios. Since a BP-oriented demand management involves many targets and variables, the results of this chapter offer one possible way to organize the analysis in terms of trade parameters, foreign conditions, and a sustainable debt–income ratio.

Notes

1 It should be noted that McCombie and Thirlwall (1997a) were the first to analyze the implications of redefining the BP constraint in terms of a stable ratio of trade deficits to income.
2 For an overview of the Brazilian trade and finance patterns in 1974–97, see Terra (1999). For an analysis of the 1990s, see Averbug and Giambiagi (2000) and Sainz and Calcagno (1999).
3 The basic idea is that the foreign good can impose a supply constraint on the home country. In this way the BP constraint is analogous to a capital or labor constraint in Harrod's (1939) closed model, which is exactly the essence of the "dual-gap" model of Chenery and Bruno (1962).
4 Note that constant labor productivity does not preclude active pricing by home and foreign firms and, in fact, changes in unit labor costs due to the pressure of trade surpluses or deficits on employment are usually part of the adjustment mechanism of growth to its BP constraint. For an analysis of markup pricing, see Taylor (1991).
5 If we define $\eta \geq 0$ as the price elasticity of the home demand for the home good, then the elasticity of substitution in the home country is $\alpha + \eta$. By analogy, the same reasoning applies to the elasticity of substitution in the foreign country. The parameters A and B are included to represent fixed effects and, in the special case where $\alpha = \gamma = 0$ and $\beta = \delta = 1$, analyzed by Chenery and Bruno (1962), they are exactly the import requirements of the home and foreign countries, respectively.
6 The adjustment mechanism is assumed but not demonstrated by Thirlwall (1979). Building upon the verbal arguments of McCombie and Thirlwall (1994), Pugno (1998) constructed a model where the employment rate "predates" the inverse of the home–foreign real exchange rate and, in this process, it makes the home growth rate converge to a level that balances trade. The causal chain is the following: (i) a trade surplus leads to an increase in the home employment rate; (ii) the higher employment rate leads to an increase in the home labor costs; and (iii) the increase in labor costs erodes international competitiveness of the home country, reducing its trade surplus. A symmetric mechanism applies to trade deficits and the steady state is reached only when trade is balanced.

7 A survey of the empirical literature on Thirlwall's Law is beyond the scope of this chapter. For a summary of the main points, see McCombie and Thirlwall (1994, ch. 5). For more recent arguments, see McCombie (1997) and Alexander and King (1998).

8 A third theoretical alternative can be found in Krugman (1989a), where $r = 0$ and δ/β converges to the ratio of supply-determined growth rates.

9 For a real-world example, see the analysis of Brazil's exchange-rate policy in 1964–97 by Bonono and Terra (1999).

10 As pointed by Moreno-Brid (1998b, p. 284), this "accounting restriction is insufficient to guarantee that the evolution of foreign capital inflows – whether in real or in nominal terms – generates a pattern of foreign indebtedness that is sustainable in the long run."

11 Neither McCombie and Thirlwall (1997a) nor Moreno-Brid (1998b) considered this potential source of instability in their unbalanced-trade version of the BP constraint.

12 By assuming that x and m are stable we obtain a stable nx but rule out the extreme case where nx is stable with x and m tending to zero or infinity.

13 In terms of Tinbergen's (1955) analysis of economic policy, the home country has two instruments (income and the real exchange rate) to achieve two targets (stable export and import ratios).

14 Given a positive growth rate in the foreign country, equations (8.15) and (8.16) give us exactly Thirlwall's Law when the income elasticity of imports equals one. In contrast, when the price elasticity of imports equals one, we have the economically unusual result of zero home growth with an appreciation of the home good.

15 Case (i) tends to happen when home imports are price inelastic ($\alpha < 1$) and case (ii) when they are price elastic.

16 Say, the ratio of budget deficits to income. Note that the intercept coefficient in equation (8.19) can incorporate a "natural" real rate of interest and an "equilibrium" or "optimal" value of g without loss of generality.

17 The exchange-rate based stabilization plans in Mexico, Argentina, and Brazil during the 1990s are a good example of such a BP-determined demand management.

18 By doing so we are merging the foreign debt of the government and private sectors of the home country and ignoring the "twin-deficits' argument that budget deficits are necessarily the driving force of current account deficits. As the recent experience of the US indicates, the business sector may also be the destabilizing agent.

19 A non-zero balance of payments can be incorporated into the analysis without loss of generality, provided that we redefine sustainable debt accumulation as a stable ratio of foreign reserves to foreign debt. For a real world example, see Barbosa-Filho (2001).

20 Note that if home imports are price inelastic and income elastic, the left-hand side of (8.23) is positive.

21 Now the home country has three instruments (q_h, r, and $x - m$) to achieve three targets (stable x, stable m, and stable d).

22 Again, the exchange-rate based stabilization plans in Mexico, Argentina, and Brazil during the 1980s and 1990s indicate that this usually involves two analytically distinct phases. First, once-for-all changes of the real exchange rate (a "maxi" depreciation or appreciation of the home currency) to put $x - m$ at the level allowed by foreign conditions. Second, a continuous demand management to keep x and m stable at such level. The second part usually breaks down in the medium run and the result is a currency crisis that starts the process all over again.

Part II
Developed countries

9   On the empirics of balance of payments constrained growth[*]

J. S. L. McCombie

Since the initial publication of Thirlwall's (1979) paper on the role of the balance of payments in constraining long-run economic growth, there have been a number of tests of this hypothesis (see Davidson, 1990–91, for an overall assessment of "Thirlwall's Law"). While these have been reviewed in McCombie and Thirlwall (1994, 1997a), it is useful to examine some new issues that have arisen and to consider some earlier matters in greater detail. Of particular relevance for the testing of the law are implications arising from recent developments in time-series analysis with regard to integration and cointegration. These issues have been carefully examined by Hieke (1997) with respect to the United States using quarterly data. I shall consider Hieke's results and those of other studies and also present some further results for the United States (as well as Japan and the United Kingdom). While my results do not lead to any dramatically different conclusions from much of the earlier work, they tie up some loose ends.

The tests of the law have generally involved a consideration of how closely estimates of balance of payments equilibrium growth rates (y_b) approximate to the observed growth rates of national income, or output (y). Since the balance of payments constraint is deemed to hold in the long run, these growth rates normally average over a number of years. The balance of payments equilibrium growth rate is calculated as either $y_b = x/\hat{\pi}$ or $y_b = \hat{\varepsilon}z/\hat{\pi}$ where x and z are the growth of exports and world income. $\hat{\varepsilon}$ and $\hat{\pi}$ are estimates of the world income elasticity of demand for a country's exports and the domestic income elasticity of demand for its imports (see Thirlwall, 1979 and Chapter 1, for the derivation of y_b). The estimates of these elasticities are taken from regression analyses of conventional export- and import demand functions. Although a central tenet of the balance of payments constrained model is that relative prices have a quantitatively small role to play in determining the growth of trade flows, the estimates of the income elasticities should be taken from the demand functions that include the relative price term. There are two reasons for this. First, the approach does not argue that relative prices have *no* effect on trade flows, only that over the long run their impact is quantitatively small. Second, to exclude the effect of relative prices is to assume

* First published in *Journal of Post Keynesian Economics*, Spring 1997.

what should be tested. The early tests of the hypothesis (e.g. Thirlwall, 1979) used the estimates from Houthakker and Magee's (1969) seminal study, which estimated import- and export demand functions using annual time-series data and the logarithms of the levels of the various variables. While their approach has been criticized as being subject to a number of potential problems (Morgan, 1970), the estimates have proved remarkably robust and have been confirmed by other studies (see, e.g. Goldstein and Khan, 1978, for the case of the income elasticity of demand for exports). More recent works (such as Bairam, 1988; Bairam and Dempster, 1991) have estimated the demand functions using proportionate growth rates and annual data.

The various approaches to the testing of the hypothesis all share a common rationale: that disparities in the income elasticities of demand primarily reflect disparities in nonprice competitiveness, which are subject to very slow change. Nonprice competitiveness reflects such supply-side characteristics as quality, after-sales service, the effectiveness of distribution networks, and so on. Consequently, while this approach stresses the importance of the growth of demand for exports in the growth process, this is a function of what may be termed a country's supply characteristics. There is, however, a marked distinction between this approach and the neoclassical emphasis on the supply side (the rate of technical progress and the growth of factors of production) in economic growth. A close relationship between y_b and y suggests that changes in relative prices are unimportant in determining trade flows, and the growth of international capital flows plays only a very small role in allowing the divergence of export and import growth rates (see McCombie and Thirlwall, 1997b, for a demonstration of the latter). It is the differences in the income elasticities of demand for exports and imports that play the crucial role in accounting for disparities in economic growth. Consequently, given that in the long run the current account (or, at least, the basic balance) must be in equilibrium, the fact that y_b closely approximates y suggests that it is income adjustments (through the Harrod foreign trade multiplier or, more generally, the Hicks supermultiplier) that ensure this occurs (McCombie and Thirlwall, 1994).

Thirlwall (1979) originally used Spearman's rank correlation coefficient to test the degree of association between y_b and y for the advanced countries over the periods, 1953–76 and 1951–73 (using slightly different data sources). This nonparametric test demonstrated that there was a significant positive relationship between the two growth rates. A more rigorous test, originally suggested by McGregor and Swales (1985), is to regress y on y_b or, alternatively, $\ln y$ on $\ln y_b$ using pooled data for a number of countries. The null hypothesis is that the intercept of the regression should not be statistically different from zero and the slope coefficient should not differ from unity. Using Thirlwall's (1979) data, they claimed that the null hypothesis was in fact rejected, hence casting serious doubts on the validity of the law. However, there are two problems with their procedure. First, the values for y_b are stochastic, since they are derived from prior estimated coefficients (namely, the $\hat{\pi}$s) which have associated standard errors. Regressing y on y_b (or $\ln y$ on $\ln y_b$) suffers from a misspecification analogous to an "errors in variables" problem. Thus, although no causality, *per se*, is implied in the regression, which variable is chosen as the regressand and which as the regressor is not immaterial. y_b should be regressed on y, and not vice versa. Second, Japan proved to have an actual growth rate that was much less than its balance of payments equilibrium growth rate. This country proved to be an outlier and it was the reason for the rejection of the null hypothesis for all the countries in the sample. The inference is that, while it is plausible that Japan was not balance of payments constrained (it was accumulating large trade surpluses over the period concerned), its inclusion in the sample led to the erroneous conclusion that no advanced country was balance of payments constrained. It should be noted that all countries in a sample are not normally simultaneously balance of payments constrained (see Chapter 5 for a theoretical model that demonstrates the implications of this proposition). Consequently, the finding that a number of individual countries are not balance of payments constrained does not refute the importance of the balance of payments in constraining the growth rates of a significant number of countries (see McCombie and Thirlwall, 1994, ch. 5).

This led McCombie (1989) to suggest an alternative test of the law. Define the hypothetical income elasticity of demand that exactly equates the actual and the balance of payments growth rates as $\pi' \equiv x/y$. Then, if π' and $\hat{\pi}$ (the least-squares estimator) are not statistically significantly different, the hypothesis that the country is balance of payments constrained has not been refuted. This has the great advantage that the test can be applied to each country separately. By this test, a significant number of advanced countries were found to be constrained by their balance of payments over the postwar period (McCombie and Thirlwall, 1994).

Two further tests of the law that have been proposed but these are not without their limitations. The first is to use, for a particular country, the current account equilibrium condition $P_d X = P_f E M$, where P_d, P_f and E are the domestic price of exports (X), the foreign price of imports (M), and the exchange rate. The export- and import-demand functions are substituted into this equation. This gives, after expressing the relationship in terms of growth rates and some rearranging,

$$y_b = \varepsilon z/\pi + (1 + \psi + \eta)(p_d - p_f - e)/\pi, \tag{9.1}$$

where $\psi\,(<0)$ and $\eta\,(<0)$ are the price elasticities of demand for imports and exports and e is the rate of change of the exchange rate. If the law is to hold, we should expect the estimate of ε/π to be statistically significant. While the estimate of $(1 + \psi + \eta)$ may also be statistically significant and negative, it should be of a size that gives only limited explanatory power to the rate of change of relative prices.

The advantage of this specification is that it enables us to test the law for individual countries using time-series data. The disadvantage is that it is essentially testing the proposition that countries are balance of payments constrained in the short run – in other words, on a yearly, or even quarterly, basis. However, it is highly probable that the growth of exports and imports may diverge substantially over such short periods and, in these circumstances, the growth of capital flows is likely to be important in accommodating the difference. A rapid upswing in the growth of domestic demand is likely to lead to an immediate worsening of the balance of payments and an increase in import growth over exports that will in the short run be financed by capital inflows. The notion of the balance of payments constraint implies that this cannot persist for very long. Eventually the rate of growth of economic activity will fall sufficiently to generate the balance of payments surplus necessary eventually to reduce the net stock of foreign debt to a level more acceptable to the international financial markets. Consequently, the failure to find that equation (9.1) gives a good statistical fit should not necessarily be taken as a refutation of the law.

Atesoglu (1993–94), however, uses a moving average to eliminate short-term fluctuations using Canadian data and finds that export growth is a significant determinant of output growth. He also explicitly includes the growth of capital flows in equation (9.1), but finds that this term is not statistically significant.

The second test was first proposed by Atesoglu (1993), who smoothed the annual growth rates of exports and income for the United States over the period 1955–90 by calculating a 15-year moving average. Using the (single) value of the income elasticity of demand for imports estimated over the full period, he calculated 21 overlapping balance of payments equilibrium growth rates. To provide a formal test of the law, he regressed the actual growth rates on the calculated values for y_b and tested the null hypothesis that the intercept and the slope did not differ significantly from zero and unity, respectively. This is an interesting test, but a couple of observations are in order. First, while an inspection of the actual and predicted growth rates shows a remarkably close correspondence (see Atesoglu, 1993, p. 512, table 1), the data display very little variation. This is inevitable given that they are generated from samples that significantly overlap. Thus, the slope coefficient is likely to be poorly determined simply because of the lack of variation in the data. The R^2 may well be very low. Hence, it would not be surprising if the law were refuted even though y and y_b were very similar in magnitude. Consequently, the failure to find a significant relationship should be interpreted with great caution. Alternatively, it could be argued on a priori grounds that the intercept should be constrained to pass through the origin (see Bairam, 1988). This is likely to give a very close fit since we are almost estimating the regression through two points.[1] I provide later an alternative test for the United States based on the use of a rolling regression, which has certain similarities to Atesoglu's procedure.

Finally, other indirect evidence is used in the interpretation of the law. The alternative hypothesis, in contrast to the law, is that the growth of exports is endogenous, determined by changes in relative prices expressed in a common currency. Hence, if there is an exogenous increase in the growth of imports, relative prices should adjust to increase the growth of exports, bringing the balance of payments back into equilibrium without requiring any income adjustment. Thus, any observed current account deficits are optimal, representing, for example, intertemporal optimization of consumption on the part of the country. A corollary of this approach is that output growth is determined by the exogenously given growth of technical change and the labor force, and the economy is always on its production possibility curve. Of relevance to this argument is Cornwall's (1977) careful study that demonstrates how, even in the Golden Age of economic growth 1950–73, the growth of the labor supply in many advanced countries was essentially endogenous. In much of continental Europe, there were either substantial reserves of labor in the agricultural sector or "guest workers" providing an additional source of labor when demand factors warranted. The United Kingdom drew heavily on immigration from the new Commonwealth countries to supplement its labor supply, especially for unskilled or semi-skilled jobs.

The estimation of the income elasticities of demand for imports

There has recently been something of a methodological revolution in time-series econometrics with the realization that many macroeconomic variables may be nonstationary. The paper that first led to a widespread appreciation of this fact was Nelson and Plosser (1982). They examined 14 macroeconomic variables ranging from the logarithm of real GNP to common stock prices over periods with starting years that ranged from 1860 to 1909, and with a terminal year of 1970. Using the now-traditional Dickey–Fuller and Augmented Dickey–Fuller (DF/ADF) tests, they concluded that only unemployment was $I(0)$ and the other variables were $I(1)$. In other words, these variables needed to be first-differenced to make them stationary. If $I(1)$ variables are to be used in regression analysis, then it becomes important to reject the hypothesis that they are not cointegrated. If they are not cointegrated, the regression will be spurious with the usual diagnostics erroneously suggesting a much closer relationship than actually exists.

These findings have obvious implications for the estimation of the import and export elasticities of demand. As I have noted, the first estimates of the import- and export demand functions were taken from regressions where the logarithmic values of the levels were used (e.g. Houthakker and Magee, 1969; Goldstein and Khan, 1978 – the latter estimated only export demand functions, but used a simultaneous equation framework that explicitly included the supply side. It is reassuring to note that their estimates did not differ greatly from those of Houthakker and Magee). More recent studies have utilized growth rates (e.g. Bairam, 1988; Bairam and Dempster, 1991; Atesoglu, 1993), although this seems to have been more a happy coincidence than because the data were $I(1)$.

Bairam (1993) was the first to note the potential problems posed by the possibility that the error structure of the log-levels (the static specification) of the import- and export demand functions might be nonstationary. Using data for five countries (Belgium, France, Germany, the Netherlands, and the United Kingdom) over the period 1970–89, he found that the variables were $I(1)$ and the static demand functions, except for the import demand function of France, were not cointegrated. However, using first differences gave almost exactly the same estimates of the income elasticities as did the use of logarithms of the levels. For convenience, I report his results in Table 9.1.

Table 9.1 Export and import income elasticities of demand

Country	Exports (ε)		Imports (π)	
	Levels	Differences	Levels	Differences
Belgium	1.87	1.89	2.06	2.06
	(16.93)	(6.90)	(12.47)	(4.76)
France	1.71	1.72	1.70	2.17
	(18.66)	(8.79)	(25.21)	(6.08)
Germany	1.28	1.17	1.86	1.46
	(3.84)	(2.66)	(11.80)	(7.87)
Netherlands	1.59	1.60	1.23	1.72
	(14.67)	(7.79)	(8.60)	(5.98)
United Kingdom	1.34	1.25	2.07	1.99
	(22.12)	(6.01)	(27.01)	(8.11)

Source: Bairam (1993).

Note
Figures in parentheses are *t* statistics.

As is to be expected, the standard errors of the static estimates are smaller than those of the dynamic coefficients. Bairam inferred that "the past research on the Harrod foreign trade multiplier and the conclusions drawn from them are still valid." Other studies for individual countries have found similar results. For example, Blecker's (1992) study of import demand functions for the United States found an income elasticity of demand of 1.67 using log-levels in a specification excluding a time trend, compared with 1.90 using first differences. Quarterly data were used over the period 1977(1)–1990(3).

It has been argued that although the use of first differences obviates the problem of nonstationarity of the residuals, long-run information is lost. Hence, the relationships should be tested to see if they are cointegrated, and, if this is the case, an error-correction model should be estimated to incorporate the short-run dynamics. This was the procedure adopted by Andersen (1993 and Chapter 10), who took a sample of 16 OECD countries. Using annual data from 1960–90, he likewise found that all the variables were $I(1)$ and that the ADF test did not reject the hypothesis of no cointegration. Nevertheless, given the low power of the ADF test and the small number of degrees of freedom, Andersen went ahead and estimated the import- and export demand functions in an error-correction model. Using the estimated income elasticities, π and ε, to calculate y_b, he found that, with pooled data for 1960–73, 1973–80, and 1980–90 and excluding Japan from the sample, regressing y_b on y gave a slope coefficient of 1.03. This did not differ significantly from unity. Paradoxically, Andersen concluded that the "close relationship *merely* holds in the very long run" (emphasis added), but this is precisely when the theory suggests it should hold.

Recently, the work of Perron (1989, 1993, 1994) has cast considerable doubt on the results of Nelson and Plosser (1982). Perron argues that, if there is a structural break in the series (resulting from, for example, an exogenous shock such as the Great Crash of 1929 or the 1973 oil price shock) and no allowance is made for these in the time series, this will bias the result in favor of not rejecting the null hypothesis of a unit root. The intuitive explanation of this is straightforward: If a series is nonstationary, it is non-trend reverting. If, however, there is a structural break in the trend and the data are stationary, after the structural break they will revert to the new, and not the old, trend. Hence, any test for unit roots that omits the change in trend will bias the test in favor of not rejecting the null hypothesis of a unit root. Of course, there is no reason why there should be only one structural break.

When Perron retested the macroeconomic variables using Nelson and Plosser's (1982) data with a single suitable structural break, he found that all but two of the variables were now $I(0)$.

In the case under consideration here, 1973–74 may well prove to be a structural break in the relationship between the levels of imports and income. Around this time, two important events occurred: Bretton Woods collapsed and a severe recession was induced by the deflationary policies adopted in the wake of the dramatic rise in the oil price. Consequently, using annual data, I tested the data for unit roots for the United States, Japan, and the United Kingdom over the period from 1952–93 with a structural break at 1973–74. Both of these shocks may have affected the income elasticities of demand, especially if there was a hysteresis effect (Blecker, 1992).

I estimated the relationship between imports and income in terms of the logarithms of levels and in first differences. This, following Bairam (1993), would show whether or not the use of log-levels or growth rates did, in fact, make any difference to the estimates of the income elasticities. (I also used a longer time period than did Bairam; this, as mentioned earlier, allowed for an explicit test for any structural breaks in the value of the income elasticities. Two of my countries, the United States and Japan, were not included in Bairam's sample.)

Perron's additive outlier model was adopted. For any trending variable y_t, the following two-step procedure was used. First, the following equation was estimated using ordinary least squares (OLS):

$$y_t = \mu + \beta t + \theta DU_t + \gamma DT_t + \tilde{y}_t, \tag{9.2}$$

where t is a time trend, DU_t is a dummy variable associated with a change in the intercept where $DU_t = 1$ if $t > 1973$ and 0 otherwise. $DT_t = t - T_b$ if $t > T_b$ and 0 otherwise, where T_b is the break date, that is, 1973. $\tilde{y}_t$ is the error term. The Perron test is based on the value of the t-statistic for testing that $\rho = 0$ in the following autoregression applied to the estimated error component $\tilde{y}_t$, namely,

$$\Delta\tilde{y}_t = \rho\tilde{y}_{t-1} + \sum_{j=0}^{k} a_j D(T_b)_{t-j} + \sum_{i=1}^{k} b_i \Delta\tilde{y}_{t-i} + e_t. \tag{9.3}$$

$D(T_b)_t = 1$ if $t - T_b + 1$ and 0 otherwise. It will be recalled that T_b is 1973.

This procedure differs from that in Perron (1989), which contained an error, later corrected in Perron (1993). The latter paper also contains the amended critical values for the t-statistic. The test statistic is, however, dependent on both T_b (in our sample, the break point is about halfway through the sample) and the number of truncation lags, k. The procedure that was adopted to determine the length of k was that of Perron (1989), which is essentially a "general to specific recursive procedure." In other words, the length of k is chosen such that the coefficient of Δy_{t-k} is statistically significant and the coefficient of the next lag, Δy_{t-k-1}, is insignificant. There are, of course, other criteria that can be used, including the Akaike Information Criterion.

Other, more restrictive, specifications of equation (9.2) may be derived by a testing-down procedure that drops either DU_t or DT_t if it is statistically insignificant. A more general procedure is to let the data determine when the most significant structural break occurs without imposing it exogenously, but that option has not been pursued here (Perron, 1994).

It should also be noted that introducing dummies to allow for the structural breaks is a more efficient procedure than splitting the sample. Perron found that when he split the sample, and tested for unit roots for each subperiod separately, the data did not, in fact, always reject the null hypothesis, even though, as noted earlier, the use of the full sample did.

Before adopting this procedure, I first undertook the standard DF/ADF tests on the various variables without allowing for a structural break. In other words, the following was first estimated:

$$\Delta y_t = \mu + \beta t + \rho y_{t-1} + \sum_{i=1}^{k} c_i \Delta y_{t-i} + u_t, \qquad (9.4)$$

and a sequential testing procedure was adopted. First, the null hypothesis that $\rho = 0$ is tested using the appropriate DF critical values, and, if this is not rejected, $\rho = \beta = 0$ is tested using the nonstandard F-statistic. If this is rejected, $\rho = 0$ is tested using the standard normal distribution. If $\rho = \beta = 0$ is not rejected, then the time trend is dropped from the regression and the testing procedure repeated with respect to ρ and μ. If the null hypothesis that $\rho = \mu = 0$ is rejected, then ρ is tested for statistical significance using the standard t-statistic. The lagged first differences enter into the regression to ensure that the error term is white noise. The Perron approach was again followed in determining the length of the lag.

The case of the United States

I begin with a consideration of balance of payments constrained growth with respect to the United States. The United States has generally been found to have an income elasticity of demand for imports that greatly exceeds the income elasticity of demand for exports, and indeed the consequences of this were singled out for specific comment in Houthakker and Magee's (1969) classic paper. They found that the ratio of $\hat{\varepsilon}$ to $\hat{\pi}$ was 0.59, which meant that, other things being equal, the United States could only grow at a rate of about 60 percent of the growth of the rest of the world without encountering an ever-increasing current account deficit.[2] Consequently, if the United States was to match the growth of the rest of the world, there would have to be a continuous improvement in its relative price competitiveness, assuming that the Marshall–Lerner condition is satisfied, unless there was an ever-increasing inflow of capital from abroad.

The proposition that the United States may be balance of payments constrained has been examined in a number of recent papers (Blecker, 1992; Atesoglu, 1993, 1995; and, most recently, Hieke, 1997). Blecker also provided a useful survey of other recent studies that have estimated import demand functions for the United States. He estimated both import- and export demand functions for the United States, using quarterly data over the 13-year period from 1977 to 1990. While he did not explicitly consider testing for the order of integration, he presented estimates using data in both log-level and first-difference form. (The Durbin–Watson statistics suggest that the log-level specifications may well not be cointegrated.) He estimated the conventional log-level and first-differences specifications both with and without time trends and also included a dummy variable to test for a possible hysteresis effect from 1985 to 1990. (This is the hypothesis that the overvalued exchange rate in the 1980s had a permanent effect in increasing imports and reducing exports; see Krugman and Baldwin, 1987.) Blecker found that autonomous imports grew at about 1.2 percent per annum from 1977 to 1985 and at about 3.2 percent from 1985 to 1990. The income elasticity of demand for imports was 2.68 when no time trend was included, but was 2.03 when it was present. When the first differences were used, the constant (which corresponds to the time trend in the log-level specification) was statistically insignificant.

Confining our attention to the estimates without the time trend, Blecker found that the ratio of the import to export elasticities was 0.62, a result remarkably close to the ratio found by Houthakker and Magee for the period 1951–66. Consequently, the relatively slow growth performance of the United States vis-à-vis the rest of the world has proved a persistent phenomenon. He also found some evidence for a hysteresis effect using the log-level specification, but not when first differences were used.

There is no doubt that the years 1983 and 1984 saw a very rapid increase in the growth of imports that may have had a hysteresis effect. The growth rate of imports in 1983 was 11 percent and in 1984, 21 percent. (However, to put this in context, 1976 and 1977 saw import growth rates of 18 percent and 11 percent, respectively.) But 1985 onward saw a return to more normal rates of import growth. A converse picture is found with respect to exports, where the period 1981 to 1985 saw a slowdown in export growth, with growth rates of −9 percent and −4 percent in 1982 and 1983, respectively. Nevertheless, 1987–89 saw a rapid turn around, with exports growing on average by 12.5 percent per annum. The inference to be drawn is that, in the short run, changes in the exchange rate may well have a significant effect on the balance of payments, with an overvaluation causing a significant deterioration in the current account. But this is not the same as saying that, in a long-run context, variations in the exchange rate can necessarily remove the balance of payments constraint. Indeed, as we shall see, there is evidence that over the postwar period as a whole the United States' trend rate of growth was close to its balance of payments growth rate.

Atesoglu (1995) found that, when estimating the import demand function separately over the period 1947–73 and over 1973–92, there was an increase in the income elasticity of demand in the second period. This offset an increase in the growth of exports in the second period and explained the slowdown in the United States' growth rate by 1 percentage point between the two periods.

Hieke (1997) used quarterly data from 1950(1) to 1990(4) and explicitly considered whether or not the import demand function was cointegrated. He also split the sample into a number of subperiods, including two subperiods with the break at 1966(4)/1967(1). Heike found that all the variables were $I(1)$. However, in both these subperiods, the import demand function was cointegrated, although, interestingly, it was not over the full period. He further found that $\hat{\pi}$ increased from 1.291 to 2.338 between the two periods, thus confirming the earlier results.

I estimated the import demand function in the traditional form where the volume of imports of goods and services was regressed on a domestic activity variable and a relative price term. Annual data were used for the period 1952–93. The variables were specified either in log-level form or in first differences of the log-levels. The domestic activity variable chosen was Gross Domestic Product (GDP). This was used in preference to, for example, total final expenditure because a significant proportion of imports are intermediate goods and hence the demand for them is likely to be related to total output. Several measures for domestic prices have been used in other studies, including the domestic expenditure deflator, the GDP deflator (although these include nontradable goods) and the price of industrial goods. Since much of international trade is intra-industry, I used the terms of trade (the ratio of the import price deflator to the export price deflator expressed in the domestic currency) as my measure.

The results of the DF tests reported in Table 9.2 would suggest that all the variables were $I(1)$. While for $\ln Y$ and $\ln M$, the F-test Φ_2 rejects the null hypothesis that $\mu = \rho = 0$, the standard t-statistic still does not reject the null of a unit root.

The position is more ambiguous once a break in the trend is allowed for in 1973. This year was just after the breakdown of Bretton Woods and when the first dramatic oil and commodity price rises occurred. In the next few years, the OECD countries were plunged into a very severe recession. The Perron tests, reported in Table 9.3, for $\ln Y$ and $\ln M$ suggest that the null hypothesis of a unit root cannot be rejected, but the decision is borderline. The τ value (i.e. the t-statistic used for testing the unit root hypothesis) for the logarithm of the terms of trade ($\ln TT$) is also low at -3.72, but no critical values are readily available because of the introduction of two structural breaks.

The results of the estimation of the log-level specification of the import demand function are reported in Table 9.4. The ADF test suggests that we cannot reject the null hypothesis of no cointegration. Nevertheless, the estimates of the income elasticity of demand are very similar to the first-difference estimates, although

Table 9.2 Dickey–Fuller unit root tests

$$\text{(i) } \Delta y_t = \mu + \beta t + \rho y_{t-1} + \sum c_i \Delta y_{t-i} + u_t$$
$$\text{(ii) } \Delta y_t = \mu + \rho y_{t-1} + \sum c_i \Delta y_{t-i} + u_t$$

	k	Equation (i)		Equation (ii)	
		τ_1	Φ_1	τ_2	Φ_2
10% critical value		*(−3.13)*	*(5.34)*	*(−2.57)*	*(3.78)*
United States					
ln Y	0	−1.60	1.69	−1.05	31.00*
ln M	0	−2.83	4.01	−0.21	16.72*
ln TT	0	−1.99	2.23	−1.06	0.58
Δln Y	0	−6.14*	18.92*	−6.16*	18.99*
Δln M	0	−6.05*	18.35*	−6.13*	18.80*
Δln TT	0	−5.52*	15.23*	−5.54*	15.35*
Japan					
ln Y	3	−1.01	3.09	−2.49	3.32
ln M	0	−1.56	4.39	−2.88*	17.21*
ln P	0	−2.34	2.93	−1.91	4.01*
Δln Y	1	−3.96*	7.92*	−2.48	3.32
Δln M	0	−7.34*	26.94*	−6.57*	21.65*
Δln P	0	−4.83*	11.28*	−4.92*	12.12*
United Kingdom					
ln Y	1	−2.59	4.02	−1.35	6.92*
ln M	1	−3.14*	4.95	−0.42	7.02*
ln TT	0	−2.36	2.99	−2.32	2.71
Δln Y	1	−5.07*	12.83*	−4.96*	12.32*
Δln M	1	−5.17*	13.39*	−5.24*	13.71*
Δln TT	0	−5.64*	15.92*	−5.56*	15.52*

Notes
Y, M, TT, and P are GDP, imports, the terms of trade, and the ratio of the GDP deflator to the import price deflator (expressed in a common currency).
* Significant at the 90% confidence level.

Equation	*Null hypothesis*	*Test static using DF distribution*
(i)	$\rho = 0$	τ_1 (*t*-ratio)
(i)	$\rho = \beta = 0$	Φ_1 (*F*-test)
(ii)	$\rho = 0$	τ_2 (*t*-ratio)
(ii)	$\rho = \mu = 0$	Φ_2 (*F*-test)

k equals number of lags.

the standard error is larger using first differences. In both specifications, there is a significant structural break in the income elasticity at 1973, with the post-1973 value significantly higher than the pre-1973 value in both regressions. It is interesting, however, that the Ramsey RESET test rejects the functional form of the log-level model but not of the first-difference specification. Moreover, there is no

Table 9.3 Perron's test for unit roots in the presence of a structural break at 1973–74

$$\text{(iii) } y_t = \mu + \beta t + \theta DU_t + \gamma DT_t + \tilde{y}_t$$
$$\text{(iv) } \Delta \tilde{y}_t = \rho \tilde{y}_{t-1} + \sum a_j D(T_b)_{t-j} + \sum b_i \tilde{y}_{t-i} + e_t$$

		Equation (iii)			Equation (iv)	
	$\hat{\mu}$	$\hat{\beta}$	$\hat{\theta}$	$\hat{\gamma}$	$\hat{\rho}$	τ_c
United States						
ln Y	14.334	0.035	0.179	−0.009	−0.502	
	(1216.60)	(38.85)	(4.94)	(−6.89)	(−3.56)	(−3.96)
ln M	11.007	0.064	—	−0.004	−0.399	
	(367.25)	(27.84)		(−2.59)	(−3.20)	(−3.65)[a]
ln TT	−0.106	−0.007	−0.715/0.355[b]	0.037	−0.471	
	(−7.36)	(−5.21)	(−5.20)/(11.64)	(6.83)	(−3.72)	(n.a.)
Japan						
ln Y	10.304	0.092	1.093	−0.053	0.422	
	(738.40)	(86.69)	(25.53)	(−2.44)	(−3.67)	(−3.96)
ln M	6.982	0.134	2.001	−0.095	−0.643	
	(161.67)	(40.84)	(15.00)	(−19.00)	(−4.22)	(−3.96)
ln P	Not applicable (see text)					
United Kingdom						
ln Y	10.177	0.024	0.110	−0.006	−0.422	
	(1076.20)	(32.86)	(3.77)	(−5.65)	(−3.95)	(−3.96)
ln M	No statistically significant break					
ln TT	Not applicable (see text)					

Notes
a Second term of equation (iv) is omitted as DU_t is not statistically significant in (iii).
b There are break points at 1973 and 1980.
τ_c is the critical value at the 10% significance level.
n.a. = not available.

statistically significant serial correlation when first differences are used, although this is not true of the log-level specification. The low Durbin–Watson statistic is further confirmation that the log-level specification is not cointegrated.

The balance of payments equilibrium growth rate (defined as $y_b = x/\hat{\pi}$) over the period 1952–73 was 2.88 percent per annum (calculated using the first-differences estimate of π), which compares with the actual growth rate of 3.36 percent. y_b for the period 1973–92 was 2.34 percent, which is almost identical to the actual growth rate of 2.29 percent. Thus, the actual growth of output was very close to the balance of payments equilibrium growth rate. These results confirm those of the other studies, which are summarized in Table 9.5, where there are also close correspondences between y and y_b.

I also tested to see whether there was any statistically significant difference between the $\hat{\pi}$ and π'.[3] It is noticeable that there was only a significant difference (for both periods) when the estimates were from log-level specifications of McCombie in this chapter and Blecker (1992), which, it will be remembered, may be misleading because of the non-cointegration. (Neither the use of an instrumental

Table 9.4 Regression results of import demand functions

(v) $\ln M = a_1 + a_2 DU + a_3 \ln Y + a_4 \ln YD + a_5 \ln TT + u_t$
(vi) $\Delta \ln M = a_3 \Delta \ln Y + a_4 \Delta \ln YD + a_5 \Delta \ln TT + u_t$

	United States		Japan		United Kingdom	
	(v)	(vi)	(v)	(vi)	(v)	(vi)
$\hat{a}_1$	14.687	—	−5.663	—	−9.650	—
	(−15.93)		(−7.08)		(−17.48)	
$\hat{a}_2$	−7.186	—	6.558	—	−5.473	—
	(−4.46)		(5.47)		(−5.64)	
$\hat{a}_3$	1.789	1.827	1.264	1.474	1.948	2.082
	(27.91)	(8.93)	(19.06)	(6.15)	(36.88)	(11.31)
$\hat{a}_4$	0.482	0.633	−0.522	—	0.510	—
	(4.48)	(1.99)	(−5.49)		(5.68)	
$\hat{a}_5$	−0.380	−0.277	−0.322	−0.113	0.131	0.102
	(−1.85)	(−1.74)	(−3.27)	(−0.82)	(0.88)	(0.71)
$\hat{\pi}_1$	1.789	1.827	1.264		1.948	
	(27.91)	(8.93)	(19.04)		(36.88)	
				1.474[a]		2.082[a]
				(6.15)		(11.31)
$\hat{\pi}_2$	2.271	2.460	0.742		2.458	
	(27.712)	(10.08)	(6.38)		(27.70)	
$\bar{R}^2$	0.994	n.a.	0.993	n.a.	0.996	n.a.
SER	0.054	0.037	0.089	0.102	0.033	0.030
Diagnostics						
A. DW	0.471	2.059	1.411	2.443	0.849	2.406
B. Ser. corr.	25.600	0.048	2.845	2.955	12.871	2.854
	(0.00)	(0.83)	(0.09)	(0.09)	(0.00)	(0.09)
C. RESET	13.740	1.199	1.145	0.866	10.547	0.842
	(0.00)	(0.29)	(0.285)	(0.352)	(0.00)	(0.36)
D. Normality	0.490	0.667	0.502	29.562	0.900	0.348
	(0.78)	(0.72)	(0.78)	(0.00)	(0.64)	(0.84)
E. Het.	1.409	0.123	0.450	0.340	0.547	1.146
	(0.24)	(0.73)	(0.51)	(0.56)	(0.46)	(0.28)
F. τ	−2.73	—	−5.08	—	−3.09	—
k	1	—	0	—	0	—

Source: OECD National Accounts (various years).

Notes
In the case of Japan, $\ln TT$ is $\ln P$, the logarithm of the GDP deflator to the import price deflator.
$\hat{\pi}_1$ and $\hat{\pi}_2$ are the estimates of the income elasticity of demand for imports over the periods 1952–73 and 1973–93, respectively.
a $\hat{\pi}$ is the estimate for the period 1952–93.
n.a. = not applicable. The OLS R^2 does not have its usual interpretation when there is no intercept.
A: Durbin–Watson statistic; B: Lagrange multiplier test of residual serial correlation ($\chi^2(1)$); C: Ramsey's RESET test using the square of the fitted values ($\chi^2(1)$); D: Bera-Jarque LM test for normality based on a test of skewness and kurtosis of residuals ($\chi^2(2)$); E: Based on the regression of squared residuals on squared fitted values ($\chi^2(1)$); F: τ is the t-value of the ADF testing the null hypothesis of no cointegration, and k is the number of lags.
B–E: Figures in parentheses are p values, elsewhere they are t statistics.

Table 9.5 The United States' balance of payments equilibrium growth rates and associated statistics

Study	Data	Method	Period	$\hat{\pi}$	π'	$|t|$	y	y_b
McCombie	Ann. ln	AR(1)	1952–73	1.78	1.49	2.59*	3.36	2.88
present	Ann. Δln	OLS	1952–73	1.83	1.49	1.66	3.36	2.80
study	Ann. ln	AR(1)	1974–93	2.42	2.51	0.67	2.29	2.11
	Ann. Δln	OLS	1974–93	2.46	2.51	0.20	2.29	2.34
Hieke	Quart. ln	OLS	1950–66	1.29	1.23	n.a.	3.87	3.67
(1997)	Quart. ln	OLS	1967–90	2.34	2.30	n.a.	2.54	2.50
	Quart. ln	OLS	1967–86	2.44	1.88	n.a.	2.63	2.04
Atesoglu	Ann. Δln	OLS	1947–73	1.32	1.49	0.36	3.36	3.88
(1995)[a]	Ann. Δln	OLS	1974–92	2.40	2.51	0.21	2.29	2.39
Atesoglu	Ann. Δln	OLS	1955–90	1.74	1.75	0.04	3.02	3.03
(1993)[a]	Ann. Δln	TSLS	1955–90	1.94	1.75	0.65	3.02	2.72
Andersen (1993)	Ann. ECM	OLS	1960–90	2.00	1.97	n.a.	3.00	2.95
Blecker	Quart. ln	OLS	1977–90	2.68	2.02	8.56*	2.70	2.03
(1992)	Quart. ln	OLS[b]	1977–90	2.85	2.02	7.50*	2.70	1.92
	Quart. Δln	OLS	1977–90	2.07	2.02	0.13	2.70	2.63
	Quart. Δln	OLS[b]	1977–90	2.08	2.02	0.16	2.70	2.63

Notes
a The import demand function includes a constant.
b Includes dummy variable to allow for a shift in the intercept post-1985 period.
$\pi' = x/y$; $y_b = x/\hat{\pi}$. $|t|$ is the absolute value of the t statistic that tests whether $\hat{\pi}$ and π' are statistically significant. * denotes that this is the case at the 95% confidence level.
Ann. is annual and Quart. is quarterly data.
ECM is error correction model.

variable approach nor, in the log-level specification, the exact ML method with an AR error structure to correct for autocorrelation made any great difference compared with the OLS results. This is the case for both the results of the United States and those of the other countries reported in Table 9.4.) The use of first differences, however, over comparable periods suggests that there is no statistically significant difference between $\hat{\pi}$ and π'. These results suggest that in the long run the United States grew at its balance of payments equilibrium growth rate, in spite of running large balance of payments deficits for a number of years. This is perhaps not surprising, since McCombie and Thirlwall (1997a) have shown that what would be considered a substantial current account deficit (of, say, 4 or 5 percent of GDP) has little effect in raising the balance of payments equilibrium growth rate.

I discussed earlier Atesoglu's procedure of regressing y on y_b using essentially a 15-year moving average as a test of whether a country was balance of payments constrained for the whole period. The use of a rolling regression is a useful procedure for examining the stability of the estimated coefficients, and this suggests a modification of Atesoglu's test. An advantage of this modification is that it may be used to determine periods when a country's growth rate is statistically significantly greater than its balance of payments equilibrium growth rate. The advantage of using a rolling regression is that it smooths out the influence of the extreme observations. The large annual variations in the growth of US imports and exports have already been noted. Since the law is a long-run relationship, there is little point in estimating the balance of payments equilibrium growth rate for only a single year and comparing it with the actual growth rate for that year – almost invariably there will be marked differences, although this has no bearing on whether or not there is a long-run balance of payments constraint.

On the other hand, the use of the rolling regression helps identify the crucial years when the country ceases to be balance of payments constrained, and vice versa. This argument may be made clearer by Table 9.6. Following Atesoglu, a 15-year window was used. The variable y in Table 9.6 is defined as the mean growth of income over each of the overlapping 15-year subperiods and y_b is the balance of payments equilibrium growth rate. The income elasticities of demand

Table 9.6 The actual and balance of payments equilibrium growth rates: the United States, 1953–93

Period[a]	y	y_b	$\hat{\pi}$	π'	$|t|$	$CA/Y(\%)$
1953–67	3.46	2.60	1.49	1.12	1.89	—
1954–68	3.40	2.63	1.53	1.18	1.62	—
1955–69	3.73	3.03	1.50	1.22	1.29	—
1956–70	3.27	3.21	1.52	1.50	0.10	−0.38
1957–71	3.30	2.75	1.51	1.26	1.06	−0.39
1958–72	3.49	2.59	1.66	1.23	1.75	−0.39
1959–73	3.85	3.54	1.80	1.66	0.62	−0.36
1960–74	3.41	3.83	1.82	2.03	0.88	−0.59
1961–75	3.21	3.20	1.92	1.91	0.02	−0.35
1962–76	3.37	2.99	2.11	1.87	0.80	−0.34
1963–77	3.31	2.81	2.15	1.83	1.04	−0.30
1964–78	3.35	2.86	2.18	1.86	1.10	−0.30
1965–79	3.19	2.67	2.27	1.90	1.25	−0.29
1966–80	2.77	2.67	2.43	2.34	0.29	0.80
1967–81	2.53	2.53	2.44	2.44	0.00	0.16
1968–82	2.19	2.20	2.44	2.44	0.02	−0.37
1969–83	2.17	1.93	2.35	2.09	0.77	−1.31
1970–84	2.42	1.81	2.54	1.90	2.02	−2.64
1971–85	2.64	1.64	2.49	1.55	3.14*	−3.11
1972–86	2.64	1.76	2.51	1.67	2.77*	−3.55
1973–87	2.53	1.85	2.49	1.82	2.16*	−3.68
1974–88	2.46	1.83	2.45	1.81	1.89	−2.62
1975–89	2.69	1.97	2.37	1.73	2.03	−1.96
1976–90	2.84	2.30	2.30	1.86	1.87	−1.66
1977–91	2.48	2.55	2.15	2.21	0.27	−0.12
1978–92	2.35	2.75	2.12	2.49	1.65	−1.13
1979–93	2.24	2.42	2.27	2.45	0.82	−1.64

Note
a The period is inclusive giving 15 observations per period. *CA/Y* is the current account deficit expressed as a percentage of GDP measured in nominal terms in the terminal year. See notes to Table 9.5 for $|t|$ and *.

used to calculate y_b were estimated using the rolling regression with growth rate data, giving 27 separate estimates of π in all.

The hypothetical balance of payments equilibrium income elasticity of demand (π') was also calculated in the usual manner and the *t*-test was used to determine whether or not there was any statistically significant difference between the two values at the 95 percent confidence level. As may be seen from Table 9.6, 1985 was the crucial year when the 15-year average growth of the United States became significantly greater than its balance of payments equilibrium growth rate. In other, words, $\hat{\pi}$ and π' do not differ significantly for the period 1970–84, whereas they do for 1971–85. It is not coincidental that 1985 was the period when the US current account moved into a substantial deficit of over 3 percent of GDP. The table indicates that for much of the 1980s the United States was growing considerably faster than its balance of payments equilibrium growth rate.

This was, however, only a temporary phenomenon and, by the early 1990s, the US 15-year average was again not significantly different from its balance of payments equilibrium growth rate. This confirms our earlier result that, over the longer period 1974–93, the growth of the United States did not significantly differ from its balance of payments equilibrium growth rate. Heike (1997) also found that, for the subperiod 1967–86, there was a discrepancy between y (2.63 percent) and y_b (2.04 percent) (see Table 9.5), whereas over the longer period 1967–90 the two growth rates were almost identical.[4]

These results demonstrate once again the importance of the distinction between the long and the short run in discussing the balance of payments equilibrium growth rate. It should be noted that these results differ somewhat from those of Atesoglu, who implicitly finds the periods ending 1970 through to 1973 are when the United States is not balance of payments constrained (see note 2). This is because the regression of y on y_b requires that these periods be omitted from the regression for the slope coefficient not to be significantly different from unity. The explanation for the difference between this and my results is that Atesoglu uses a single value of the income elasticity of demand for imports ($\hat{\pi} = 1.914$) in calculating the various values of y_b.

A study by Godley and Milberg (1994) that carefully examined the capital account of the United States suggests that, in the early 1990s, the United States faced a potentially serious balance of payments constraint. They describe the possible impact of this balance of payment constraint as follows:

> While quite substantial changes in policy are now required to set the U.S. primary deficit on an acceptable path, the scale of the problem, and measures which are required, will become much larger – if things are allowed to drift. If the current account deficit grew to 4–5 percent of GDP, and net foreign indebtness to 40 percent, the policy initiatives then necessary would be twice as draconian as they are now. If the United States were driven to adopt the deflationary solution, unemployment would surely be driven up beyond the levels that obtain in Europe at present. These could, in turn, translate into another era of depression throughout the world.
>
> (Godley and Milberg, 1994, p. 46)

The case of Japan

Japan was undoubtedly the early postwar economic growth success story, and the reasons for the success are many and varied. In the early postwar years, the deliberate borrowing of technology from the advanced countries through, for example, the Japanese productivity missions to the United States and Europe was of unquestionable importance. The intervention in industry and guidance from the government through such organizations as MITI have often been cited as major factors in Japan's economic success, notwithstanding recent studies that attempt to play down the role of state intervention (see Boltho, 1985, for a discussion of this debate and criticism of the latter position). There was also a deliberate development strategy that was not based on static comparative advantage, but on the development of industries that required intensive use of capital and technology. One significant element of the growth strategy was the emphasis placed on the role of international trade. On the import side, this consisted of explicit protectionism in the form of tariffs and quotas in the 1950s and 1960s to protect what were seen as the strategic industries, followed in later years by the more subtle "administrative protection." On the export side, foreign markets were targeted and a major objective was to increase market share in foreign markets. However, it should be emphasized that Japan cannot be viewed as a good example of conventional "export-led growth," at least through the workings solely of the Harrod foreign trade multiplier, if only because of the relatively low share of exports in GDP. In 1952, exports, in current prices, were less than 5 percent of Japan's GDP and, although export growth rapidly outstripped the growth of output, 40 years later its share had only doubled to 10 percent. The importance of the export strategy was rather that it made possible the growth of output of key industries that were high tech (for their day) at a more rapid rate than could have been warranted by the growth of the domestic market. Japan demonstrates the successful working of the Hicks supermultiplier (McCombie and Thirlwall, 1994, ch. 6). The rapid growth of exports, by preventing a balance of payments crisis, allowed a rapid and uninterrupted rate of domestic capital accumulation and product innovation and development.

The ADF tests in Table 9.2 suggest that $\ln Y$ and $\ln P^5$ are $I(1)$. However, $\ln M$ is $I(0)$ since Φ_2 is statistically significant and so also is the estimate of ρ by the asymptotic standard t-statistic (although this result must be treated with some caution). The Perron test shows that, after allowing for a structural shift, as in the case of the United States, $\ln Y$ and $\ln M$ are borderline $I(0)/I(1)$ (Table 9.2). The problem with the logarithm of the relative prices is that there are several structural breaks in its trend. Japan experienced a secular decline in the logarithm of its relative prices from 1952 until 1972, when there was a marked increase associated with the commodity and oil price rises. This reversal peaked in 1975, after which there was a decline until about 1978. After this year, there was another dramatic rise until about 1982, after which the secular decline resumed. Because of this multiplicity of structural breaks, Perron's procedure was not followed.

Given the low power of the ADF tests, I again regressed the import demand functions in both log-levels and first differences and the results are reported in Table 9.3.

Table 9.7 Japan's balance of payments equilibrium growth rates and associated statistics

Period	Data	y	y_b	x	$\hat{\pi}$	π'	$|t|$
1952–73	ln	8.71	10.26	12.97	1.264	1.489	3.39*
1974–93	ln	3.52	8.84	6.56	0.742	1.864	9.65*
1952–73[a]	ln	8.71	10.15[b]	12.97	n.a.	n.a.	n.a.
1974–93[a]	ln	3.52	6.18[b]	6.56	n.a.	n.a.	n.a.
1952–93	Δln	6.17	6.67	9.83	1.474	1.593	0.50

Notes
a Regression includes a time trend and a dummy to allow for a structural change in the time trend over the post-1973 period.
b $y_b = (x - \hat{m}_0)/\hat{\pi}^*$ where $\hat{m}_0$ is the coefficient of the time trend, expressed as a percentage growth rate.
* Statistically significant at the 95% confidence level.
n.a. The test of the hypothesis that $\hat{\pi} = \pi'$ is not applicable.

Considering first the log-level specification, the critical value of the DF τ statistic suggests that the null hypothesis of no cointegration is rejected. There is also a similarity with the US results in that there is a statistically significant structural shift in the income elasticity of demand after 1973. From Tables 9.4 and 9.7, it may be seen that the value of $\hat{\pi}$ is 1.264 for 1952–73, which is low compared with other countries but consistent with other estimates for the early postwar period (Houthakker and Magee's [1969] estimate is 1.213). However, the value for 1974–93 seems surprisingly low at 0.742. It may be seen also that the average balance of payments equilibrium growth rate over the years 1954 to 1973 was 10.26 percent per annum, which exceeds the actual growth rate of 8.71 percent. There is a statistically significant difference between $\hat{\pi}$ (1.264) and π' (1.489), with an absolute t-statistic value of 3.39. In the second period, 1974–93, the difference between y and y_b is even more marked – namely, 3.52 and 8.84 percent per annum. Not surprisingly, the difference between $\hat{\pi}$ (0.742) and π' (1.864) is also statistically significant.

When a time trend is introduced, no significant structural break is found in the trend at 1973, but there is a small structural break in the estimate of the income elasticity of demand. (The full results are not reported here.) The estimate for 1952–73 is 1.644 and for 1974–93 is 1.661 (which is over double the value obtained when no time trend is included). There is a statistically significant autonomous decline of imports of 3.72 percent per annum. An inclusion of a time-trend in the log-level specification (and a constant in the growth rate specification) of the import demand function necessitates a slightly different interpretation of the law. The exogenous growth rate of imports (m_0) derived from these specifications should be interpreted as the growth (which may be negative) due to the relative nonprice competitiveness of the country concerned. In these circumstances, we should expect relatively little variation between countries in the associated estimate of the income elasticity of demand for imports (which we shall denote by π^*). The balance of payments equilibrium growth rate is now given by $y_b = (x - m_0)/\pi^*$. The use of this equation and these estimates still gives Japan's balance of payments equilibrium growth rate well in excess of its actual growth rate (see Table 9.7).

The use of first differences, without a constant term, shows that there is no statistically significant structural break at 1973, suggesting that the choice of specification – that is, whether to use first differences or log-levels – is important. The estimated income elasticity is 1.474, which gives a value of y_b of 6.67 percent per annum over the period 1952–93 (compared with a value for y of 6.17 percent). There is, however, perhaps surprisingly, no statistical difference between $\hat{\pi}$ and π' (the absolute value of the *t*-statistic is 0.50). Introducing a constant to capture the autonomous growth of imports gives a value of -2.88 percent per annum, but this is not statistically significantly different from zero.

Thus, to conclude, the evidence is somewhat mixed. The growth of Japan is always below its balance of payments equilibrium growth rate, which is consistent with Japan's accumulation of current account surpluses over the postwar period. Nevertheless, in the case of the first-difference specification, the difference between y and y_b is, perhaps surprisingly, not statistically significant. The use of log-levels always gives a significant difference between y and y_b.

The case of the United Kingdom

The United Kingdom has often been seen as balance of payments constrained for much of the postwar period. Under the fixed exchange rate system prior to 1972, the United Kingdom experienced a typical "stop-go" growth pattern, with periodic sterling crises at the height of a boom leading to the rapid introduction of deflationary policies. The problems of UK macroeconomic policy at this time have been cogently discussed by Kaldor (1971). The year 1976 saw a massive sterling crisis and the calling in of the International Monetary Fund (IMF). The deflationary policies that were insisted on by the IMF as a condition of support for sterling led to a marked slowdown in growth, so that the United Kingdom could be better described as policy-constrained rather than balance of payments constrained (see McCombie 1993 and Chapter 5). This persisted with the introduction of the deflationary monetary policies of the Thatcher government in 1979, and it is only since the late 1980s that the balance of payments has posed problems once again.

As for the empirical estimates, the DF/ADF tests reported in Table 9.1 suggest that $\ln Y$, $\ln M$, and $\ln TT$ are all $I(1)$. Although the F-test, Φ_2, rejects the hypothesis that $\rho = \mu = 0$, the standard *t*-statistic does not reject the hypothesis that $\rho = 0$.

From Table 9.3, it may be seen that Perron's test allowing for a structural break suggests that $\ln Y$ is $I(0)$. There was no statistically significant break in the $\ln M$ series. The $\ln TT$ series suffers from the problem, noted earlier with respect to Japan, that there are a number of structural breaks associated with the 1973–74 and 1979 oil price rises. Bearing in mind, once again, the low power of these tests, I estimated a conventional import demand function in log-level form. The results are reported in Table 9.4. I found a significant structural break with the

Table 9.8 The United Kingdom's balance of payments equilibrium growth
            rates and associated statistics

Period	Data	y	y_b	x	$\hat{\pi}$	π'	$|t|$
1952–73	ln	2.42	2.37	4.62	1.948	1.909	0.74
1974–93	ln	1.35	1.46	3.58	2.458	2.652	2.18*
1952–73[a]	ln	2.42	2.22[b]	4.62	n.a.	n.a.	n.a.
1974–93[a]	ln	1.35	0.95[b]	3.58	n.a.	n.a.	n.a.
1952–93	Δln	1.90	1.97	4.11	2.082	2.169	0.45

See Table 9.7 for explanatory notes.

import income elasticity increasing from 1.948 over the period 1952–73 to 2.458
in 1974–93.

The null hypothesis of no cointegration was not rejected by the DF statistic, so
some care must be taken in interpreting the results. The values for y, y_b, x, $\hat{\pi}$,
and π' are reported in Table 9.8, together with the absolute value of the t-statistic
based on the null hypothesis that $\hat{\pi} = \pi$. It can be seen that in both periods y
and y_b are close together. $\hat{\pi}$ and π' are not statistically different over the period
1952–73, but this is not the case in the post-1973 period, suggesting that y_b is
significantly greater than y, which is to be expected if the United Kingdom were
policy-constrained.

A time trend, t, was included, together with a dummy time trend taking a
value of zero for the period 1952–73 and one for the period 1974–93. Both time
trends proved statistically significant and the autonomous growth rates of imports
were 1.45 percent per annum and 2.23 percent per annum for the two respective
periods. (The full results are not reported here.) The value of the income elasticity
of demand for imports fell to 1.423. From 1952 to 1973, y_b at 2.22 percent per
annum is virtually the same as the actual growth rate. The balance of payments
equilibrium growth rate for the post-1973 period is substantially lower than the
actual growth rate, contradicting the results earlier. It should be noted that the
estimate of 0.95 percent per annum for y_b is close to the value found by Turner
(1988) (see McCombie and Thirlwall, 1994, ch. 10).

When first differences are used, which is the preferred specification, no statistically significant structural shift in the income elasticity of demand is found in the
post-1973 period, and the estimates suggest that y and y_b were very close over the
whole postwar period. There was no statistically significant difference between π
and π'.

Conclusions

I have reviewed some of the tests of the balance of payments equilibrium growth
hypothesis and have presented some further empirical evidence for the United
States, Japan, and the United Kingdom. I conclude that, over much of the postwar
period, the growth rates of the United States and the United Kingdom were close
to their balance of payments equilibrium growth rates. The evidence suggests that

Japan, on the other hand, grew more slowly than its balance of payments equilibrium growth rate, which is consistent with the large current account surpluses it
was acquiring over much of the postwar period. However, when its import elasticity of demand was estimated using first differences, the possibility that even
Japan was growing near its balance of payment equilibrium growth rate cannot be
ruled out.

Notes

1 The result of regressing y_b on y using Atesoglu's data is:

$$y_b = 1.899 + 0.409y \quad R^2 = 0.200$$
$$\quad\;(3.39) \quad (2.18)$$

and the slope coefficient differs significantly from unity at the 95 percent confidence
level. (Atesoglu similarly finds that the slope coefficient is significantly different from
unity when y is regressed on y_b.)
   Constraining the intercept to zero gives the result:

$$y_b = 1.037y.$$
$$\quad(32.00)$$

(The R^2 is not reported as it does not have its conventional meaning when there is no
intercept in the regression.) The slope coefficient now does not differ significantly from
unity.
   Atesoglu (1993) found that when y is regressed on y_b with an intercept present, but with
the separate periods ending with 1970 to 1973 omitted, the slope coefficient also is not
significantly different from unity. "These findings provide strong support for Thirlwall's
Law" (Atesolglu, 1993, p. 512).
2 Strictly speaking, the United States could grow no faster than the growth of its major
trading partners, weighted by the United States' export shares in these markets. However,
the two measures are highly correlated.
3 It will be recalled that π' is the hypothetical income elasticity of demand for imports
calculated by $\pi' = x/y$.
4 I am grateful to Hubert Hieke for a helpful discussion about this point and also about
Atesoglu's test.
5 Since, in the case of Japan, imports have a large component of raw materials, I used the
GDP price deflator as a proxy for domestic prices.

10 The 45°-rule revisited*

P. S. Andersen

Introduction

A number of recent studies have dealt with the 45°-rule (also referred to as Harrod's foreign trade multiplier or Thirlwall's Law) which compares actual demand (or real output) growth ($d\hat{d}_i$) with a warranted rate ($d\hat{d}^*$) defined so as to keep the external current account in equilibrium without changes in the real effective exchange rate. Thirlwall (1979) uses a rank correlation test between $d\hat{d}_i$ and $d\hat{d}^*$ and finds a significant value. McCombie (1989) relies on a more indirect test by comparing import elasticities obtained from time-series regressions with the import elasticities required to keep the current account in balance. For the period 1954–73 he finds that for 11 out of 15 countries the two elasticities are not significantly different, and Bairam (1990), applying the same test to 15 low-income countries for the period 1961–85, finds the 45°-rule confirmed except for 4 oil exporting countries. Krugman (1989) compares $d\hat{d}_i$ with $d\hat{d}^*$ in a cross-country regression for 13 countries over the period 1955–65 and finds an R^2 of 0.75, with most observations closely clustered around a 45°-line. However, when Krugman repeats this exercise for the period 1970–86 on the basis of revised elasticity estimates and a smaller country sample, the R^2 falls to only 0.32. McGregor and Swales (1991) obtain a rather higher R^2 for the same period using a sample of 19 countries, but the regression coefficient is significantly below the expected value of unity and the intercept term is significant. By suppressing the latter Bairam (1988) estimates a regression coefficient near unity but only when the calculation of $d\hat{d}^*$ is based on actual rather than estimated values for exports.

These last results suggest that while the 45°-rule is useful as a condition for balanced growth, it is less useful in describing actual developments, especially under a regime of flexible exchange rates. Indeed, external imbalances in many countries are non-stationary or show a distinct time trend (Andersen, 1990) and it is well known that real exchange rates have not been constant. Moreover, most of the elasticities presented in the literature are based on merchandise trade only (or confined to manufactured goods), whereas total trade flows include a rising share of

* First published in *Applied Economics*, October 1993.

services and non-factor payments. It might also be argued that some of the earlier samples were rather small and that the results proved very sensitive to the inclusion (or exclusion) of extreme observations, usually the United States and Japan.

The purpose of this chapter is to provide a more up-to-date and extensive evaluation of the 45°-rule. To achieve this, export and import equations for 16 industrial countries were estimated using annual national accounts data for the period 1960–90, and then the income elasticities were applied to calculate warranted growth rates for various subperiods, and assess changes in countries' external positions.

Theoretical model

Most empirical estimates of export and import equations are made on the assumption that exports and imports are imperfect substitutes for domestic goods and services and rely on the following two equations in describing country i's trade with the rest of the world (Goldstein and Khan, 1985):

$$M_i = f(DD_i, P_i, P_m E) \tag{10.1}$$

and

$$X_i = g(DD_w, P_w, P_x/E),$$

where M_i is the volume of imports by country i, X_i the volume of exports from country i, DD_i the domestic demand in country i, in current prices, DD_w the domestic demand in the rest of the world, in current prices, P_i the domestic demand deflator in country i, P_w the domestic demand deflator in the rest of the world, P_m the import prices measured in the currency of the rest of the world, P_x the export prices measured in the currency of country i and E is the exchange rate measured in units of country i's currency and approximated by the effective exchange rate.

Assuming further that the two equations are homogeneous of degree zero in nominal income and prices and can be approximated by a log-linear specification, equation (10.1) can be rewritten as

$$\begin{aligned} m_i &= a_1 dd_i + a_2[p_i - (p_m + e)], \\ x_i &= a_3 dd_w + a_4[p_w - (p_x - e)] \\ &\text{with } a_i \geq 0 \quad \text{for } i = 1 \dots 4. \end{aligned} \tag{10.2}$$

Small letters are used to denote logs and in the case of *dd, m* and *x* also denote variables in real terms. Differentiating the two equations with respect to time and denoting percentage rates of change by '$\hat{\ }$' equation (10.2) becomes

$$\begin{aligned} \hat{m}_i &= a_1 \hat{dd}_i + a_2(\hat{p}_i - \hat{p}_m - \hat{e}), \\ \hat{x}_i &= a_3 \hat{dd}_w + a_4(\hat{p}_w - \hat{p}_x + \hat{e}). \end{aligned} \tag{10.3}$$

If the current external account is initially in equilibrium, maintenance of equilibrium requires $\hat{m}_i + \hat{p}_m = \hat{x}_i + \hat{p}_x - \hat{e}$ or

$$(a_3 d\hat{d}_w - a_1 d\hat{d}_i) = a_2(\hat{p}_i - \hat{p}_m - \hat{e}) - a_4(\hat{p}_w - \hat{p}_x + \hat{e})$$
$$+ \hat{p}_m - \hat{p}_x + \hat{e} \tag{10.4}$$

but on the further assumption that $\hat{p}_i = \hat{p}_x$ and $\hat{p}_m = \hat{p}_w$, equation (10.4) can be simplified to

$$(a_3 d\hat{d}_w - a_1 d\hat{d}_i) = (a_2 + a_4 - 1)\hat{e}', \tag{10.5}$$

where e' is the real effective exchange rate measured as $P_i/(P_w E)$ or $P_x/P_m \cdot E$.[1]

The left-hand side of equation (10.5) may be restated as

$$d\hat{d}_i/d\hat{d}_w = a_3/a_1 \quad \text{or} \quad d\hat{d}_i = d\hat{d}_w a_3/a_1 = d\hat{a}^* \tag{10.6}$$

with $d\hat{a}^*$ to be interpreted as the 'warranted rate' of domestic demand growth, that is, the rate of 'home' *DD* growth consistent with external balance and real exchange rate stability. Hence, for $a_3 > a_1$ country *i* can grow faster than the rest of the world without encountering any external problems, while for $a_3 < a_1$ country *i* will have to keep domestic demand growth below that of the rest of the world to avoid a rising external deficit. In both cases satisfaction of equation (10.6) implies that in a graph with actual and warranted demand growth measured along the two axes, $d\hat{d}_i$ and $d\hat{a}^*$ would be close to the 45°-line (see Krugman, 1989).

Specification and data

Before discussing the empirical results, a few words about the specification and the data used. Since equation (10.6) essentially refers to a long-run phenomenon and is unlikely to be satisfied on a year-to-year basis, the elasticities were estimated with the long-term relations given in equation (10.2) as the co-integration equations in the two-step procedure proposed by Engle and Granger (1987). In a second step, these were then complemented by error-correction equations to capture the short-run dynamics and assess the adjustment process.

dd_i was measured as total domestic demand in country *i* and dd_w as a trade-weighted average of domestic demand in the other countries included in the sample. $p_i - (p_m + e)$ was measured by the ratio between the domestic demand deflator and the import deflator and $p_w - (p_x - e)$ by relative unit labour costs. While the activity variable in the export equation is uncontroversial, the relative price variable should ideally have been measured by a weighted average of export prices and home market prices in the other countries relative to the export price of country *i*, and our only excuse for using relative unit labour costs is that this variable is more readily available.[2] As regards the import equation, several alternative specifications might be considered depending on the use of imported goods and services. For final goods the appropriate determinants are domestic demand and the ratio between the deflator for domestic output sold in the domestic market and import prices. In the case of intermediate goods a better measure of activity would be total demand (i.e. including exports), while relative prices might be proxied by some measure of domestic costs over import prices. A breakdown of imports into final and intermediate goods and services is, however, not available in the national accounts and a further drawback is that the alternative measures of $p_i - (p_m + e)$ are not obtained when the homogeneity assumption is imposed on equation (10.1). On the other hand, when dd_i and $p_i - (p_m + e)$ are measured as mentioned earlier, there is a risk of biased coefficients.[3]

Empirical results

Table 10.1 shows the estimated trade elasticities with income elasticity ratios largely in line with the main findings of the literature (see Houthakker and Magee, 1969; Goldstein and Khan, 1985): the United States[4] and the United Kingdom have low elasticity ratios (in both cases reflecting a low export elasticity combined with a high import elasticity), while Japan is at the other extreme, largely due to a very high export elasticity. For Germany the ratio is estimated near unity, while Canada, France and Italy appear to be more favourably placed. For some of the smaller countries the ratios deviate rather markedly from earlier consensus estimates. Thus, for The Netherlands and Switzerland the ratio is estimated at around one, compared with earlier values of 0.8–0.9, whereas for Australia, Austria, Denmark and Sweden our estimates may be on the low side. On average, however, the use of national accounts as opposed to trade data seems to have only a marginal effect on the ratio.

By contrast, the long-run price elasticities are in many cases significantly different from those reported elsewhere. A common finding in the literature is that the Marshall–Lerner condition is satisfied, whereas in Table 10.1 it just holds for only 2 of the 16 countries and in several cases neither exports nor imports were significantly influenced by relative price changes or the latter had only a transitory effect.[5] For a few of the countries with low price elasticities, the short-run coefficients obtained from the error-correction equations are somewhat higher, but for the 16 countries there is, on average, virtually no difference between the short- and long-run elasticities.

A second problem concerns the diagnostic statistics of the co-integration and error-correction equations.[6] The former yield R^2 values of 0.97 or higher and with a few exceptions also satisfy the Bhargava (1986) condition for co-integration. However, for most countries the Dickey and Fuller (1979) condition for multivariate regressions (Engle and Yoo, 1987) is not satisfied and for several countries the error-correction terms in the first-difference equations are rather low and in three cases not statistically significant.

To what extent are these unexpected results invalidating the model and the test of the 45°-rule? As regards the relative price elasticities, others (see Bairam, 1988) have also found low or insignificant elasticities. Moreover, as can be seen from equations (10.4) and (10.5), the validity of the 45°-rule is not dependent

Table 10.1 Long-run trade elasticities

Countries	Relative prices[a]			Domestic demand[b]			Diagnostic statistics[c]					
	$e_{X,RP}$	$e_{M,RP}$	Sum	$e_{X,DDW}$	$e_{M,DDi}$	Ratio	DW(X)	DW(M)	DF(X)	DF(M)	ECM(X)	ECM(M)
United States	−0.43	−0.17	−0.60 (−0.73)	1.34	2.00	0.67 (0.72)	0.26	0.51**	−1.43	−3.12	−0.22	−0.30***
Japan	−0.75	−0.21	−0.96 (−0.80)	3.82	1.25	3.05 (2.17)	0.45**	0.50**	−1.75	−2.05	−0.17*	−0.31**
Germany	−0.49[d]	−0.06[d]	−0.55[d] (−0.28)[d]	1.86	2.02	0.92 (1.04)	1.22***	1.20***	−3.42*	−3.50*	−0.61***	−0.38***
France	−0.18[d]	−0.22	−0.22 (−0.20)	2.25	1.83	1.23 (1.17)	0.21	0.78***	−1.89	−3.17	−0.15	−0.45***
United Kingdom	−0.12[d]		−0.12[d] (−0.22)[d]	1.42	1.81	0.78 (0.73)	0.88***	0.64***	−3.84*	−3.53*	−0.60***	−0.39***
Italy	−0.21[d]	−0.22	−0.22 (−0.09)	2.08	1.62	1.28 (1.28)	0.62***	0.51**	−2.22	−2.29	−0.26**	−0.34***
Canada	−0.18	−0.50	−0.68 (−0.40)	1.96	1.47	1.32 (1.05)	0.85***	1.18***	−4.30**	−5.81***	−0.38*	−0.53***
Australia	−0.32	−0.38	−0.70 (−1.06)	1.30	1.25	1.05 (1.61)	0.91***	0.83***	−3.26	−2.95	−0.46**	−0.33**
Austria	−0.53[d]	−0.33	−0.33 (−0.19)	2.30	1.85	1.25 (1.47)	0.49*	0.66***	−2.48	−2.31	−0.37***	−0.31**
Belgium	−0.09[d]	−0.17[d]	−0.26[d] (−0.25)[d]	1.89	1.82	1.04 (1.04)	0.71***	0.85***	−2.46	−2.73	−0.39***	−0.30*
Denmark	−0.41	−0.14	−0.55 (−0.23)	1.52	1.48	1.03 (1.33)	0.50**	0.95***	−1.22	−3.33	−0.14*	−0.40**
Finland	−0.23	−0.05	−0.28 (−0.53)	1.80	1.35	1.33 n.a.	0.36*	1.45***	−2.01	−3.98***	−0.25**	−0.67***
The Netherlands	−0.08[d]	−0.15[d]	−0.23[d] (−0.25)[d]	1.95	1.86	1.05 (0.89)	0.26	0.34*	−1.96	−2.42	−0.23**	−0.23**
Spain	−0.53	−0.23	−0.76 (−0.84)	2.94	1.89	1.55 n.a.	0.65**	0.46**	−2.25	−2.66	−0.47***	−0.32***
Sweden	−0.45	−0.10	−0.55 (−0.70)	1.55	1.75	0.90 (1.24)	1.22***	1.35***	−3.54*	−4.25***	−0.63***	−0.59***
Switzerland	−0.09[d]	−0.95	−0.95 (−0.18)	1.49	1.37	1.09 (0.78)	0.93***	0.75***	−3.41	−2.68	−0.39*	−0.27***
Average	−0.41	−0.29	−0.57 (−0.50)	1.97	1.65	1.22 (1.25)	—	—	—	—	−0.36	−0.38

Source: OECD National Accounts. Vol. 1.

Notes

   * Indicate 10% level of significance for one-tailed test.
   ** Indicate 5% level of significance for one-tailed test.
   *** Indicate 1% level of significance for one-tailed test.
   a Figures in brackets are the sum of the price elasticities obtained from the error-correction equation and RP refers to relative prices as defined in the text. For several countries coefficients of the correct sign were only obtained when relative prices were entered as first differences (second differences). These are marked with a 'd' and are not included in the sums or in the averages.
   b Figures in brackets are taken from Goldstein and Khan (1985).
   c DW refers to Durbin–Watson statistics for the export (DW(X)) and import (DW(M)) equations; DF to t-values for the Dickey–Fuller test applied to the export (DF(X)) and import (DF(M)) equations; and ECM to the coefficients of the error-correction terms in the export (ECM(X)) and import (ECM(M)) equations.

on satisfying the Marshall–Lerner condition. On the contrary, low relative price elasticities (or constant relative prices) make the 45°-rule look more plausible. Hence, unless the low relative price elasticities reflect measurement or specification errors there should be no bias to the income elasticities which are the crucial parameters for the 45°-rule. In fact, the ratios of the income elasticities proved robust to various specification changes.

The ambiguous results with respect to the co-integration conditions are far more serious to the validity of the model and the 45°-rule. The problem could be related to the weak response to relative price changes but the explanation is more likely to be found in the effects of variables not included in the model. In line with previous analysts (see Thirlwall, 1979; McCombie, 1992) it has been implicitly assumed that the estimated income elasticities also capture the effects of non-price competition and changes in the composition of exports and imports, whereas the absence of co-integration suggests that this assumption does not hold. Consequently, the model is misspecified and considering also the non-stationarity of the current account balances in most of the countries in the sample, the test of the 45°-rule could stop right here. Nonetheless, since the income elasticities ratios given in Table 10.1 are not very different from those used in earlier tests it seems relevant and appropriate to analyse the 45°-rule from different angles and search for further explanations.

Further evaluations of the 45°-rule

As a first step in explicitly testing the 45°-rule, the long-run elasticities were used in calculating warranted growth rates and in setting up Table 10.2. For the 1960–73 period $d\hat{d}$ and $d\hat{d}^*$ differed on average by 0.7 percentage points and by 1 point or less in all countries except Japan, Australia and Austria. In Australia, the positive growth differential was accompanied by a major improvement in the current account, while in Japan the effect of the growth differential mainly appeared as a real appreciation. Relatively, large differences between $d\hat{d}$ and $d\hat{d}^*$ were also recorded in Italy, Finland and Sweden. In the latter case the current external account improved by almost 3.5 per cent relative to GNP, whereas Italy experienced a deterioration and the same is true for Finland despite a depreciating exchange rate. Nevertheless, other countries with $d\hat{d}$ and $d\hat{d}^*$ close to the 45°-line saw major changes in their external accounts, though partly as a result of extreme positions in either the initial or the final year. Finally, the United States and the United Kingdom show small growth differentials accompanied by real depreciations and stable or slightly worsening external accounts, whereas Germany managed to keep the fall in its balance of payments (BP) to only 0.2 per cent despite a real appreciation of almost 3 per cent per year.

For the 1973–80 period, all countries except the United Kingdom and Canada experienced a deterioration in their terms of trade, and on average the current accounts declined by 2 per cent relative to GNP. The largest changes were concentrated among the smaller countries but in most cases as a result of terms-of-trade changes rather than excessive domestic demand growth. Among

Table 10.2 Actual and warranted demand growth and external developments (percentage change, annual rate)

Countries	1960–73					1973–80					1980–90				
	$d\hat{d}$	$d\hat{d}^*$	reer	tot	BP	$d\hat{d}$	$d\hat{d}^*$	reer	tot	BP	$d\hat{d}$	$d\hat{d}^*$	reer	tot	BP
United States	4.0	3.8	−2.9	−0.1	−0.0	1.7	1.8	−1.3	−5.1	−0.2	3.1	1.9	−1.5	0.3	−2.0
Japan	9.7	13.1	2.2	−0.1	−0.5	2.7	5.9	0.5	−8.0	−1.0	4.1	8.0	2.6	1.3	2.3
Germany	4.5	4.7	2.9	0.9	−0.2	2.3	1.9	−0.2	−1.9	−3.1	1.7	2.3	0.6	0.9	4.9
France	5.4	5.8	0.6	0.4	−0.9	2.2	2.6	0.3	−3.8	−1.2	2.3	2.9	−1.1	0.7	−0.1
United Kingdom	3.2	3.9	−2.0	−0.3	−1.0	0.5	1.7	3.8	0.6	3.4	3.1	1.8	−0.5	0.3	−4.1
Italy	5.2	6.2	0.2	−0.4	−2.1	3.4	2.7	−1.6	−2.3	−0.7	2.3	3.1	1.9	1.5	0.7
Canada	5.3	6.0	−1.1	0.3	2.9	4.1	2.4	−1.6	1.5	−0.6	3.0	4.0	1.8	0.0	−2.9
Australia	5.1	6.5	0.9	1.0	4.9	2.9	2.4	−2.5	−2.8	−2.3	2.6	3.5	−0.0	−0.2	−0.1
Austria	4.8	6.0	−0.3	0.3	0.8	2.8	1.9	0.7	−1.5	−2.4	2.1	2.8	−0.9	0.5	3.2
Belgium	4.7	5.0	0.8	0.1	1.8	2.5	2.1	−0.6	−1.1	−6.3	1.5	2.3	−2.7	0.2	5.5
Denmark	4.6	4.7	−0.4	0.4	−0.6	0.6	2.0	−0.6	−2.3	−2.0	1.2	2.5	0.5	−0.0	4.5
Finland	5.0	6.0	−2.3	0.1	−1.0	2.6	2.6	1.0	−1.6	−0.8	3.2	3.2	1.6	1.1	−2.4
The Netherlands	5.0	4.9	1.6	0.5	1.1	2.3	2.2	0.1	−1.2	−5.3	1.3	3.4	−1.6	0.4	5.3
Spain	7.7	7.5	3.2	1.9	−2.7	1.9	3.3	3.9	−2.5	−2.8	3.3	4.0	1.2	1.4	−1.7
Sweden	3.6	4.4	−0.3	−0.5	3.3	1.9	1.9	0.8	−2.0	−6.4	1.8	2.2	−0.2	0.4	0.2
Switzerland	4.8	5.2	−1.7	0.9	−0.3	0.8	2.4	1.9	−0.3	−1.2	2.3	2.6	−0.0	1.6	4.3
Average[a]	5.2	5.9	—	0.3	0.3	2.2	2.5	—	−2.3	−2.1	2.4	3.1	—	0.9	1.1

Notes
$d\hat{d}$ = domestic demand.
$d\hat{d}^*$ = domestic demand (trade-weighted average) in major trading partners, multiplied by the elasticity ratios given in Table 10.1.
reer = real effective exchange rate based on unit labour costs.
tot = terms of trade, national account deflators.
BP = current external account as percentage of GNP, measured as cumulative change between initial and final year.
a Unweighted.

the larger countries, Germany suffered a major deterioration as domestic demand growth outpaced that of its major trading partners and in Canada excessive demand growth more than offset the gains from terms-of-trade and exchange rate movements. The United Kingdom was the only country to achieve an improvement in its external account and did so mainly by compressing domestic demand growth. In the United States and Japan low domestic demand growth also had a dampening effect on the external account, while in France policies were not sufficiently tight to offset the effects of a large terms-of-trade loss. Italy, on the other hand, managed to more or less stabilize the external account in conditions of rapid domestic demand growth. On the whole, for this period it is difficult to relate BPs changes systematically to growth differentials, exchange rate movements and terms-of-trade changes, partly because countries adopted very different policies to cope with the external shocks.

A main feature of the 1980s has, of course, been the marked deterioration in the US current account position which can be ascribed entirely to excessive domestic demand growth. Excessive domestic demand growth was also a feature of UK developments, while most other countries benefited from a positive growth differential and in several cases this occurred through a compression of domestic demand growth until late in the period. In particular, large differentials and associated external gains were recorded by Austria, Belgium, Denmark and the Netherlands, while Germany achieved an external gain of almost 5 per cent of GNP despite a relatively small growth differential. As in the previous periods, Japan also benefited from rapid growth of external demand, and Spain initially saw an improvement in the current account due to a favourable impact of relative demand and terms-of-trade developments, but later in the period BP fell sharply.

Table 10.3 shows cross-country regressions for various periods and thus provides a more direct test of the 45°-rule. For the overall period regressing

Table 10.3 Actual and warranted growth of demand (cross-country regressions)

Period	c	$d\hat{d}$	R^2	SE	Deviation $\geqslant 1SE^a$
1960–73	−0.97	1.32	0.88	0.74	JP(+) NL(−), ES (−)
	(1.5)	(10.7)			
1973–80	1.91	0.26	0.00	1.00	JP (+)
	(3.1)	(1.0)			
1980–90	0.65	1.03	0.30	1.22	US(−), JP(+), GB(−), NL(+)
	(2.6)	(2.7)			
1960–90	−1.60	1.62	0.86	0.61	US(−), JP(+), CA(−), DK(+), ES(−)
	(2.6)	(9.7)			
1960–90[b]	0.33	1.03	0.81	0.32	US(−), AU (+), DK (+)
	(0.7)	(37.8)			

Notes
Results obtained by regressing $d\hat{d}^*$ on $d\hat{d}$, using the figures shown in Table 10.2.
a A(−) implies that actual growth exceeds the warranted rate.
b Without Japan.

$d\hat{a}^*$ on $d\hat{a}$[6] yields an R^2 of 0.86 but a negative intercept term and a regression coefficient significantly above unity, neither of which is predicted by the hypothesis. Repeating the regression without Japan reduces the regression coefficient to unity and produces an insignificant intercept term. There are, however, a few large deviations, as actual growth in the United States has exceeded the warranted rate by more than one standard error, whereas in Denmark and Austria actual growth has been well below the rate predicted by the 45°-line.

A second feature of Table 10.3 is that, while for the overall period the 45°-rule is not rejected when Japan is excluded, the fit is much less close for the three subperiods.[7] In fact, the overall result seems to have been strongly influenced by developments during 1960–73, when nominal exchange rates were largely fixed and the terms-of-trade were stable. $d\hat{a}$ and $d\hat{a}^*$ were uncorrelated in the 1970s and for the 1980s R^2 is much lower than for the 1960s, with four countries showing rather large deviations between actual and predicted growth rates. Evidence of shifts in the hypothesized relationship between $d\hat{a}$ and $d\hat{a}^*$ can also be seen from the simple correlation coefficients displayed in Table 10.4. For the 1960s $d\hat{a}-d\hat{a}^*$ is uncorrelated with changes in the terms-of-trade, exchange rates and the external account, implicitly confirming the high R^2 shown in Table 10.3. Indeed, for this period the only significant correlation is between exchange rate and terms-of-trade movements, with the (positive) sign indicative of largely offsetting effects with respect to the current account. For the 1970s terms-of-trade changes and growth differentials are positively, albeit weakly, correlated, suggesting that countries experiencing large (small) losses were more (less) likely to tighten policies and thus partly explaining the absence of any significant relationship between $d\hat{a}$ and $d\hat{a}^*$. The 1980s is the most interesting period as $d\hat{a}-d\hat{a}^*$ is significantly and negatively correlated with changes in the external account. One interpretation of this result might be that because countries co-ordinated their monetary policies but pursued very different fiscal policies, large differences in demand growth and in the policy mix occurred, which in turn were reflected in movements in the external accounts.

Table 10.4 Simple correlation coefficients

	1960–73				1973–80				1980–90			
	$d\hat{a}-d\hat{a}^*$	*reer*	*tot*	*BP*	$d\hat{a}-d\hat{a}^*$	*reer*	*tot*	*BP*	$d\hat{a}-d\hat{a}^*$	*reer*	*tot*	*BP*
$d\hat{a}-d\hat{a}^*$	1				1				1			
reer	0.24	1			−0.42	1			−0.11	1		
tot	0.31	0.61**	1		0.18	0.05	1		−0.13	0.53*	1	
BP	−0.40	−0.03	−0.13	1	−0.21	0.15	0.14	1	−0.58*	−0.20	0.18	1

Notes
Correlation coefficient based on cross-country regression, using the figures in Table 10.2.
 * Significant at 5%.
** Significant at 1%.

Conclusion

Taken together, the evidence presented in Tables 10.2–10.4 clearly shows that the hypothesis of a close relationship between $d\hat{d}$ and $d\hat{d}^*$ merely holds in the very long run and even then a $1:1$ ratio between $d\hat{d}$ and $d\hat{d}^*$ is only obtained when excluding Japan. In the short to medium term, actual and warranted demand growth do not appear to be very closely correlated. Moreover, even if $d\hat{d}$ and $d\hat{d}^*$ were linked in a $1:1$ ratio, it cannot be assumed that the current accounts would remain stable, especially after 1973 when countries were exposed to large external shocks in the form of terms-of-trade and exchange rate fluctuations. Finally, as pointed out in Iwata (1989), the 45°-rule ignores the influence of changes in domestic saving and investment behaviour which can be independent of $d\hat{d}$ and $d\hat{d}^*$.

Notes

1 That is '$\hat{e}$' > 0 implies a deterioration in country i's competitive position.
2 Additional tests using relative consumer prices and wholesale prices produced only marginal changes.
3 In some further experiments total demand was used in the import equations for Germany and The Netherlands and produced income elasticities lower than those reported here. However, the fall largely corresponded to the faster growth of total demand compared with domestic demand. Measuring $p_i - (p_m + e)$ by the deflator for domestic output sold at home relative to import prices, led to a decline in the standard error for both countries and a significant relative price coefficient for The Netherlands, whereas for Germany it remained insignificant.
4 One exception to this general finding is Heikie and Hooper (1988), who include measures of relative supplies in US trade equations and find export and import elasticities of about the same size.
5 One reason for this result could be that services are less price sensitive than goods and thus lower the average price elasticitiy of foreign trade. However, the estimates reported by Barrell and Wren–Lewis (1989) for the G-7 countries do not support this hypothesis.
6 Before estimating the co-integration equations, the data generating processes were determined and all the variables of equation (10.2) were found to be integrated of order 1. These estimates, as well as details of the results given in Table 10.1, are available upon request.
7 Excluding Japan improved the estimates of 1960–73, while less satisfactory results were obtained for the more recent subperiods.

11 A new approach to the balance of payments constraint: some empirical evidence*

José A. Alonso and Carlos Garcimartín

One of the main aims of growth theory has been to explain why growth rates differ across countries and over time. The pioneering studies trying to answer this question were based on a neoclassical framework and, as a result, concluded that most growth differences could be explained by the diversity of growth rates of the inputs that made up the production function. In recent years, a new approach, the so-called endogenous growth theory, has stressed the role played by the production function. Thus, endogenous growth theorists argue that not only does growth vary across countries because of their *dynamic* resource endowment, it also varies to an important extent according to the *form* of the production function. Both approaches, however, are supply-side oriented and give no role to demand. When a country has factors to be employed and a production function, it is assumed that it will grow and no attention needs to be paid to where the goods produced are consumed. Nevertheless, this is only true under the unrealistic assumption that there is only one sector in the economy. In a previous study, one of the authors showed that, in an economy with more than one sector and different degrees of returns to scale, demand plays a crucial role in growth since it affects the endogenous process.[1] Thus, in order to explain why growth varies across countries and over time, it is necessary to pay attention not only to the discrepancies in the growth of inputs and to the shape of the production function but also to the form of the demand function.

This being true for a closed economy, it also holds for an open economy. In order to grow, a country that trades with the rest of the world not only needs inputs. It also needs to be able to sell the new goods produced. Because of the structure of consumption, a country cannot consume every new good produced and it needs to exchange some of them for other goods that better fit domestic demand patterns. Since in a pure neoclassical framework every country can sell the goods produced at the international price, this fact does not add anything new to the standard one-sector theory. But if price elasticity is not infinite, the country must reduce either the selling price – thus worsening the terms of trade – or potential output.

* First published in *Journal of Post Keynesian Economics*, Winter 1998–99.

Traditionally, the demand-side oriented approach to growth based on Harrod's study argues that prices do not play an important role and that the adjustment process is carried out mainly through changes in output. Thus, a country's capacity to grow could be constrained by the balance of payments. More specifically, Thirlwall (1979) assumes that the long-run rate of growth can be proxied by the ratio of export and import income elasticities multiplied by the foreign growth rate. In this chapter, we maintain that the assumption defended by Thirlwall (1979) that prices do not matter in determining the equilibrium income is neither necessary nor sufficient to affirm that growth is constrained by the balance of payments. Our aim is to develop a new approach to the Keynesian balance of payments growth constraint theory that avoids some theoretical and empirical shortcomings of former studies based on Thirlwall's framework.

Neoclassical versus Keynesian approach to production and growth

According to neoclassical theory, input supply is an exogenous variable that, together with the form of the production function, determines output, that is to say,

$$Y = f(L, H), \tag{11.1}$$

where Y stands for output, L is labor, and H refers to other inputs. Taking logs and derivatives with respect to time, we obtain the dynamic version of equation (11.1),[2]

$$\dot{y} = g(\dot{l}, \dot{h}), \tag{11.2}$$

This equation illustrates one of the main conclusions of the neoclassical theory of growth: Excluding technical change, an increase in output depends exclusively on the growth of inputs. It also implies that every increase of input generates a corresponding increase of output. This is guaranteed by the full employment assumption.

In contrast to neoclassical theory, the Keynesian approach to growth considers that the exogenous variable is not the amount of inputs but the quantity of output, which in turn determines the level of employment. If output requires an amount of inputs that exceeds the quantity available, then the economy is supply-constrained. If, on the other hand, employment falls short of input supply, growth is demand-constrained. That is, in the case of labor,

$$
\begin{aligned}
L &= f_1(Y, H) &&\text{if } f_1(Y, H) < S^L \\
L &= S^L &&\text{if } f_1(Y, H) \geq S^L,
\end{aligned}
\tag{11.3}
$$

where L is the labor employed and S^L is the total supply of labor. To simplify and without any loss of generality we can consider the case where total supply of labor does not grow. Writing equation (11.3) in dynamic terms gives,

$$\dot{l} = g_1(\dot{y}, \dot{h}) \quad \text{if } L_0 e^{g_1(\dot{y}, \dot{h})} \le S^L$$
$$\dot{l} = s^L - l_0 \quad \text{if } L_0 e^{g_1(\dot{y}, \dot{h})} > S^L,$$

(11.4)

where l_0 stands for the log of labor employed in the initial time considered. In other words, according to the Keynesian approach, an increase in output results in an increase in the level of employment and only if output requires a quantity of inputs above the amount available is the economy resource-constrained.

Harrod's multiplier and Thirlwall's Law

The first important contribution to a balance of payments constrained growth theory was the model developed by Harrod (1933), who thought that exports played the role of the independent variable which governed output and employment. A later version of Harrod's model was developed by Thirlwall (1979). According to this model, the trade balance is supposed to be in equilibrium in the long run, so,

$$XP = MP^*,$$

(11.5)

where X denotes export volume, M import volume, P the domestic price level, and P^* the foreign price level, both expressed in a common currency. In addition, the trade functions are defined as

$$X = A \left(\frac{P}{P^*} \right)^\gamma Y^{*\varepsilon};$$
$$M = B \left(\frac{P^*}{P} \right)^\eta Y^\pi,$$

(11.6)

where A and B are constants, Y^* and Y stand for world and domestic income, respectively, η and γ are price elasticities of imports and exports, respectively, and π and ε are import and export income elasticities, respectively. Taking logs and time derivatives, we can get the dynamic version of equation (11.6),

$$\dot{x} = \gamma(\dot{p} - \dot{p}^*) + \varepsilon \dot{y}^*;$$
$$\dot{m} = \eta(\dot{p}^* - \dot{p}) + \pi \dot{y}.$$

(11.7)

Plugging equation (11.7) into the dynamic version of equation (11.5), we obtain the rate of growth of income consistent with trade balance equilibrium:

$$\dot{y} = \frac{(1 + \gamma + \eta)(\dot{p} - \dot{p}^*) + \varepsilon \dot{y}^*}{\pi}.$$

(11.8)

The long-run rate of growth of output is thus determined by foreign income growth and changes in relative prices. It is important to note that, for an external constraint to exist, both foreign income growth and relative price changes must be exogenous. As far as foreign income is concerned, this seems quite realistic, especially for small countries, so the real assumption refers to relative prices. In fact, according to the neoclassical theory, equation (11.8) should be written as:

$$(\dot{p} - \dot{p}^*) = \frac{\pi\dot{y} - \varepsilon\dot{y}^*}{(1 + \eta + \gamma)}, \tag{11.9}$$

where the exogenous variables are foreign and domestic income, the latter depending on the resource endowment. In other words, in the Keynesian approach, trade is balanced thanks to changes in the level of income: As long as there is a trade deficit, income falls in order to reduce imports. On the other hand, in the neoclassical theory, the deficit is eliminated through a reduction in relative prices, assuming that the Marshall–Lerner condition holds.

In Thirlwall's model, relative prices do not play any role for two reasons that are, to some extent, mutually incompatible. The first refers to the stability of relative prices in the long run so that PPP theory holds. The second suggests that price elasticities are very small, so the term $(1 + \eta + \gamma)$ is close to unity. Hence, according to Thirlwall, equation (11.8) may be written as:

$$\dot{y} = \frac{\varepsilon\dot{y}^*}{\pi}. \tag{11.10}$$

an expression that is known in the literature as Thirlwall's Law. The meaning of this equation is that, in the long run, growth depends only on external income growth multiplied by the ratio of income export and import elasticities.

The law has been tested by, among others, Thirlwall (1979), McGregor and Swales (1985, 1986, 1991), Bairam (1988), McCombie (1989, 1992), Bairam and Dempster (1991), and Atesoglu (1993, 1994, 1995) over a varied range of countries, and, generally speaking, the empirical work seems to support Thirlwall's Law. In other words, for many countries growth seems to be demand-constrained rather than resource-constrained.

In Thirlwall's pioneering study, the theory was tested applying the Spearman's rank correlation coefficient to the actual and hypothetical rate of growth (calculated according to equation (11.10)). After criticisms of this method by McGregor and Swales (1985), the law is now usually tested as follows: First, equation (11.6) is estimated in order to obtain income elasticities for exports and imports; second, the hypothetical growth rate is calculated from equation (11.10); finally, a regression of hypothetical growth is run on actual growth:

$$\dot{y} = a + b\dot{y}_b + e, \tag{11.11}$$

where y_b is hypothetical income, a is a constant, and e is the error term. If Thirlwall's Law holds, a should equal zero and b should equal one.

Some limits on Thirlwall's approach

Although Thirlwall's model has been generally supported by empirical research, in our opinion it suffers from both theoretical and empirical shortcomings that may make its conclusions less tenable.

Three types of shortcomings are worth noting here: (a) Trade functions may not be properly defined for countries that experience significant changes in the structure of their output; (b) the empirical methodology used to test Thirlwall's Law shows some econometric shortcomings – the variables are commonly measured by growth rates instead of levels; income is assumed to be either an exogenous variable in the import function or an endogenous one in the equilibrium growth equation; the estimate of equation (11.10) includes a nondeterministic variable ($\varepsilon y^*/\pi$); and (c) the null impact of relative prices on growth is not necessary to justify the balance of payments constraint hypothesis. The approach to balance of payments constrained growth developed in this study tries to avoid these shortcomings.

However, before we present our approach, it is useful to clarify some of the previous topics by means of the following model specified by Alonso (1999) to analyze the effect of the external constraint on the Spanish economy.

In this study the trade functions are defined as:

$$X = A\,(RPX)^\gamma\, Y^{*\varepsilon}\, G^\delta;$$

(11.12)

$$M = B\,(RPM)^\eta\, Y^\pi,$$

(11.13)

where RPX and RPM are the relative price ratios for exports and imports, respectively, and G is a technological index that tries to capture the significant change Spanish exports have experienced in recent years.[3] It is important to note that, for countries showing structural change, the exclusion of this effect may lead to erroneous estimates of trade functions and, as we shall show later, to misleading conclusions about the determinants of growth.[4]

To avoid the loss of information regarding the long-term relationship between the variables, both equations were estimated by cointegration using Johansen's methodology based on Maximum Likelihood for VAR(p) processes. The following results were obtained:

$$\varepsilon = 2.128; \quad \gamma = -1.332; \quad \delta = 0.187; \quad \pi = 1.332; \quad \eta = -0.752.$$

Since all the parameters were statistically significant,[5] these figures show that, apart from income, trade is sensitive to both relative prices and technology. Therefore, we should use the augmented (and static) version of equation (11.8), that is,

$$ybc = \frac{a - b + px - pm + \gamma\,rpx - \eta\,rpm + \varepsilon y^* + \delta g}{\pi},$$

(11.14)

to verify if the actual income adjusts to the income level consistent with balance of payments equilibrium. Since the external constraint alludes to a long-term relationship, the estimation should be made with the variables in levels. Consequently, the following relationship was estimated through cointegration:

$$y = c + \beta ybc + \xi, \tag{11.15}$$

where the error term is modelled as an AR (2). The results were (with all parameters being significant):

$$y = 2.078 + 0.895 ybc + \xi;$$
$$\xi_t = 1.097\xi_{t-1} - 0.419\xi_{t-2};$$
$$R^2 = 0.986; \quad DW = 2.27.$$

Since β was not significantly different from 1, the estimates support the existence of a long-term relationship between actual and balance of payments constrained income defined as in equation (11.14). But, since relative prices (which have changed by about 40 percent during the period considered in this study) are included in that expression, one can conclude, according to Thirlwall's approach, that growth is not constrained by balance of payments. Yet this would be misleading.

In fact, it is possible to draw the opposite conclusion from the same estimates. In accordance with the usual procedure, a regression was made using Thirlwall's methodology (i.e. equation (11.10)). The results obtained showed the following relationship:

$$\dot{y} = 0.0001 + 1.0158\dot{y}_{BS},$$
$$R^2 = 0.41; \quad SER = 0.024,$$

where $\dot{y}_{BS}$ stands for the rate of growth of output computed according to equation (11.10). The intercept was not significantly different from zero and the coefficient of $\dot{y}_{BS}$ was not significantly different from one, thus supporting Thirlwall's Law. This is due, however, not to the irrelevance of prices but to the compensating effect of technology: During the period considered, the worsening of relative prices in Spain was balanced by the improvement of technology, thus maintaining the country's overall competitiveness level. Not taking these two variables into consideration – prices and structural change, proxied by technology – may confirm Thirlwall's Law erroneously.

To sum up, the Spanish case reveals, first of all, how important it is to include in trade functions a variable capturing structural change. Second, it demonstrates the inadequate simplification entailed in an a priori exclusion of relative prices in the equilibrium equation. In addition, the misleading conclusion about the equilibrium income with and without relative prices clearly reveals the limits stemming from traditional Thirlwall's methodology.

A new approach to balance of payments constrained growth

The causes of an economy's balance of payments constraint are a low absolute value of the price elasticities of foreign trade and /or the independence of relative prices from the balance of payments disequilibria. Thus, the impact of relative prices on the growth rate does not hinder the effect of the balance of payments constraint. Consequently, this hypothesis cannot be tested through the degree of correlation between actual and Thirlwall's Law rate of growth (defined as in equation (11.10)).

In fact, the main difference between the neoclassical approach to growth and the Keynesian-oriented balance of payments constraint hypothesis is the variable by means of which the balance of payments equilibrium is achieved. Let us stress this fact by showing the dynamic version of the balance of payments equilibrium equation, which includes the export and import functions as indicated in equation (11.6):

$$(1 + \gamma + \eta)(\dot{p} - \dot{p}^*) + \varepsilon \dot{y}^* = \pi \dot{y}. \tag{11.16}$$

To simplify, we can consider the case where foreign income remains constant. For this equation to hold when there is a trade balance deficit, either relative prices or income, or both, must decrease. This is the fundamental question: Which variable changes in the presence of a trade balance disequilibrium? In other words, which is the endogenous variable? According to neoclassical theory, adjustment occurs through changes in relative prices, while in Keynesian theory this role is mainly played by income. Consequently, the equations that should be tested in order to identify the correct approach to growth are:

$$\dot{y} = \alpha_1 (x - m + p - p^*), \tag{11.17}$$

versus

$$(\dot{p} - \dot{p}^*) = \alpha_2 (x - m + p - p^*). \tag{11.18}$$

The meaning of equation (11.17) is that income changes when the trade balance is not in equilibrium. On the other hand, equation (11.18) refers to the neoclassical approach, so that the variable that changes when trade is out of balance is prices, not income. If Keynesian theory turns out to be correct, α_1 must be positive, while if the neoclassical explanation of growth is right, α_2 must be positive and α_1 not significantly different from zero.

From an econometric point of view, it is not possible to estimate equations (11.17) and (11.18) correctly. The reason is that, when we estimate these equations, we are assuming that exports and imports are exogenous variables but, by hypothesis, we also assume that they depend on prices and income. Hence, exports and imports cannot be considered exogenous variables. Thus, the correct technique to distinguish between the neoclassical and Keynesian approaches is to estimate two systems of equations where variables adjust to their partial equilibrium level. These systems are:

$$\dot{y} = \alpha_1(x - m + p - p^*)$$
$$\dot{x} = \alpha_2(x - x^e)$$
$$x^e = a + \gamma(p - p^*) + \varepsilon y^* \qquad (11.19)$$
$$\dot{m} = \alpha_3(m - m^e)$$
$$m^e = b + \eta(p - p^*) + \pi y,$$

versus

$$(\dot{p} - \dot{p}^*) = \alpha_4(x - m + p - p^*)$$
$$\dot{x} = \alpha_5(x - x^e)$$
$$x^e = a + \gamma(p - p^*) + \varepsilon y^* \qquad (11.20)$$
$$\dot{m} = \alpha_6(m - m^e)$$
$$m^e = b + \eta(p - p^*) + \pi y,$$

where superscript e refers to the partial equilibrium level of the variable. System (11.19) is built to test the Keynesian hypothesis of balance of payments constraint, which is supported as long as α_1 is positive, while the aim of system (11.20) is to test the neoclassical approach of resource constraint, which is supported as long as α_4 is positive. Parameters α_i measure the speed of adjustment of the variables to their partial equilibrium levels and $1/\alpha_i$ is the mean time lag, defined as the time necessary for about two-thirds of the discrepancy between the observed value of the variable at time t and its equilibrium value to be eliminated.[6] Partial stability requires positive values for $\alpha_2, \alpha_3, \alpha_5,$ and α_6.

The empirical evidence

In this section, we test the two alternative hypotheses, the neoclassical versus the Keynesian, over a group of 10 OECD countries for the period 1965–94. The first problem we had to deal with was that of defining relative prices in systems (11.19) and (11.20). Because we were aware that they are only proxies of price competitiveness, we decided to use the following ratios:

$$PRX = \frac{PX}{P*}; \qquad (11.21)$$

$$PRM = \frac{PM}{P}, \qquad (11.22)$$

where PRX and PRM are relative prices of exports and imports, respectively, PX stands for export prices, P^* is an index of foreign prices (in national currency), PM

is import prices, and P is domestic prices. Therefore, equation systems (11.19) and (11.20) become:

$$\dot{y} = \alpha_1(x - m + px - pm)$$
$$\dot{x} = \alpha_2(x^e - x)$$
$$x^e = a + \gamma(prx) + \varepsilon y^* \qquad (11.23)$$
$$\dot{m} = \alpha_3(m^e - m)$$
$$m^e = b + \eta(prm) + \pi y,$$

and

$$(\dot{prx}) = \alpha_4(x - m + prx + p^* - pm)$$
$$(\dot{prm}) = \alpha_5(x - m + prx + p^* - pm)$$
$$\dot{x} = \alpha_6(x^e - x) \qquad (11.24)$$
$$x^e = a + \gamma(prx) + \varepsilon y^*$$
$$\dot{m} = \alpha_7(m^e - m)$$
$$m^e = b + \eta(prm) + \pi y.$$

The estimates obtained for systems (11.23) and (11.24) are shown in Tables 11.1 and 11.2.

According to the results shown in Table 11.1, the parameter α_1 is significantly different from zero and shows the correct sign for 8 of the 10 countries included in the sample. The exceptions are the United States and France. With respect to the United States, this result is not so surprising, since this country also raised problems in previous studies that estimated equation (11.11) using cross-section data. On the other hand, the evidence of no relationship between balance of payments equilibrium and income growth in the case of France is more difficult to explain – especially given the results obtained for the rest of the sample.[7]

Regarding price elasticities, 15 of the 20 parameter estimates show the correct sign and are significantly different from zero at a 95 percent probability level (16 at a 90 percent probability level). Six countries show negative and significant elasticities for exports and imports (7 countries at a 90 percent probability level). Only in the case of France is neither export price elasticity nor import price elasticity significant. For all the countries in the sample price elasticities show a low absolute value.

With most price elasticities being significant, one may wonder if prices do indeed adjust to balance of payments disequilibria. According to the results in Table 11.2, the answer would appear to be no. There is no evidence of a relationship between relative prices and the balance of payments, not even in the countries where there was no evidence of an income adjustment process (the United States and France). These two empirical findings (low price elasticities and no price adjustment to a balance of payments disequilibria) might explain why relative prices may not

Table 11.1 Income adjustment (A) System (11.23) (asymptotic t-ratios in brackets)

Country	α_1	α_2	α_3	γ	η	ε	π
Germany	0.15 (4.15)	0.58 (2.80)	3.92 (2.64)	−0.73 (2.09)	−0.11 (0.96)	1.54 (12.45)	1.90 (31.90)
Canada	0.12 (2.11)	1.40 (2.85)	0.46 (2.45)	−0.37 (4.68)	−0.98 (3.44)	1.51 (18.61)	1.57 (10.35)
Spain	0.16 (3.85)	0.23 (1.97)	2.26 (3.50)	−0.59 (2.08)	−0.58 (2.59)	2.18 (2.98)	1.88 (16.10)
United States	−0.06 (1.78)	0.81 (4.12)	2.22 (2.83)	−0.47 (5.25)	−0.41 (10.36)	1.39 (10.69)	2.02 (53.41)
France	−0.05 (1.18)	0.22 (2.17)	0.8 (2.57)	−0.05 (0.17)	−0.29 (1.26)	1.42 (3.87)	1.76 (25.24)
Netherlands	0.13 (2.53)	1.99 (3.53)	1.34 (2.86)	−0.29 (5.30)	−0.37 (3.21)	1.27 (40.28)	1.33 (12.97)
Italy	0.16 (3.09)	1.74 (3.82)	1.40 (3.86)	−0.63 (4.73)	−0.44 (11.67)	1.35 (24.51)	1.42 (35.50)
Japan	0.19 (5.04)	0.97 (4.31)	1.03 (5.76)	−1.45 (3.87)	−0.59 (6.80)	1.89 (17.06)	0.96 (14.97)
Great Britain	0.11 (2.38)	0.61 (2.42)	1.87 (3.45)	−0.25 (1.86)	−0.29 (4.68)	0.94 (7.33)	1.77 (30.36)
Sweden	0.09 (1.98)	0.95 (2.56)	1.30 (2.25)	−0.28 (1.58)	−0.29 (2.70)	1.09 (8.47)	1.65 (14.69)
(Expected sign)	+	+	+	−	−	+	+

Source: Author's own calculation

Table 11.2 Price adjustment (B) System (11.24) (asymptotic t-ratios in brackets)

Country	α_4	α_5	α_6	α_7	γ	η	ε	π
Germany	-0.001 (0.56)	-0.001 (0.86)	0.85 (3.40)	3.36 (2.51)	-0.87 (3.74)	-0.11 (1.01)	1.41 (16.08)	1.82 (26.92)
Canada	-0.01 (1.63)	0.001 (1.19)	1.99 (2.97)	0.76 (2.59)	-0.37 (5.77)	-1.04 (3.80)	1.44 (20.53)	1.35 (8.19)
Spain	-0.004 (1.14)	-0.001 (0.77)	0.26 (2.20)	1.87 (3.51)	-0.82 (1.98)	-0.42 (1.80)	2.21 (2.76)	1.72 (3.38)
United States	-0.01 (2.01)	0.0 (0.39)	0.92 (4.68)	2.02 (1.78)	-0.42 (6.47)	-0.49 (13.08)	1.50 (16.08)	1.99 (79.16)
France	-0.07 (0.83)	-0.001 (0.65)	0.37 (3.55)	2.52 (2.55)	-0.56 (2.55)	-0.33 (5.66)	1.25 (3.03)	1.56 (38.01)
Netherlands	-0.001 (0.49)	-0.001 (0.47)	2.02 (3.57)	2.45 (2.11)	-0.32 (6.45)	-0.28 (2.89)	1.25 (43.97)	1.41 (16.16)
Italy	-0.003 (0.67)	-0.001 (0.52)	0.94 (2.50)	3.56 (3.17)	-0.70 (3.48)	-0.35 (10.80)	1.34 (17.57)	1.36 (43.62)
Japan	-0.001 (0.53)	-0.003 (0.79)	0.54 (3.44)	0.71 (3.53)	-1.83 (3.53)	-0.60 (5.22)	1.76 (10.55)	0.79 (8.22)
Great Britain	-0.005 (1.45)	-0.001 (0.69)	0.48 (2.18)	2.36 (3.82)	-0.35 (2.11)	-0.28 (5.20)	0.89 (6.03)	1.81 (37.16)
Sweden	-0.004 (0.91)	0.0 (0.10)	0.80 (2.79)	0.80 (2.25)	-0.26 (1.85)	-0.31 (2.36)	0.99 (7.93)	1.44 (11.62)
(Expected sign)	+	−	+	+	−	−	+	+

Source: Author's own calculations.

be as important as the neoclassical theory of growth suggests. Furthermore, since price elasticities are so low, the change in relative prices that a country should experience to achieve balance of payments equilibrium could be a completely unrealistic assumption. In the earlier model, it is not possible to estimate these changes, since they include two different relative prices indicators. A simple but clearly incorrect way to avoid this problem is to suppose that export and import prices follow the same trend as domestic and foreign prices, respectively. In this context, the rate of change of relative prices consistent with balance of payments equilibrium is

$$(\dot{p} - \dot{p}^*) = \frac{\pi \dot{y} - \varepsilon \dot{y}^*}{(1 + \gamma + \eta)}. \tag{11.25}$$

Applying this relationship, we find that to experience a 4 percent rate of growth of income while the OECD grows at 2 percent requires a fall in relative prices that is only feasible in the case of Japan, 0.06 percent. Canada, which shows the second highest price elasticity and also has an above-average ratio of income elasticities, should reduce its relative prices by 8.5 percent per year. In the rest of the countries prices should decrease at a higher rate.

The steady-state rate of growth

The steady-state rate of growth of income according to system (11.23) is (see Appendix A):

$$\lambda_y = \frac{\lambda_{px} - \lambda_{pm} + \gamma \lambda_{prx} - \eta \lambda_{prm} + \varepsilon \lambda_{y^*}}{\pi}, \tag{11.26}$$

which is equivalent to that in equation (11.8). Using the estimates of the model (Table 11.1), we obtain the following rates of growth for the countries exhibiting a balance of payments constraint (Figures 11.1–11.8).

Table 11.3 comprises the actual and steady-state rates of growth over the period 1965–94. The contribution of prices and foreign income to each steady-state rate of growth is also shown.

The table shows that the contribution of relative prices is low for every country, reaching on average 9 percent in absolute value. The highest share of the relative price effect is displayed by Japan, while Spain shows the lowest.

The speed of income adjustment

We have stated earlier that the reciprocal of α_i (the so-called mean time lag) indicates the time required for about two-thirds of the discrepancy between actual and equilibrium level of the variable i to be eliminated. Using the figures of Table 11.1, we obtained the results shown in Table 11.4.

According to these figures, trade variables adjust to their equilibrium levels at a higher speed than income does. We can thus conclude that the adjustment path

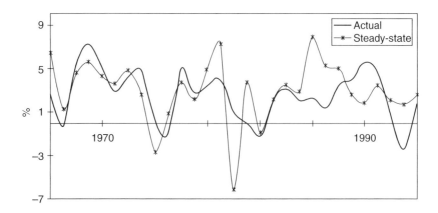

Figure 11.1 Actual and steady-state yearly rate of growth of Germany.

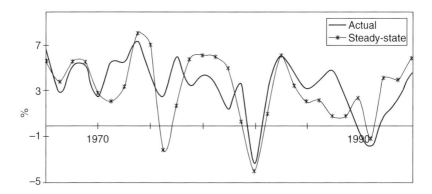

Figure 11.2 Actual and steady-state yearly rate of growth of Canada.

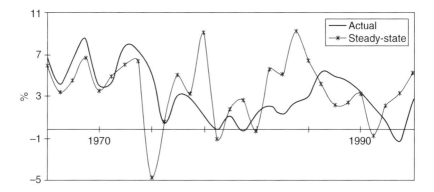

Figure 11.3 Actual and steady-state yearly rate of growth of Spain.

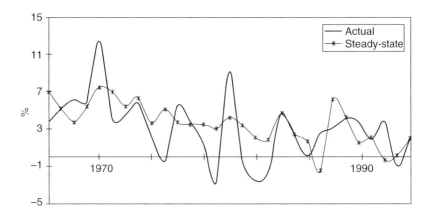

Figure 11.4 Actual and steady-state yearly rate of growth of the Netherlands.

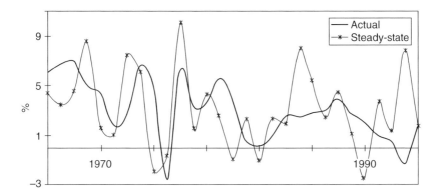

Figure 11.5 Actual and steady-state yearly rate of growth of Italy.

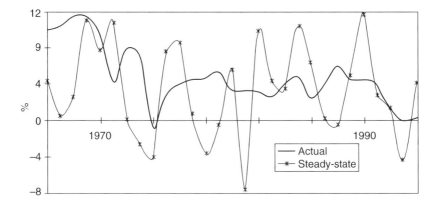

Figure 11.6 Actual and steady-state yearly rate of growth of Japan.

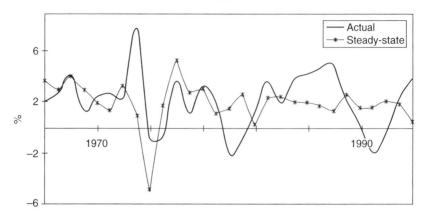

Figure 11.7 Actual and steady-state yearly rate of growth of Great Britain.

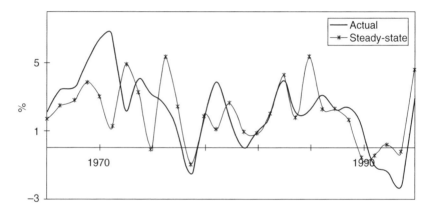

Figure 11.8 Actual and steady-state yearly rate of growth of Sweden.

followed by income determines the evolution of imports, especially in the cases of Sweden, Great Britain, and Canada. It should also be noted that the speed of adjustment of exports reflects the efficiency of the economic system to confront changes in the overall economic environment. In this sense, the most efficient economies are Italy, the Netherlands, Canada, Japan, and Sweden, while the worst performance corresponds to Spain.

Conclusion

Throughout this study we have made the case for a new approach to the balance of payments constrained growth theory since, in our opinion, some of the previous work done in this field displays certain theoretical and econometric shortcomings. The methodology presented in the chapter tries to test the balance of payments constraint hypothesis by identifying the variable by means of which the balance

Table 11.3 Actual and steady-state rates of growth, 1965–94

Country	Actual (%)	Steady-state (a)(%)*	Contribution to (a)(%)**	
			Of relative prices	*Of foreign income*
Germany	75	87	12	88
Canada	101	96	6	94
Spain	99	110	2	98
Netherlands	92	107	16	84
Italy	90	92	4	96
Japan	144	157	−18	118
Great Britain	62	56	11	89
Sweden	63	60	−3	103

Notes

* The level of significance of the parameters is 90 percent.
** The contribution of relative prices is defined as the share of

$$\frac{\lambda_{px} - \lambda_{pm} + \gamma\lambda_{prx} - \eta\lambda_{prm}}{\pi}$$

in the steady-state rate of growth. The contribution of income is the share of $\varepsilon\lambda\gamma^*/\pi$ in that rate.

Table 11.4 Speed of adjustment

Country	Mean time lag (years)		
	y	*x*	*m*
Germany	6.6	1.7	0.3
Canada	8.3	0.7	1.6
Spain	6.2	4.5	0.4
Netherlands	7.7	0.5	0.7
Italy	6.2	0.6	0.7
Japan	5.3	1.0	1.0
Great Britain	9.1	1.6	0.5
Sweden	11.1	1.0	0.8

of payments equilibrium is achieved. The empirical evidence seems to support income as the adjustment variable, which means that growth is indeed balance of payments constrained. On the other hand, relative prices do not play a significant role in economic growth, for price elasticities are low and relative prices seem to be basically independent from balance of payments disequilibria.[8] To sum up, the main conclusion obtained in this study is similar to that derived from Thirlwall's Law: long-run economic growth depends not only on a country's resource endowment but also on its ability to satisfy both domestic and foreign demand.

Appendix A: analytical solution of the model

We will solve the equations only for the steady-state growth rates of model (11.23); with regard to systems (11.21), (11.22), and (11.24), the same methodology applies. The model is

$$\dot{y} = \alpha_1(x - m + px - pm)$$
$$\dot{x} = \alpha_2(x^e - x)$$
$$x^e = a + \gamma(prx) + \varepsilon y^* \qquad (11.23)$$
$$\dot{m} = \alpha_3(m^e - m)$$
$$m^e = b + \eta(prm) + \pi y,$$

To find its solution we shall apply the method of undetermined coefficients. Assuming that all variables – exogenous (P, PX, PM, P^*, and Y^*) as well as endogenous (X, M, Y) – grow at a constant rate, each variable at time t can be defined as

$$i_t = i_0 e^{\lambda_i t}, \quad i = PM, PX, P, P^*, Y, Y^*, X, M. \qquad (11.27)$$

Substitution of (11.24) into (11.23) yields

$$\lambda_y = \alpha_1(x_0 + \lambda_x t - m_0 - \lambda_m t + px_0 + \lambda_{px} t - pm_0 - \lambda_{pm} t), \qquad (11.28)$$
$$\lambda_x = \alpha_2[-x_0 - \lambda_x t + a + \gamma(prx_0 + \lambda_{prx} t) + \varepsilon(y_0^* + \lambda_{y^*} t)], \qquad (11.29)$$
$$\lambda_m = \alpha_3[-m_0 - \lambda_m t + b + \eta(prm_0 + \lambda_{prm} t) + \pi(y_0 + \lambda_y t)]. \qquad (11.30)$$

For these expressions to be identically satisfied, the coefficients of t must be zero, so

$$0 = \alpha_1(\lambda_x - \lambda_m + \lambda_{px} - \lambda_{pm}) t, \qquad (11.31)$$
$$0 = \alpha_2[-\lambda_x + \gamma(\lambda_{prx}) + \varepsilon(\lambda_{y^*})] t, \qquad (11.32)$$
$$0 = \alpha_3[-\lambda_m + \eta(\lambda_{prm}) + \pi(\lambda_y)] t, \qquad (11.33)$$

From (11.26) we can obtain the following equations:

$$\lambda_x = \lambda_m - \lambda_{px} + \lambda_{pm}, \qquad (11.34)$$
$$\lambda_x = \gamma\lambda_{prx} + \varepsilon\lambda_{y^*}, \qquad (11.35)$$
$$\lambda_m = \eta\lambda_{prm} + \pi\lambda_y, \qquad (11.36)$$

which is a three-equation system with three unknowns whose solution is

$$\lambda_y = \frac{\lambda_{px} - \lambda_{pm} + \gamma\lambda_{prx} - \eta\lambda_{prm} + \varepsilon\lambda_{y^*}}{\pi}, \qquad (11.37)$$
$$\lambda_x = \gamma\lambda_{prx} + \varepsilon\lambda_{y^*}, \qquad (11.38)$$
$$\lambda_m = \gamma\lambda_{prx} + \varepsilon\lambda_{y^*} + \lambda_{px} - \lambda_{pm}. \qquad (11.39)$$

Thus, as far as income is concerned, the same conceptual solution is reached as found in equation (11.8).

Appendix B: stability

With regard to partial stability of system (11.23), every single variable included in this model is stable for the 8 countries revealing an income adjustment process. The parameter α_1 is positive, which means that income decreases when there is a trade balance deficit, reducing imports and forcing the trade balance to move to its equilibrium. Also the parameters α_2 and α_3 are positive, which means that both imports and exports decrease when they are above their equilibrium levels and rise when they are below them.

To analyze the general stability of the model, let us write equation (11.19) as

$$\dot{y} = \alpha_1(x - m) + \alpha_1(px - pm)$$
$$\dot{x} = \alpha_2(x^e) - \alpha_2(x)$$
$$x^e = a + \gamma prx + \varepsilon y^*$$
$$\dot{m} = \alpha_3(\pi y - m) + \alpha_3(b + \eta prm).$$

(11.40)

It will be stable if all the roots of the characteristic equation of the matrix

$$\begin{pmatrix} 0 & \alpha_1 & -\alpha_1 \\ 0 & -\alpha_2 & 0 \\ \alpha_3\pi & 0 & -\alpha_3 \end{pmatrix}$$

are negative in their real parts. Using the parameters estimated earlier, we obtain the roots shown in Table 11.5.

Table 11.5 Stability

Country	Roots (t-ratio)		
	Real		Imaginary
Germany	−0.32 (3.7)	−0.58 (2.8)	−3.60 (2.4)
Canada	−1.40 (2.8)	−0.23 (2.4)	— +/−0.18 (1.4)
Spain	−0.23 (2.6)	−0.41 (3.0)	−5.85 (3.1)
Netherlands	−0.16 (2.5)	−1.5 (3.0)	−1.99 (3.5)
Italy	−0.28 (2.0)	−1.12(2.3)	−1.74 (3.8)
Japan	−0.26 (2.4)	−0.48 (2.3)	−0.63 (2.4)
Great Britain	−0.23 (2.1)	−0.61 (2.4)	−1.64 (2.6)
Sweden	−0.17 (2.6)	−0.95 (2.5)	−1.13 (1.8)

Appendix C: on relative prices indicators

The relative prices indicators were constructed as follows:

$$PRX_i = \frac{PX_i}{P_j^*}; \tag{11.41}$$

$$PRM_i = \frac{PM_i}{P_i}, \tag{11.42}$$

where PX_i, PM_i, and P_i are exports, imports, and Gross Domestic Product (GDP) deflators, respectivley, of country i, and P_j^* is a weighted GDP price deflator of the countries receiving imports from i. Then

$$P_j^* = \frac{\sum_i P_j w_{ij}}{e_{ij}}, \tag{11.43}$$

where P_j stands for the GDP deflator of country j, e_{ij} is the exchange rate of the currencies i and j, and w_{ij} is the weight that the country j represents in the exports of i, as a five-year average. The weight w_{ij} is defined as

$$w_{ij} = \frac{X_{ij}}{X_i}, \tag{11.44}$$

where X_{ij} are the exports from country i to country j and X_i are total exports of country i. To build these indicators, we used only OECD countries, which means that for country i the evolution of relative prices with respect to non-OECD countries is considered as the weighted average of those of the OECD countries. The error stemming from this assumption is proportional to the weight of non-OECD as markets for the exports of country i. This problem was particularly important for Japan, since non-OECD countries received as an average of the period considered about 40 percent of Japanese exports. In this case we decided to use the real terms of trade for Japan developed by the International Monetary Fund (IMF). But, since this indicator is not available prior to 1972, for the years 1965–71 we used the relative prices ratio developed earlier.

Appendix D: data sources

Y	Real domestic GDP. National Accounts.
Y^*	Real OECD GDP. OECD.
X	Real exports of goods and services. National Accounts.
M	Real imports of goods and services. National Accounts.
PX	Export price deflator. National Accounts.
PM	Import price deflator. National Accounts.
P	GDP price deflator. National Accounts.
e	Exchange rate. IMF.
X_{ij}	Exports from country i to country j. National Accounts.

Notes

1 See Garcimartín (1997).
2 Throughout this work we will denote logs by lower-case letters where the dotted variables denotes their time derivative.
3 Relative price ratios are defined as follows:

$$RPM = MPD/GPD \quad RPX = XPD/XPD^*,$$

where *MPD* and *XPD* are the import and export price levels, respectively; *GPD* is the domestic price level; and *XPD** is a weighted export price level of the countries competing with Spanish exports.
4 The study of the composition of trade shows that these changes are not so important in the case of imports (Bairam, 1993).
5 The exclusion contrast of variables from cointegration vectors confirms the significance of all the estimated components, which indicates that none can be excluded from cointegration relationship.
6 See Gandolfo (1981) for a detailed description of the econometric and analytical analysis of differential equation systems. Also see Appendix A for the analytical solution of system (11.19) and Appendix B for the conditions required for stability.
7 It must be noted that in the case of France we faced convergence problems in the estimation.
8 The existence of deficiencies in the usual price competitiveness indicators leads us to suggest than improvements should be made in these indicators.

12 An application of Thirlwall's Law to the Spanish economy*

Miguel A. León-Ledesma

Post Keynesian growth theory argues that, far from being constrained by the exogenous increase of factors of production, growth is demand determined. In the model developed by Thirlwall (1979) and Thirlwall and Hussain (1982), and debated in McGregor and Swales (1985, 1986, 1991), Thirlwall (1986), and McCombie (1989, 1992), the growth of demand is limited by the current (or basic) balance of payments deficit. The expenditure of a country or region cannot indefinitely grow faster than income since, sooner or later, the external deficits generated must be corrected through a reduction of economic growth because there is a limit to capital inflows (and government transfers in the case of regions). The existence of a balance of payments constraint at different rates of expenditure growth between countries will determine differences in growth rates in the long run. Only exports, as an autonomous component of aggregate demand, are capable of increasing an economy's expenditure without generating external disequilibrium. Hence, the growth rate of modern open economies is fundamentally determined by export growth (given the propensity to import).[1]

This chapter is concerned with the application of Thirlwall's (1979) model to the growth experience of the Spanish economy over the period 1965–93. It will briefly outline the model, then refer to the estimation of the import demand function, and test the validity of the model for the Spanish economy.

Thirlwall's model

In Thirlwall's (1979) model, the rate of growth consistent with a balance of payments equilibrium is obtained by means of import- and export demand functions and a balance of payments equilibrium condition, where all the variables are expressed in growth rates. The equations are as follows:

$$x_t = \eta(p_{ft} + e_t - p_{dt}) + \varepsilon z_t, \tag{12.1}$$

$$m_t = \psi(p_{dt} - p_{ft} - e_t) + \pi y_t, \tag{12.2}$$

$$p_{dt} + x_t = p_{ft} + m_t + e_t, \tag{12.3}$$

* First published in *Journal of Post Keynesian Economics,* Spring 1999.

where x_t, m_t, y_t, and z_t are the rates of growth of real exports, imports, domestic income, and world income, respectively. p_{dt} is the rate of growth of domestic prices, p_{ft} is the rate of growth of import prices, and e_t is the rate of change of the exchange rate. Hence, $(p_{dt} - p_{ft} - e_t)$ is the rate of change of the real terms of trade for the country. The parameters η, ψ, ε, and π are the price elasticity of demand for exports, the price elasticity of demand for imports, the world income elasticity of demand for exports, and the income elasticity of demand for imports, respectively.

The strict version of the model states that relative prices stay invariant in the long run; that is, $(p_{ft} + e_t - p_{dt}) = 0$. The existence of this dynamic equalization is not attributed to the neoclassical law of one price, as pointed out by Thirlwall (1986), but to the fact that international prices are fixed in oligopolistic markets where product differentiation and quality competition are the dominant entrepreneurial strategies. Therefore, prices play a minor role in international market competition and, hence, have little variation through time (*sticky relative prices*).[2] Given this assumption, substituting equations (12.1) and (12.2) into (12.3), we obtain:

$$y_{bt} = \frac{\varepsilon z_t}{\pi}, \tag{12.4}$$

or, alternatively,

$$y_{bt} = \frac{x_t}{\pi}. \tag{12.5}$$

The final statement of the model is that $y_t = y_{bt}$ – known as Thirlwall's Law – that is, the long-run growth of an economy is determined by the rate of growth of exports and the income elasticity of demand for imports.

Data and estimation

To test Thirlwall's Law for the Spanish economy, we have estimated an import function for the Spanish economy over the period 1964–94 in order to estimate the value of π to be used for obtaining the value of y_{bt}. The estimated relation is:

$$m_t = \alpha + \pi y_t + \psi pr_{t-1} + u_t,$$

where m_t is the rate of growth of real imports of goods and services; y_t is the rate of growth of real Gross Domestic Product (GDP); and pr_{t-1} is relative import prices, measured as the difference between the rate of growth of the GDP deflator and the import deflator, lagged one period (to reflect the lagged effect of changes in relative prices on imports). This variable reflects the changes in relative import prices.

Data were obtained from *Historical Series* of the Spanish Ministry of Economy and from the *Financial Accounts of the Spanish Economy (1985–1994)* of the Spanish Central Bank. Before proceeding to estimation, following Fuller (1976) and Dickey and Fuller (1979), the possible existence of a unit root in all the series

Table 12.1 Values of *t*-ratio for the DF and ADF tests (critical values in parenthesis)*

Variable	DF	ADF(1)
m_t	$-5.287(-3.12)^{**}$	$-4.963(-3.12)^{**}$
y_t	$-1.732(-1.60)^{***}$	$-1.690(-1.60)^{***}$
pr_t	$-4.159(-3.00)$	$-3.588(-3.00)$
x_t	$-3.627(-3.00)$	$-2.300(-3.00)$
cp_t (private consumption growth rate)	$-3.355(-3.12)^{**}$	$-3.328(-3.12)^{**}$

Notes
 * Fuller (1976) and Dickey and Fuller (1981) critical values.
 ** Since change in the mean is detected, Perron's (1990) critical values were used.
 *** Critical value at 10%.

used was tested. Since the data are growth rates, only the existence of one unit root was tested. The results of the tests, with the *t*-ratios, are presented in Table 12.1. For that purpose we used the simple Dickey–Fuller (DF) and the Augmented Dickey–Fuller (ADF) tests (critical values in parenthesis). Following a sequential testing procedure for y_t, a model without a time trend and constant was used. A model with constant and without trend was chosen for pr_t. For m_t, however, a change in the mean was detected for the years 1986, 1987, and 1988 (which could be related with the Spanish incorporation into the EU in 1986). The application of DF and ADF would tend to accept the null hypothesis of the presence of a unit root in the series. To correct this effect, a dummy variable for these years was included in the DF test, and the critical values provided by Perron (1990) were used. The results show that neither m_t nor pr_t has a unit root, leading us to assume $I(0)$ series (stationarity). For the growth of GDP, however, we can only assume $I(0)$ at the 90 percent confidence level. Hence, the stationarity of all the variables included in the regression of the import function is accepted.

Following Bairam (1988) and Atesoglu (1993), there could be simultaneity between y_t and m_t. Thus, for the estimation procedure, the two-stage least squares (2SLS) method was chosen.[3] The instrumental variables used were the rate of growth of real exports, private consumption, and relative prices.[4] A dummy variable for the years 1986, 1987, and 1988 is included to allow for the provisional effect on the rate of growth of imports of Spanish entry into the EU in 1986. The results are (*t*-ratios in parenthesis):

$$m_t = -0.276 + 1.916y_t + 0.150pr_{t-1} + 8.185D_t.$$
$$\quad(-0.145) \quad (4.195) \quad (1.304) \quad\quad (2.195)$$

Sargan's test $(\xi^2) = 0.108$
LM test of serial correlation $(\xi^2) = 0.621$

The Sargan test of misspecification of the model and the instrumental variables show that the model is jointly significant, and correction for residual autocorrelation is not necessary.[5] GDP growth and the dummy variable are significant at the 95 percent level, while neither the constant nor the relative price change variable is significant. The results support the hypothesis that relative prices are insignificant in determining international trade flows, as in Bairam (1988) and Bairam and Dempster (1991).

Thirlwall's Law for the Spanish economy

In order to test Thirlwall's Law for the Spanish economy from 1965 to 1993, we follow the procedure of Atesoglu (1993, 1994). Since the theory establishes a long-run relationship between the balance of payments condition and the growth rate of the economy, it makes no sense to test it year by year, but rather for longer periods.

Thus, we have taken the mean decennial rates of growth of the variables in overlapping periods starting from 1965–74 and ending in 1984–93. The balance of payments equilibrium growth rate of income has been obtained from expression (12.5) above, using the income elasticity from the estimated import function. The results are provided in Table 12.2. Column 1 shows the average actual growth rate of GDP; column 2 shows the growth of exports, column 3 the estimated balance of payments equilibrium growth rate, and the last column gives the difference between the balance of payments equilibrium growth rate and the actual growth rate.

Table 12.2 Actual and balance of payments equilibrium growth rates

Period	y_t	x_t	y_{bp}	$y_{bp} - y_t$
1965–74	6.41	12.85	6.71	0.29
1966–75	5.89	12.43	6.49	0.59
1967–76	5.49	11.00	5.74	0.25
1968–77	5.39	12.03	6.28	0.89
1969–78	4.89	10.48	5.47	0.58
1970–79	4.01	8.79	4.59	0.57
1971–80	3.73	7.18	3.75	0.02
1972–81	3.21	6.60	3.44	0.23
1973–82	2.52	5.74	2.99	0.48
1974–83	1.91	5.75	3.00	1.09
1975–84	1.52	7.03	3.67	2.15
1976–85	1.64	7.35	3.83	2.19
1977–86	1.67	6.97	3.64	1.97
1978–87	1.89	6.35	3.32	1.43
1979–88	2.23	6.03	3.15	0.92
1980–89	2.68	5.99	3.12	0.44
1981–90	2.93	6.08	3.17	0.24
1982–91	3.17	6.03	3.15	−0.02
1983–92	3.12	6.28	3.28	0.16
1984–93	2.83	6.10	3.18	0.35

The results show that, for the period analyzed, the Spanish economy's growth rate has been very close to the estimated balance of payments constrained growth rate. The periods where the divergence is more evident correspond to those when monetary instability was greater (i.e. mid-1970s and early 1980s), a fact that this strict version of the model cannot accommodate. Inflationary pressures generating an adverse movement in terms of trade combined with a sudden change in the long-run capital inflows[6] – which became large and negative. These factors, together with deflationary demand management policies to fight the high inflation rate, reduced Spain's growth rate below its potential given by its current balance of payments. Figure 12.1 shows the divergence between actual and equilibrium rates of growth, together with the relative price changes and the rate of growth of nominal long-run capital flows for the 20 overlapping periods analyzed. The figure shows the sudden change of capital inflows and the adverse relative price movements.

The correlation coefficient between the actual and the equilibrium growth rate is near 90 percent (89.23). If the 1975–84, 1976–85, and 1977–86 periods are removed, the coefficient is 96.2 percent.

However, as pointed by McGregor and Swales (1985), the use of a correlation coefficient is not sufficient to make solid assertions about the empirical validity of the law. It is necessary to apply tests on the parameters of the model. Their proposed test consists of estimating the following regression:

$$y_t = a + by_{bt} + u_t.$$

For the law to be statistically relevant, the constant must be equal to zero and b must equal one. That regression gives us the following results:

$$y_t = -0.966 + 1.05y_{bt}.$$
$$(-1.791) \ (8.380)$$

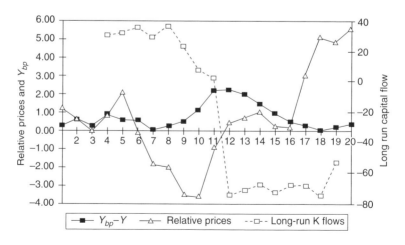

Figure 12.1 Prediction error versus relative prices and capital flows (rates of growth).

At the 95 percent confidence level, b is not significantly different from one, while a is not statistically different from zero. If we remove the 3 periods of greater monetary instability, 1975–84, 1976–85, and 1977–86, the results of the same regression are:

$$y_t = -0.485 + 0.996y_{bt}.$$
$$(-1.521) \quad (13.669)$$

The results strongly support the theory; $a = 0$ and $b = 1$ at the 95 percent confidence level. The model passes the McGregor–Swales test, but the use of that test, according to McCombie (1989), suffers from an important problem: The use of y_{bt} in the regression, since it is a variable obtained from the estimated value of π, introduces an associated standard error in the regressor. This fact leads to biased OLS estimates of the parameter of y_{bt}. A solution to this problem is to calculate the "mean balance of payments equilibrium income elasticity of imports" as follows: $\pi^* = x_t/y_t$, for each overlapping period and then obtain the mean π^* of the 20 observations. Once that value is obtained, the hypothesis of equivalence of the estimated π^* and π is tested. If both elasticities are not statistically different, that will also be true for y_t and y_{bt}. The mean value of π^* obtained for the 20 periods is 2.58, which is not statistically different from π estimated at the 95 percent confidence level. If, again, the 1975–84, 1976–85, and 1977–86 periods are removed from the exercise, we can support the fulfillment of the law at any confidence level (the value of π^* obtained is 1.92, with 1.91 the estimated value of π).

Conclusions

This chapter has examined a Keynesian model of growth where the growth of income for a country or region is determined by demand factors. Ultimately, it is the balance of payments that poses a limit on demand growth, and that determines why growth rates differ.

The test of this model for the Spanish economy from 1965 to 1993 shows that Spain's rate of growth has been very similar to that predicted by the theory. Although for the periods that cover the two energy crises, the movement of relative prices and long-run capital flows could have been expected to have played a role, the long-run regularity shows that the adjustment to balance of payments equilibrium came via income. The evidence in favor of this model is also supported by the existence of unemployed resources. The rate of unemployment at the end of 1976 was 4.6 percent, which rose to 20.9 percent in 1986 and 23.9 percent in 1994, and the labor participation rate was 51.13 percent in 1976, 47.9 percent in 1986, and 49.8 percent in 1994. Before 1976, migration of Spanish labor force to foreign countries was about 1.15 million between 1960 and 1976, which shows that migration was the safety valve for unemployed and underemployed labor force. Moreover, the endogencity of capital accumulation prevents the economy from being constrained by capital inputs. These facts together yield strong evidence in support of Thirlwall's Law that growth is demand determined by the balance of payments position rather than supply constrained as in neoclassical theory.

Notes

1 This model constitutes an export-led model of growth with a full macroeconomic the-oretical base. Most of the early works relating exports to growth were just a statistical relation between both variables, where causality tests were applied. The theoretical base was missing in these studies.

2 It is worth noting that the argument of the quantitative unimportance of relative price movements may also be seen in the low price elasticities of imports and exports. The Marshall–Lerner condition that the sum of price elasticities exceed unity may only just be met, making price movements quantitatively unimportant. This can also be related with the nonprice competition strategies dominating international trade flows.

3 Previous estimations using simple OLS gave implausibily low values of the income elas-ticity of demand for imports. This result may be attributed to some degree of endogeneity of the income variable that tends to bias the value of the income parameter downward.

4 Before proceeding to estimation, we also tested the possible existence of a unit root in the instrumental variables. The DF result showed the stationarity of the rate of growth of exports at the 5 percent confidence level, using a model with a constant and no time trend. The ADF, however, did not allow us to assert the stationarity of the export growth series. In the private consumption growth rate, mean change was detected for the years 1976–85 and 1992–94, and, henceforth, the method proposed by Perron (1990) was used, together with his critical values. The results reflect the stationarity of the series at the 5 percent confidence level. The results of both tests are provided in Table 12.1.

5 At this point it is worth noting that, in 2SLS estimations, the R^2 and DW tests do not have the usual interpretation, as in OLS.

6 A model of balance of payments constrained growth with capital flows was developed by Thirlwall and Hussain (1982). In accordance with this model, for some countries, the limit on growth could be the basic balance deficit (i.e. including long-run capital flows). These countries could grow above the equilibrium rate of growth for long periods because of the existence of strong long-run capital inflows. In the case of Spain, although just for some periods, these capital inflows could have had some influence, especially when strong and sudden inflows and outflows have taken place.

Part III
Developing countries

13 Balance of payments constrained growth and developing countries: an examination of Thirlwall's hypothesis[*]

Jonathan Perraton

Introduction

'Thirlwall's Law' of balance of payments constrained growth postulates that a country's growth rate is determined by the ratio of the income elasticity of demand for its exports to its income elasticity of demand for imports multiplied by world income growth. Although tested extensively for developed countries, it has been tested much less for developing countries.[1] It has often been claimed that the balance of payments is a significant constraint on developing countries' growth. Previous tests of Thirlwall's hypothesis for developing countries used small samples and dated estimates, whilst the econometric techniques used to derive the parameters may not have been robust. This chapter examines Thirlwall's hypothesis and argues that the objections often levelled at it may not apply to many developing countries. It then provides new estimates of Thirlwall's hypothesis for a large sample of developing countries. Many studies have used export variables to explain differences in developing countries' growth rates and taken positive results as support for neoclassical growth models. Testing Thirlwall's hypothesis can indicate whether the positive impact of exports on growth primarily operates through relieving an external demand constraint.

Thirlwall's hypothesis is now well known (e.g. McCombie and Thirlwall, 1994, 1997b). Current account equilibrium will be maintained over time if the domestic currency values of imports and exports grow at the same rate. Demand for a country's exports and imports are assumed to be stable functions of relative prices and income. The income elasticities are assumed to capture the influence of non-price factors on demand. If relative prices do not vary between countries, then the current account equilibrium growth rate for each country will be determined by the ratio of the world's income elasticity of demand for its exports to the country's income elasticity of demand for imports. This chapter tests whether Thirlwall's hypothesis holds for a large sample of developing countries since 1973. The section, 'Theoretical issues', considers several theoretical issues concerning the hypothesis in the developing country context. The section, 'Modelling

* First published in *International Review of Applied Economics*, Vol. 17, No. 1, 2003.

framework', discusses modelling issues for deriving the demand elasticities. The section, 'Empirical estimates', presents estimates for the sample countries. The last section concludes.

Theoretical issues

Several possible objections have been raised to Thirlwall's hypothesis; these are considered here in the developing country context.

Amongst developed countries, growth rates are strongly correlated with the growth rate of total factor productivity. McCombie and Thirlwall (1994, ch. 2) argue that an external demand constraint on growth is consistent with this observation if productivity is determined in accordance with 'Verdoorn's Law'. Others have argued that this is not plausible. In particular, Krugman (1989a) shows that differences in income and productivity growth rates determined by supply-side factors could give rise to apparent differences in income elasticities of demand consistent with the empirical predictions of Thirlwall's hypothesis. This can occur when the growth process takes the form of expanding numbers of imperfectly competitive firms. Although not explicitly directed at Thirlwall's hypothesis, Krugman's argument can be seen as modelling some criticisms of Thirlwall's hypothesis from McGregor and Swales (1985, 1986, 1991).

Whether 'Verdoorn's Law' is a plausible hypothesis to underpin Thirlwall's hypothesis may be a less important question with developing countries. Growth accounting indicates that even the Asian newly industrialising economies (NIEs) have not experienced particularly high-productivity growth, with growth being primarily generated by high rates of factor accumulation (Young, 1995). Since even the NIEs rely heavily on imported capital goods, Thirlwall's hypothesis can be rationalised for developing countries if growth is dependent on import capacity. Imports of capital goods are central to developing countries' growth, with limited possibilities for substituting domestic production for imports of capital goods (Marquez, 1985; Lee, 1995). Incorporating imports into aggregate production function models of growth demonstrates that growth may in principle be constrained by external demand (Bardhan, 1970, ch. 4; Bochove, 1982; Ziesemer, 1995).

Beyond the particular features of Krugman's (1989a) model, Krugman's critique raises a more general point. Thirlwall's hypothesis presumes that countries' patterns of trade endure over time and it is this that produces stable elasticities of demand. Others have argued that the high-estimated income elasticities of demand for Asian NIEs' exports are an artefact, reflecting changing patterns of exports as they develop new products for export and upgrade existing ones (Muscatelli *et al.*, 1994, 1995). Although the Asian NIEs have seen significant shifts in their export patterns over this period, this appears to be the exception rather than the rule amongst developing countries (Lafay, 1992; Chow and Kellman, 1993; Noland, 1997). For other developing countries, patterns of exports appear to be much more stable over time, indicating the lock-in of comparative advantage implied in Thirlwall's hypothesis. Accordingly, the section 'Empirical estimates', examines whether tests of Thirlwall's hypothesis are sensitive to the inclusion of the Asian NIEs.[2]

The concept of a balance of payments constraint on growth would be meaningless if these economies were small countries in the trade theory sense, that is, if they faced infinitely elastic demand for their exports. Although some studies find that developing countries approximate to the small country case, the estimates supporting this are not robust and other estimates indicate that developing economies are not small countries in the trade theory sense and therefore do face demand constraints on their export growth. These issues are dealt with further in the section, 'Modelling framework', but there are at least four main reasons why developing economies may not be small countries in the trade theory sense. First, some are already major world exporters of certain products. This can be seen with certain primary commodities, but also now with some manufactures. Table 13.1 lists those developing countries which have at least a 10 per cent share of world trade in various manufactures (defined at the SITC 3-digit classification level). Second, the term 'small' can be misleading: even where countries have small shares in world trade they may still export differentiated products and thus face imperfect competition. Third, developing countries may face protection against their exports. Fourth, the small country hypothesis neglects institutional features of world markets. Developing country exports, especially of manufactures, are often sold through marketing contracts with developed country purchasers. This can create important barriers to entry for developing country exporters and insider–outsider relationships to developed country markets for these exporters (Mody and Yilmaz, 1997).

Provided that the export- and import demand functions are properly specified, Thirlwall's hypothesis can be tested against the data. Importation of capital equipment can provide a theoretical justification for external demand determining income and productivity growth rates. Although it is possible that causality may run from growth to changes in trade patterns in a manner consistent with empirical tests of Thirlwall's hypothesis, as Krugman suggests, this is likely to apply to a small group of developing countries at most.

Modelling framework

Since Thirlwall's hypothesis assumes that demand for imports and exports are stable functions of income and their relative price, tests of the hypotheses have typically estimated functions of the following general forms for each country:

$$M = f(Y, P_m, P_d), \tag{13.1}$$

$$X = g(Y_w, P_x, P_w, E), \tag{13.2}$$

where M, X and Y are real values of imports, exports and income for the domestic country, P_m is an index of the domestic price of imports and P_d is a domestic price index. For the export function, Y_w is world real income, P_x is an index of the domestic price of exports, P_w is a world export price index and E is the nominal

Table 13.1 Selected countries' shares of world manufactured exports, 1993–94

Country	Commodity	SITC	Share of world exports (%)
China	Cotton fabrics	652	15.1
	Textile articles nes	658	19.3
	Radio receivers	762	13.1
	Travel goods, handbags	831	24.7
	Mens outwear not knit	842	19.4
	Womens outwear not knit	843	17.9
	Underwear not knit	844	19.8
	Outwear knitted	845	12.2
	Undergarments knitted	846	11.6
	Headgear	848	20.5
	Footwear	851	17.9
	Watches and clocks	885	10.4
Hong Kong	Outwear knitted	845	11.2
	Watches and clocks	885	10.1
Indonesia	Veneers, etc.	634	33.6
Korea	Leather goods	611	10.0
	Woven man-made fibre	653	19.7
	Knitted fabrics	655	11.5
	Ships and boats	793	13.8
Malaysia	Veneers, etc.	634	11.3
	Radio receivers	762	16.5
	Sound recorders	763	10.6
Mexico	Television receivers	761	11.6
	Electrical distribution equipment	773	13.9
Singapore	Auto data process equipment	752	14.4
	Radio receivers	762	14.0
	Sound recorders	763	11.1
Taiwan	Knitted fabrics	655	22.1
	Special textile fabric	657	13.6
	Television receivers	761	10.6

Source: UNCTAD, *Handbook of International Trade and Development Statistics 1995* (New York: United Nations, 1997), Table 4.4.

exchange rate. However, it cannot simply be assumed that demand for imports and exports for developing countries take the standard forms of (13.1) and (13.2).

The first problem with estimating import demand functions for developing countries is protection. Tariffs imply that prices faced by domestic consumers differ from border prices; if they vary over the estimation period, and the data used are for border prices, then the estimates of the price elasticity will be biased. Where countries operate quantitative restrictions on imports, domestic consumers face demand rationing. Time-varying levels of protection would affect the errors in estimates of import demand functions, but this could be misdiagnosed as serial correlation. However, in the absence of direct time series data on protection, there is no clear solution to this and it is more appropriate to test directly whether functions of the form (13.1) provide good estimators. Some studies incorporate lagged foreign exchange reserves into the function as an indicator of foreign exchange shortage and assume that the authorities adjust protection in response, but this is not robust (Faini *et al.*, 1992b).

Net capital flows could introduce instability into import demand functions in developing countries. Under Thirlwall's hypothesis, net capital inflows, by increasing import capacity, would raise income in proportion given by the income elasticity of demand for imports. Thus, capital flows would determine income levels and not affect the income elasticities of demand for imports. If this holds then the import demand functions could still be stable with capital flows. Mirakhor and Montiel (1987) find some evidence of stability in import demand functions for developing countries since the 1960s. The estimates later test for a structural break. Further, the section, 'Empirical estimates', examines the performance of those sample countries which borrowed extensively to see whether their growth rates systematically exceeded that predicted by Thirlwall's hypothesis.

Turning to export demand, Riedel claims that estimates from standard procedures give implausibly large estimates of income elasticities and implausibly low estimates of price elasticities, with differences in export growth rates apparently explained by differences in income elasticities of demand (Riedel, 1988; Athukorala and Riedel, 1996). Obviously export growth being largely determined by growth in world demand is in accordance with Thirlwall's hypothesis, although it is not always the case that estimated income elasticities are simply correlated with export growth rates (Mody and Yilmaz, 1997). Riedel claims that strong estimates for income elasticities of demand for exports are due to trending in the data, but obviously this should be dealt with by appropriate attention to its time-series properties. He proposes normalising estimates of (13.1) so that export price is the dependent variable and testing whether the coefficient on export volume is significant; if it is not, one cannot reject the hypothesis that the economy is a small country in the trade theory sense. However, this normalisation only provides a weak test of the small country hypothesis and one which is biased towards accepting it; even so, estimates reject the small country hypothesis for many developing countries (Faini *et al.*, 1992a; Muscatelli *et al.*, 1994). In previous studies both high-estimated income elasticities and apparent support for the small country hypothesis when (13.1) is normalised for export price appear to be due to trending in the data. Appropriate estimation should avoid this. As noted earlier, if a country's export composition changes significantly over the period for which export demand is estimated then the apparent estimated income elasticity may be misleading. Hence, we examine whether tests for Thirlwall's hypothesis are sensitive to including countries for which this may be the case.

Overall, although there are potential difficulties with estimating import- and export demand functions for developing countries, it is still appropriate to estimate these and test whether they have the classical statistical properties. Estimates of import- and export demand functions used in past studies of Thirlwall's hypothesis usually did not test for unit roots and consequently the results from these estimations may not be robust. Testing for unit roots with these data found that the series were usually I(1). Consequently, import- and export demand functions for each country are estimated here using an error correction specification of the standard forms (13.1) and (13.2). This should also address some of the concerns noted earlier with the estimation of export demand functions. From these results we can derive the long-run income elasticities of demand, which are appropriate for testing Thirlwall's hypothesis.

Having derived the parameters for each sample country, the next step is to test Thirlwall's hypothesis. A distinction can be drawn between 'weak' and 'strong' forms of Thirlwall's hypothesis. Taking π to denote the income elasticity of demand for imports and ε to denote the world income elasticity of demand for exports, and using lower-case letters to denote rates of change of variables, Thirlwall's hypothesis can be expressed as follows. From initial balance of payments equilibrium and assuming no relative price changes, a country's balance of payments constrained growth rate is determined by the ratio of the income elasticities multiplied by the world income growth rate: countries cannot exceed this without falling relative prices or capital inflows. (Note, too, that the relative price of domestic production would have to fall continuously to raise the balance of payments equilibrium growth rate, assuming the Marshall–Lerner condition was satisfied.) Thus the 'strong' form of Thirlwall's hypothesis predicts that a country's growth rate will approximate to:

$$y = \left(\frac{\varepsilon}{\pi}\right) y_w. \tag{13.3}$$

If the actual growth of exports can be assumed to approximate to the rate determined by external demand growth, particularly where it may be difficult to derive robust estimates of the export demand elasticities, the 'weak' form of Thirlwall's hypothesis can be tested as predicting that a country's growth rate will approximate to:

$$y = \left(\frac{x}{\pi}\right). \tag{13.4}$$

Thirlwall's hypothesis is straightforward to test if we can assume away net capital movements and changes in relative prices between the sample countries and the rest of the world. For developed countries these may be reasonable approximations. But whilst it may be realistic to assume that developing countries cannot engineer persistent changes in their relative prices to improve their trade performance, it is not realistic to assume that developing countries experienced no relative price changes over this period. On the contrary, most of the sample countries experienced significant terms of trade movements. On capital inflows, a country's current account deficit cannot grow indefinitely and thereby relieve their external constraint on growth. A period of net borrowing would be expected to be followed by a period of trade surplus during repayment; as such exports must grow in line with imports over an extended period. Further, attempting to relieve the balance of payments constraint by external borrowing risks falling into a debt trap. Nevertheless, many of these countries experienced significant capital flows at times during this period and these would have been expected to affect their growth rates. Thirlwall advocates incorporating capital flows into his scheme by computing the weighted average of the real growth rate of capital inflows and export volume, and dividing this by the income elasticity of demand for imports (Thirlwall and Hussain, 1982; McCombie and Thirlwall, 1994, ch. 3). This would not be a robust procedure here as the growth rate of capital flows fluctuated widely for many of these countries; for many countries net capital flows fluctuated between deficit and surplus, making calculation of their growth rate impossible. Over the period as a whole most of the countries were not systematic net borrowers. Consequently, we focus here on incorporating the impact of terms of trade changes, but later we examine whether foreign borrowing in the 1970s boosted growth rates in the main debtor countries.

Terms of trade changes will affect the balance of payments constrained growth rate both directly through their effect on import capacity and indirectly through any relative price effect on demand (Thirlwall and Hussain, 1982; McCombie and Thirlwall, 1994, ch. 3). To simplify the exposition, assume an aggregate price level for all home goods (P) and all foreign goods (P_w). As the economy grows over time balance of payments equilibrium implies:

$$p + x = p_w + m + e. \tag{13.5}$$

The demand functions for imports and exports imply:

$$m = \eta(p_w + e - p) + \pi y, \tag{13.6}$$
$$x = \psi(p - p_w - e) + \varepsilon y_w. \tag{13.7}$$

Substituting (13.6) and (13.7) into (13.5) and solving for the balance of payments constrained growth rate gives:

$$y = \frac{(1 + \eta + \psi)(p - p_w - e) + \varepsilon y_w}{\pi}. \tag{13.8}$$

In principle therefore we could estimate both the pure terms of trade effect, the change in the terms of trade divided by the income elasticity of demand for imports and the price adjustment. However, since the price data are likely to be less accurate than the income data, less reliance can be placed on the estimated price elasticities. Therefore, we estimate a modified balance of payments constrained growth rate by adding the pure terms of trade effect to the estimates of (13.3) and (13.4); any major price adjustment to demand is clearly not within the logic of Thirlwall's hypothesis.

Empirical estimates

It seems appropriate to test Thirlwall's hypothesis for the period since 1973 given evidence of structural breaks in macroeconomic series around then, not least in trade series (Ben-David and Pappell, 1997). The sample is those low- and middle-income countries for which consistent data are available, excluding predominantly oil exporters and countries with a population below one million. Sources are given in the 'data appendix'. In this section, we report estimates of import- and export demand elasticities and use these to test Thirlwall's hypothesis; we also use estimates of import elasticities from an earlier study for comparison. A Chow test for a structural break in 1981 is included; any date would be somewhat arbitrary, but this divides the sample by a major slowdown in the world economy and the onset of the 1980s debt crisis. Data are available for trade in goods and nonfactor services and for merchandise imports and exports alone; where reasonable results cannot be obtained for imports or exports of goods and nonfactor services, the function was estimated for merchandise imports or exports only. For imports of goods and services a domestic index of import prices is used, which should reflect changes in tariff rates as well as changes in border prices and the exchange rate. Out of a sample of 51 countries, it was only possible to derive reasonable estimates of the import demand function for 34. These include 10 where the Chow test for a structural break was significant at the 10 per cent level, 7 of which were also significant at the 5 per cent level. Earlier studies were also unable to obtain reasonable estimates of import demand functions for many developing countries (cf. Faini *et al.*, 1992b). Some countries, especially in Africa, experienced profound economic dislocation over this period. Others may not have experienced such difficulties, but their development processes entailed major structural change and/or shifts in their trade policy; either of which could lead to instabilities in demand functions. The widespread shift away from import-substituting industrialisation policies amongst many of these countries since the 1970s may have affected these elasticities. Growth may or may not still be limited by the balance of payments, but this cannot be tested in terms of Thirlwall's hypothesis where we cannot obtain stable estimates for the income elasticities of demand.

Of the 34 countries for which statistically significant estimates of the import demand function could be obtained, in 27 cases it was possible to produce statistically significant estimates of the export demand function. This includes 11 countries where the Chow test for a structural break is significant at the 10 per cent level, 7 of which are also significant at the 5 per cent level. We have emphasised that changes in export composition may lead to misleading estimates of income elasticities. This would not necessarily lead to a structural break, but a structural break may indicate a significant change in the composition of a country's exports. Accordingly, we examine later whether the tests of Thirlwall's hypothesis are sensitive to the inclusion of estimates where there is evidence of a structural break.

For comparison, we also use estimates of import elasticities for developing countries from Senhadji (1998), who tests a slightly different specification for data over 1960–93.[3] Although these estimates do not include tests for structural breaks, the comparison does allow us to examine how sensitive tests of Thirlwall's hypothesis are to different estimates of the demand elasticities and a slightly different country sample.

Table 13.2 Tests of 'weak' form of Thirlwall's hypothesis, 1973–95

	Export volume growth (x)	Income elasticity of demand for imports (π)	Predicted growth rate (x/π)	Actual growth rate	Annual terms of trade change (tot)	Pure terms of trade effect (tot/π)	Predicted growth rate plus pure terms of trade effect
Argentina	4.61	3.01	1.53†	1.16	−3.36	−1.12	0.42
Bangladesh	7.99	1.29	6.19	4.37	−1.44	−1.12	5.08†
Bolivia	1.10	0.50	2.20†	1.12	−1.85	−3.70	−1.50
Brazil	7.98	1.77	4.51†	2.94	−2.21	−1.25	3.26†
Burundi	3.43	0.61	5.62†	3.43	−5.12	−8.39	−2.77
Cameroon	9.42	0.88	10.70	3.64	−2.76	−3.14	7.57
Cote d'Ivoire	3.13	1.95	1.61	0.75	−1.64	−0.84	0.76†
Costa Rica	6.05	1.76	3.44†	3.32	−1.78	−1.01	2.43†
Dominican Rep.	6.53	1.15	5.68	3.32	−2.28	−1.98	3.70†
Ecuador	4.35	0.24	18.13	3.31	0.74	3.08	21.21
El Salvador	0.55	3.26	0.17	0.81	−3.17	−0.97	−0.80
Guatemala	0.41	0.69	0.59†	2.25	−2.66	−3.86	−3.26
Haiti	0.77	1.96	0.39	0.23	−1.50	−0.77	−0.37
Honduras	2.11	0.56	3.77†	3.46	−1.75	−3.13	0.64†
India	5.88	0.88	6.68	4.84	−1.25	−1.42	5.26†
Jamaica	−0.22	1.51	−0.15	0.65	−1.09	−0.72	−0.87
Kenya	3.21	1.84	1.74†	3.21	−2.25	−1.22	0.52
Korea	11.96	0.70	17.09	8.49	−0.46	−0.66	16.43
Madagascar	−0.69	11.00	−0.06†	0.49	−2.32	−0.21	−0.27†
Malaysia	10.49	1.66	6.32†	6.67	−0.75	−0.45	5.87†
Mali	4.14	0.87	4.76	2.27	0.15	0.17	4.93
Mauritius	6.82	1.17	5.83†	5.15	−0.48	−0.41	5.42†
Nicaragua	−2.48	0.27	−9.19	−1.93	−3.68	−13.63	−22.81
Pakistan	8.77	0.83	10.57	6.10	−2.61	−3.14	7.42†
Panama	4.73	0.26	18.19	3.06	−0.82	−3.15	15.04
Peru	1.54	0.94	1.64†	0.99	−3.48	−3.70	−2.06
Philippines	6.50	0.92	7.07†	2.49	−1.58	−1.72	5.35†
Senegal	2.75	0.98	2.81†	2.50	−0.96	−0.98	1.83†
Sri Lanka	5.31	1.44	3.69†	4.65	−1.89	−1.31	2.38†
Thailand	12.78	1.45	8.81†	7.65	−1.87	−1.29	7.52†
Togo	0.67	5.00	0.13†	1.60	−4.71	−0.94	−0.81†
Trinidad	6.63	1.43	4.64	0.62	−0.97	−0.68	3.96
Turkey	12.56	2.11	5.95†	4.47	−1.04	−0.49	5.46†
Uruguay	5.60	2.78	2.01†	1.61	−1.40	−0.50	1.51†

Table 13.2 reports the long-run income elasticities of demand for imports, together with the predicted and actual growth rates. The 'weak' form of Thirlwall's hypothesis can be tested in one of two ways: first, by testing whether the estimated income elasticity of demand for imports is significantly different from the value required to make the estimated growth rate equal to the actual growth rate. Second, it can be tested by estimating actual growth rates as a function of predicted ones: if Thirlwall's hypothesis holds, then a regression of actual on predicted growth rates

should yield an intercept term of zero and a slope coefficient of unity. McCombie and Thirlwall (1994, ch. 5) argue that it is more appropriate to regress predicted growth rates as a function of actual growth rates: since the predicted growth rate is derived from estimates of the parameters it is subject to errors and therefore produces an error in variables problem. Further, unless the surpluses and deficits amongst the sample countries cancel out the results from such a regression will be biased and may lead to rejection of the hypothesis even where the majority of sample countries are balance of payments constrained.

In Table 13.2, a † indicates that we cannot reject the hypothesis that the estimated income elasticity of demand for imports is equal to the value required to make the estimated growth rate equal to the actual growth rate on a Wald test at the 95 per cent level. Thus, for 19 countries of the sample – a majority – we cannot reject the weak form of Thirlwall's hypothesis.

Regressing the predicted growth rates as a function of the actual rates gave the following result (t-statistics in parentheses):

$$\text{Predicted Growth Rate} = -0.11 + 1.67 \text{ Actual Growth Rate,}$$
$$-(0.09) \ (5.30)$$
$$R^2 = 0.47 \quad \bar{R}^2 = 0.45 \quad SEE = 4.07 \quad F = 28.05,$$

where the Wald test rejects the joint hypothesis that the intercept coefficient is zero and the slope coefficient is unity at the 1 per cent level. Here the 'weak' form of Thirlwall's hypothesis overpredicts the actual growth rate where it was above 0.16 (which it was for all but one of the sample countries).

Table 13.2 also reports estimates of the balance of payments constrained growth adjusted for terms of trade movements. Again, a † indicates that we cannot reject the hypothesis that the estimated income elasticity of demand for imports is equal to the value required to make the estimated growth rate equal to the actual growth rate on a Wald test at the 95 per cent level. For 18 countries we cannot reject Thirlwall's hypothesis. Regressing the adjusted predicted growth rates as a function of the actual growth rates gave the following result:

$$\text{Predicted Growth Rate} = -3.05 + 2.03 \text{ Actual Growth Rate,}$$
$$(-1.96) \ (4.79)$$
$$R^2 = 0.42 \quad \bar{R}^2 = 0.40 \quad SEE = 5.46 \quad F = 22.96,$$

where the Wald test only rejects the joint hypothesis that the intercept coefficient is zero and the slope coefficient is unity at the 10 per cent level. The overall fit is slightly poorer than for the unadjusted 'weak' form. For this sample the 'weak' form of Thirlwall's hypothesis adjusted for terms of trade effects overpredicts the growth rate where the actual growth rate was above 2.96 (which it was for 17 countries). Excluding those countries where the Chow test indicated a structural break in their import demand functions did not significantly affect the regression tests of the 'weak' form of Thirlwall's hypothesis whether or not this was adjusted for terms of trade movements.

Table 13.3 Tests of 'weak' form of Thirlwall's hypothesis, 1973–95 (Senhadji data)

	Export volume growth (x)	Income elasticity of demand for imports (π)	Predicted growth rate (x/π)	Actual growth rate	Annual terms of trade change (tot)	Pure terms of trade effect (tot/π)	Predicted growth rate plus pure terms of trade effect
Argentina	4.61	1.21	3.81	1.16	−3.36	−2.78	1.03†
Benin	1.20	4.91	0.24†	3.19	−1.71	−0.35	−0.10†
Brazil	7.98	1.24	6.44	2.94	−2.21	−1.78	4.65
Burundi	3.43	1.63	2.10†	3.43	−5.12	−3.14	−1.04
Cameroon	9.42	1.01	9.33	3.64	−2.76	−2.73	6.59
Chile	8.69	1.87	4.65†	4.65	−2.79	−1.49	3.16
Colombia	6.36	1.09	5.83	3.94	−2.52	−2.31	3.52†
Congo	6.10	0.87	7.01†	4.81	1.57	1.80	8.82
Costa Rica	6.05	1.21	5.00†	3.32	−1.78	−1.47	3.53†
Cote d'Ivoire	3.13	0.96	3.26	0.75	−1.64	−1.71	1.55
Dominican Rep.	6.53	0.86	7.59	3.32	−2.28	−2.65	4.94
El Salvador	0.55	1.47	0.37	0.81	−3.17	−2.16	−1.78
Gambia	3.28	1.51	2.17†	3.28	−2.87	−1.90	0.27†
Haiti	0.77	2.79	0.28†	0.23	−1.50	−0.54	−0.26
Honduras	2.11	0.74	2.85†	3.46	−1.75	−2.36	0.49†
India	5.88	1.33	4.42†	4.84	−1.25	−0.94	3.48†
Indonesia	3.64	0.98	3.71	6.32	−0.17	−0.17	3.54
Kenya	3.21	1.14	2.82†	3.21	−2.25	−1.97	0.84
Korea	11.96	1.32	9.06†	8.49	−0.46	−0.35	8.71†
Madagascar	−0.69	0.52	−1.33†	0.49	−2.32	−4.46	−5.79
Malawi	3.11	1.14	2.73†	2.78	−1.60	−1.40	1.32
Mauritania	2.81	2.83	0.99†	2.03	−1.49	−0.53	0.47†
Mauritius	6.82	2.25	3.03†	5.15	−0.48	−0.21	2.82†
Mexico	7.49	1.31	5.72	2.92	−0.76	−0.58	5.14
Morocco	4.40	1.23	3.58†	4.13	−0.06	−0.05	3.53†
Nicaragua	−2.48	0.57	−4.35	−1.93	−3.68	−6.46	−10.81
Pakistan	8.77	0.82	10.70	6.10	−2.61	−3.18	7.51
Panama	4.73	0.99	4.78	3.06	−0.82	−0.83	3.95
Paraguay	9.27	1.58	5.87	4.66	−1.52	−0.96	4.91†
Peru	1.54	0.50	3.08	0.99	−3.48	−6.96	−3.88
Philippines	6.50	2.25	2.89†	2.49	−1.58	−0.70	2.19†
Thailand	12.78	1.67	7.65†	7.65	−1.87	−1.12	6.53†
Trinidad	6.63	0.50	13.26	0.62	−0.97	−1.94	11.32
Turkey	12.56	1.78	7.06†	4.47	−1.04	−0.58	6.47†
Uruguay	5.60	5.48	1.02†	1.61	−1.40	−0.26	0.77†
Zambia	−1.40	0.34	−4.12	0.61	−2.76	−8.12	−12.24

Testing the 'weak' form of Thirlwall's hypothesis using the estimates of the income elasticity of demand for imports in Senhadji (1998) gave the results reported in Table 13.3. Again we can test the hypothesis in two ways. Constructing 95 per cent confidence intervals for the income elasticity of demand for imports from their *t*-statistics, we cannot reject the hypothesis that the estimated income elasticity of demand for imports is equal to the value required to make the estimated growth rate equal to the actual growth rate for 20 of the 36 sample countries, a clear majority. Alternatively, regressing the predicted growth rate as a function of the actual growth rate gave the following result:

$$\text{Predicted Growth Rate} = 0.86 + 0.99 \text{ Actual Growth Rate,}$$
$$(0.93) \quad (4.11)$$
$$R^2 = 0.33 \quad \bar{R}^2 = 0.31 \quad SEE = 3.09 \quad F = 16.88,$$

where the Wald test cannot reject the joint hypothesis that the intercept coefficient is zero and the slope coefficient is unity. Thus these estimates provide more support for Thirlwall's hypothesis than estimates from elasticities derived in this study, although the overall fit of this function is poorer. Adding the pure terms of trade effect to this predicted growth rates gives the modified predicted growth rates as earlier. In this case, 16 of the estimated elasticities – slightly under half – fell within their confidence intervals, and so we could not reject Thirlwall's hypothesis. Again, regressing this as a function of actual growth rates gave the following result:

$$\text{Predicted Growth Rate} = -2.52 + 1.47 \text{ Actual Growth Rate,}$$
$$(-2.26) \quad (5.03)$$
$$R^2 = 0.43 \quad \bar{R}^2 = 0.41 \quad SEE = 3.74 \quad F = 25.29,$$

where the Wald test only rejects the joint hypothesis that the intercept coefficient is zero and the slope coefficient is unity at the 10 per cent level. However, the overall fit of this regression is stronger than for the unadjusted 'weak' form of Thirlwall's hypothesis. For this sample the 'weak' form of Thirlwall's hypothesis adjusted for terms of trade effects tends to underpredict the actual growth rate as it would overpredict it when the actual growth rate was above 5.36, which it was for only 4 of the 36 sample countries.

Values for the long-run income elasticity of demand for exports are derived[4] and used to provide estimates of the 'strong' form of Thirlwall's hypothesis as reported in Table 13.4. We can only test the 'strong' form of Thirlwall's hypothesis by regressing predicted growth rates as a function of actual ones: we lack the sampling theory to construct confidence intervals for estimates of both the import and export income elasticities of demand. Regressing the predicted growth rates as a function of the actual growth rates gave the following result:

$$\text{Predicted Growth Rate} = 0.85 + 1.28 \text{ Actual Growth Rate,}$$
$$(0.94) \quad (5.49)$$
$$R^2 = 0.55 \quad \bar{R}^2 = 0.53 \quad SEE = 2.67 \quad F = 30.18,$$

where the Wald test rejects the joint hypothesis that the intercept coefficient is zero and the slope coefficient is unity at the 1 per cent level. However, the fit of this regression is stronger than for the 'weak' form (on a smaller sample). Thus the 'strong' form of Thirlwall's hypothesis tends to overpredict the actual growth rate

Table 13.4 Tests of 'strong' form of Thirlwall's hypothesis, 1973–95

	Income elasticity of demand for exports (ε)	Income elasticity of demand for imports (π)	Predicted growth rate $((\varepsilon/\pi)^*$ world growth rate)	Actual growth rate	Annual terms of trade change (tot)	Pure terms of trade effect (tot/π)	Predicted growth rate plus pure terms of trade effect
Argentina	1.31	3.01	1.41	1.16	−3.36	−1.12	0.30
Bolivia	0.23	0.50	1.50	1.12	−1.85	−3.70	−2.21
Brazil	1.92	1.77	3.53	2.94	−2.21	−1.25	2.28
Burundi	0.99	0.61	5.27	3.43	−5.12	−8.39	−3.12
Cote d'Ivoire	0.38	1.95	0.63	0.75	−1.64	−0.84	−0.21
Costa Rica	2.77	1.76	5.12	3.32	−1.78	−1.01	4.10
Dominican Rep.	1.91	1.15	5.40	3.32	−2.28	−1.98	3.42
Ecuador	0.61	0.24	8.26	3.31	0.74	3.08	11.34
Haiti	0.57	1.96	0.95	0.23	−1.50	−0.77	0.18
Honduras	0.78	0.56	4.53	3.46	−1.75	−3.13	1.40
India	1.92	0.88	7.09	4.84	−1.25	−1.42	5.67
Jamaica	0.55	1.51	1.18	0.65	−1.09	−0.72	0.46
Kenya	0.63	1.84	1.11	3.21	−2.25	−1.22	−0.11
Korea	3.11	0.70	14.44	8.49	−0.46	−0.66	13.78
Madagascar	0.71	11.00	0.21	0.49	−2.32	−0.21	−0.001
Malaysia	3.24	1.66	6.34	6.67	−0.75	−0.45	5.89
Mali	1.33	0.87	4.97	2.27	0.15	0.17	5.14
Mauritius	2.24	1.17	6.22	5.15	−0.48	−0.41	5.81
Pakistan	2.63	0.83	10.30	6.10	−2.61	−3.14	7.15
Panama	1.21	0.26	15.13	3.06	−0.82	−3.15	11.97
Peru	0.69	0.94	2.39	0.99	−3.48	−3.70	−1.32
Senegal	0.65	0.98	2.16	2.50	−0.96	−0.98	1.18
Sri Lanka	2.63	1.44	5.94	4.65	−1.89	−1.31	4.62
Thailand	3.83	1.45	8.58	7.65	−1.87	−1.29	7.29
Trinidad	1.78	1.43	4.05	0.62	−0.97	−0.68	3.37
Turkey	3.42	2.11	5.27	4.47	−1.04	−0.49	4.77
Uruguay	1.49	2.78	1.74	1.61	−1.40	−0.50	1.24

for this sample. Excluding the Asian NIEs did not significantly affect the results, nor did excluding those countries where a Chow test indicated a structural break in either their import- or export demand functions.

Adjusting the predicted growth rates from the 'strong' form of Thirlwall's hypothesis by adding the pure terms of trade effect as before and regressing the results against the actual growth rates gave the following result:

$$\text{Predicted Growth Rate} = -0.62 + 1.29 \text{ Actual Growth Rate,}$$
$$(-0.57) \ (4.59)$$
$$R^2 = 0.46 \quad \bar{R}^2 = 0.44 \quad SEE = 3.21 \quad F = 21.07,$$

where the Wald test cannot reject the joint hypothesis that the intercept coefficient is zero and the slope coefficient is unity, although the overall fit of the regression is poorer than for the unadjusted form. Excluding either the Asian NIEs, or those countries where Chow tests indicated a structural break in their estimates of the import- or export demand function, did not significantly affect this result. Thus, the estimates here support Thirlwall's hypothesis in its 'strong' form as an explanation of growth rate differences once the impact of terms of trade movements on import capacity are taken into account.

To assess the impact of capital flows here we examine a subgroup of the sample that borrowed heavily during the 1970s to see whether this boosted their growth rate by relieving a balance of payments constraint during that period. This subgroup includes those classified as Heavily Indebted Countries in the 1980s, but since this might bias the sample towards countries that made inefficient use of their loans it also includes those classified as Market Borrowers.[5] Interestingly, of the 12 countries in this subgroup, for only 3 did the Chow test indicate a structural break in their import demand functions. This would suggest that capital inflows did not alter the income elasticities of demand for imports in most borrowing countries. Tables 13.5 and 13.6 report the actual growth rates during the 1973–81 period for these countries, together with estimated growth rates from the 'weak' and 'strong' forms of Thirlwall's hypothesis, respectively. In each case, the mean predicted growth rate was higher than the mean actual growth rate, the reverse of what would be expected if capital flows enabled countries to grow more rapidly than the balance of payments constrained rate. Again, a † indicates that we cannot reject the hypothesis that the estimated income elasticity of demand for imports is equal to the value required to make the estimated growth rate equal to the actual growth rate: this is the case for 5 countries on the standard test and 6 once adjusted

Table 13.5 Tests of 'weak' form of Thirlwall's hypothesis for debtor countries, 1973–81

	Export volume growth (x)	Income elasticity of demand for imports (π)	Predicted growth rate (x/π)	Actual growth rate	Annual terms of trade change (tot)	Pure terms of trade effect (tot/π)	Predicted growth rate plus pure terms of trade effect
Argentina	7.97	3.01	2.65	1.84	−6.58	−2.19	0.46
Bolivia	−2.97	0.50	−5.94	3.21	7.91	15.82	9.88
Brazil	8.76	1.77	4.95†	5.71	−5.41	−3.06	1.89†
Cote d'Ivoire	8.08	1.95	4.14†	5.57	4.97	2.55	6.69†
Ecuador	0.30	0.24	1.25†	6.28	12.12	50.50	51.75
Korea	15.65	0.70	22.36	8.80	−2.24	−3.20	19.16
Malaysia	7.97	1.66	4.80	7.53	5.55	3.34	8.14†
Panama	7.79	0.26	29.96	5.02	4.09	15.73	45.69
Peru	6.74	0.94	7.17†	2.84	−6.20	−6.60	0.57†
Philippines	10.38	0.92	11.28†	5.61	−6.57	−7.14	4.14†
Trinidad	1.21	1.43	0.85	6.89	6.70	4.68	5.53†
Uruguay	10.28	2.78	3.70†	4.27	−6.09	−2.19	1.51

Table 13.6 Tests of 'strong' form of Thirlwall's hypothesis for debtor countries, 1973–81

	Income elasticity of demand for exports (ε)	Income elasticity of demand for imports (π)	Predicted growth rate $((\varepsilon/\pi)^*$ world growth rate)	Actual growth rate	Annual terms of trade change (tot)	Pure terms of trade effect (tot/π)	Predicted growth rate plus pure terms of trade effect
Argentina	1.31	3.01	1.54	1.84	−6.58	−2.19	−0.65
Bolivia	0.23	0.50	1.62	3.21	7.91	15.82	17.44
Brazil	1.92	1.77	3.83	5.71	−5.41	−3.06	0.77
Cote d'Ivoire	0.38	1.95	0.69	5.57	4.97	2.55	3.24
Ecuador	0.61	0.24	8.97	6.28	12.12	50.50	59.47
Korea	3.11	0.70	15.68	8.80	−2.24	−3.20	12.48
Malaysia	3.24	1.66	6.89	7.53	5.55	3.34	10.23
Panama	1.21	0.26	16.43	5.02	4.09	15.73	32.19
Peru	0.69	0.94	2.59	2.84	−6.20	−6.60	−4.00
Trinidad	1.78	1.43	4.39	6.89	6.70	4.69	9.08
Uruguay	1.49	2.78	1.89	4.27	−6.09	−2.19	−0.30

for terms of trade movements. However, in only 3 cases under the standard test, and 2 cases once adjusted for terms of trade movements, did the actual growth rate significantly exceed the predicted growth as one would expect if capital flows relieved a balance of payments constraint. Regressions of the predicted growth rates as a function of actual growth rates produced insignificant F-statistics for any form of Thirlwall's hypothesis except for the 'strong' form, which is reported as:

$$\text{Predicted Growth Rate} = -2.50 + 1.49 \text{ Actual Growth Rate,}$$
$$(-0.60) \quad (1.99)$$
$$R^2 = 0.28 \quad \bar{R}^2 = 0.21 \quad SEE = 4.98 \quad F = 3.98,$$

where the Wald test cannot reject the hypothesis that the intercept term is zero and the slope coefficient is unity. Thus, overall the results of applying Thirlwall's hypothesis to debtor countries over 1973–81 are poor.[6] This is consistent with other evidence that there were wide variations in the efficiency with which developing countries used foreign borrowing over this period.

Conclusions

This study has derived elasticities of demand for exports and imports for a large sample of developing countries and used the income elasticities to test Thirlwall's hypothesis of balance of payments constrained growth. Previous studies in this area typically have not examined the time-series properties of the data and used rather basic econometric techniques. In this study, the import- and export demand functions were estimated using error-correction techniques and long-run elasticities derived from these. It was only possible to derive reasonable estimates of the import demand function for 34 of the 51 sample countries; of these 34 it was only possible to derive reasonable estimates for 27 countries. This illustrates the wider problem, not generally considered with tests of Thirlwall's hypothesis, of deriving stable elasticities of demand for countries undergoing significant structural change in their development process. Tests of the hypothesis are also sensitive to estimates of the parameters. Despite these reservations we found that for a majority of countries we could not reject Thirlwall's hypothesis in its 'weak' form. We also found a strongly significant relationship between the actual growth rates and their values predicted from Thirlwall's hypothesis. We were unable to accept the restriction that the intercept term was zero and the slope coefficient was unity for the 'weak' form of the hypothesis, although this was accepted for an alternative set of estimates of income elasticities of demand. Although estimates of the 'strong' form of the hypothesis for this sample also did not accept the restriction that the intercept term was zero and the slope coefficient was unity, this restriction was accepted once the direct effects of terms of trade changes on import capacity were included. Some possible explanations for weaknesses in these results do not appear to be supported by the data. Tests of Thirlwall's hypothesis were not significantly affected by excluding countries with structural breaks in their import- or export demand functions. Nor did excluding the East Asian NIEs significantly affect the results. Capital flows would be expected to lead to actual growth rates deviating from those predicted by Thirlwall's hypothesis, but this does not appear to hold systematically for those sample countries where capital inflows would be expected to have had the greatest impact. Capital flows may still account for some of the failures of Thirlwall's hypothesis to hold, but the results here are also consistent with other evidence of inefficient use of capital inflows during the 1970s. These failures may also reflect the poor quality of data for many developing countries. Further, the import- and export demand functions were estimated with a small number of years' data and we have limited knowledge of the robustness of these estimates with small samples. Overall, though, we do find some support for Thirlwall's hypothesis as an explanation for growth rate differences. Many studies have taken positive associations between export and GDP growth rates amongst developing countries as indicative of the gains from outward orientation in a supply-side neoclassical growth model. Evidence in support of Thirlwall's hypothesis here suggests that the positive impact of exports on GDP growth may operate primarily through relieving an external demand constraint.

Data appendix

All country data are annual data derived from World Bank, *World Data 1995* CD-ROM, supplemented by World Bank, *World Development Indicators 1997* CD-ROM for 1994–95 data. The income variable was GDP at market prices in 1987 domestic prices. The import and export price indices were derived from the implicit deflator of imports and exports of goods and services in 1987 domestic prices, except for merchandise exports and imports where the price indices provided were used. The domestic price variable was the domestic absorption deflator. World income and price data are from IMF, *International Financial Statistics Yearbook*, 1997. The price deflators were the unit value indices for exports of the world, developing country and non-oil developing countries.

Notes

1 See McCombie and Thirlwall (1994, 1997b) and the symposium in the *Journal of Post Keynesian Economics*, Vol. 19 No. 3 (1997). For tests of developing countries see Thirlwall and Hussain (1982), Bairam (1990) and Bairam and Dempster (1991).
2 These are usually defined as Hong Kong, Indonesia, Malaysia, Korea, Singapore, Taiwan and Thailand. For Hong Kong and Singapore exports often exceeded GDP and for Taiwan data were not available. Estimates are therefore confined to the other 4 economies.
3 Senhadji (1998) uses GDP net of exports as the income variable, but this is strongly correlated with GDP.
4 Estimates can be seen in the original article.
5 Classifications from IMF (1989).
6 There was no significant relationship between the predicted and actual growth rate either when the import demand elasticities from Senhadji (1998) were used instead.

14 The balance of payments constraint and growth rate differences among African and East Asian economies*

M. Nureldin Hussain

Introduction

The term 'balance of payments constraint' refers to the situation where a country's performance in external markets and the response of the world to this performance, constrain the growth of the country to a rate which is below the rate required for addressing domestic economic problems such as the prevalence of unemployment and underemployment, and the existence of idle resources and capacity (see McCombie and Thirlwall, 1994). The balance of payments constrained growth-rate model postulates that the balance of payments position of a country is the main constraint on economic growth, because it imposes a limit on demand to which supply can adapt. It states that no open economy can grow faster, in the long run, than the rate consistent with balance of payments equilibrium on current account unless it can finance ever-growing deficits. Export performance is crucial because no other component of aggregate demand provides the foreign exchange to pay for import requirements associated with the expansion of output. In its basic form, the balance of payments constrained growth rate model is epitomized by the 'dynamic Harrod foreign-trade multiplier' (also known as Thirlwall's Law or the 45 degree rule) pioneered by Thirlwall (1979). On the assumptions of constant relative prices and no capital flows, the basic dynamic Harrod foreign-trade multiplier postulates that the growth rate of a country can be predicted by the rate of growth of its volume of exports divided by its income elasticity of demand for imports. In its extended form introduced by Thirlwall and Hussain (1982), the model incorporates two factors that might cause a country's growth rate to deviate from the rate predicted by the basic dynamic Harrod foreign trade multiplier namely, changes in the terms of trade and capital flows.

The purpose of this chapter is to apply the balance of payments constrained growth model, in its basic and extended forms, to a sample of African and East Asian countries. The countries of East Asia, led by Japan, have had remarkable growth experiences during the postwar period. However, the impressive development record of Asian countries has been checked by the currency and financial

* First published in the *African Development Review*, June 1999.

crises, which have afflicted the region since 1997. Nonetheless, the success of these countries in achieving sustained rapid growth prior to the crises merits further investigation.[1] Some of these Asian countries still rely heavily on capital imports, while others have passed this stage and have managed to accumulate huge balance of payments surpluses and/or become capital exporters in their own right. In contrast, most African countries have been able to build growing current account deficits financed by capital inflows, which might allow them to grow faster than otherwise would be the case. However, what African countries might gain from capital inflows, they may lose by the adverse terms-of-trade effect; indeed, the former might be partly in response to the latter. In view of this, the chapter attempts to address the following empirical issues:

- to quantify the contribution of capital flows to the growth of African as compared to Asian countries;
- to explain growth rate differences among African and Asian countries by quantifying the individual and combined contributions of export growth, capital flows and changes in the terms of trade in each country's case;
- to quantify the net effect of capital inflows and the terms of trade in the case of African countries; and
- to measure the extent to which the actual growth rates of African and Asian countries deviate from those predicted by the basic and extended dynamic Harrod foreign-trade multipliers.

The chapter is organized as follows. The section, 'The model', gives a brief account of the balance of payments constrained growth rate theory and a formal derivation of the basic and extended Harrod foreign trade multipliers. The section, 'Estimation and verification', estimates the basic parameters of the model, applies the models to a sample of African and Asian countries and tests the statistical validity of the models' predictions. The section, 'Interpretation of results', discusses and interprets the empirical results and provides estimates of the counterfactual balance of payments which is a measure of what would have been the rate of real income growth in the absence of capital flows. The section uses the results obtained to throw more light on the issue of balance of payments constrained growth. The section, 'Comparing African with Asian countries', draws a comparison, in the context of the model, between the growth experiences of African and South East Asian countries. The conclusions and policy implications are provided in the last section.

The model

The model of the balance of payments constrained growth offers a Keynesian demand-side explanation of the process of economic growth and growth rate differences among countries. The theory places emphasis on demand as the main vehicle of growth, rather than factors of production and technical change as in the neoclassical doctrine. It postulates that increases in the labour force, capital stock and technical change are largely endogenous, adjusting passively to the changes in the economy that are brought about by changes in demand (see Thirlwall, 1979; Thirlwall and Hussain, 1982; McCombie, 1985a).

The balance of payments on current account, B, can be written as:

$$B = X - M, \tag{14.1}$$

where X and M are the values of exports and imports of goods and services measured in a common currency, respectively. Starting from a position of an initial equilibrium in the current account, the rate of growth in the balance can be written as:

$$b = x - m, \tag{14.2}$$

where lower-case letters denote the rate of growth of the variables. The demand for exports and imports depends on relative prices and real income. Assuming constant relative prices, the demand for exports and imports will be determined by world income and domestic income in conjunction with the respective income elasticities of demand for exports and imports. Assuming constant relative prices, the rate of change in the balance of payments starting from initial equilibrium can be expressed as:

$$b = \sigma w - \pi y, \tag{14.3}$$

with $x = \sigma w$ and $m = \pi y$, where σ is the income elasticity of demand for the country's exports, w is the rate of growth of world income, π is the country's income elasticity of demand for imports and y is its real income growth rate. From equation (14.3) it can be seen that movements in the balance of payments depends on the relative size of the income elasticities of demand for exports and imports and on the differential income growth rate between the country and the rest of the world. If a country has an income elasticity of demand for imports which is larger than its income elasticity of demand for exports (i.e. $\pi > \sigma$), any attempt by that country to grow at a rate which is equal to the rate of growth of the rest of the world (i.e. $w = y$), will cause the balance of payments to deteriorate.[2] In the absence of capital inflows to bridge the emerging deficit in the balance of payments, and with the rate of growth of exports determined exogenously by the rate of growth of world income, and the values of σ and π constant, it is the rate of growth of domestic real income that must adjust downwards to maintain equilibrium between the growth of imports and exports. In this case, the rate of growth of the country is said to be constrained by the balance of payments and the values of σ and π play the crucial role in determining the balance of payments constrained growth rate. From equation (14.3) the rate of growth which is consistent with balance of payments equilibrium can be obtained as:

$$y^{**} = \sigma w / \pi. \tag{14.4}$$

This result is based on the restrictive assumptions of constant relative prices and no capital flows.

An extended version of the model can be obtained by relaxing these two assumptions (see Thirlwall and Hussain, 1982). The starting point of the extended model is the balance of payments accounting identity that the balance of payments must balance:

$$P_d X + K = P_f ME, \tag{14.5}$$

where X is the volume of exports; P_d is the domestic price of exports; M is the volume of imports; P_f is the foreign price of imports; E is the exchange rate measured as the domestic price of foreign currency, and K is the value of nominal capital flows measured in domestic currency. $K < 0$ measures capital outflows and/or accumulation of reserves, and $K > 0^3$ measures capital inflows. Taking rates of change of the variables of equation (14.5) gives:

$$\Theta(p_d + x) + \tau k = p_f + m + e, \tag{14.6}$$

where the lower-case letters represent rates of growth of the variables and Θ and τ represent the proportions of the total import bill 'financed' by export earnings and capital flows, respectively (i.e. $\Theta = P_d X/(P_d X + K)$ and $\tau = K/(P_d X + K)$). Assuming the conventional multiplicative import- and export demand functions with constant elasticities, we have:

$$M = a(P_f E/P_d)^\varepsilon Y^\pi, \tag{14.7}$$

$$X = b(P_d/P_f E)^\beta W^\sigma, \tag{14.8}$$

where a and b are constants; ε is the price elasticity of demand for imports ($\varepsilon < 0$); β is the price elasticity of demand for exports ($\beta < 0$); Y is the level of real domestic income; W is the level of real 'world' income; π is the income elasticity of demand for imports ($\pi > 0$); and σ is the income elasticity of demand for exports ($\sigma > 0$). From equations (14.7) and (14.8) and taking rates of change of variables, denoted by lower-case letters, we have:

$$m = \varepsilon(p_f + e - p_d) + \pi y, \tag{14.9}$$

$$x = \beta(p_d - e - p_f) + \sigma w. \tag{14.10}$$

Substituting equations (14.5) and (14.6) into (14.2) gives:

$$\Theta[p_d + \beta(p_d - e - p_f) + \sigma w] + \tau k = p_f + \varepsilon(p_f + e - p_d)$$
$$+ \pi y + e. \tag{14.11}$$

The extended Harrod foreign trade multiplier can be obtained by solving equation (14.11) for the rate of growth of real domestic income (y):

$$y^* = [(1 + \Theta\beta + \varepsilon)(p_d - e - p_f) + \Theta\sigma w + \tau(k - p_d)]/\pi. \tag{14.12}$$

A version of the extended model that exhibits the effect of export performance on the balance of payments constrained growth rate can be obtained by substituting in equation (14.12) for growth in real world income, w, from the export equation (14.10). This yields:

$$y^* = [(1 + \varepsilon)(p_\mathrm{d} - e - p_\mathrm{f}) + \Theta x + \tau(k - p_\mathrm{d})]/\pi. \tag{14.13}$$

This is the model we apply to compare the growth performance of Asia and Africa.

Estimation and verification

Estimates of import price and income elasticities

The first step for fitting the model is to estimate import demand functions for the selected African and Asian countries. Empirically, there is no one correct a priori specification of the import demand function. It is suggested that investigators must proceed on a trial-and-error basis according to the data available, their reliability and the purpose of the study (see Leamer and Stern, 1970; Thirlwall and Gibson, 1992). To estimate price and income elasticities of demand for imports, two empirical specifications of the import demand functions are considered. The first is the traditional function which is based on the logarithmic transformation of the import demand function given by equation (14.7). That is:

$$\log M = \log a + \varepsilon \log(P_\mathrm{f} E/P_\mathrm{d}) + \pi \log(Y), \tag{14.14}$$

where all the variables are defined as earlier. The second is the adjustment to equilibrium specification which is a transformation of equation (14.14) based on the hypothesis that it takes time for imports to adjust to the desired level (see Thirlwall and Gibson, 1992). The adjustment to equilibrium specification allows for the estimation of short- and long-run import elasticities. This specification is given by:

$$\log M_t = \delta \log a + \delta\varepsilon \log(P_\mathrm{f} E/P_\mathrm{d})_t + \delta\pi \log(Y)_t$$
$$+ (1 - \delta) \log M_{t-1}, \tag{14.15}$$

where, δ is the coefficient of adjustment and $\delta\varepsilon$, $\delta\pi$ are the short-run elasticities. The long-run elasticities can be obtained by imposing the equilibrium condition where $\log M_t = \log M_{t-1}$. This gives:

$$\varepsilon = \delta\varepsilon/(1 - (1 - \delta)) \quad \text{and} \quad \pi = \delta\pi/(1 - (1 - \delta)). \tag{14.16}$$

Another estimation problem is the representation of domestic prices in an import demand equation. Ideally, the relative price variable should be the ratio of import prices and the price of domestic import-substitutes measured in a common currency. As these prices are not available, three price indices – namely, export prices, GDP deflator and consumer prices – are considered as proxies. For each country, experiments with these two specifications and the three domestic price proxies are conducted and the best results are reported. The volume of imports is measured as imports of goods and services in constant 1987 prices, and real income is measured by GDP in constant 1987 prices. All the data that are used for estimation are obtained from World Bank *World Tables 1992*.

Fitting the model

To fit the model, the price and income elasticities of demand for imports are used for the countries where the traditional import demand function gave the best results. For the countries where the adjustment to equilibrium specification gave the best results, use is made of the long-run income elasticities of demand for imports. In addition to these basic parameters, the values of Θ and τ, the rates of growth of the terms of trade, real export volume and real capital inflows are required to fit the extended model. The terms of trade is measured as the ratio of export to import prices measured in a common currency. Export volume is measured as exports of goods and services in constant 1987 prices. Real capital inflows (outflows) are measured as the current account balance with an opposite sign deflated by the consumer price index. For each country in the sample, the rates of growth of these variables are measured as the average annual growth rate over the relevant time period. The values of Θ and τ are measured as averages for the time period considered. All the data used in the calculation are obtained from World Bank *World Tables 1992* and International Monetary Fund (IMF) *International Financial Statistics*. Using the obtained growth rates, and the price and the income elasticities of demand for imports, the basic and the extended model are fitted and the results are shown in Table 14.1.

For all the countries, Table 14.1 gives data over the relevant time period on the terms of trade effect measured as $[(1 + \varepsilon)(p_d - e - p_f)]/\pi$; the export volume effect measured as $\Theta x/\pi$; the effect of the rate of growth of real capital flows measured as $\tau(k - p_d)/\pi$; the rate of growth predicted by the extended model measured as the sum of the effects of the terms of trade, export volume and real capital flows; the actual growth rate; and the rate of growth predicted by the basic model measured as (x/π). Before discussing the results obtained, it is imperative to test the validity of the models' predictions.

Testing the validity of the models' predictions

A casual inspection of Table 14.1 reveals that in most cases both the basic and the extended models seem to yield estimates which are close to the actual growth rate. The perennial question, however, is how close is close. Formally, there are two methods to test the predictive power of the model. The first is the regression method introduced by McGregor and Swales (1985) and modified by McCombie (1989). The second is what can be called the individual country method introduced by McCombie (1989). The application of these two methods to the sample of African and Asian countries is discussed later.

Table 14.1 Results of applying the basic and extended dynamic Harrod foreign trade multiplier (in percentage points)

	Terms of trade effect	Export volume effect	Real capital flows effect	Extended y^*	Actual y	Basic y^{**}	Period
African countries							
Algeria	10.15	4.21	−8.72	5.64	4.90	4.38	1972–90
Benin	1.44	0.96	1.35	3.75	2.90	1.48	1973–90
Burkina Faso	−5.17	3.03	5.63	3.50	4.20	8.66	1974–89
Burundi	1.69	3.21	−1.26	3.65	5.60	5.95	1971–90
Cameroon	−1.12	7.08	0.00	5.97	5.50	7.23	1972–89
Congo	0.42	3.88	2.38	6.67	6.59	4.31	1971–90
Côte d'Ivoire	0.39	4.23	0.81	5.43	4.50	3.88	1971–88
Egypt	−2.37	4.36	7.31	9.30	6.90	6.91	1973–90
Ethiopia	−0.09	0.74	2.53	3.17	2.20	0.95	1974–86
Gabon	0.49	6.81	0.04	7.33	5.10	5.49	1972–90
Ghana	−3.81	0.15	2.88	−0.79	1.40	0.16	1971–90
Kenya	−0.50	1.62	5.59	6.71	6.24	1.67	1971–90
Lesotho	−3.43	6.62	1.55	4.74	4.40	7.70	1974–86
Madagascar	−0.10	0.06	0.95	0.91	0.48	0.09	1971–90
Mauritania	0.68	1.58	0.42	2.69	2.30	2.40	1974–89
Mauritius	0.92	5.13	0.19	6.23	5.80	5.46	1975–90
Morocco	−1.34	2.83	3.47	4.96	4.62	4.16	1973–90
Niger	−5.07	1.79	3.47	0.20	0.81	2.52	1971–90
Nigeria	2.37	1.28	−1.17	2.48	2.50	1.30	1973–90
Senegal	0.23	1.56	1.05	2.83	2.67	1.97	1971–90
Sierra Leone	−0.23	−0.67	2.65	1.75	1.58	−0.84	1971–88
Somalia	−1.10	0.18	5.00	4.07	3.40	0.37	1971–90
South Africa	−1.03	1.32	7.74	8.03	2.42	1.14	1974–90
Sudan	0.14	1.13	1.92	3.20	3.10	2.18	1976–88
Tanzania	0.33	−0.55	5.01	4.79	2.90	−0.93	1972–88
Togo	0.08	2.31	0.61	3.00	2.90	2.38	1972–87
Tunisia	0.87	5.24	1.48	7.59	5.69	6.10	1971–90
Zambia	−0.31	−1.29	0.58	−1.02	1.40	−1.28	1971–88
Zimbabwe	−2.40	2.23	−1.24	−1.41	3.23	2.19	1977–90
Asian countries							
China	−0.02	6.43	0.26	6.67	8.20	6.36	1976–89
India	−0.85	3.16	1.96	4.27	4.31	4.00	1971–90
Hong Kong	−0.07	8.34	1.01	9.28	9.07	8.26	1971–90
Indonesia	1.82	3.18	5.76	10.76	8.24	2.89	1971–90
Japan	−1.42	9.73	−4.63	3.68	4.20	8.44	1971–90
Korea, Rep. of	−0.81	13.47	−2.49	10.17	9.11	14.64	1971–90
Malaysia	−0.69	6.60	2.21	8.12	7.08	6.16	1971–90
Pakistan	−0.44	4.28	4.40	8.24	5.04	7.50	1971–90
Philippines	0.22	2.00	0.26	2.48	3.70	2.22	1971–90
Srilanka	−0.65	2.33	3.00	4.68	4.30	2.99	1971–90
Thailand	0.96	5.45	2.61	9.02	6.80	6.20	1971–90

Note
y^* and y^{**} are the average growth rates predicted by the extended and basic models, respectively, and y is the actual growth rate.

The modified McGregor and Swales method

McGregor and Swales (1985) suggest that the predictive power of the model can be measured by regressing the actual growth rate (y) on the predicted growth rate y^{**} (or y^* in case of the extended model) and testing whether the regression coefficient is equal to unity and the constant term is equal to zero. If these two conditions are satisfied, then the predicted growth rate will be considered as a good estimate of the actual growth rate. McCombie (1989) criticizes the McGregor and Swales test on the grounds that the independent variable y^{**} (or y^*) is itself calculated using estimated parameters (π in the case of the basic model and π and ε in the case of the extended model) and hence is subject to errors. To the extent that this causes an 'error in variables' problem, the McGregor and Swales test will yield a biased estimate of the coefficient. He suggests the modification of the test by using inverse least squares, that is, regressing y^{**} (or y^*) on y and test whether or not the coefficient of the equation is equal to unity and the constant term is equal to zero. The result of applying the modified McGregor and Swales method to the basic and extended models are reported in Tables 14.2 and 14.3 respectively.

Table 14.2 shows that for the group of African countries in the sample, the basic model proved to be a good predictor of the actual growth rate as the constant term is not statistically different from zero and the coefficient on y is not different from unity at the 95 per cent level of confidence. The same is true for the group of Asian countries. However, when the full sample of African and Asian countries is tested, the result is inconclusive. That is, while the constant term fails the test as it is statistically different from zero, the coefficient on y passes the test with a value which is statistically equal to unity.

McCombie (1989) argues that if the countries in the sample have diverse experiences regarding the effects of capital inflows and the terms of trade, it will be inappropriate to test the validity of the basic model using a cross-section regression

Table 14.2 Estimated coefficients of regressing the prediction of the basic model (y^{**}) against the actual growth rate (y)

Dependent variable	Constant	y	R^2	$|t'|$
y^{**}				
African countries	−1.08	1.123		
	(−1.31)	(5.57)	0.53	0.62*
Asian countries	0.89	0.86		
	(0.28)	(1.79)	0.26	0.30*
Full sample	−0.87	1.09		
	(6.46)	(6.70)	0.54	0.56*

Notes
Data for these regressions are obtained from Table 14.1. Figures in parentheses are the usual t-statistics.
$|t'|$ is the absolute value of the t-statistic based on the null hypothesis that the coefficient on y is unity.
* denotes that the null hypothesis cannot be rejected at the 95 per cent level of confidence.

Table 14.3 Estimated coefficients of regressing the prediction of the
extended model (y^*) against the actual growth rate (y)

Dependent variable	Constant	y	R^2	$|t'|$
y^*				
African countries	−0.38	1.19		
	(−0.50)	(6.38)	0.60	1.02*
Asian countries	−0.27	1.15		
	(−0.17)	(4.87)	0.73	0.63*
Full sample	−0.30	1.16		
	(−0.50)	(9.61)	0.71	1.33*

Notes
Data for these regressions are obtained from Table 14.1. Figures in parentheses
are the usual *t*-statistics.
$|t'|$ is the absolute value of the *t*-statistic based on the null hypothesis that the
coefficient on *y* is unity.
* denotes that the null hypothesis cannot be rejected at the 95 per cent level of
confidence.

analysis. In this case, he argues, the cross-section test, because of a number of outliers, may lead to the rejection of the model for all the individual countries. He
suggests that the cross-section test is more appropriate for the extended model
which includes the effects of capital flows and the terms of trade. The results of
the cross-section test applied for the extended model lend support to McCombie's
argument. It can be seen from Table 14.3 that in the regression test of the sample of
African countries, the sample of Asian countries and the full sample, the constant
term is statistically not different from zero and the coefficient on *y* is statistically
equal to unity. It can be inferred from this test that the growth rate predicted by
both the basic and extended model can be considered as good estimates of the
actual growth rates. However, the predictive power of the extended model appears
to be superior in the case of the full sample of African and Asian countries.

It must be noted, however, that the McGregor and Swales regression test suffers from two other major shortcomings which the modification introduced by
McCombie (1989) does not resolve. First, there may be systematic over-prediction
or underprediction if the sample of the countries under consideration is not complete in the sense that their balance of payments surpluses or deficits do not cancel
out (Thirlwall, 1986). Second, the method, by its very nature, cannot show whether
the model is valid or not for each individual country separately.

McCombie's individual country method

A more satisfactory test that avoids the earlier objections is the method introduced
by McCombie (1989) which determines whether the actual and predicted growth
rates are statistically significantly different from each other for each individual
country separately. The first step is to calculate, for each country, the implied
balance of payments equilibrium income elasticity of demand for imports $\pi^\wedge$ (i.e.

the income elasticity of demand for imports that would make the predicted growth rate equal to the actual growth rate). Then, the calculated $\pi^\wedge$ will be compared with the estimated income elasticity of demand for imports from time-series regression analysis (π') for the country under consideration. This comparison is conducted by calculating the t statistic from the standard error of π' for the null hypothesis that $\pi^\wedge$ is equal to π' and ascertaining whether or not the null hypothesis is rejected at the 95 per cent confidence level. If $\pi^\wedge$ is found to be not statistically different from π', it follows that the actual and predicted growth rates are not statistically different from each other.

To apply this test to the sample of countries under consideration, the implied balance of payments equilibrium income elasticity of demand for imports $\pi^\wedge$, is calculated for the basic and extended models as in equations (14.17) and (14.18) below.

$$\pi^\wedge = x/y, \tag{14.17}$$

$$\pi^\wedge = [(1+\varepsilon)(p_d - e - p_f) + \Theta x + \tau(k - p_d)]/y. \tag{14.18}$$

The estimated income elasticities and the results of the test for the basic and extended models are shown in Table 14.4.

For the basic model, it may be seen that, of the full sample of 40 African and Asian countries, 22 countries have a predicted growth rate which is not statistically different from the actual growth rate. Of these 22 countries, 17 are African (out of the sample of 29 African countries) and 5 are Asian (out of the sample of 11 Asian countries). However, of the remaining 18 countries, 7 fail the test by a marginal discrepancy. These are Benin, Burkina Faso, Congo, Senegal, Tanzania, Ghana and Malaysia. As for the extended model, the test shows that for 29 of the full sample of 40 countries, the predicted growth rate is statistically equal to the actual growth rate. Of these 29 countries, 23 are African and 6 are Asian. Also, of the 11 countries that fail the test, 3 do so by a very small discrepancy. These are Malaysia, Philippines and Thailand.

Of the full sample of 40 countries, there are 18 countries where both the basic and the extended models gave statistically accepted predictions of the actual growth rate. These are the countries where the effects of terms of trade and capital flows are minimal or where the two effects worked in opposite directions tending to push the actual growth rate back to that predicted by the basic model. There are 11 cases where only the extended model yields statistically valid predictions and there are 4 cases where only the basic model gives statistically valid predictions.

Thus, there are 33 countries of the full sample where at least one of the two versions of the model gives a prediction which is not statistically different from the actual growth rate. As a percentage of the full sample the extended model has valid prediction in about 73 per cent of the cases compared with 55 per cent for the basic model. It can be concluded, according to the results of the individual country test, that the extended model which includes the effects of the terms of trade and real capital inflows, performed better in predicting the actual growth rate than the basic model.

Table 14.4 Application of McCombie's individual country test

	Estimated income elasticity π'	Implied income elasticities			Test results	
		Standard error	$\pi^\wedge$ for the extended model	$\pi^\wedge$ for the basic model	Extended model $|t'|$	Basic model $|t'|$
African countries						
Algeria	0.73	0.22	0.84	0.65	0.50*	0.35*
Benin	1.97	0.44	2.54	1.00	1.31*	2.20
Burkina Faso	0.64	0.31	0.53	1.31	0.34*	2.18
Burundi	0.86	0.24ª	0.56	0.91	1.24*	0.22*
Cameroon	0.84	0.12	0.90	1.09	0.49*	2.06*
Congo	1.44	0.22ª	1.46	0.94	0.08*	2.24
Côte d'Ivoire	1.20	0.12	1.45	1.04	2.06*	1.37*
Egypt	0.81	0.08	1.09	0.81	3.52	0.02*
Ethiopia	2.77	0.22	3.99	1.20	5.56	7.11
Gabon	1.37	0.31	1.97	1.47	1.94*	0.34*
Ghana	2.79	0.93	−1.57	0.31	4.69	2.67
Kenya	0.98	0.13ª	1.05	0.26	0.57*	5.51
Lesotho	1.19	0.10	1.28	2.08	0.92*	8.92
Madagascar	2.22	1.00	4.20	0.40	1.98*	1.83*
Mauritania	1.87	0.42	2.18	1.95	0.75*	0.20*
Mauritius	1.23	0.16	1.32	1.16	0.60*	0.46*
Morocco	1.37	0.37	1.47	1.23	0.27*	0.37*
Niger	0.92	0.15ª	0.27	3.46	4.33	16.93
Nigeria	2.70	0.96	2.68	1.40	0.02*	1.35*
Senegal	2.26	0.25ª	2.40	1.67	0.54*	2.37
Sierra Leone	1.54	0.73	1.71	−0.82	0.23*	3.25
Somalia	2.44	0.42	2.92	0.26	1.14*	5.14
South Africa	1.38	0.94	4.55	0.64	3.38	0.77*
Sudan	1.57	0.50	1.62	1.10	0.10*	0.94*
Tanzania	3.01	1.48	4.97	−0.97	1.33*	2.69
Togo	1.93	0.37	2.00	1.59	0.19*	0.93*
Tunisia	1.34	0.56	1.79	1.44	0.79*	0.17*
Zambia	1.11	2.69	−0.80	−1.01	0.71*	0.78*
Zimbabwe	1.64	0.33ª	−0.72	1.11	7.14	1.60*
Asian countries						
China	1.76	0.54	1.43	1.37	0.61*	0.73*
India	1.53	0.13	1.52	1.42	0.11*	0.88*
Hong Kong	1.39	0.08	1.42	1.26	0.40*	1.55*
Indonesia	1.97	0.08	2.58	0.69	7.54	16.02
Japan	0.94	0.17	0.82	1.88	0.68*	5.56
Korea, Rep. of	1.12	0.06	1.25	1.80	2.17*	11.34
Malaysia	1.55	0.09	1.78	1.35	2.52	2.23
Pakistan	0.82	0.13	1.34	1.22	3.91	3.01
Philippines	2.48	0.30ª	1.72	1.54	2.53	3.13
Sri Lanka	1.34	0.26ª	1.46	0.93	0.46*	1.58*
Thailand	2.05	0.26ª	2.72	1.87	2.27	0.62*

Notes

$|t'|$ is the absolute value of the *t*-statistic based on the null hypothesis that the π' is equal to $\pi^\wedge$.

a The standard error for these countries where the stock-adjustment specification is used, is the one of the coefficient on log M_{t-1}.

* Indicates that $\pi^\wedge$ is not statistically different from π'.

Interpretation of results

Classifying the results according to McCombie's test

To throw more light on the models' predictions, it is useful to divide the countries in the sample according to the results of the McCombie test. This gives the following four groups:

Group I   Countries where both the basic and the extended models yield statistically accepted predictions;[4]

Group II   Countries where only the extended model yields statistically valid predictions;[5]

Group III   Countries where only the basic model yields statistically valid predictions;[6] and

Group IV   Countries with no valid predictions.

These groups are shown in Table 14.5. To measure the extent to which the models overpredict/underpredict the actual growth rate, the table calculates, for each country, the difference between the predicted and actual growth rates; and for each group, it calculates the absolute mean deviation of the actual growth rate from that predicted by the two models.

Group I

For the first group where both models give valid predictions, it can be observed that, on average, changes in the terms of trade raises the balance of payments constraint on real income growth by 0.66 per cent per annum, while real capital inflows raises it by 0.41 per cent per annum. Adding these to the effect of export volume of 3.72 per annum, the extended model gives a prediction of the real income growth rate of 4.79 per annum. This is to be compared with an actual growth rate of 4.60 per cent and with a prediction of the basic model of 4.01 per cent per annum. For all the countries in this group, the mean absolute deviation of the actual growth rate from the growth rate predicted by the extended model is 0.82 per cent, while the mean absolute deviation of the actual growth rate from the prediction of the basic model is 0.83 per cent. This gives additional support to the result of the McCombie test that the predictions of the two models, in the case of Group I countries, are not statistically different from the actual growth rate.

Group II

This group includes 12 countries with statistically valid predictions of the extended model. It can be seen that, on average, the terms of trade effect is unfavourable, constraining countries in their growth by 0.63 per cent per annum, while capital inflows are favourable, enabling the countries to grow by 1.64 per cent per annum. The contribution of the export volume effect to growth is relatively large, amounting to 3.78 per cent per annum. Accordingly, the extended model predicts a rate of growth of real income of 4.79 per cent, to be compared with an actual average

Table 14.5 Arrangement of countries in accordance with McCombie's individual country test (in percentage points)

	Terms of trade effect	Export volume effect	Real capital flows effect	y^*	y	y^{**}	$y^* - y$	$y^{**} - y$
Countries with valid predictions for both basic and extended models								
Algeria	10.15	4.21	−8.72	5.64	4.90	4.38	0.74	−0.52
Burundi	1.69	3.21	−1.26	3.65	5.60	5.95	−1.95	0.35
Cameroon	−1.12	7.08	0.00	5.97	5.50	7.23	0.47	1.73
Côte d'Ivoire	0.39	4.23	0.81	5.43	4.50	3.88	0.93	−0.62
Gabon	0.49	6.81	0.04	7.33	5.10	5.49	2.23	0.39
Madagascar	−0.10	0.06	0.95	0.91	0.48	0.09	0.43	−0.39
Mauritania	0.68	1.58	0.42	2.69	2.30	2.40	0.39	0.10
Mauritius	0.92	5.13	0.19	6.23	5.80	5.46	0.44	−0.34
Morocco	−1.34	2.83	3.47	4.96	4.62	4.16	0.34	−0.46
Nigeria	2.37	1.28	−1.17	2.48	2.50	1.30	−0.02	−1.20
Sudan	0.14	1.13	1.92	3.20	3.10	2.18	0.10	−0.92
Togo	0.08	2.31	0.61	3.00	2.90	2.38	0.10	−0.52
Tunisia	0.87	5.24	1.48	7.59	5.69	6.10	1.90	0.41
Zambia	−0.31	−1.29	0.58	−1.02	1.40	−1.28	−2.42	−2.68
China	−0.02	6.43	0.26	6.67	8.20	6.36	−1.53	−1.84
India	−0.85	3.16	1.96	4.27	4.31	4.00	−0.04	−0.31
Hong Kong	−0.07	8.34	1.01	9.28	9.07	8.26	0.21	−0.81
Malaysia	−0.69	6.60	2.21	8.12	7.08	6.16	1.04	−0.92
Sri Lanka	−0.65	2.33	3.00	4.68	4.30	2.99	0.38	−1.31
Average	0.66	3.72	0.41	4.79	4.60	4.08	(0.82)	(0.83)
Countries with valid predictions for the extended model								
Benin	1.44	0.96	1.35	3.75	2.90	1.48	0.85	−1.42
Burkina Faso	−5.17	3.03	5.63	3.50	4.20	8.66	−0.70	4.46
Congo	0.42	3.88	2.38	6.67	6.59	4.31	0.08	−2.28
Kenya	−0.50	1.62	5.59	6.71	6.24	1.67	0.47	−4.57
Lesotho	−3.43	6.62	1.55	4.74	4.40	7.70	0.34	3.30
Senegal	0.23	1.56	1.05	2.83	2.67	1.97	0.16	−0.70
Sierra Leone	−0.23	−0.67	2.65	1.75	1.58	−0.84	0.17	−2.42
Somalia	−1.10	0.18	5.00	4.07	3.40	0.37	0.67	−3.03
Tanzania	0.33	−0.55	5.01	4.79	2.90	−0.93	1.89	−3.83
Japan	−1.42	9.73	−4.63	3.68	4.20	8.44	−0.52	4.24
Korea, Rep. of	−0.81	13.47	−2.49	10.17	9.11	14.64	1.06	5.53
Philippines	0.22	2.00	0.26	2.48	3.70	2.22	−1.22	−1.48
Average	−0.63	3.78	1.64	4.79	4.48	3.95	(0.66)	(3.14)
Countries with valid predictions for the basic model								
Egypt	−2.37	4.36	7.31	9.30	6.90	6.91	2.40	0.01
Ghana	−3.81	0.15	2.88	−0.79	1.40	0.16	−2.19	−1.24
South Africa	−1.03	1.32	7.74	8.03	2.42	1.14	5.61	−1.28
Zimbabwe	−2.40	2.23	−1.24	−1.41	3.23	2.19	−4.64	−1.04
Thailand	0.96	5.45	2.61	9.02	6.80	6.20	2.22	−0.60
Average	−1.73	2.70	3.86	4.83	4.15	3.32	(3.41)	(0.83)
Countries with no valid predictions								
Ethiopia	−0.09	0.74	2.53	3.17	2.20	0.95	0.97	−1.25
Niger	−5.07	1.79	3.47	0.20	0.81	2.52	−0.61	1.71
Indonesia	1.82	3.18	5.76	10.76	8.24	2.89	2.52	−5.35
Pakistan	−0.44	4.28	4.40	8.24	5.04	7.50	3.20	2.46
Average	−0.94	2.49	4.04	5.59	4.07	3.47	(1.82)	(2.69)

Note
Figures in parentheses are absolute mean deviation of actual growth rate from that predicted by the two models.

rate of growth of 4.48 per cent and with the rate predicted by the basic model of 3.9 per cent. The mean absolute deviation of the actual growth rate from the growth rate predicted by the extended model is small amounting to 0.66 per cent, while the mean absolute deviation of the actual growth rate from the prediction of the basic model is large amounting to 3.14 per cent. This confirms the result of the McCombie test that the basic model in the case of Group II countries is not a good predictor of the actual growth rate. The result implies also that the net terms of trade and capital inflow effect are quantitatively important, causing the actual growth rate to deviate from the prediction of the basic model.

Group III

This group includes five countries where only the basic model yields statistically valid predictions. It can be observed that, on average, the basic model predicts a growth rate of 3.32 per cent per annum to be compared with an actual growth rate of 4.15 per cent and with the prediction of the extended model of 4.83 per cent. The mean absolute deviation of the actual growth rate from the growth rate predicted by the extended model is large, amounting to 3.41 per cent, while the mean absolute deviation of the actual growth rate from the prediction of the basic model is 0.83 per cent. This confirms the earlier result that the extended model is not a good predictor of the actual growth rate in the case of the countries in this group.

Group IV

Although the predictions of both the basic and extended models in the case of the four countries in this group are not statistically valid, the discrepancies between the predicted and the actual rates are not very large. On average, the extended model predicts an average growth rate of 5.59 per cent per annum, to be compared with an actual growth rate of 4.07 per cent and a prediction of the basic model of 3.47 per cent. The mean absolute deviation of the actual growth rate from the growth rate predicted by the extended model is 1.82 per cent, compared with the mean absolute deviation of the actual growth rate from the prediction of the basic model which amounts to 2.69 per cent.

Estimates of the counterfactual balance of payments constrained growth rate

The extended model which incorporates the effect of the terms of trade and capital flows may be a good predictor of the actual growth rate, but by incorporating the effect of capital flows, it does not measure the 'true' balance of payments constrained growth rate. To tackle this issue, a measure of what would have been the rate of growth in the absence of capital flows is required. This may be defined as the rate of growth of real income that would have prevented further deterioration (improvement) in the initial current account deficit (surplus) with no *nominal* capital inflows.[7] This can be obtained from equation (14.13) by setting $k = 0$.

Table 14.6 Estimates of the counterfactual balance of payments constrained growth rate (percentage points)

Country	Counterfactual growth rate A	Actual growth rate B	Difference (A − B)
African countries			
Algeria	13.82	4.90	8.92
Benin	1.34	2.90	−1.56
Burkina Faso	−3.52	4.20	−7.72
Burundi	−0.36	5.60	−5.96
Cameroon	4.32	5.50	−1.18
Congo	4.11	6.59	−2.48
Côte d'Ivoire	5.24	4.50	0.74
Egypt	−4.19	6.90	−11.09
Ethiopia	−0.07	2.20	−2.27
Gabon	8.79	5.10	3.69
Ghana	−4.13	1.40	−5.53
Kenya	0.74	6.24	−5.50
Lesotho	1.86	4.40	−2.54
Madagascar	−1.73	0.48	−2.21
Mauritania	0.66	2.30	−1.64
Mauritius	5.49	5.80	−0.31
Morocco	−0.37	4.62	−4.99
Niger	−4.89	0.81	−5.70
Nigeria	3.58	2.50	1.08
Senegal	1.14	2.67	−1.53
Sierra Leone	−6.76	1.58	−8.34
Somalia	−8.22	3.40	−11.62
South Africa	1.78	2.42	−0.64
Sudan	−8.92	3.10	−12.01
Tanzania	−3.14	2.90	−6.04
Togo	2.28	2.90	−0.62
Tunisia	5.36	5.69	−0.33
Zambia	−1.30	1.40	−2.70
Zimbabwe	−0.05	3.23	−3.28
Asian countries			
China	6.40	8.20	−1.80
Hong Kong	8.32	9.07	−0.75
India	1.10	4.31	−3.21
Indonesia	5.65	8.24	−2.59
Japan	9.20	4.20	5.00
Korea, Rep. of	11.85	9.11	2.74
Malaysia	6.11	7.08	−0.97
Pakistan	−1.31	5.04	−6.35
Philippines	1.63	3.70	−2.07
Sri Lanka	−0.08	4.30	−4.38
Thailand	5.99	6.80	−0.81

That is:

$$y_B = [(1 + \varepsilon)(p_d - e - p_f) + \Theta x - \tau p_d]/\pi. \tag{14.19}$$

It can be observed from equation (14.19) that if τ is positive, domestic inflation measured by p_d will reduce the balance of payments constrained growth rate y_B. Table 14.6 shows the computation of y_B and compares it with the actual growth rate, y. It may be seen that of the 40 countries in the sample, the counterfactual balance of payments constrained growth rate y_B is negative for 16 countries; 2 of them are Asian countries (Pakistan and Sri Lanka) and 14 are African countries.[8] For these countries, the result implies that, had it not been for nominal capital inflows, the rate of growth of real income would have been negative. The negative growth rate implies a cut down the rate of growth of imports below that of exports to keep the absolute gap between exports and imports (equal to the initial value of K) unchanged. It is interesting to note that four African oil-exporting countries in the sample (Algeria, Cameroon, Gabon and Nigeria) show a positive and relatively large y_B.

Resource constrained and balance of payments constrained growth

It is worth introducing the discussion in this section by citing the experience of Japan which typifies the case of a disequilibrium country with a large balance of payments surplus. In the case of Japan, as it may be recalled, the extended model predicts the growth rate of Japan as 3.68 per cent, compared with an actual rate of 4.2 per cent (see Table 14.4). The basic model, which gives an estimate of 8.44 per cent, overpredicts the actual growth rate by a large margin. It is interesting to note that most of the studies that apply the basic model to the economy of Japan find that the model gives an overprediction of the actual growth rate. For instance, Thirlwall (1979), who applies the model for developed countries over the period 1953–76, arrives at a prediction of a balance of payments constrained growth rate for Japan of 13.2 per cent, compared with an actual growth rate of 8.6 per cent.

Recently, Bairam and Dempster (1991), who estimate the model for a sample of developed and developing countries, arrive at an estimate of 11.3 per cent for Japan over the period 1961–85, compared with an actual rate of growth of 7.4 per cent. To explain the large gap between the actual growth rate and the balance of payments equilibrium growth rate as predicted by the basic model, Thirlwall (1979) raises the possibility that countries such as Japan might not be balance of payments constrained. Conducting his analyses in the context of developed countries, he suggests that if the estimate of the basic model for a country is larger than the actual growth rate, this might imply that the country is making a balance of payments surplus. In his own words:

> While a country cannot grow faster than its balance-of-payments equilibrium growth rate for very long, unless it finances an ever-growing deficit, there

is little to stop a country growing slower and accumulating large balance-of-payments surpluses. This may particularly occur where the balance-of-payments equilibrium growth rate is so high that a country simply does not have the physical capacity to grow at that rate. This typifies many oil producing countries and would also seem to typify the experience of Japan...

(Thirlwall, 1979: 239)

To throw more light on these issues, use can be made of the estimates of the counterfactual balance of payments constrained growth rate, y_B, in comparison with actual growth rates. For each country, the difference between the counterfactual rate, y_B, and the actual rate, y, provides inferences about the balance of payments position over the time period considered – with a negative average growth rate in the current account indicated by $y_B - y < 0$ and a positive average growth rate in the current account indicated by $y_B - y > 0$. The difference, $y_B - y$, (with an opposite sign) can also be interpreted as measures of the contribution of *nominal* capital flows to the actual growth rate. Examining Table 14.6, it is clear that the actual rate of growth of all the countries in the sample (with the exception of Algeria, Côte d'Ivoire, Gabon, Nigeria, Japan and the Republic of Korea) exceeds the hypothetical rate, y_B. This indicates that these countries had to incur current account deficits (financed by capital inflows) to grow at a rate higher than their 'true' balance of payments constrained growth rate. Appreciating the fact that most deficit countries in the sample have idle human and natural resources, they can be approximated to a situation where the actual growth rate is lower than the capacity growth rate implying growing unemployment and/or underemployment, but larger than the balance of payments equilibrium growth rate, implying growing balance of payments deficit. [9]

The group of countries with appreciable[10] positive average growth rate in the current account includes Japan, the Republic of Korea and the oil-exporting countries of Algeria and Gabon. In the case of Japan, our estimate confirms Thirlwall's earlier assertion that Japan's growth rate is unconstrained by the balance of payments. It is argued that the economy of Japan approximates to the situation where the country's balance of payments constrained growth rate lies well above the capacity growth rate allowing the actual growth rate to equal the capacity growth rate without balance of payments difficulties arising (Thirlwall, 1979). Based on our results, it might be suggested that the Republic of Korea (with an actual rate of growth well below the balance of payments equilibrium growth rate) approximates to Japan's position.

McCombie (1989) suggests that such countries in Japan's position, may be described as *resource constrained*. He argues that while there is a large growth of demand for Japanese goods in the world market, there is a maximum rate at which these goods can be produced. This maximum rate is set by factors such as the speed of intersectoral mobility of labour, especially from agriculture to manufacturing and the rate of production of the capital goods industry. Thus, countries such as Japan and probably the Republic of Korea, are said to be growing at their capacity growth rate.

A measure of the potential growth which is constrained by resources for the surplus countries of Japan and Korea might be provided by the difference between y and y_B. This gives a potential growth rate of about 5 per cent per annum for Japan and 2.6 per cent per annum for the Republic of Korea. Had it not been for the resource constraint, the results suggest that Japan would have been able to grow at an annual rate of about 9 per cent, while the Republic of Korea would have been able to grow at an annual rate of about 12 per cent without encountering balance of payments problems. Whether these countries will be able to realize this potential and accelerate growth would depend on whether the buoyancy of demand at full employment will raise the capacity growth rate to a higher level. This can occur through a number of mechanisms. For instance, the ability to import more may increase capacity by making domestic resources more productive; the supply of labour may increase by the entry into the labour market of people previously outside or from abroad; and the factors of production may move from low productivity to high-productivity sectors (McCombie and Thirlwall, 1994).

The remaining countries, with actual growth well below the counterfactual balance of payments equilibrium growth rate, are the two oil-exporting countries of Algeria and Gabon. It might be suggested that growth in these two countries was not constrained by the balance of payments during the time period considered.[11] In the case of Gabon, for instance, our result indicates that Gabon could have grown at a rate of 8.8 per cent per annum without encountering balance of payments problems. However, the country has been growing at a slower rate of 5 per cent per annum and, hence, accumulating surpluses. Even though Gabon has one of the highest per capita incomes in Africa, it will be difficult to argue that the country did not want to grow faster. It will also be difficult to argue, as in the case of Japan and the Republic of Korea, that Gabon was resource constrained. Unless the accumulation of surpluses was a policy target in its own right, domestic policies might be the predominant constraint on growth in Gabon. The same argument might also be relevant to Algeria.

Comparing African with Asian countries

In an attempt to explore the main sources of growth underpinning the Asian success story, and draw development policy lessons to be applied to the troubled countries of Africa, this section investigates the comparative growth performance of the two groups of countries. Table 14.7 divides the sample into African and Asian countries and arranges countries within each group, in descending order, according to actual real income growth. The table also shows the prediction of the extended model with its terms of trade, export volume and real capital flows effects.

It may be seen from the table that in the case of both African and Asian countries, the terms of trade effect is adverse, reducing the growth rate by 0.27 per cent per annum for African countries and 0.18 per cent per annum for Asian countries. If African oil-exporting countries are excluded, the adverse terms of trade effect reduces the growth rate of African countries by 0.84 per cent per annum. It is interesting to note that the adverse terms of trade effect, in the case of Japan, is

Table 14.7 Comparing African with Asian countries (in percentage points)

	Actual rate of growth	Terms of trade effect	Export volume effect	Real capital flows effect	Growth rate predicted by the extended model
African countries					
Algeria	4.90	10.15	4.21	−8.72	5.64
Benin	2.90	1.44	0.96	1.35	3.75
Burkina Faso	4.20	−5.17	3.03	5.63	3.50
Burundi	5.60	1.69	3.21	−1.26	3.65
Cameroon	5.50	−1.12	7.08	0.00	5.97
Congo	6.59	0.42	3.88	2.38	6.67
Côte d'Ivoire	4.50	0.39	4.23	0.81	5.43
Egypt	6.90	−2.37	4.36	7.31	9.30
Ethiopia	2.20	−0.09	0.74	2.53	3.17
Gabon	5.10	0.49	6.81	−0.04	7.33
Ghana	1.40	−3.81	0.15	2.88	−0.79
Kenya	6.24	−0.50	1.62	5.59	6.71
Lesotho	4.40	−3.43	6.62	1.55	4.74
Madagascar	0.48	−0.10	0.06	0.95	0.91
Mauritania	2.30	0.68	1.58	0.42	2.69
Mauritius	5.80	0.92	5.13	0.19	6.23
Morocco	4.62	−1.34	2.83	3.47	4.96
Niger	0.81	−5.07	1.79	3.47	0.20
Nigeria	2.50	2.37	1.28	−1.17	2.48
Senegal	2.67	0.23	1.56	1.05	2.83
Sierra Leone	1.58	−0.23	−0.67	2.65	1.75
Somalia	3.40	−1.10	0.18	5.00	4.07
South Africa	2.42	−1.03	1.32	7.74	8.03
Sudan	3.10	0.14	1.13	1.92	3.20
Tanzania	2.90	0.33	−0.55	5.01	4.79
Togo	2.90	0.08	2.31	0.61	3.00
Tunisia	5.69	0.87	5.24	1.48	7.59
Zambia	1.40	−0.31	−1.29	0.58	−1.02
Zimbabwe	3.23	−2.40	2.23	−1.24	−1.41
Average	3.66	−0.27	2.45	1.80	3.98
Average excluding oil exporters*	3.40	−0.84	1.99	2.49	3.64
Asian countries					
China	8.20	−0.02	6.43	0.26	6.67
Hong Kong	9.07	−0.07	8.34	1.01	9.28
India	4.31	−0.85	3.16	1.96	4.27
Indonesia	10.76	1.82	3.18	5.76	7.58
Japan	4.20	−1.42	9.73	−4.63	3.68
Korea, Rep. of	9.11	−0.81	13.47	−2.49	10.17
Malaysia	7.08	−0.69	6.60	2.21	8.12
Pakistan	5.04	−0.44	4.28	4.40	8.24
Philippines	3.70	0.22	2.00	0.26	2.48
Sri Lanka	4.30	−0.65	2.33	3.00	4.68
Thailand	6.80	0.96	5.45	2.61	9.02
Average	6.60	−0.18	5.91	1.31	6.74
Average excluding Japan and Korea	6.58	0.03	4.46	2.39	6.70

Source: Table 14.3

Note

* The oil exporters that are excluded are Algeria, Cameroon, Congo, Gabon and Nigeria.

above that of non-oil African countries. This result should not be puzzling, since the deterioration in the terms of trade for a large country like Japan might be considered as an indication of improved price competitiveness in the international market.[12] In view of this, what really matters is the extent to which this deterioration in the terms of trade (improved competitiveness) stimulates the demand for exports and hence increases the growth of the volume of exports.

The outstanding difference in performance between African and Asian countries is in the domain of export performance relative to the income elasticity of demand for imports. In the case of Asian countries, the export volume effect increases the growth rate, on average, by about 6 per cent per annum. Whereas in the case of the sample of African countries, the contribution of the export volume effect to the growth rate amounts, on average, to about 2.6 per cent per annum. For non-oil African countries, the contribution of the export volume effect is about 2.0 per cent. There are 5 African countries which have an export performance that approximates to the Asian average. These are Cameroon, Gabon, Mauritius, Tunisia and Lesotho. In the latter case, however, the export volume effect is largely offset by the adverse terms of trade effect. The combined terms of trade effect and export volume effect (the net export effect) increases the income growth rate of Asian countries, on average, by 5.7 per cent per annum. The comparable figures are 2.2 per cent for the sample of African countries and 1.2 per cent for non-oil African countries.

Real capital inflows increase the average rate of growth of African countries by 1.8 per cent per annum, whereas they increase the growth rate of non-oil African countries by an average of about 2.5 per cent per annum. It is interesting to note that the contribution of real capital inflows to real income growth, in the case of non-oil African countries, is larger than the contribution of exports. This amounts to 125 per cent of the export volume effect and to 216 per cent of the combined terms of trade and export volume effects.

In the case of Asian countries, real capital inflows increase the growth of income, on average, by an annual amount of 1.3 per cent. If the two surplus countries of Japan and the Republic of Korea are excluded, this figure increases to about 2.4 per cent per annum, which is virtually equal to the comparable average for non-oil African countries. Yet, while Asian countries (excluding Japan and Korea) record an actual average rate of growth of 6.6 per annum, the actual average rate of growth of non-oil African countries is only 3.4 per cent.

The explanation of this growth rate differential between this group of Asian countries and non-oil African countries must be found in their differing perfor-mance in external markets. For the group of Asian countries (excluding Japan and Korea), the terms of trade effect is virtually neutral, increasing the annual rate of growth by a small amount of 0.03 percentage points. The combined terms of trade and export volume effect increases the growth rate by about 4.66 per cent per annum. For the group of African countries (excluding oil-exporters), the terms of trade effect is adverse and relatively large, and the combined terms of trade and export volume effect increases the rate of growth by only 1.2 per cent per annum.

The differing performance in external markets between African and Asian coun-tries might be attributed to the differing characteristics of goods produced by

African and Asian countries which determine the income elasticity of demand for the country's exports and the country's propensity to import. Goods produced can generally be characterized into two basic groups:

- those whose production is based on nature-given comparative advantage (mainly primary products); and
- those whose production is based on man-made comparative advantage (mainly knowledge-intensive manufactured goods).

It can be argued that it is the latter group of goods that generates a bigger stimulus to growth, for they are characterized by a high income elasticity of demand.[13] As the world's income grows, so increasingly does the demand for knowledge-intensive manufactured goods. Thus, it would be expected that the higher the ratio of manufactured goods in total exports, the higher the growth of the net export effect and the higher the contribution of export growth to real income growth.

Table 14.8 shows the net export effect and the shares of primary products and fuel plus manufactured exports in the total merchandise exports. In general, it can be observed that the higher the share of primary products in total merchandise exports the lower the net export effect. Conversely, the higher the share of fuel plus manufactured goods in total merchandise exports, the higher the net export effect.

Individually, all Asian countries have a lower share of primary products and a higher net export effect than the respective averages for non-oil African countries. The only Asian country that approximates to the case of non-oil African countries, is Sri Lanka with a primary product share of 72 per cent and a net export effect of 1.7 per cent. The comparable average figures for Asian countries (excluding Japan and Korea) are 43 and 4.5 per cent.

In order to test more directly the relationship between the characteristics of exported goods, the net export effect and actual growth rates, Table 14.9 shows – for the full sample of African and Asian countries – the correlation coefficients between the share of manufactured goods in total merchandise exports, the share of primary goods in total merchandise exports, the net export effect and actual real income growth.

It is evident from the correlation coefficients that the higher the share of manufactured exports, the higher the net export effect and the higher the actual rate of growth. The correlation coefficient between the share of manufactured goods and the net export effect is positive and large amounting to 75 per cent, whereas the share of manufactured goods and the growth rate show a correlation coefficient of 61 per cent. It is also evident that the higher the share of primary products, the lower the net export effect and the lower the rate of income growth. The correlation coefficient between the share of primary products and the net export effect is negative and large amounting to −75 per cent, whereas the share of primary products and real income growth show a negative correlation coefficient of −61 per cent. The correlation between the net export effect and the actual rate of growth is 66 per cent, indicating that the net export effect which is a product of the terms of trade effect, export volume effect and the income elasticity of demand for imports,

Table 14.8 The rate of growth, net export effect and the shares of primary products and manufactured goods in merchandise exports

	Annual average (percentage points)*		Percentage of merchandise exports Average*	
	Actual growth rate	Net export effect	Primary products	Fuel + manufactured goods
African countries				
Egypt	6.90	1.99	43.0	57.0
Congo	6.59	4.29	14.6	85.4
Kenya	6.24	1.12	68.8	31.2
Mauritius	5.80	6.05	75.8	24.2
Tunisia	6.59	6.11	23.0	77.0
Burundi	6.50	4.90	98.0	2.0
Cameroon	5.50	5.97	66.3	33.7
Gabon	5.10	7.29	21.3	78.7
Algeria	4.90	14.36	5.2	94.8
Morocco	4.62	1.48	69.0	31.0
Côte d'Ivoire	4.50	4.62	83.7	16.3
Burkina Faso	4.20	−2.13	94.7	5.3
Somalia	3.40	−0.92	96.9	3.1
Zimbabwe	3.23	−0.17	66.3	33.7
Sudan	3.10	1.28	99.0	1.0
Benin	2.90	2.40	75.4	24.6
Tanzania	2.90	−0.22	81.6	18.4
Togo	2.90	2.39	87.1	12.9
Senegal	2.67	1.78	71.4	28.6
Nigeria	2.50	3.65	8.0	92.0
Mauritania	2.30	2.27	96.0	4.0
Ethiopia	2.20	0.64	93.9	6.1
Sierra Leone	1.58	−0.91	88.7	11.3
Zambia	1.40	−1.60	98.0	2.0
Ghana	1.40	−3.66	97.0	3.0
Niger	0.81	−3.28	96.6	3.4
Madagascar	0.48	−0.04	86.9	13.1
Average	3.66	2.18	70.6	29.4
Average excluding oil exporters	3.40	1.15	77.9	22.1
Asian countries				
Korea, Rep. of	9.11	12.66	9.0	91.0
Hong Kong	9.07	8.27	3.0	97.0
Indonesia	10.76	5.00	30.0	70.0
China	8.20	6.41	17.0	83.0
Malaysia	7.08	5.90	59.0	41.0
Thailand	6.80	6.41	69.0	31.0
Pakistan	5.04	3.83	35.0	65.0
India	4.31	2.31	38.5	61.5
Sri Lanka	4.30	1.68	72.0	28.0
Japan	4.20	8.31	2.0	98.0
Philippines	3.70	2.21	61.2	38.8
Average	6.60	5.73	36.0	64.0
Average excluding Japan and Korea	6.58	4.49	42.8	57.2

Source: Net export effect is obtained from Table 14.1. The rate of growth and the shares of manufactured goods and primary products in total merchandise exports are calculated from World Bank *World Tables 1992*.

Note
* For the time period considered for each country see Table 14.1.

Table 14.9 Correlation coefficients between the share of manufactured goods, the share of primary goods, the net export effect and real income growth

	Share of manufactured exports	Share of primary product exports	Net export effect	Real income growth
Share of manufactured exports	1.00	−1.00	0.75	0.61
Share of primary products exports		1.00	−0.75	−0.61
Net export effect			1.00	0.66
Real income growth				1.00

Source: Computed from Table 14.8.

is positively and strongly related to actual growth rates. Thus, while large shares of manufactured goods are associated with large net export effects, the latter are associated with high growth rates.

Based on these findings, it can be argued that rapid growth in East Asia was made good by the promotion of manufactured exports which have high income elasticities of demand in the world market. There may be disagreement, therefore, with the often expressed view that a basic lesson emerging from the East Asian experience which is applicable to African countries is to produce according to comparative advantage, implying nature-given comparative advantage. It is true that some Asian countries, in the early stages of growth, relied on the exportation of natural resource-intensive products, but the emphasis was on resource-intensive *manufactures* rather than agricultural primary goods and unprocessed minerals and raw materials. The Philippines, for instance, focused on manufactured wood products and clothing; Thailand focused on textiles, clothing and processed food. However, these countries concentrated more, as they advanced, on knowledge-intensive manufacturing and less on resource-intensive manufacturing activities. The basic lesson emerging from the Asian experience is that comparative advantage is not static, it is dynamic and can be created and acquired.

Conclusions and policy implications

In the preceding analysis, the dynamic Harrod foreign trade multiplier in its basic and extended forms was applied to a sample of African and Asian countries. It was found that the extended model – which incorporates the effects of the terms of trade and capital inflows – performed better than the basic model, which does not incorporate these two effects. Yet, the basic model, because of its simplicity, remains an interesting law of growth.

The results obtained from applying the models indicate that the explanation of the poor performance of African countries must be found, primarily, in the low magnitudes of their dynamic Harrod foreign trade multipliers as determined by the respective income elasticities of demand for exports and imports. These income elasticities, which also capture the elements of non-price competition, are the direct product of the characteristics of the goods produced – for example, whether they are primary goods or manufactured goods. As it is well known, primary products, such as those produced and exported by African countries, tend to have an income elasticity of demand of less than unity (Engel's Law), while most industrial products have an income elasticity greater than unity. Thus, it is only logical to find that most African countries have a low dynamic Harrod foreign trade multiplier, given their excessive dependency on exports of primary commodities and imports of manufactured goods. This, as the results of this chapter show, would constrain their growth to low rates that can only be surpassed if these countries are able to finance ever-increasing external deficits.

In a nutshell, the balance of payments constitutes a 'structural' problem in the context of African countries. Structural in the sense that it is inherent in the structure of production and the characteristics of the goods produced. For African countries with low rates of export growth combined with high income elasticities of demand for imports, the implications of the results must be that the goods produced by them are not 'income-attractive' either to the home or external markets. To accelerate their growth rate, they would need to raise the balance of payment constraint on growth by shifting to the production of more attractive exports and by reducing the income elasticity of demand for imports. In addition to maintaining sound economic fundamentals, this calls for the adoption of active visionary planning to engineer new comparative advantage through industrial transformation and create export market niches in selected products that capture larger proportions of world income growth.

Notes

1 See, for instance, World Bank (1993).
2 For a formal statement of these relationships see McCombie and Thirlwall (1994) and Thirlwall (1979).
3 This is based on the implicit assumption that current account deficits are not financed from foreign exchange reserves. In a long-term model this assumption is plausible as no country can finance an ever-growing deficit without capital inflows.
4 To this group we add Malaysia where the McCombie test is almost satisfied in the case of both the basic and extended model.
5 To this group we add the Philippines where the prediction of the extended model is almost valid.
6 To this group we add Ghana where the prediction of the basic model is almost valid.
7 A derivation of such a growth rate but with no terms of trade effect can be found in McCombie and Thirlwall (1994: 248).
8 Burundi, Madagascar, Morocco, Sudan, Zambia, Burkina Faso, Sierra Leone, Somalia, Tanzania, Egypt, Ghana, Zimbabwe, Ethiopia and Niger.
9 For the relationships between the balance of payments constrained growth rate, the actual growth rate and the capacity growth rate, see McCombie and Thirlwall (1994), and Thirlwall (2001).
10 This excludes Côte d'Ivoire and Nigeria where the estimated average growth rate in the current account is positive but relatively small.

11 The classification of whether a country is balance of payments constrained or not is not static; it varies from time to time according to the country's performance in international markets. For instance, Algeria and Gabon whose growth could be described as being balance of payments unconstrained during the 1970s and 1980s are presently facing balance of payments problems which can be partly attributed to the sharp decline in the dollar price of oil.

12 One measure of price competitiveness is the ratio of export prices to that of competing countries. In a large country such as Japan, the import price is considered to be a good proxy for the price of competing countries, hence, the terms of trade (the ratio of export prices to import prices measured in a common currency) can be treated as a measure of price competitiveness.

13 Note that in the context of our model the growth of export volume is given by $x = \beta(p_d - e - p_f) + \sigma w$. If the terms of trade is ignored the growth of export volume will be determined by the size of the income elasticity of demand for exports ($= \sigma$) and the growth of world income ($= w$).

15 The chronicle of economic growth in Southeast Asian countries: does Thirlwall's Law provide an adequate explanation?*

M. Ansari, N. Hashemzadeh, and Y. Xi

Thirlwall (1979, 1982) has formally shown a close association between the growth of output and the dynamic Harrod foreign trade multiplier using data for a number of developed countries. As he puts it:

> In the long run, no country can grow faster than at that rate consistent with balance of payments equilibrium on current account, and if the real terms of trade do not change much, this rate is determined by the rate of growth of export volume divided by the income elasticity of demand for imports. Attempts to grow faster than this rate mean that exports cannot pay for imports, and the economy comes up against a balance of payments constraint on demand, which affects the industrial sector's ability to grow as fast as labor productivity.
>
> (1982, p. 33)[1]

Over the last two decades, there have been numerous attempts to test the validity of Thirlwall's proposition using both time-series and cross-section data.[2] The main reason for the ongoing interest in the subject is that Thirlwall's hypothesis has amounted to a substantive challenge to the mainstream view that economic growth is supply-determined. As Cripps and Tarling have aptly put it, "The mainstream economic theory has tended to assume that capitalist economies are, to a sufficient degree of approximation, efficient in their use of resources at each point of time and that this efficiency is the result of market competition. This implies that growth depends on the provision of more resource inputs and on advances in knowledge" (1973, p. 1).

This chapter examines the applicability of Thirlwall's proposition to the economic experience of four Southeast Asian countries: Indonesia, Malaysia, Thailand, and the Philippines. Several considerations have provided the motivation for this study. First, Young (1994) has argued that contrary to popular opinion, economic performances of the four Asian tigers – namely, Hong Kong, Korea, Singapore, and Taiwan – do not look as spectacular as it is made out to

* First published in *Journal of Post Keynesian Economics*, Summer 2000.

be if one looks at *output per worker* rather than *output per capita*. He makes this distinction on the ground that a change in per capita output reflects a change in the living standards while a change in output per worker reflects a change in productivity. But more importantly, and most relevant to this study, Young maintains that the economic growth in these countries can be attributed more to the *static* neoclassical gains from factor accumulation and sector reallocation rather than to *dynamic* gains from outward-oriented policies. Nevertheless, Young's reaffirmation of the validity of the neoclassical growth paradigm has been refuted by numerous authors, who tend to emphasize the potential gains associated with outward-looking trade and commercial policies (see e.g. the World Bank, 1987; Balassa, 1988; Krueger, 1990).

This chapter contributes to the literature in several ways. First, it uses more recent data and a different sample period to see whether results from previous studies of the hypothesis can be replicated. Second, we expand on the earlier contributions by Thirlwall and Hussain (1982) and Bairam and Dempster (1991) by adding Malaysia to the pool of countries for which Thirlwall's hypothesis has been tested. To our best knowledge, the validity of Thirlwall's hypothesis has never been investigated with respect to Malaysia. Third, we address the statistical properties of the input data before proceeding with testing the hypothesis. This is a critical step because macroeconomic variables often need to be appropriately transformed to correct for nonstationary variances and possibly differenced or detrended to correct for nonstationary means.[3] The rest of the chapter is organized as follows: The section, "A comparative analysis of the macroeconomic profiles" gives a brief overview of the important macroeconomic aggregates in Indonesia, Malaysia, Thailand, and the Philippines. The next section discusses the theoretical framework and the methodology used for testing Thirlwall's hypothesis. Results obtained from our estimation are presented and analyzed in the last section.

A comparative analysis of the macroeconomic profiles

To date, most academic studies have tested Thirlwall's hypothesis in the context of developed industrialized economies and only a handful in the context of developing countries. There are only two studies that have attempted to examine the applicability of Thirlwall's hypothesis to the countries under study. Bairam and Dempster (1991) studied 11 developing countries including Indonesia, Thailand, and the Philippines. Thirlwall and Hussain (1982) studied a sample of 20 developing countries, including Thailand and the Philippines. In the case of Malaysia, the validity of Thirlwall's Law has never been investigated.

Income growth

In this section, we present a brief macroeconomic profile of these 4 countries. With the exception of Thailand, these countries have had a history of colonial rule.[4] All 4 are the original members of the Association of Southeast Asian Nations (ASEAN) formed by the Bangkok Declaration in 1967. They are also members of the Asia-Pacific Economic Cooperation (APEC) forum. At the time of their independence,

Table 15.1 Per capita GNP in Southeast Asian countries

	1970	1980	1990	1996	1970–96
Per capita GNP	$	$	$	$	Growth*
Indonesia	80	470	560	1,080	4.63
Malaysia	390	1,690	2,360	4,370	3.78
Philippines	230	650	730	1,160	1.50
Thailand	210	670	1,470	2,960	3.85
Average	228	870	1,280	2,393	3.44
Low income countries	—	—	—	490	—
East Asia and Pacific	—	—	—	890	—
Middle income countries	—	—	—	2,590	—

Source: Figures for 1970, 1980, and 1990 are from World Bank, *World Tables 1991*, and for 1996 from World Bank, *World Development Indicators 1998*.

Note
* Annual average growth rates.

these countries represented some of the most economically depressed nations in the world with comparatively low per capita income and a concomitant low standard of living. As shown in Table 15.1, decades after their independence, the average per capita income for the group as a whole was less than US$230 in 1970. Besides, there have been some wide intercountry variations in per capita income. In 1990, for instance, among the group of 4, Indonesia, with per capita income of $560, ranked the lowest, while Malaysia, with per capita income of $2,360, ranked the highest. Notwithstanding, all of the 4 economies managed to grow their per capita income significantly over the 1970–96 period. During this period, Indonesia with an annual average growth in per capita income of over 4.6 percent, led the group followed by Thailand, Malaysia, and the Philippines in that order. Furthermore, by 1996, the per capita income in all of the four countries was substantially higher than the average per capita income of the low-income countries and the East Asian and Pacific countries. By the same year, the per capita income of Malaysia and Thailand surpassed the average per capita income of the middle income countries. It is worth noting that the impressive growth in the per capita income in these countries was happening concurrently with a high rate of population growth during 1970–96 period. Our estimates show that over the period under study, Indonesia's population rose by 63 percent, Malaysia's by 100 percent, Thailand's by 64 percent, and the Philippines' by 89 percent.

Export growth

In as much as the emphasis in this study is on the importance of exports for generating economic growth, it is instructive that we examine the growth pattern of these countries with respect to both real gross domestic product (GDP) and real exports. As Table 15.2 indicates, these countries, as a group, have experienced significant growth in real GDP and real exports in recent years. With the exception of

Table 15.2 GDP and export growth[a] in Southeast Asian countries

	GDP		Export[b]	
	1980–90	*1990–95*	*1980–90*	*1990–95*
Group one				
Indonesia	6.1	7.6↑	5.3	21.3↑
Malaysia	5.2	8.7↑	11.5	17.8↑
Philippines	1.0	2.3↑	2.9	10.2↑
Thailand	7.6	8.4↑	14.3	21.6↑
Group average	5.0	6.8↑	8.5	17.7↑

Source: World Bank, *World Development Indicators, 1997.*

Notes
Arrows indicate period over period increase in growth rates of GDP and exports.
a Annual average growth rates in real terms.
b Merchandise trade only.

the Philippines, each one individually has recorded significant growth in both sub-periods. Likewise, the growth rates of both real GDP and real exports in the second subperiod have exceeded those during the first subperiod, indicating acceleration in the growth process. The data also show a definite positive association between growth rates of real GDP and merchandise export volume in both subperiods.

Theoretical framework and methodology

Theoretical framework

The neoclassical view on the determinants of economic growth had its origin in Say's law, which postulates that supply creates its own demand. Income generated by the production process is ultimately spent on the purchase of goods and services so produced. In this framework, saving does not disrupt the circular flow because offsetting changes in the interest rate ultimately reestablish the saving-investment equality. Similarly, wage adjustment ensures full employment of labor, and in the goods market prices adjust continuously to ensure equilibrium. Given full employment of labor and capital and exogenous technological progress, the rate of factor augmentation and technological progress will then determine a country's rate of economic growth. Although most neoclassical economists do not dismiss some connection between demand-side factors and economic growth, they do suggest that economic growth is not demand-driven in the long run. Likewise, the Keynesians and the Post Keynesians, who emphasize the demand-side factors in determining economic growth, do not dismiss the relevance of the supply-side factors. They simply believe that in the long run, supply factors are not binding and growth is primarily demand-constrained. They point out that supply factors in the long run are endogenous, and therefore, can be augmented. Labor resources, for instance, can be augmented through changes in productivity, participation rate, work hours, and migration, all of which tend to respond to growth in output. Similarly, investment is widely believed to respond to growth in output through the accelerator mechanism. Even domestic saving is positively influenced by the investment opportunities. Moreover, supply of capital can be augmented through inducement to save and invest domestically as well as through inducement to attract direct investment from abroad. Finally, trade is widely seen as an effective conduit for international diffusion of technology, a process that is further aided by the growth in multinational corporations.

Thirlwall singles out foreign exchange reserves as the only demand-side factor with the potential to constraining growth in the long run. This is especially true in case of the developing countries. As Thirlwall puts it, "there are not many countries in the world, particularly developing countries, that could not utilize (or generate) more domestic resources given the greater availability of foreign exchange" (1997, p. 380). Furthermore, he emphasizes the crucial importance of exports as a component of demand which "can provide the foreign exchange to pay for the import content of other components of demand – consumption, investment, and government expenditure" (1997, p. 380).

Drawing upon the idea of the Harrod foreign trade multiplier, Thirlwall develops a dynamic version of the multiplier using two assumptions: In the long run (1) capital inflows cannot finance payments deficits, and (2) changes in terms of trade or real exchange rate cannot provide a lasting relief from payments problem.[5] Subject to these assumptions, Thirlwall's Law is captured by the following equation:

$$q^* = (1/\pi)x, \tag{15.1}$$

where $q^* = $ rate of growth of real income consistent with balance of payments equilibrium, $\pi = $ income elasticity of demand for imports, $x = $ rate of growth of export, and $(1/\pi) = $ the dynamic Harrod foreign trade multiplier. Alternatively, equation (15.1) can be written as $q^* = (h/\pi)z$, where $h = $ income elasticity of demand for exports and $z = $ rate of growth of world income.[6]

Methodology

In general, a multistage procedure is used to test Thirlwall's hypothesis.[7] First, the income elasticity of import demand is estimated from an appropriately defined regression model. In the second stage, the rate of growth of real income consistent with balance of payments equilibrium (q^*) is computed using equation (15.1). In the third stage, the predicted value of growth in real income (q^*) is compared to the actual growth rate (q) using an appropriate statistical test. A significant concurrence between the two rates of growth is interpreted as evidence in support of Thirlwall's Law.

The approximate measure of income elasticity of demand for imports needed for computing q^* has been obtained using a variety of methods. Earlier studies estimated an import demand function using variables in logarithm form (see e.g. Houthakker and Magee, 1969; Goldstein and Khan, 1978), while later studies (see e.g. Bairam, 1988; Bairam and Dempster, 1991; Atesoglu, 1993, 1994, 1995) used either growth rates or first differences of the logarithm of the variables. However, earlier studies testing Thirlwall's hypothesis did not benefit from recent advances made in the field of time-series analysis. As it is now widely recognized, the validity of certain statistical tests, including tests for causality and cointegration, depend on the assumption that the input data is a realization of a stationary process or a process which has been rendered stationary by appropriate transformations. Bairam (1993), for the first time, treated the issue of nonstationarity in an explicit manner. However, in the absence of cointegration, he was unable to further examine other defining characteristics of his data before proceeding with his analysis. To make the data stationary, Bairam decided to transform the variables to first differences. Andersen (1993 and Chapter 10) made a full use of the recent literature on time-series analysis. He tested for both unit roots and cointegration. After confirming that import demand and real income were cointegrated, Anderson procccdcd with an error-correction model to separate the short-run behavior of the income elasticity of demand for imports from its long-run value.

There have been three other studies in recent years, which bear mention in this regard. McCombie (1997), after testing for stationarity, used a two-step cointegration test as suggested by Engle and Granger (1987). McCombie, after finding no cointegration between the import demand and real income time series, used the traditional regression method to estimate the income elasticity of demand for imports. Heike (1997), like McCombie, also tested for stationarity and cointegration. However, unlike McCombie, he found the variables to be cointegrated and hence he obtained his income elasticity of demand for imports from a cointegrating equation. Atesoglu (1997) followed a similar methodology for testing stationarity in the data set but instead of using two-step Engle and Granger methodology to test for cointegration, he used the Johansen procedure and examined cointegration between real income and real exports.

Empirical results

Unit root and cointegration test

We have used annual data from 1970 to 1996, yielding a total of 27 observations. The following considerations led us to choose 1970 as the starting year. First, a common sample period was considered important for making a meaningful intercountry comparison of the results. Some of the required data series were not available for all the countries for the earlier years. Furthermore, these countries began to show marked improvements in their economic performance only over this sample period. Third, so that we may keep our findings untainted from the influence of the recent financial crisis plaguing this region since 1997, we chose 1996 as the cut off date.

Since a time series can have a stochastic trend or a deterministic trend, we use the Dickey–Fuller (DF) and Augmented Dickey–Fuller (ADF) tests both with and without trend to check for stationarity. All variables have been transformed to natural logarithms except the relative price variable (rp), which is defined as the difference between the growth rate of foreign prices (p_f) and domestic prices (p_d). Results from these tests show that the export, import, and income variables are all difference stationary with a single order of integration. However, relative price variable is stationary with zero order of integration, or $I(0)$. We then test for the existence of a long-run equilibrium relationship between income and export variables for each country. Using the procedure suggested by Johansen and Juselius (Johansen, 1988; Johansen and Juselius, 1990), we tested the hypothesis of no cointegration between the time series using a deterministic trend and up to three lags.[8] The test results are presented in the Appendix. Based on the trace statistics the null hypothesis of no cointegration is not rejected in any of the cases. We therefore concluded that these two variables are not cointegrated. One of the conditions for conducting cointegration test is that all variables in the system should have a common order of integration. Since income and import variables were found to be $I(1)$ and relative price variable to be $I(0)$, we did not employ cointegration test using these variables.

Empirical results from equation (15.1)

Having established that import, income, and relative price variables have different order of integration, and therefore it is not appropriate to employ cointegration methodology to estimate an import demand function, we proceeded to estimate a traditional import demand function of the following form:

$$m_t = \beta_0 + \beta_1 y_t + \beta_2 rp_t + e_t, \tag{15.2}$$

where growth rate of real import (m_t) is the dependent variable and growth rates of real income (y_t) and real relative price variable (rp_t), as defined earlier, are the explanatory variables, while e_t is the error term satisfying the standard econometric conditions. Estimation results based on annual data from 1970 to 1996 are presented in Table 15.3.

All estimations were first carried out using the ordinary least squares techniques (OLS). However, a significant degree of first order serial correlation in the error terms was detected in the case of Malaysia. Therefore, the equation has been reestimated using the generalized least squares techniques (GLS) in order to achieve increased efficiency. This seems to alleviate the problem. As the table shows, both the income and the price coefficients have the expected signs in all four countries. The income coefficient is statistically significant at the 10 percent level for Indonesia and at the 1 percent level for Malaysia, Thailand, and the Philippines. Although the price coefficient in each case has the expected sign, it is statistically significant only in case of the Philippines. It is worth noting that our estimation produced an adjusted R^2 of 0.02 for Indonesia, which is very low. This warrants caution in interpreting the results. We re-estimated the import demand function for Indonesia by dropping the relative price variable as well as by applying lags on the price variable. Nevertheless, this did not produce any improvement in the R^2

Table 15.3 Regression results from equation (15.2), 1970–96

Country	Method	Constant	y_t	rp_t	R^2	DW
Indonesia	OLS	−9.75	2.98	−0.15	0.02	2.30
		(−0.70)	(1.55)***	(−0.79)		
Malaysia	AR(1)	−4.90	2.25	−0.09	0.30	1.81
		(−0.77)	(3.08)*	(−0.35)		
Philippines	OLS	1.39	1.92	−0.49	0.47	2.17
		(0.46)	(3.34)*	(−3.88)*		
Thailand	OLS	−12.92	2.86	−0.17	0.38	1.92
		(−2.08)**	(3.79)*	(−0.88)		

Notes
∗ significant at the 1 percent, ∗∗ 5 percent, and ∗ ∗ ∗ 10 percent levels using a one-tail test.
Numbers in parentheses are the *t*-values. The critical values for d_l and d_u for testing for the
presence of serial correlation for sample size 27 were, respectively, 1.24 and 1.56.

Table 15.4 Actual and predicted growth rates and their deviations

Country	x	q	q^*	$q - q^*$
Indonesia	16.3	6.90	5.47	1.43
Malaysia	14.5	7.40	6.44	0.96
Philippines	9.9	3.70	5.16	−1.46
Thailand	13.0	7.60	4.55	3.05
Average	13.4	6.40	5.41	0.99

Notes
x − export growth, q = GDP growth, and q^* − balance of payments
constrained growth rate, all in real terms. Numbers pertain to the sample
period, 1970–96.

value. We have done two things to test the robustness of our results for Indonesia.
First, as a diagnostic check, we applied DF and ADF unit root tests on the residuals
from equation (15.2). We found the residuals to be white noise.[9]

Based on the estimated income elasticity of demand for imports for these
countries, the predicted growth rates (q^*) using equation (15.1) are computed and
presented in Table 15.4. A close examination of the table corroborates the following
findings. First, for the group as a whole the average difference between actual (q)
and the predicted (q^*) growth rate is less than 1 percentage point. Second, the
deviation of actual from the predicted growth rate ranges from −1.46 percentage
point in the case of the Philippines to 3.05 percentage points in case of Thailand.
We use the *t*-test to measure the statistical difference between the two means.

The results from the *t*-test show that in the case of Indonesia, Malaysia, and
the Philippines the null hypothesis of no difference is not rejected at any reasonable
level of significance. In the case of Thailand however, the difference is large
enough to reject the null hypothesis. Hence, Thirlwall's proposition does not seem
to hold in the case of Thailand. For the remaining three countries, results from the
t-test clearly imply that the differences between the predicted and the actual growth

rates are random. We, therefore, surmise that Thirlwall's proposition cannot be rejected for these countries. The main policy implication is that these countries should continue to follow the outward-looking growth strategy with emphasis on export performance for a continued high rate of economic growth.

The results show that for Thailand, Thirlwall's simple model considerably underpredicts the growth rate of real income. One explanation may be that during the 1970–96 period, Thailand's foreign trade sector experienced extreme volatility which forced a currency devaluation and request for assistance from the International Monetary Fund (IMF) in the mid-1980s. Thailand's trade deficit as a percent of GDP, which showed a remarkable and consistent improvement over the period 1970–82, started to deteriorate from 1983. This situation continued until 1995 that resulted in a decline in earnings from exports of tin, sugar, and tapioca. Quota restrictions imposed by other nations on textiles originating in Thailand also contributed to this phenomenon. This large and persistent deterioration seemed to have resulted in an unusually low q^*, causing a large positive deviation of actual from the predicted rate of growth.

Appendix

Table 15.5 Results of Johansen and Juselius cointegration tests

Cointegrating vector		Likelihood ratios		
Null	Alternate	One lag	Two lags	Three lags
Indonesia				
$r = 0$	$r = 1$	7.39	8.50	7.61
		(0.23)	(0.25)	(0.17)
$r \leq 1$	$r = 2$	0.33	0.63	2.50
		(0.01)	(0.02)	(0.09)
Malaysia				
$r = 0$	$r = 1$	12.30	13.83	19.97
		(0.29)	(0.33)	(0.46)
$r \leq 1$	$r = 2$	3.96	4.04	5.68
		(0.15)	(0.15)	(0.22)
Philippines				
$r = 0$	$r = 1$	6.50	10.46	16.48
		(0.20)	(0.27)	(0.44)
$r \leq 1$	$r = 2$	0.40	2.19	1.97
		(0.01)	(0.08)	(0.07)
Thailand				
$r = 0$	$r = 1$	13.82	8.53	5.16
		(0.40)	(0.26)	(0.18)
$r \leq 1$	$r = 2$	0.11	0.76	0.12
		(0.00)	(0.03)	(0.00)

Numbers are the likelihood ratio test statistics, which are also called trace statistics. Numbers in parentheses are the eigenvalues, which are used in obtaining trace statistics. For details, see Eviews, *Version 3 User's Guide*, p. 511. All tests cover the sample period, 1970–96.

Notes

1 Thirlwall believes that in the short run, a balance of payment deficit can be financed by capital inflows. However, in the long run, a rising deficit as percentage of GDP and the concomitant reaction by the international financial community will force the country to make adjustments. Fluctuations in terms of trade or real exchange rate may also provide the needed adjustments in the short run.

2 McCombie (1997) presents an excellent synopsis of the literature on the subject and it also contains an exhaustive list of previous studies.

3 Most previous studies including Bairam (1993), Andersen (1993), Atesoglu (1997), Heike (1997), and McCombie (1997), have addressed this issue.

4 Indonesia was a Dutch colony until 1949, while Malaysia was a British colony until 1957. The Philippines was a Spanish colony until 1899 and remained under the American control until 1946.

5 The second implies either that price elasticities are very small or that the Marshall–Lerner condition is just satisfied.

6 For a discussion and derivation of these equations, see Atesoglu (1993), and McCombie and Thirlwall (1994). We have decided to work with equation (15.1) because income elasticity of demand for imports (π) is believed to be more stable than income elasticity of demand for exports (h).

7 Alternatively, the model can be tested by directly estimating a form of equation (15.1), see Atesoglu (1993–94, 1997).

8 The use of two-step Engle and Granger methodology for testing cointegration has been criticized on several grounds. For a detailed discussion of this issue, see Murthy and Phillips (1996).

9 Very often differencing can cause a loss of long-term information contained in the data, which might result in low R^2. In order to check if this is in fact true, we reestimated the import demand function for Indonesia using a double log formulation. The R^2 value shot up to 0.95, as expected. Also, the calculated value of q^* based on the new income elasticity of demand for imports produced a much narrower difference between q and q^*, providing even stronger evidence in support of Thirlwall's Law for Indonesia.

16 Thirlwall's Law and beyond: the Latin American experience[*]

Julio López G. and Alberto Cruz B.

According to Thirlwall's well-known model of balance of payments constrained growth, output growth is demand-determined, provided demand is below supply capacity, which is normally the case in capitalist economies. However, the balance of payments situation can restrict the growth of aggregate demand because a country cannot persistently undergo an ever-increasing current account deficit. From this general idea, "Thirlwall's Law" is derived as follows.

Let y stand for the rate of growth of domestic real income compatible with external equilibrium. It can be shown that the following relation holds (see, Thirlwall, 1999 or Heike, 1997, for details):

$$y = \frac{(1 + \eta + \psi)(p_d - p_f - e) + \varepsilon z}{\pi},\tag{16.1}$$

where z is the proportional rate of growth of world real income; $\eta(<0)$ and $\varepsilon(>0)$ are the price and income elasticity of exports; and $\psi(<0)$ and $\pi(>0)$ are the price and income elasticity of imports. Also, p_d is the rate of growth of the average price of exports, p_f is the rate of growth of the average price of imports in foreign currency, and e is the rate of growth of the nominal exchange rate (say, pesos per dollar).

Now suppose, following McCombie and Thirlwall (1994), that the real terms of trade, or real exchange rate (RER), remains constant in the long run – that is, $(p_d - p_f - e) = 0$. Then equation (16.1) becomes:

$$y = \frac{\varepsilon z}{\pi},\tag{16.2}$$

or (on the same assumption):

$$y = \frac{x}{\pi}.\tag{16.3}$$

This last equation has come to be known as "Thirlwall's Law."

* First published in *Journal of Post Keynesian Economics*, Spring 2000.

Most studies carried out under this theoretical framework maintain or assume that the terms of trade do not play an important role in long-run growth.[1] The purpose of this chapter is to investigate this hypothesis for selected Latin American countries, specifically, Argentina, Brazil, Colombia, and Mexico (Latin American economies, for short). We are interested in whether comparative prices (and the real exchange rate) are important, and if so, how important, in determining the rate of growth with external equilibrium in Latin America. We regard the real exchange rate as an economic policy variable that, under certain conditions, a country can manage in order to achieve the desired growth rate of output with external balance.

In order to evaluate, and later to discuss in more depth, Thirlwall's Law, we proceed as follows: First, we confirm statistical support for "Thirlwall's Law" for Latin American economies. Second, we show the existence of a stable long-run relationship between gross domestic product (GDP) and the RER for the four economies we have selected. Third, we estimate an equation for the trade balance (TB) and discuss the relationship between the RER and aggregate demand. Finally, we shall consider some economic policy issues emerging from our statistical analysis.

Since we support our reasoning with econometric analysis, it seems appropriate to state clearly the scope and limits of our research. What interests us is some theoretical and economic policy issues related to the theory of balance of payments constrained growth. The purpose of our econometric work is to show the plausibility of the assumed relation between economic variables rather than to discover the particular values of the parameters. In fact, to estimate the values of the parameters adequately would require a complete model, with a larger set of variables, which is beyond the scope of this chapter.

"Thirlwall's Law" in Latin America

As a preliminary step for evaluating Thirlwall's Law, we provide some background information on foreign trade and growth for our group of countries on the basis of two sets of figures. Also, Tables 16.4 and 16.5 (see Appendix) shows some macroeconomic and trade variables for our group of countries.

First, Figures 16.1–16.4 show the evolution of exports, imports, and real output. Output is in constant domestic prices and exports and imports are in constant US dollars.[2] The period spans 1965–96, and lower-case letters denote logarithms of the variables.

In general terms for Latin American economies, the three variables show an upward trend, but with structural breaks. The long-term rate of growth of output clearly declines beginning in the early 1980s in Argentina, Brazil, and Mexico, while in Colombia the structural break is not apparent.

In the long term, all three variables seem to be correlated, but this is not necessarily the case for each particular year. Instability in the growth rate is much more noticeable for exports and imports than for output, and year-to-year fluctuations are stronger for imports than for exports and for output. This result can be rationalized on the basis of the structural characteristics of these economies.

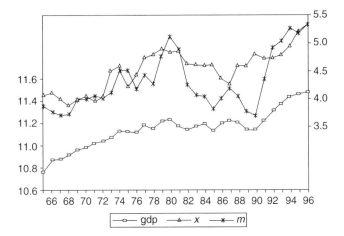

Figure 16.1 Argentina, gdp, exports (*x*), and imports (*m*), 1965–96.

Source: *International statistics yearbook*, IMF, 1995, 1966.

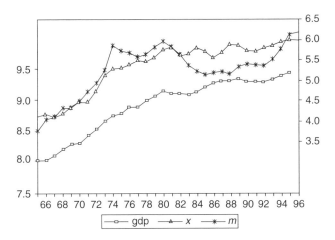

Figure 16.2 Brazil, gdp, exports (*x*), and imports (*m*), 1965–96.

Source: *International statistics yearbook*, IMF, 1995, 1966.

Indeed, Latin American economies share three common features. The first is a higher-than-average import coefficient of investment, the second is a high income elasticity of demand for foodstuffs, and the third is a low supply elasticity of domestic agricultural production. Accordingly, economic upswings, which are normally associated with a fast rise in investment, are accompanied with a large demand for imported investment goods. This goes together with disequilibrium between

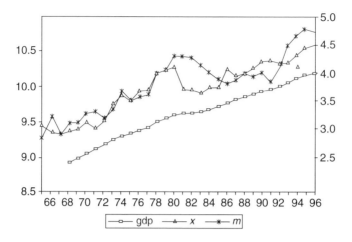

Figure 16.3 Colombia, gdp, exports (*x*), and imports (*m*), 1965–96.

Source: *International statistics yearbook*, IMF, 1995, 1966.

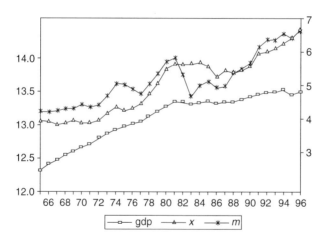

Figure 16.4 Mexico, gdp, exports (*x*), and imports (*m*), 1965–96.

Source: *International statistics yearbook*, IMF, 1995, 1966.

domestic supply and demand for foodstuffs, which translates into a large demand for agricultural imports and TB disequilibrium. On the other hand, economic down-swings, which are normally accompanied by a fall in investment, will provoke a decline in imports proportionally larger than in output.

The next set of Figures, 16.5–16.8, show the evolution of the RER[3] and the TB, where RER is in logarithms and the TB is in levels.

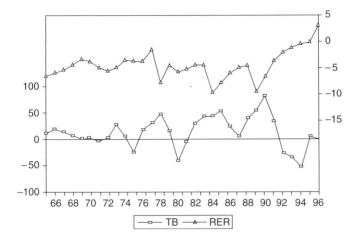

Figure 16.5 Argentina, TB, and RER, 1965–96.

Source: *International statistics yearbook*, IMF, 1995, 1966.

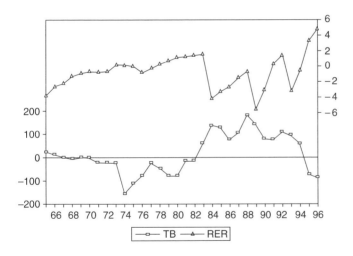

Figure 16.6 Brazil, TB, and RER, 1965–96.

Source: *International statistics yearbook*, IMF, 1995, 1966.

Notice, in the first place, that in Latin American economies the RER has been subject to large fluctuations and also to an upward trend. Thus, it would be difficult to claim the existence of an "equilibrium long-run RER."[4]

On the other hand, the TB and the RER seem to move in opposite directions; a worsening of the TB normally follows an appreciation of the RER. Again, the

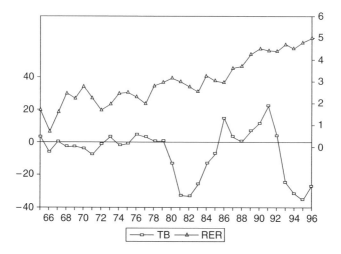

Figure 16.7 Colombia, TB, and RER, 1965–96.

Source: *International statistics yearbook*, IMF, 1995, 1966.

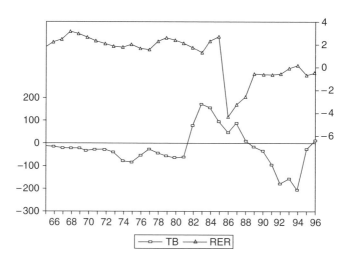

Figure 16.8 Mexico, TB, and RER, 1965–96.

Source: *International statistics yearbook*, IMF, 1995, 1966.

association seems to be strong in the long run, but not necessarily so in each particular year. It goes without saying that this association should be accepted cautiously because the TB is the result of a complex set of variables (more on this later).

In order to assess Thirlwall's growth model, we need to establish that the growth rates of exports and output maintain a stable long-run economic relationship, for which purpose we shall use a few econometric techniques: Augmented Dickey–Fuller (ADF) unit roots tests, and vector autoregresion (VAR), and Johansen's cointegration analysis. ADF tests are useful to determine the order of integration of the time series, and to confirm that cointegration analysis can be used. VAR models and the Johansen procedure allow us to analyze the hypothesis of the presence of stable long-run relationships between the variables of the model and to find out the number of relationships (see Charemza and Deadman, 1997; Cardero and Galindo, 1997).

According to the ADF tests, GDP is a nonstationary $I(1)$ series for Argentina, while for the remainder of the economies (the US GDP series is taken as a proxy for world output), GDP is a series whose order of integration is $I(2)$. The TB is $I(1)$ for all the countries, except for Argentina where the order of integration is $I(0)$. And the RER is $I(0)$ for Brazil, $I(1)$ for Argentina and Colombia, and $I(2)$ for Mexico.[5] These results testify that the Johansen cointegration procedure is a good starting point for testing the presence of long-run relationships among these variables.

Next, for each of our selected countries we estimated a VAR for domestic output and exports (Y_t is [the log of] domestic output in constant domestic units, X_t is [the log of] exports in constant dollars).[6]

The results of VAR estimates for GDP and real exports, subjected to the Johansen procedure, point to the existence of cointegrating vectors for each one of our four countries.[7] Cointegration of output with exports allows us to confirm the validity of Thirlwall's Law for the countries under consideration. Moreover, Granger causality tests for uniequational models with output and exports (not reported here) show that, for all countries (except Mexico), causality runs from exports to output – that is, higher exports tend to stimulate higher output. This result may be due to the expansionary effects of exports on domestic demand, but it may also suggest that export surges tend to encourage an expansionary demand policy – as hinted by Thirlwall.

Table 16.1 reports the results of the cointegration vector for GDP and exports. It also shows both the "equilibrium" π^e and the estimated π, long-run elasticities of imports with respect to domestic income (π^e is the inverse of the (long-run) elasticity of exports with respect to output, while π is the estimated cointegrating vector in the VAR for output and imports).

Notice that in Argentina, Colombia, and Mexico, the estimated elasticities of imports tend to exceed the "equilibrium" elasticities of imports. The latter country is the most outstanding example of this disparity, insofar as the growth of imports exceeded by far its "equilibrium" value. In Mexico, a growth rate of exports of 1 percent, say, was associated with a growth rate of output of 2.2 percent. Thus, to maintain foreign trade equilibrium (i.e. equality between the growth rates of exports and imports), the elasticity of imports with respect to output π^e should have been 0.45. However, the actual elasticity of imports was well above that figure, namely, 1.3. The two big crises (1982 and 1995) Mexico suffered in the period under consideration were the direct outcome of this disequilibrium.

Table 16.1 Normalized cointegration vectors (VAR of output and exports),
and import coefficients

Country	b_1	π^e	π
Argentina (1965–96)	0.41	2.4	2.8
Brazil (1965–95)	0.59	1.6	1.03
Colombia (1968–96)	1.7	0.56	1.8
Mexico (1965–96)	2.2	0.45	1.3

Notes
The vectors are normalized for domestic GDP ($Y = 1$).
b_1 is the elasticity of exports, π^e and π are the elasticities of imports.
The years for which VARs were estimated are shown in parentheses. The value of the
constant is not introduced. GDP (in constant units) and the real exports and imports
(in US constant dollars) are in logarithms.

The RER and output growth

As mentioned, Thirlwall derives his well-known equation $y = x/\pi$, under the
assumption that the RER (or the real terms of trade) can be assumed constant
in the long run (see Thirlwall, 1999). Nevertheless, as shown earlier, in Latin
America the RER has undergone important fluctuations during the period under
consideration. These fluctuations affect the competitiveness of tradeable goods
and therefore the balance of payments associated with any given output level and
growth rates. By the same token, they modify the level and rate of growth of output
in external equilibrium.

In order to analyze if and how the RER affects domestic output in the long run,
we estimated a VAR with domestic output (Y) and the RER (RER_t is [the log of]
the RER).

Using the Johansen procedure, we found one cointegration vector for each
of our countries. In other words, a stable long-run relationship between domestic output and the RER was found. The normalized vectors are given in
Table 16.2.

The sign associated with the RER variable indicates whether the impact of
variations of the RER on domestic output was negative or positive during the
period of study. In the case of Colombia and Mexico, the sign was positive,
which would indicate that a rise in the RER helped to achieve a higher growth
rate of output in the long run. Argentina and Brazil are in a different situation
because, from the negative signs for the RER, we can infer that a higher RER was
accompanied with a lower rate of growth of output.

The negative association between the RER and output can be due to two
alternative causes, or a combination of both. On the one hand, the so-called
Marshall–Lerner condition may not be fulfilled. On the other hand, a currency
depreciation, which raises the RER, may bring about a fall of domestic demand
large enough to offset the improvement of the TB. In the next section we analyze
these points.

Table 16.2 Normalized cointegration vectors. VAR of output
           and the RER

Country	β_1
Argentina (1965–94)	−1.7
Brazil (1980–95)	−0.05
Colombia (1968–96)	0.16
Mexico (1965–94)	0.50

Notes
The vector is normalized for domestic GDP (Y = 1).
β_1 is the elasticity of output with respect to the RER.
The years for which VAR were estimated are shown in parentheses.
The value of the constant is not introduced. GDP (in constant units)
   and the RER are in logarithms.

The RER, the TB, and effective demand

In order to verify if the Marshall–Lerner condition is fulfilled in our group of countries, we estimate a VAR for the TB. We thus estimate a VAR including the TB (TB_t is the TB in constant dollars), world output (Y_t^* is world output),[8] the domestic GDP (Y_t is the domestic GDP in constant units), and the RER (RER_t is the RER).[9] All the variables, except the TB, are in logarithms.[10]

If the Johansen procedure shows the existence of a long-run relationship between the selected variables, and the parameter for the RER is statistically significant, then we can claim that the RER influences the TB – and also, very likely, the level of output at external equilibrium. Besides, we could also know immediately whether or not the Marshall–Lerner condition is fulfilled. Table 16.3 shows the results of the estimates for the VAR in our selected countries.[11]

In general terms, the results show once more that, for the Latin American economies, stable long-run relationships between the selected variables exist. Further, we can see that in all cases the TB is positively associated with international output and negatively associated with the domestic output. However, its association with the RER is positive in Argentina and Colombia, but negative in Brazil and Mexico.

The Brazilian and Mexican economies, then, do not seem to follow the pattern commonly assumed in mainstream economic thought: A higher RER (i.e. a real depreciation) appears to worsen the TB. We can then understand why we found a negative association between output and the RER in Brazil. The reason is simply that the Marshall–Lerner condition is not fulfilled in that country.

But what about Argentina where, even though the Marshall–Lerner condition is fulfilled, output appears to be negatively associated with the RER?[12] As mentioned earlier, this negative association is probably the result of the harmful impact of a higher RER on domestic demand.[13] Let us now analyze this point.

Currency depreciation is the most common option for raising the RER. We shall argue that currency depreciation may depress domestic demand, even

Table 16.3 Normalized cointegration vectors for the VAR ($TB_t, \beta_1 Y_t^*, \beta_2 Y_t, \beta_3 RER_t$)

Country	β_1	β_2	β_3
Argentina (1968–96)	76.7	−118	1.05
Brazil (1967–95)	52.7	−42	−38.7
Colombia (1971–96)	493	−856	135
Mexico (1969–96)	351	−230	−114

Notes
The vector is normalized for the TB ($TB = 1$). The years for which VAR were estimated are shown in parentheses. The value of the constant is not introduced. GDP is in constant units, TB is in constant dollars, and RER is the real exchange rate.

when obstacles to expanding or redirecting supply limit its potential benefits for domestic producers. Let us first consider the demand aspects involved.

On the one hand, the initial price hike triggered by the currency depreciation can provoke uncertainty as to the future stability of prices and the exchange rate, which may depress private investment. This is particularly the case when drastic currency depreciation and accelerating inflation take place after a period of stability, and when a collapse of the previous optimistic scenario provokes a dramatic worsening of expectations.

Investment can be further discouraged due to the rise in the debt ratios of firms – especially when they are indebted in foreign currency – and due also to the rise in the interest rate, which normally follows a currency depreciation. Unless banks are willing to expand lending and unless there is an accommodating monetary policy, firms will find it difficult to finance their extra needs of working and fixed capital ensuing from higher prices. Finally, currency depreciation raises the supply price of imported capital goods, thus reducing expected profitability.

In addition, depreciation of the currency also depresses private consumption. Higher-income groups may not be terribly harmed by the inflationary shock induced by the currency depreciation, because they can reduce their savings rather than expenditure. But since money wages are normally not fully adjusted to past inflation, consumption per worker will fall and a shift from wages to profits will take place.

In sum, private investment, as well as domestic consumption, are reduced with the depreciation of the currency. Our findings suggest that, in cases such as Argentina's, these negative effects on internal demand may not necessarily be offset by the improvement in the TB brought about by the depreciation.[14] The price elasticity of demand for exports and for import substitutes may be quite high, but supply limitations normally limit the capacity of domestic producers to take full advantage of latent demand and higher profit margins.

Indeed, semi-industrialized economies usually have large unutilized capacities in the manufacturing sector, but in specific industries, or in sectors such as infrastructure or agriculture, capacities may be insufficient or inadequate. Thus, bottlenecks normally appear at early stages of output expansion, which prevent full response to potential demand. Furthermore, exports, and even substitution of imports, may be limited because firms may not have adequate marketing channels to access and satisfy potential customers. Thus, they may be unable to substitute foreign for domestic demand when the latter contracts.

Proponents of currency depreciation accept that it may in some (infrequent) cases bring about a fall in demand and in output. But they tend to downplay this effect with the argument that this fall will be short lived. Export growth, so the argument goes, will eventually drag investment down and aggregate demand growth with it.

Our results suggest that this view is unwarranted and that the contractionary impact of currency depreciation may indeed be long lasting. One possible explanation would emphasize the negative impact of a fall in profitability and in the degree of utilization of the productive capacities on investment; but this is a point that deserves a deeper analysis and cannot be further pursued here.[15]

Some economic policy issues

We have been able to show that Thirlwall's Law is relevant for Latin American economies, in that output growth closely tracks export growth in the long run and, moreover, higher exports tend to cause higher output. However, we also found significant departures from Thirlwall's original assumptions. On the one hand, the RER has varied greatly during the period under consideration, without it having any tendency to return to a supposed "long-run equilibrium value." More important, the level of the RER was found to be statistically significant for the level of output at external equilibrium – however, the sign of the association differed as between different countries.

Thirlwall's assumptions about the constancy of the RER in the long run, or its lack of statistical significance for the level of output at external equilibrium, have strong policy implications. Indeed, he concludes: "Differences in the income elasticity of demand for exports and imports reflect the non-price characteristics of goods." He goes on to argue: "In balance-of-payments-constrained countries, supply-side policies are needed to change the structure of production in the broad sense of allocation of resources between primary and secondary production and between tradeable and nontradeable goods, and in the specific sense of the characteristics of the goods produced" (Thirlwall, 1997, p. 383).

Now, it is undeniable that supply-side measures such as the ones suggested by Thirlwall are necessary in order to be able to achieve a higher rate of growth with external equilibrium. But we should also be aware that the benefits of such "structural" measures are rather delayed. The rate of growth of a country implementing an industrial policy of the sort hinted at by Thirlwall could possibly be enhanced, but the process would be protracted. Moreover, a considerable part of the inherited capital equipment may go unused because it cannot be "modernized."

By contrast, the benefits accruing from price (and cost) competition could be reaped at a much earlier date – though probably not in the very short run. More precisely, if the TB were positively associated with the RER – that is, if the Marshall–Lerner condition holds – then a country with idle capacity and an unoccupied work force could expand output and employ its idle resources in the short or middle term. It would pay for the requisite additional imports with higher exports made possible thanks to its more competitive RER, and the latter may allow even old capital equipment to become profitable as well as competitive. Of course, once the rate of exchange has been stabilized, the growth rate of output would cease to accelerate, but then output would be growing from a higher plateau.

Our results suggest that the RER may indeed be significant for output at external equilibrium for some Latin American economies. This would imply that those countries where the Marshall–Lerner condition is fulfilled could achieve a faster rate of growth of output if they pursued a policy whereby their RER is kept at a competitive level. However, our results also suggest that a higher RER, by itself, is no guarantee that output will be higher. Rather, in some cases, it is associated with a lower level of output, even when the Marshall–Lerner conditions are fulfilled.

In conclusion, our previous reasoning indicates that management of the RER should be extremely cautious. More specifically, it points out, in the first place, that any country should first of all carefully inquire whether or not the TB is positively associated with the RER, both at a general level and for particular sectors and branches of the economy. In the second place, our results suggest that management of the exchange rate should be combined with a demand policy capable of preventing the shift from wages as well as the depression of domestic demand that could arise with a higher rate of exchange. But to analyze which specific measures would comprise this policy mix is beyond the scope of the present paper (see, however, López, 1998, and López and Mántey, 1999).

Appendix

Table 16.4 Average rates of growth of GDP, exports, and imports, percent per annum

		GDP	M^a	X^b
Argentina	1966–81	2.4	6.5	4.9
	1982–95	2.0	1.8	2.3
Brazil	1966–81	6.7	12.9	10.3
	1982–95	2.4	2.1	1.3
Colombia	1969–81	5.2	8.8	4.1
	1982–95	3.8	3.4	5.0
Mexico	1966–81	6.6	10.7	11.0
	1982–95	0.81	4.6	5.8

Notes
a Imports
b Exports.

Table 16.5 Main export markets (percentages), 1990–96

		Export markets
Argentina	1990	USA = 13.7
	1991	Brazil = 12.4
	1995	Brazil = 26.1
	1996	Brazil = 27.7
Brazil	1990	USA = 24.6
	1992	USA = 19.8
	1994	USA = 20.5
	1996	USA = 19.4
Colombia	1990	USA = 44.4
	1992	USA = 43.6
	1994	USA = 38.7
	1996	USA = 40
Mexico	1990	USA = 70
	1991	USA = 79.5
	1992	USA = 81.1
	1994	USA = 85
	1995	USA = 90.8
	1996	USA = 84

Notes

1 McCombie and Thirlwall (1994) argue that the empirical evidence suggests that, over a long period of time, movements in similarly measured prices in a common currency are comparatively small. However, they, as well as Thirlwall in most of his papers, consider mainly the case of developed countries. A host of researchers have used "Thirlwall's Law" to explain economic growth in the long run. For developed economies, see, e.g. Atesoglu (1993, 1997), McCombie and Thirlwall (1994), Heike (1997), and McCombie (1997). For developing economies, see, e.g. Moreno-Brid (1999) and McCombie and Thirlwall (1994). All these studies have been carried out under the (implicit) assumption that the real terms of trade or the RER remain constant in the long run. For a criticism of this assumption and a different modeling procedure, see Alonso and Garcimartin (1998–99).

2 It seems more adequate to consider exports and imports in dollars because this is the currency in which Latin American foreign payments have to be met. We take domestic output in constant domestic prices because no long-run series for domestic output in Purchasing Power Parity units are available for our sample of countries.

3 We follow the Latin American convention and define the RER as $RER = E(P^*/P)$, where E is the nominal exchange rate (say pesos per dollar), P^* the international price index, and P the domestic price index. Hence, a rise in RER denotes a currency depreciation, and a rise in price competitiveness.

4 Thirlwall (1997, p. 380) says, "the terms or trade or real exchange rate may fluctuate in the short term, but in the long run it appears to remain relatively stable." But here again he has in mind mostly industrialized countries.

5 ADF tests are known to have low power for alternatives close to the unit root (Spanos and McGuirk, 1999), and here we use them only as a first approximation. The results of ADF tests can be obtained from the authors.

6 The VAR is defined as a set of statistical assumptions related to the stochastic process of the vector **V** (where **V** includes the variables of the VAR) defined as (Spanos, 1986): (i) Markov (p), (ii) second-order stationarity, and (iii) normality. All estimated VARs were subjected to misspecification analysis. This is necessary in order to specify a statistical model that adequately captures the systematic information in the data – or, what amounts to the same, that the assumptions of the VAR are not rejected by the data. Only those estimates not rejected by the misspecification tests are reported in this paper. All the econometric work was carried out with PC FIML 9 (see Doornik and Hendry, 1997).

7 Incidentally, imports and domestic output also cointegrate. The results of the cointegration analysis can be obtained from the authors.

8 US GDP in constant dollars is always taken as a proxy for world output. It would have been more precise to construct a different estimate for world demand for each country, with trade partners weighted according to their weights in exports. But the necessary figures were not available.

9 The ordering of the variables selected for the VAR can affect the final results. We tried different orderings, and the results were rather similar. We present here the results for the TB as the first variable.

10 Since the TB is sometimes negative, we could not use logarithms for the TB to estimate the elasticities directly. In any event, we also estimated the VAR with the logarithm of exports less the logarithm of imports, but our statistical results were less robust.

11 Misspecification tests for the VAR and the results of the cointegration analysis are available from the authors. In cases when more than one cointegration vector was found, we show in Table 16.3 only the cointegration vector with the greatest characteristic value. A graphical analysis shows that these cointegrating vectors satisfied also the condition of (second-order) stationarity.

12 And what about Mexico, where despite the fact that the Marshall–Lerner condition is not fulfilled, output is positively associated with the RER? See later.

13 Of course, a thorough analysis of the relationship between output growth and the external sector for Argentina (or for any of our countries, for that matter) would require a comprehensive model of their economies.

14 The Krugman and Taylor paper (1978), where these problems are formally analyzed, is still very much worth reading. See also Taylor (1988) and, on the Mexican experience, see for example J. López (1998), and Castro *et al.* (1997).

15 Regarding the case of Mexico, our statistical findings could be rationalized with the argument that a currency depreciation increases government revenues, which are immediately spent. Thus, the rise of government expenditure more than offsets the negative effect of a higher RER on the TB and on demand (see Krugman and Taylor, 1978).

17 Balance of payments constrained growth in Central America: 1950–96*

Juan Carlos Moreno-Brid and Esteban Pérez

The growth path of most Latin American economies in the postwar era experienced drastic shifts. In the case of some Central American countries, important turning points in their economic growth trajectories have been associated with political and social instability and with radical changes in macroeconomic policy. The civil strife and, most important, the armed conflicts in Guatemala (1963–96), El Salvador (1979–92), and Nicaragua (1974–79, 1981–90) had severe negative effects on their economies and, to a certain extent, on those of Honduras and Costa Rica. The Central American peace process, whose origins can be traced back to the formation of the Contadora Group (1983) and that is currently undergoing its final phase, has undoubtedly improved the economic prospects and performance of the region.[1] Despite the effects of these social and political events on the fluctuations of output, it has been argued that, from a long-term perspective, the evolution of exports and the terms of trade can be seen as fundamental determinants of Central America's economic growth (Oman and Wignaraja, 1991; ECLAC, 1993, 1995; Taylor, 1993).

Table 17.1 Growth rates of real GDP, exports, and terms of trade for Central American countries, 1950–96 (annual averages, in percentages)

Country	GDP	Exports	Terms of trade
Costa Rica	4.7	5.8	−0.04
El Salvador	3.4	3.3	−0.00
Guatemala	3.8	4.4	−1.21
Honduras	3.8	2.7	−0.60
Nicaragua	2.6	3.4	−1.40

Source: ECLAC (1997).

Note
Data were available for Honduras for 1950–94 and for the rest of the countries for 1950–96.

* First published in *Journal of Post Keynesian Economics*, Fall 1999.

Table 17.1 suggests that, during 1950–96, there was a close association between the rate of growth of real gross domestic product (GDP) and of exports and, to a lesser extent in some periods, with the terms of trade. As an example, in this period Costa Rica achieved the fastest average annual rate of expansion of real GDP (4.7 percent) and of exports (5.8 percent), with close to no deterioration in terms of trade (−0.04 percent). Nicaragua, the most laggard economy in the region in terms of the expansion of real GDP (2.6 percent), experienced the harshest deterioration in its terms of trade (−1.4 percent).

The purpose of this chapter is to examine the extent to which long-term economic growth in 1950–96 in each of these five Central American nations may be explained by the evolution of exports and the terms of trade. It seeks to investigate whether the balance of payments constraint, as formulated by Thirlwall, has been a key determinant of the long-term economic growth of each of these countries.

Theoretical framework

The notion of the balance of payments setting an upper ceiling to the long-run rate of expansion of economic activity has its theoretical underpinnings in the seminal work of A. P. Thirlwall, who in 1979 introduced a simple theoretical macroeconomic model that essentially set Harrod's analysis of the foreign trade multiplier in a dynamic context. His pioneering model, based on the hypothesis that current account deficits cannot be indefinitely financed and must eventually be canceled out, concludes that the long-term rate of expansion of aggregate demand – and thus of domestic economic activity – is constrained by the availability of foreign exchange. Applying such a model to empirical analysis of selected advanced economies, he concluded that their long-term economic growth is essentially determined by the income elasticity of import demand and by the rate of expansion of their exports (Thirlwall, 1979). His results suggested that, in the case of most advanced countries, neither foreign capital flows nor the terms of trade exert a major significant influence on their long-term rates of economic growth.

The analytical framework that emerged from his contribution came to be known as the balance of payments constrained growth model (hereafter, BPC model). To an important extent it has its intellectual roots in the work of Allyn Young, Myrdal, and Verdoorn, which underlined the crucial role of aggregate demand on the economic growth process. Such perspective stands in stark contrast with conventional neoclassical views that see technical progress and the supply of factors of production as the determinants of long-term economic growth, with no major role played by aggregate demand or financial constraints.

The revision that took place in the last ten years in growth theory, triggered by the work of Romer (1986) and Lucas (1988), questioned the main tenets of standard neoclassical interpretations of economic growth. But the mainstream analytical framework that has been reconstructed does not adequately address the issue that economic growth in developing nations may be severely limited by the availability of foreign exchange due to heavy dependence of investment on imported machinery.[2]

The pioneering BPC model was subsequently revised explicitly to allow for a persistent disequilibrium in the balance of payments and, therefore, to make it more adequate to reflect the experience of "developing countries [that] are often able to build up ever-growing current account deficits financed by capital inflows" (Thirlwall and Hussain, 1982, pp. 500–501).

The model, thus revised, led to the same basic conclusion – namely, that long-term economic growth has an upper limit given by the country's availability of foreign exchange. But it now stressed that, in the case of LDCs, such availability is determined by the evolution of the net inflow of foreign capital as well as by factors previously identified in the BPC model's simple version: exports, the terms of trade, and the income elasticity of imports.

The next section succinctly presents the algebraic expressions of the model of the balance of payments constraint that served as the theoretical basis for the econometric study, carried out in this chapter, of the economic growth trajectories of the five Central American countries in 1950–96.

The analytical model of balance of payments constrained growth

The analytical model put forward by Thirlwall and Hussain (1982, see Chapter 3) may be summarized by the following system of five equations, representing a two good, small, open economy:[3]

$$px + ef^* = p^*em; \tag{17.1}$$

$$\theta = px/(px + ef^*); \tag{17.2}$$

$$\theta(\hat{p} + \hat{x}) + (1 - \theta)(\hat{f} + \hat{e}) = \hat{p}^* + \hat{e} + \hat{m}; \tag{17.3}$$

$$\hat{x} = \eta(\hat{p} - \hat{p}^* - \hat{e}) + \pi\hat{w}, \quad \text{with } \eta < 0, \pi > 0; \tag{17.4}$$

$$\hat{m} = \phi(\hat{p}^* + \hat{e} - \hat{p}) + \xi\hat{y}, \quad \text{with } \phi < 0, \xi > 0. \tag{17.5}$$

Equation (17.1) is the standard balance of payments identity, with x standing for real exports, m for real imports, p for price of domestic goods (exports) in local currency, p^* the price of imports in units of foreign currency, and f^* the current account deficit of the balance of payments in units of foreign currency (by definition, it is equal to net nominal foreign capital inflows); e is the nominal exchange rate in units of local currency per unit of foreign currency.

The second expression is an identity introduced for notational purposes in order to ease some algebraic formulations. It defines θ as the initial share of exports in the total inflow of foreign exchange measured at current prices. Equation (17.3) gives the continuous time expression of the balance of payments, and it is easily derived by differentiating equation (17.1) with respect to time (the notation ˆ represents a continuous rate of change).

The model is closed with equations (17.4) and (17.5), which correspond to the dynamic expressions of the conventional export- and import demand functions with constant, income and price, elasticities. That is, they specify the rates of change of the demand for real exports x and real imports m, where y stands for real domestic income, w for world's real income, η and π for the price and income elasticities of exports, and ϕ and ξ for the price and income elasticities of imports.

Solving the system of equations (17.1)–(17.5) in terms of the rate of growth of domestic income gives the expression that constitutes, in fact, the fully developed formulation of the balance of payments constrained rate of economic growth as identified by Thirlwall and Hussain:

$$\hat{y}_b = \frac{\theta\pi\hat{w} + (1-\theta)(\hat{f} + \hat{e} - \hat{p}) + (\theta\eta + \phi + 1)(\hat{p} - \hat{p}^* - \hat{e})}{\xi}. \tag{17.6}$$

Equation (17.6) specifies the long-term rate of growth of domestic income $\hat{y}_b$ as a linear function of the rates of growth of the world's real income $\hat{w}$, of foreign capital flows in real terms $\hat{f} + \hat{e} - \hat{p}$, and of the evolution of the terms of trade $\hat{p} - \hat{p}^* - \hat{e}$, with the weights of aggregation of the three terms given by the price and income elasticities of imports and of exports and the share of exports in the total availability of foreign exchange.

Substituting $\theta = 1$ in equation (17.6) leads to the expression of balance of payments constrained growth of domestic income for the case when foreign capital inflows are assumed away or considered not significant:

$$\hat{y}_b = \frac{\pi\hat{w} + (\eta + \phi + 1)(\hat{p} - \hat{p}^* - \hat{e})}{\xi}. \tag{17.7}$$

If the expression of $\pi\hat{w}$ given in equation (17.4) is substituted into equation (17.7), the balance of payments constrained rate of economic growth $\hat{y}_b$ is specified as a linear combination of the rate of growth of exports $\hat{x}$ and of the terms of trade:

$$\hat{y}_b = \frac{\hat{x} + (\phi + 1)(\hat{p} - \hat{p}^* - \hat{e})}{\xi}. \tag{17.8}$$

Note that expression (17.8) could have been obtained too as the solution of the subsystem of four equations: (17.1), (17.2), (17.3), and (17.5); in other words, by leaving exports as exogenously determined. Finally, if the terms of trade are assumed to remain constant in the long term, the balance of payments constrained rate of economic growth is determined as a function of only the rate of growth of exports and the income elasticity of imports. This expression is usually referred to in the literature as Thirlwall's Law:

$$\hat{y}_b = \frac{\hat{x}}{\xi}. \tag{17.9}$$

Equation (17.9) ends this brief review of the basic analytical framework of the BPC model developed by Thirlwall and his associates. In this process, different specifications for the long-term rate of economic growth – compatible with balance of payments equilibrium – have been identified. These specifications differ in their assumptions concerning the long-term evolution, or significance, of the terms of trade and of the net foreign capital inflows. Equation (17.6) allowed for a significant influence of both factors. On the other hand, equations (17.7) and (17.8) gave room for changes in the terms of trade, but under the assumption that in the long run the capital account of the balance of payments must be zero. And equation (17.9) did not assume any relevant influence either of the terms of trade or of net capital inflows on long-term economic growth.

These formulations provide the theoretical framework for the present study of the long-term economic growth in the selected Central American countries. Given our interest in the relationship between such long-term economic growth and the evolution of exports and of the terms of trade, we have focused on testing the empirical relevance of the BPC model as expressed in equation (17.8). But, to do so, and following standard practice in the empirical studies within the BPC tradition, it was necessary to express equation (17.8) in its corresponding first-difference log-linear functional form:

$$\Delta \log(y_b) = \alpha \Delta \log(x) + \beta \Delta \log(p/ep^*), \tag{17.10}$$

where, for notational purposes, two identities were introduced: $\alpha = 1/\xi$ and $\beta = (\phi + 1)/\xi$.

The next section presents and interprets the results of the econometric estimation of a stochastic formulation of equation (17.10),[4] for each Central American country, applying cointegration techniques with time-series data covering 1950–96.[5] In so doing, we attempt to examine the implications for cointegration analysis for the three variables mentioned earlier, rather than using a stepwise procedure to test for the long-run relationship between two variables – say, GDP and exports – and then add a third one – terms of trade – in order to assess its overall contribution.[6]

Testing the BPC model in five Central American economies: 1950–96

The BPC model encapsulated in equation (17.8), and in its corresponding first difference log-linear form in equation (17.10), postulates a stable relationship between the long-run rates of growth of GDP y_b, exports x, and the terms of trade p/p^*e. Formally, stability of a linear relationship among a group of variables means that, even though the time series for each individual variable may not gravitate toward its mean and may show infinite variance over time – that is, exhibit nonstationarity – the linear combination of these variables will tend to return to its mean and to show fluctuations of constant amplitude about it, that is, it will be stationary (Cuthbertson *et al.*, 1992).

Since the last decade, cointegration analysis has become the standard tool to test for the presence of stable long-term relations among sets of variables. It consists of a two-step procedure. The first step is to establish the order of integration of each variable – that is, the number of times that the variable must be first-differenced to obtain a stationary series. In this chapter, the order of stationarity was determined with the Dickey–Fuller statistic (DF) and the augmented Dickey–Fuller statistic (ADF).

Once it has been verified that the variables have compatible orders of integration, the second step consists of determining whether there is at least one linear combination of them that is stationary. In such case, the variables are said to be cointegrated and the specific values of the stationary linear combinations are called the cointegrating vectors. This step was carried out with the Johansen procedure, that is, a maximum-likelihood method to test for the existence of a stable long-run relationship between sets of variables.

Table 17.2 shows the results of the unit-root tests for GDP, exports X, and the terms of trade TOT in logarithmic form in levels and first differences for all Central American countries, for 1950–96 with the exception of Honduras. The estimations for Honduras were carried out for 1950–94. In all cases, the three variables were found to be integrated of order one, $I(1)$, in first differences at a 5 percent level of significance. The Box–Pierce (BP) and Ljung-Box statistics (LB) indicate that the integration residuals for these $I(1)$ variables are not correlated.

Following standard practice, prior to applying the Johansen cointegration procedure, it was necessary to identify the best lag length for the corresponding vector autoregressive systems (VARs). Such identification was done on the basis of the Akaike information criterion (AIC) and the adjusted likelihood ratio (ALR), considering up to a maximum length lag of six years. Table 17.3 reports the results for the best lag length thus calculated, that is, two years for Honduras, and one year for the other four countries.

As Table 17.4 shows, the BP statistic for twelve residuals computed for the optimal lag structure of the VARs suggest that the yielded parameters were not inconsistent (Taylor, 1991; Charemza and Deadman, 1992).

The outcome of the Johansen cointegration procedure is given in Table 17.5. As column two shows, for each country the trace of the stochastic matrix indicated the existence of at least one stationary, linear combination of the first difference of the logarithms of real GDP, exports, and the terms of trade. Indeed, for all cases, the null hypothesis of no cointegrating vectors was rejected but the hypothesis of having at least one such vector could not be rejected, at the 5 percent significance level. These results tend to validate the key claim of the BPC model, as expressed in equation (17.8), concerning the long-run association between the growth of GDP, exports, and the terms of trade.

The third column in Table 17.5 shows the cointegrating vector for each country that was chosen on the basis of theoretical considerations. As shown by equation (17.10), the coefficient for the export variable (ΔLX) corresponds to the inverse of the income elasticity of imports $1/\xi$, and the coefficient for the terms-of-trade variable ($\Delta LTOT$) corresponds to $(\phi+1)/\xi$, where ϕ and ξ are the estimated price and income elasticities of imports, respectively. Both elasticities, as well as the observed and the balance of payments constrained rates of growth of real GDP in annual terms for the 1950–96 period, are given in Table 17.6. The observed rate of growth of GDP was calculated with the data at constant dollar prices for each country. The estimated rate of growth of output was derived from the estimated coefficients of the respective cointegrating vectors reported in Table 17.5.

Table 17.2 Unit root test for real GDP, exports, and the terms of trade in Central American Countries, 1950–96 (variables in logs)

Country	Variable	DF(ADF)	n
Costa Rica	$\Delta LGDP$	−1.23*	3
	$\Delta^2 LGDP$	−5.80	0
	ΔLX	−0.50*	1
	$\Delta^2 LX$	−8.57	0
	$\Delta LTOT$	−2.69*	2
	$\Delta^2 LTOT$	−4.89	3
Guatemala	$\Delta LGDP$	−1.28*	1
	$\Delta^2 LGDP$	−3.88	0
	ΔLX	−1.54*	3
	$\Delta^2 LX$	−3.94	2
	$\Delta LTOT$	−1.70*	0
	$\Delta^2 LTOT$	−6.10	0
El Salvador	$\Delta LGDP$	−1.81*	1
	$\Delta^2 LGDP$	−3.16	0
	ΔLX	−1.48*	0
	$\Delta^2 LX$	−6.02	0
	$\Delta LTOT$	−2.01*	0
	$\Delta^2 LTOT$	−6.95	0
Honduras	$\Delta LGDP$	−0.38*	0
	$\Delta^2 LGDP$	−5.92	0
	ΔLX	−0.94*	0
	$\Delta^2 LX$	−6.02	0
	$\Delta LTOT$	−1.94*	3
	$\Delta^2 LTOT$	−3.22	2
Nicaragua	$\Delta LGDP$	−3.13	0
	$\Delta^2 LGDP$	−4.77	0
	ΔLX	−1.73*	0
	$\Delta^2 LX$	−6.68	0
	$\Delta LTOT$	0.28*	8
	$\Delta^2 LTOT$	−4.00	7

Notes

n is the number of lags selected in the unit root regression to ensure "white noise" residuals. BP and LB statistics – not reported here – were computed up to 12 lags showing no evidence of autocorrelation between the integration residuals. The symbol Δ denotes first differences and the symbol Δ^2 the double application of the first difference operator; the asterisk denotes "not significant" at a 5% level confidence level (no asterisk indicates significance at that level). Tests for the variables in log-levels – though not reported here – showed nonsignificant ADF coefficients. All results were computed with TSP.

Table 17.3 Akaike information criteria (AIC) and adjusted likelihood ratios (ALR) for 0 to 6 VAR lag structure for Central American countries

Country	Test diagnostic		Lag order
	AIC	ALR	
Costa Rica	165.44	46.13*	1
El Salvador	126.54	44.48*	1
Guatemala	175.08	33.79*	1
Honduras	168.48	30.18*	2
Nicaragua	85.21	39.96*	1

Note
AIC and ALR were computed with Microfit 4.0. The ALR is distributed as a chisquare with 54 and 45 degrees of freedom for 1 and 2 lags, respectively. The asterisk denotes non-significance at a 5% confidence level.

Table 17.4 Residual diagnostics of chosen VAR lag for $\Delta LGDP$, ΔLX, $\Delta LTOT$ for Central American countries

Country (VAR lag length)	Variable	BP(12)
Costa Rica (1)	$\Delta LGDP$	7.58*
	ΔLX	5.85*
	$\Delta LTOT$	17.36*
El Salvador (1)	$\Delta LGDP$	4.75*
	ΔLX	12.87*
	$\Delta LTOT$	6.80*
Guatemala (1)	$\Delta LGDP$	9.12*
	ΔLX	11.20*
	$\Delta LTOT$	9.92*
Honduras (2)	$\Delta LGDP$	2.47*
	ΔLX	5.98*
	$\Delta LTOT$	8.71*
Nicaragua (1)	$\Delta LGDP$	12.38*
	ΔLX	11.32*
	$\Delta LTOT$	18.09*

Note
BP(12) = BP statistic for twelve residual autocorrelations. The asterisk denotes not significant at the 5% confidence level.

Note that in all cases the estimated income elasticities of imports were positive and fell between 1.10 (Costa Rica) and 3.70 (Honduras). For El Salvador, Guatemala, and Nicaragua, they took the values of 1.75, 1.35, and 2.04, respectively. In turn, as expected, the estimates for the price elasticities of imports were always negative, with magnitudes within the range of −0.44 (El Salvador) and

Table 17.5 Johansen cointegration procedure for selected Central American countries, 1950–96

Country and lag	Johansen cointegration test result				Estimated cointegrating vector
	HO	*H1*	*LRS*	*5% CV*	
Costa Rica, 1	$r = 0$	$r = 1$	43	18	$\Delta LGDP = 0.91\Delta LX$
	$r \leq 1$	$r = 2$	37	11	$+0.48\Delta LTOT$
El Salvador, 1	$r = 0$	$r = 1$	43	18	$\Delta LGDP = 0.57\Delta LX$
	$r \leq 1$	$r = 2$	37	11	$+0.32\Delta LTOT$
Guatemala, 1	$r = 0$	$r = 1$	43	18	$\Delta LGDP = 0.74\Delta LX$
	$r \leq 1$	$r = 2$	30	11	$-0.07\Delta LTOT$
Honduras, 2	$r = 0$	$r = 1$	37	18	$\Delta LGDP = 0.27\Delta LX$
	$r \leq 1$	$r = 2$	15	11	$-0.01\Delta LTOT$
Nicaragua, 1	$r = 0$	$r = 1$	59	18	$\Delta LGDP = 0.49\Delta LX$
	$r \leq 0$	$r = 2$	37	11	$-0.31\Delta LTOT$

Note
The lag structure for each country was chosen on the basis of the results of Table 17.3. LRS is the likelihood ratio statistic; 5% CV stands for the 5% significance level critical value.

Table 17.6 Central America, income and price elasticities of imports, and observed GDP growth (y_{obs}) and balance of payments constrained one (y_e)

Country	Income elasticity ξ	Price elasticity ϕ	y^*_{obs}	y^{**}_e
Costa Rica	1.10	−0.47	4.7	5.3
El Salvador	1.75	−0.44	3.4	1.9
Guatemala	1.35	−1.01	3.8	3.3
Honduras	3.70	−1.04	3.8	0.7
Nicaragua	2.04	−1.63	2.6	2.1

Notes
* Actual average annual growth rates of GDP in percentages.
** BPC rate of growth calculated from the estimated cointegration vector and the observed rates of growth of real exports and of the terms of trade during 1950–96 for Costa Rica, El Salvador, Guatemala, Nicaragua, and during 1950–94 for Honduras.

−1.63 (Nicaragua). With the exception of Honduras, the income elasticity of imports estimated here are in line with the results of previous estimates of the import demand function for Latin American countries (Bairam, 1997).[7]

With the exception of El Salvador and Honduras, the observed growth rates of GDP are rather close (below one percentage point) to the balance of payments constrained ones. The discrepancies between the actual and the estimated rates of growth of GDP for Guatemala, Costa Rica, and Nicaragua do not seem significant, given that the sample covers more than forty years that include important changes in economic policy such as the opening of domestic markets to foreign trade, the

Table 17.7 Relative contributions of exports and of the terms of trade to the balance of payments constrained growth of GDP, 1950–96

Country	BPC growth of GDP y_e	Export contribution $\alpha \Delta LX$	Terms of trade contribution $\beta \Delta LTOT$
Costa Rica	5.26 (100%)	5.28 (100%)	−0.02 (0.0%)
El Salvador	1.88 (100%)	1.88 (100%)	0.00 (0.0%)
Guatemala	3.34 (100%)	3.26 (98%)	0.08 (2%)
Honduras	0.73 (100%)	0.73 (100%)	0.00 (0.0%)
Nicaragua	2.10 (100%)	1.67 (80%)	0.43 (20%)

dismantling of protectionism, and periods of civil strife and prolonged economic instability – the Nicaraguan hyperinflation is a case in point (see note 1).

For El Salvador and Honduras, the BPC equilibrium rate of growth is well below the actual rate; this suggests that both economies were able to overcome their balance of trade constraints. For El Salvador, this may be partly explained by private remittances that represented on average 9 percent of GDP for 1990–95 (World Bank, 1995). For Honduras, official aid – especially during the 1980s – was an important factor in alleviating the country's restrained access to foreign exchange.

Although, as shown earlier, evidence was found in all five cases of a statistically significant long-term association between the rate of growth of GDP and that of exports and the terms of trade, it was deemed convenient to assess the relative magnitude of the contribution of these two factors to economic growth in each country. Such assessment is useful, given the ongoing debate within the BPC literature on the quantitative relevance (apart from the statistical significance) of including – or not – the terms of trade as an explanatory variable of long-term economic growth (see, among others, McGregor–Swales, 1991; McCombie, 1992; Heike, 1997; McCombie and Thirlwall, 1997b).

Table 17.7 shows, for each of the five countries, the relative contribution of exports and of the terms of trade to the balance of payments constrained rate of growth of GDP derived with the cointegrating vectors estimated here. The results indicate that, with the exception of Nicaragua, the relative contribution of the terms of trade to the BPC growth of GDP was negligible. And even for Nicaragua itself, their contribution was 20 percent, much lower than that of exports (80 percent). This evidence tends to corroborate an important insight of the BPC model in its basic form – that is, à la Thirlwall's Law given by equation (17.9) – in the sense that it "gives limited explanatory power to the rate of change of relative prices as a determinant of the rate of growth of output" (McCombie, 1997, p. 351).[8]

Conclusions

The aim of this chapter was to examine with the aid of cointegration techniques the empirical validity of the BPC model – in its version including exports and the terms of trade as determinants of long-term economic growth – for Central American countries during the period 1950–96.

The empirical analysis found strong evidence of a long-run association between the rates of growth of real GDP and of real exports and the terms of trade for all Central American countries, thus lending support to the BPC model as a relevant tool of analysis of the long-term growth trajectories of these small, open economies. The estimated parameters of the cointegrating vectors also suggested that exports, rather than the terms of trade, are by far the most relevant explanatory variable of the rate of growth of output. Moreover, the results indicate that the countries with the fastest long-term rates of expansion of GDP compatible with balance of payments equilibrium in 1950–96 tended to be those with relatively lower income elasticities of imports and higher growth of exports.

In addition, we found strong support for the BPC model for Guatemala, Costa Rica, and Nicaragua, in the sense that the results – for the period analyzed – showed that Thirlwall's point equilibrium rate of growth of output does not differ substantially from its observed value, suggesting that it may act over time as a center of gravity of the actual rate of growth of output. However, the relevance of the BPC model, in the version tested here, was not so robust for the case of El Salvador and Honduras which, through private remittances and official aid, respectively, were able to overcome the restrictions imposed by the balance of payments constraint on their long-term economic growth path. Whether the more complete version of the BPC model introduced by Thirlwall and Hussain to capture the influence of foreign capital movements will give better explanations of the economic growth path followed by the economies of El Salvador and Honduras remains to be examined.

Notes

1 The armed conflict in Guatemala started in 1963 and lasted for 33 years. Its origins can be traced to the overthrow of the democratically elected president, Jacobo Arbenz, in 1954. The peace process, which began in 1986 under the auspices of President Vinicio Cerezo, fully materialized with the signing of the peace agreement under the presidency of Alvaro Arzú. El Salvador suffered a civil war that began in 1979 and ended with the 1992 peace agreement. Nicaragua experienced a civil war (1974–79) that ended with the overthrow of self-imposed dictator Anastasio Somoza Debayle (1979), a transition from a peace to a war economy (1981–90), a period of hyperinflation (1987–91), and several drastic stabilization attempts characterized by maxi-devaluations among which the most important are the Mayorga and Lacayo Plans (1990 and 1991, respectively). The Contadora Group, which was formed in January 1983 and comprised Mexico, Venezuela, Colombia, and Panamá, represented a Latin American diplomatic initiative with the aim of achieving a peaceful solution to the Central American conflict (Dunkerley, 1988).
2 Critical reviews of the "New Growth" theory may be found in Kurz and Salvadori (1995), Skott and Auerbach (1995), Srinivasan (1995), Taylor (1996), and McCombie and Thirlwall (1997b).
3 The assumption of being a small open economy allows prices of tradables to be treated as exogenously given; that is, as independent of the country's supply of exports or demand of imports. For notational purposes, upper-case Z denotes variables in current prices, lower-case z in constant prices; asterisks denote variables measured in units of foreign currency, and hats $(\hat{z})$ denote rates of change of z.
4 For the econometric estimation, a disturbance term "v_t" is added to the right-hand side of equation (17.10), and its distribution is assumed to have standard properties for regression analysis.

5 Readers interested in having access to the data should contact the authors directly at éperez@un.org.mx or brid@un.org.mx

6 Using a stepwise procedure may not necessarily be the most adequate approach, for it may not reveal the weight of each variable in a given cointegrating relationship. The importance of the variables included in a long-run relationship is determined by computing their relative contribution to a determined cointegration equation. In our case, the contributions of exports and terms of trade to the balance of payments constrained growth equation, as embodied in equation (17.10), are shown in Table 17.7.

7 Bairam (1997) reports earlier findings of an income elasticity of imports of 1.48 for Brazil (1964–85) and of 1.91 for Colombia (1961–85).

8 The reader must keep in mind that the model used in the empirical exercises carried out in this paper was based on an expression of BPC growth that did not allow for an independent influence of the RER (which in this version is equivalent to the terms of trade) on real exports. A more thorough analysis of the relative influence of the terms of trade on the long-term rate of economic expansion will be done in the future, but focusing on equation (17.7). This equation gives an expression of the BPC rate of growth that captures the influence on real imports as well as on real exports.

18 Balance of payments constrained economic growth: the case of Mexico*

Juan Carlos Moreno-Brid

Background

From 1940 to 1981 Mexico experienced spectacular economic growth, with its gross domestic product (GDP) expanding in real terms at a speed that outpaced that of the United States of America (US), its powerful neighbour. In those four decades, in spite of its rapid demographic expansion, Mexico cut down nearly ten percentage points in the gap of its GDP per capita *vis-à-vis* the US. From being equivalent to 22 per cent of the US average in 1939, Mexico's GDP per capita climbed to represent 30 per cent of the US figure in 1981, measured in constant dollars (Maddison, 1995).

However, the evolution of the Mexican economy since 1982 has been plagued by stagnation and instability. Upswings in economic activity, though moderate by historic standards, have been recurrently interrupted by balance of payments crisis. The result has been a dismal performance in terms of economic growth. Real GDP declined in 1982–87, and averaged an annual increase of just 2.4 per cent in 1988–97, more than four points below its average in 1950–75 (see Table 18.1). Such sluggish behaviour pushed back its catching-up process with the US economy. By 1997, Mexican GDP per capita in constant dollars represented approximately 24 per cent of the US, a relative gap similar to the one prevailing nearly sixty years ago.

Sustaining high long-term economic growth should be a top priority in the national agenda. The economy needs to expand at least at 6 per cent per year in real terms, just to create the jobs required by the 3.3 per cent annual increase in its labour force.[1] Economic expansion must be even stronger in order to significantly improve the living standards of the tens of millions of Mexicans that live in extreme poverty.[2] If the economy does not soon enter a path of high and sustained growth, the nation's social fabric may be severely damaged.

In the last ten years, economic growth has again became a fashionable topic for academic research, originating a vast literature on the, so-called, New Growth theory. This theory differs from the conventional one, based on Solow's seminal

* First published in the *Banca Nazionale del Lavoro Quarterly Review*, December 1998.

contributions, in claims regarding, *inter alia*, the convergence of levels of real income per capita and the impact of the savings rate on long-term economic growth. However, both theories identify technical progress and the supply of factors of production as the main determinants of long-term economic growth.

Notwithstanding their valuable contributions, their focus on the supply side fails to recognize the influence of financial constraints and of aggregate demand on economic growth (Skott and Auerbach, 1995; Taylor, 1996). This neglect questions their relevance for the analysis of growth processes in developing economies, whose fixed capital formation strongly depends on imported machinery and equipment. Such dependence implies that access to foreign exchange tends to be a relevant constraint on fixed investment and, therefore, on economic growth. In fact, the experience of the Mexican economy, and many other countries in Latin America, is a dramatic proof that apparently sound economic growth trajectories can be derailed by sudden changes in the availability of foreign exchange. Shocks in the terms of trade or in the net inflow of foreign capital have radically altered the growth path of many economies in the region.

The availability of foreign exchange is recognized as a key determinant of long-term economic growth by some, non-neoclassical, analytical perspectives. "Two Gap" Models, rooted in the work of Chenery, and the balance of payments constraint models (BPC-model hereafter), extending Harrod's work on the foreign-trade multiplier, are examples of these perspectives. Some of their tools have gained acceptance as useful instruments to analyse economic growth processes when markets do not necessarily clear (Taylor, 1996).

The chapter covers four sections besides this introduction. The section, "The balance of payments constraint: an analytical model", puts forward a revised version of the balance of payments constraint model to include a notion of long-term equilibrium that guarantees a positive and sustainable path of external indebtedness. The section, "Balance of payments constrained growth in Mexico", applies this version of the BPC-model to explain main turning points in Mexico's economic growth path since 1950. The last section summarizes the conclusions.

The balance of payments constraint: an analytical model

The work of Thirlwall has been a path-breaking contribution to highlight the role of the balance of payments as a determinant of long-term economic growth. Based on the proposition that the current account deficit cannot be indefinitely financed, Thirlwall (1979) built a parsimonious model, known as the BPC-model, showing that the lack of foreign exchange sets a fundamental limit to the long-run expansion of domestic income.

In 1982, with Hussain, he modified the BPC-model in order to examine the influence of foreign capital movements, and concluded that long-run economic growth has an upper ceiling given by the evolution of net foreign capital inflows, net exports and the terms of trade. Their model, however, imposed no restriction on the trajectory of foreign capital flows except for the accounting principle equating the consolidated debit and credit items in the balance of payments. Therefore, it did not ensure that the path of external indebtedness is sustainable. But, as Mexico's economic history painfully attests, external capital may be financing the foreign exchange needs of economic booms but, simultaneously, fueling an excessive accumulation of foreign debt that sooner or later will explode into a balance of payments crisis that plunges the economy into a recession.

Aware of this problem, McCombie and Thirlwall (1997a) once more modified the BPC-model by incorporating in it an additional constraint given by a long-term constant ratio of the *stock* of external debt to GDP. They only examined the case of constant terms of trade, and showed how the introduction of this constraint necessarily leads to a different expression of Thirlwall's Law. We will come back to this expression later, but it should be stressed that the present chapter adopts a different approach and goes beyond the previous contributions to the BPC-literature in various ways.

First of all, it limits external indebtedness to preserve a long-term constant ratio of the *current account deficit* to nominal income or GDP. Such specification, not considered by other authors in the BPC-literature, seems to better reflect the position of international financial institutions regarding what are – and are not – sustainable paths of foreign indebtedness. Indeed, the "Washington Consensus" has recognized that one main lesson to be derived from the Mexican crisis of 1994 is that "[...] the current account is a key variable that should not get out of line" (Edwards, 1995, p. 302). Moreover, current account deficits of around 5–8 per cent of GDP, and certainly higher, have been singled out as a matter of serious concern by senior officers of the International Monetary Fund (IMF) (Fischer, 1997) and the World Bank (Burki and Edwards, 1995).[3]

Second, the analytical model here put forward leads to a formulation of the BPC-growth rate that: (a) differs from the canonical expressions derived by Thirlwall and his associates for the case of unrestricted foreign capital flows, and (b) generalizes the expression obtained by McCombie and Thirlwall (1997a) for the case of constant terms of trade.

Third, the present chapter carries out an empirical application of the revised BPC-model to examine the Mexican economy's growth path in 1950–97 and to offer an explanation of its slowdown since 1982.

A BPC-model with a sustainable path of external indebtedness

The rate of economic growth compatible with a constant long-term ratio of the current account deficit to nominal income is derived by the following system of equations:

$$dx/x = \eta(dp/p - dp^*/p^*) + \pi \, dw/w \tag{18.1}$$

$$dm/m = \phi(dp^*/p^* - dp/p) + \xi \, dy/y \tag{18.2}$$

$$\mu = p^* m/(p^* m - px) \tag{18.3}$$

$$0 = \mu \, dm/m - (\mu - 1) \, dx/x - \mu(dp/p - dp^*/p^*) - dy/y. \tag{18.4}$$

The first two equations are the standard export- and import demand functions with constant elasticities, but expressed in terms of their rates of change, where x stands for real exports, m for real imports, p for domestic prices, p^* for foreign prices, w for world's real income, y for real domestic income, $\eta < 0$ and $\pi > 0$ for the price and income elasticities of exports, and $\phi < 0, \xi > 0$ for the respective elasticities of imports. To ease the exposition, the nominal exchange rate was taken to be fixed and equal to one. We shall refer to the price ratio p/p^* as the terms of trade, and its upward (downward) movement as an improvement (deterioration). Note that this version of the BPC-model does not distinguish between the real exchange rate and the terms of trade.

The third equation is just an identity defining μ as the ratio of nominal imports to the current account deficit. The fourth equation establishes the equilibrium condition for the balance of payments in terms of a long-term constant ratio of the current account to nominal income. It is derived from the balance of payments identity, but written in terms of proportions of nominal income:

$$B = (p^*m - px)/py = (M - X)/Y, \qquad (18.5)$$

where M and X stand for total imports and exports of goods and services (factor and non-factor ones) and B is the initial ratio of the current account deficit relative to domestic nominal income Y. Taking differentials on both sides of expression (18.5) and equating them to zero leads to the following expression of the long-term equilibrium condition of economic growth with a sustainable path of foreign indebtedness:

$$0 = (M/Y)\,dm/m - (X/Y)\,dx/x - [(M - X)/Y]\,dy/y$$
$$+ (M/Y)(dp^*/p^* - dp/p). \qquad (18.6)$$

The BPC-growth rate of real domestic income y_{ca} in our revised model is obtained by solving the system of equations (18.1)–(18.4):

$$y_{ca} = \frac{(\mu - 1)\pi\,dw/w + [\mu(\eta + \phi + 1) - \eta](dp/p - dp^*/p^*)}{\xi\mu - 1}. \qquad (18.7)$$

Multiplying numerator and denominator of equation (18.7) by $1/\mu$ and, defining θ as the export/import ratio at nominal prices[5] leads to an equivalent, but perhaps easier to interpret, expression of y_{ca}:

$$y_{ca} = \frac{\theta\,\pi\,dw/w + (\theta\eta + \phi + 1)(dp/p - dp^*/p^*)}{\xi - (1 - \theta)}. \qquad (18.8)$$

Equation (18.8) shows that, if foreign capital inflows expand in tandem with domestic nominal income, then the long-term growth of *real* income y_{ca} is determined by the initial export/import ratio, the income and price elasticities of exports and imports, the rate of expansion of the world economy and the evolution of the terms of trade.

If the terms of trade are assumed to be constant in equation (18.8), then the BPC-growth rate would be given by the following expression:

$$y_{ca} = \frac{\theta \pi \, dw/w}{\xi - (1 - \theta)},$$ (18.9)

or equivalently:[6]

$$y_{ca} = \frac{\theta \, dx/x}{\xi - (1 - \theta)}.$$ (18.10)

If the current account is zero, then equation (18.10) leads to the canonical expression typically referred to as "Thirlwall's Law":

$$y_{ca} = \frac{dx/x}{\xi}.$$ (18.11)

Returning to equation (18.8) note that the long-term income multiplier of the world economy's growth is equal to $\theta\pi/[\xi - (1 - \theta)]$ and, in turn, the multiplier of the terms of trade equals $(\theta\eta + \phi + 1)/[\xi - (1 - \theta)]$. The sign of the first one depends exclusively on $\xi - (1 - \theta)$ because its numerator $(\theta\pi)$ is always nonnegative. But the sign of the second multiplier is given by $\xi - (1 - \theta)$ and also by the "weighted" Marshall–Lerner expression: $\theta\eta + \phi + 1$. Note that neither of these signs are a priori determined.

Whether the weighted Marshall–Lerner expression has a positive or a negative sign must be empirically determined. But, as we show later, $\xi - (1 - \theta)$ will likely be non-negative. To see this, one should examine three different positions of the current account balance: surplus, zero or deficit.

First, when the current account is in surplus – a situation that applies to economies which systematically transfer capital abroad – θ is greater than one and, therefore, $\xi - (1 - \theta)$ would be positive.

Second, if the current account is zero, then $\theta = 1$, and thus $\xi - (1 - \theta)$ is reduced to ξ which, by assumption, is greater than zero. In this case, the BPC-growth y_{ca} in equation (18.8) is reduced to the formulation put forward by Thirlwall in 1979:

$$y_{ca} = \frac{\pi \, dw/w + (\eta + \phi + 1)(dp/p - dp^*/p^*)}{\xi}.$$ (18.12)

The third, and final, case corresponds to a current account in deficit, that is, $\theta < 1$. To determine the sign of $\xi - (1 - \theta)$, let us substitute in it the full expressions of ξ and θ, thus obtaining its equivalent formulation:

$$\xi - (1 - \theta) = (dm/m)/(dy/y) - [1 - (px/p^*m)].$$ (18.13)

Therefore $\xi < (1 - \theta)$ if, and only if:

$$\frac{dm + m - x(p/p^*)}{y + dy} < \frac{m - x(p/p^*)}{y}, \tag{18.14}$$

which, multiplying both sides by p^*/p, lead to:

$$\frac{p^*(dm + m) - px}{p(y + dy)} < \frac{p^*m - px}{py}. \tag{18.15}$$

The left hand side of (18.15) is the current account deficit/domestic income ratio in period $t + dt$, assuming that exports remain at the level they were in the previous period t. Its right-hand side corresponds to the same ratio, but for period t. Both ratios are calculated at prices p and p^*. Thus, (18.15) states that if $\xi - (1 - \theta) < 0$, then an increase in domestic economic activity will bring about a *reduction* in the current account deficit as a *proportion* of domestic income. That is, higher growth of the domestic economy – even with constant exports – would tend to reduce the pressure on the current account of the balance of payments. Moreover, in this case the long-term income multiplier of external demand (dw/w) would be *negative*, implying that *ceteris paribus* an expansion of foreign demand would trigger a contraction in domestic economic activity! Such perverse dynamics question the empirical relevance of the case $\xi < 1 - \theta$ for the analysis of economic growth in developing countries.

Therefore, it may be safely assumed that ξ is not smaller than $1 - \theta$. This implies that the long-term income multiplier of external demand (dw/w) is positive and inversely related to the magnitude of the export/import ratio θ. In other words, if two economies have the same initial level of income, identical elasticities of foreign trade and the same trajectory of the terms of trade, then the economy with a higher ratio of the current account deficit as a proportion of domestic income will have faster long-term growth.[7]

A graphical representation of the BPC-model

The BPC-model, here introduced as the set of equations (18.1)–(18.4), may be diagrammatically represented in the space of combinations of the growth rates of real domestic income (dy/y) and imports (dm/m):

Line B is given by the solution of equations (18.1) and (18.4), and thus depicts the set of combinations of growth rates of income and imports consistent with keeping constant the current account deficit as a proportion of domestic nominal income:

$$B = \{(dy/y, dm/m)|0 = dm/m - \theta\pi dw/w - (\eta\theta + 1)(dp/p - dp^*/p^*)$$
$$- (1 - \theta)dy/y\}.$$

Its slope in the $(dy/y, dm/m)$ space is equal to $1 - \theta$; *ergo* not greater than one but may be negative if the current account is in surplus. Figure 18.1 pictures it

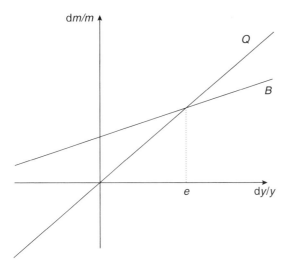

Figure 18.1

with a positive intercept, which may correspond to the case of constant terms of trade and an expanding world economy. Points below (above) *B* have a decreasing (increasing) ratio of the current account deficit relative to income.

Line *Q* is the graph of the import demand function given by equation (18.2):

$$Q = \{(dy/y, dm/m)|0 = dm/m - \phi(dp^*/p^* - dp/p) - \xi dy/y\}.$$

Its slope is positive and is equal to the income elasticity of imports ξ. Its intercept at the origin $(0, 0)$ mirrors the assumption of constant terms of trade. To the right (left) of *Q* the growth path of real income is associated with a decreasing (increasing) import-income ratio. Following the argument of the previous section, it is assumed that $\xi > 1 - \theta$ and, thus, line *Q* is depicted as steeper than line *B*. The intersection of lines *B* and *Q* determines the equilibrium growth rate of real income y_{ca} and of real imports, consistent with a long-term constant ratio of the current account deficit relative to income.

In Figure 18.1, an increase in the income elasticity of imports will be represented as a counterclockwise rotation in line *Q*. A slowdown in the world's economic growth will be captured as a downward shift of line *B*. Persistent improvements in the terms of trade would be mirrored as upward displacements of both lines *B* and *Q*. An increase in the long-term ratio of the current account deficit relative to nominal income – that is, in the ratio that is a priori considered adequate by the international financial community – would displace line *B*, making its upward trend steeper and, at the same time, reducing its vertical intercept.[8]

Balance of payments constrained growth in Mexico

The BPC-model summarized by equations (18.1)–(18.4), and illustrated by Figure 18.1, helps to understand the role played by the availability of foreign exchange in shaping main turning points in the Mexican economy's growth path. For this purpose, it is convenient to divide the evolution of Mexico's growth trajectory since 1950 in four periods: import substitution 1950–76; oil boom 1977–82; international debt crisis 1982–87; trade liberalization and structural reform from 1988 onwards.

Table 18.1 shows selected indicators of Mexican macroeconomic performance during these four periods.[9] Its first three rows report average rates of growth of real GDP, exports and imports. Row 4 shows the implicit income elasticity of imports as given by the ratio of the rates of growth of real imports and GDP. This figure is merely a crude estimate of the true income elasticity, but serves here for illustrative purposes.

The fifth row applies equation (18.11) to obtain the BPC-growth rate of GDP as given by Thirlwall's Law, that is, as the ratio of the growth of exports (row 2) and the implicit income elasticity of imports (row 4). Notice that this calculation gives the rate of growth of GDP consistent with equilibrium in the balance of payments, assuming away the influence of changes in foreign capital inflows or in the terms of trade. Row 6 registers the difference between the actual growth of GDP (row 1) and the BPC-estimated one (row 5). The last rows, 7 and 8, report the evolution of the terms of trade and the current account/GDP ratio.

The slowdown in Mexico's economic growth since 1982 is evident. In 1950–75, real GDP expanded at an average rate of 6.6 per cent at constant pesos. In 1976–81, its expansion was faster, driven by an ambitious industrialization programme financed by oil exports and foreign loans. The era of high growth ended in 1982 with the collapse of oil revenues and the drastic exclusion of Mexico from the international financial markets. Since then the economy has been, on average, rather stagnant. In 1982–87, Mexico's GDP declined in real terms. It grew again in 1988–94, but at a slow pace, both in terms of its historical standards as well as in relation to demographic expansion.

Moreover, in 1994, external factors plus domestic political instability and inadequate monetary policies resulted in a massive loss of foreign exchange reserves that detonated a severe balance of payments crisis in December, pushing the economy into an acute contraction. GDP fell 7 per cent in real terms in 1995, its sharpest collapse in more than fifty years. However, assisted by a financial package put together by the IMF and the United States Treasury, Mexico's economic activity strongly rebounded in 1996 and 1997, and real GDP per capita managed to surpass by 0.6 per cent its 1994 level (ECLAC, 1998). It would be desirable that such recovery heralds the beginning of a new era of sustained and high economic growth, and is not just one more episode in its, by now traditional, stop-go performance.

Table 18.1 suggests that the engine of growth of the Mexican economy in 1950–75 was located in the internal market, as exports grew at a slower pace

Table 18.1 Mexico: real GDP, exports and imports: 1950–97[a] (average annual rates of growth, %)

	1950–75	1976–81	1982–87	1988–94	1988–97[b]
1. GDP ($\hat{y}$)	6.56	7.03	−0.13	2.79	2.41
2. Exports ($\hat{x}$)	4.16	12.06	8.32	4.12	8.61
3. Imports ($\hat{m}$)	6.24	14.29	−10.25	17.67	13.48
4. Income elasticity of imports (implicit value of $\xi = 3/1$)	0.95	2.03	77.15	6.34	5.59
5. Balance of payments constrained growth of GDP ($\hat{y}_{ca} = 2/4$)	4.37	5.94	0.11	0.65	1.54
6. Growth gap, $(1) - (5) = (\hat{y} - \hat{y}_{ca})$	2.19	1.09	−0.24	2.14	0.87
7. Terms of trade (p_x/p_m).					
Average (1975 = 100)	93.8	109.0	90.1	81.1	80.5
Average annual change	0.4	4.0	−8.5	2.1	1.8
8. Current account balance, % nominal GDP[c]	−2.30	−3.98	0.91	−4.87	−3.72

Notes

a Figures in real terms at 1980 Mexican pesos were calculated by the author based on data from INEGI, Banco de México and ECLAC (1998).

b Preliminary.

c Negative figures stand for current account deficits.

than GDP. The oil boom changed this pattern, and exports augmented at a much faster pace than domestic demand. Exports' strong dynamism continued even after the collapse of the oil market in 1982. In 1982–87, they expanded at an annual average rate of 8.3 per cent driven by the external sales of non-oil products as Mexican firms entered foreign markets to try to compensate for the collapse in domestic demand. In the following years exports have kept growing at a faster pace than GDP, becoming one of the most dynamic elements of demand.

The trajectory of imports followed that of GDP, but with sharper fluctuations. Table 18.1 suggests that the implicit income elasticity of imports increased in the second half of the 1970s. Comparing periods of high economic activity, it is seen that the income elasticity of imports in 1950–76 was half of its value in 1976–81, and one-sixth of its value in 1988–94. The increased penetration of imports during the oil boom was caused by the lack of spare capacity brought about by the accelerated expansion of the domestic economy, the appreciation of the real exchange rate and, also, by the elimination of some of the trade restrictions in Mexico's domestic market (Bazdresch and Levy, 1991).

The high income elasticity of imports in 1988–94 was the result of the drastic trade liberalization strategy implemented by Mexico, the pent-up demand for imports in the previous five years of economic stagnation, and the real exchange rate appreciation. But the extraordinarily high magnitude of the implicit income elasticity merits deeper analysis. First of all, it must be stressed that it has been derived just as a quotient of the observed rates of growth of GDP and imports;

a procedure that fails to capture the effect of changes in relative prices and the price elasticity.[10]

Second, to a certain extent, a temporary but strong surge in imports could be expected with the drastic trade liberalization strategy implemented in Mexico in 1985. After decades of severely restricted access to imports, Mexican consumers had a significant pent-up demand for foreign goods. And it may also reflect a certain breakdown of internal linkages in domestic production, with domestic producers being forced out of business by the competition of imports.

In any case, the BPC-model shows that a high income elasticity of imports puts pressure on the export sector to generate more foreign exchange to avoid excessive foreign indebtedness. Persistent weakening of the internal linkages in the domestic productive structure may accentuate the pattern of recurrent balance of payments crisis. Moreover, if the export sector fails to generate sufficient foreign exchange, and access to foreign capital is restricted, the economy may end up stuck in a long-term platform of slow growth. Clearly, the deterioration in the terms of trade could further hinder the prospects of sustaining high rates of economic growth.

The BPC-model suggests that the grip of the balance of payments on Mexico's economic growth tightened after 1982. As the estimates shown in Table 18.1 indicate, during 1950–75 and 1976–81 the Mexican economy could grow at annual rates of 4.4 and 5.9 per cent, respectively, without a fortiori incurring excessive foreign indebtedness (assuming away changes in the capital account or in the terms of trade). In contrast, they indicate that, on average, from 1982 onwards a persistent expansion of GDP above 2 per cent pressures the balance of payments, notwithstanding the dynamic growth of exports.

According to the data in Table 18.1, the ceiling set by the simple BPC-model on the rate of growth of GDP was not always fully binding. The sixth row shows that in the three subperiods where the Mexican economy did grow, foreign capital flows helped to finance the actual expansion of GDP over and above the limit set by the simple BPC-model.

In 1950–75 and 1976–81, international capital flows were a major source of foreign exchange to Mexico, providing external resources equivalent to 2.3 and 4 per cent of GDP. In contrast, in 1982–87 the repayment of foreign debt obligations – and perhaps capital flight too – were a heavy burden on Mexico's growth prospects. The amortization of international debt plus the lack of fresh external finance resulted in an average net transfer of capital abroad of approximately 1 per cent of GDP. In addition, on average, in these five years the terms of trade suffered a substantial fall.

There is a consensus that the external debt rescheduling in the late 1980s, by actively reinserting Mexico into the international capital market, was a key factor for the resumption of its economic growth (van Wijnbergen, 1991; Armendáriz and Armendáriz, 1995). Table 18.1 shows that in 1988–94 foreign capital inflows represented, on average, close to 5 per cent of GDP.

The role played by the availability of foreign exchange, in shaping key turning points in Mexico's economic growth, may be illustrated with the diagram introduced earlier of the revised BPC-model.

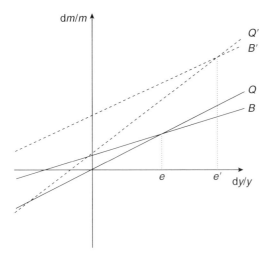

Figure 18.2

In Figure 18.2 the growth path of the Mexican economy during 1950–75 is represented by the solid lines B and Q, and the effect of the oil boom in 1976–82 is seen as shifting them to lines B' and Q'. The position of these pairs of lines (B, Q and B', Q') is not based on econometric specifications, but is only drafted to reflect the stylized facts of the changing influence of the balance of payments constraint on Mexico's economic growth.

The upward movement in line B to B' reflects the faster expansion of exports in 1976–82 than in the previous subperiod. Its counterclockwise rotation mirrors the willingness of the international capital markets to invest more heavily in Mexico and, thus, to finance a higher current account deficit as a proportion of domestic income. In turn, the counterclockwise drift in line Q to Q' reflects an increase in the income elasticity of imports, and its upward shift captures the effect of the terms of trade improvement (or real exchange rate appreciation, in this model).

As Figure 18.2 shows, the combined outcome of the changes brought about by the oil boom and the massive inflow of foreign capital in 1976–82 was faster long-term economic growth in Mexico (from e to e').

But when the oil boom and the inflow of international capital proved to be short-lived, Mexico's high economic growth became unsustainable. The massive net transfer of capital abroad and the deterioration of the terms of trade that Mexico suffered in 1982–87 are captured in Figure 18.3 as displacing lines B' and Q', to B'' and Q''.

Mexico's new role as a source of net transfers of capital abroad is captured by the radical shift in line B' to B'', from being upward sloping to downward sloping. In turn, the downward shift in line Q' to Q'' reflects the lower terms of trade (here equivalent to a depreciation of the real exchange rate).

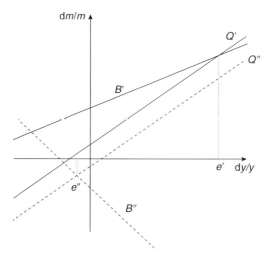

Figure 18.3

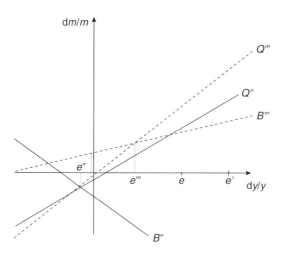

Figure 18.4

The outcome, as Figure 18.3 illustrates, was a drastic halt in economic growth – from e' to e'' – in order to generate the necessary foreign exchange outflows to meet foreign debt obligations. As depicted in the figure, the shift in the import function was insufficient to impede a decline in economic activity ($e'' < 0$).

The change in the balance of payments constraint on the Mexican economy from 1982–87 to 1988–94 is captured in Figure 18.4.

The shift in line B'' to B''' illustrates the favourable reinsertion of the Mexican economy in the international capital markets, bringing about a massive net inflow of foreign capital. The clockwise movement and upward displacement in line Q'' to Q''' mirror, respectively, an increase in the income elasticity of imports and an improvement in the terms of trade (appreciation of the real exchange rate). The combined impact of these phenomena was a resumption of long-term economic growth at a rate e''' which, however, was far lower than the average rates of expansion registered by the Mexican economy during 1950–75 and 1976–81.

Conclusions

The analytical model put forward in this chapter showed that, adopting a long-term constant ratio of the current account to nominal GDP, led to a modification of the long-term income multipliers – of external economic activity and of the terms of trade – of the BPC-model. Using this revised model to examine the stylized facts of Mexico's growth path in 1950–97, it was seen that the slowdown in its economic growth seems to be, ultimately, traced to the inability to generate sufficient foreign exchange to finance a robust and persistent growth of real domestic output.

During the second half of the 1970s, and up to most of 1982, Mexico's economic strategy was based on the assumption that oil exports would provide sufficient foreign exchange to build a platform of high and sustained economic expansion. The economy grew spectacularly for some years, but the current account deficit soared and eventually exploded in a balance of payment crisis and stagnation.

In the mid-1980s, the Mexican government launched a macroeconomic reform that, allegedly, would ensure strong and persistent economic growth. A key assumption was then that massive foreign capital inflows, induced by the North American Free Trade Agreement (NAFTA), would bring in sufficient foreign capital to transform Mexico's productive structure in order to place exports as its engine of growth. Exports indeed expanded, but not enough to pull the rest of the economy onto a path of high and sustained growth. On average, the response of Mexico's GDP since the radical macroeconomic reform began to be implemented in the mid-1980s has been far from dynamic. In general, domestic sales have shown a weak response, affected by the intense penetration of imports. Moreover, the moderate rate of expansion of the domestic economy in 1988–94 has been associated with marked deterioration in the current account of the balance of payments, which ended up in a severe foreign exchange crisis in December 1994 that pushed the Mexican economy to its worst fall in more than fifty years.

There are no guaranteed recipes to remove the balance of payments constraint on Mexico's economic growth. The option, apparently favoured by the administration of President Zedillo (1995–2000), is to try to reduce the economy's high dependence on foreign savings by directly promoting domestic savings, mainly by reforming the pension system. Other views, not so optimistic about the existence of a strong causal relation going from domestic savings to aggregate economic growth, are more inclined to try to build institutional arrangements and to implement policies that help to boost the productivity and competitiveness of

Mexico's business sector both in the international as well as in the domestic market. Both views may supplement each other, helping to remove different obstacles on Mexico's road to economic development. In any case, the evaluation of the relative benefits, costs and limitations of alternative policies to promote Mexico's economic growth goes way beyond the objectives of this chapter.

Notes

1 Labour force figures are taken from OECD (1996). Other estimates of the GDP growth required to absorb the labour supply can be found in Ros (1997) – around 4.5 per cent – and Dussel (1995), who puts it close to 10 per cent.

2 According to official data, more than 13 million Mexicans lived in conditions of extreme poverty in 1992 (ECLAC – INEGI 1993). It is estimated that their number today is much higher.

3 Evidently, the evolution of the current account deficit/GDP ratio affects the ratio of the *stock* of foreign debt relative to GDP. However, as mentioned earlier, the former ratio has been singled out as a key indicator of macroeconomic performance. One reason for this may be the availability of reliable data on the current account (*flows*), in contrast with the difficult access to data on the total *stock* of foreign debt.

4 Equation (18.4) is immediately derived by multiplying both sides of the expression (18.6) by $(\mu Y)/M$, where μ was defined in equation (18.3) as $M/(M - X)$, assuming $M - X$ is non-zero.

5 Note that by definition $\mu = 1/(1 - \theta)$.

6 This expression coincides with the one derived by McCombie and Thirlwall (1997a) where they introduced in the standard BPC-model the assumptions of: (a) a given long-term ratio of the *stock* of external debt to GDP, and (b) constant terms of trade.

7 I am grateful to H. Escaith for pointing out the need to stress that this conclusion does not necessarily hold if the BPC-model explicitly allows for changes in foreign interest rates.

8 An analysis of the dynamic properties and stability conditions of the BPC-model may be found in Moreno-Brid (1998b) or, within a framework that explicitly includes the labour market, in Pugno (1998). It may be mentioned that the former was written without being aware of the results of McCombie and Thirlwall (1997a).

9 For in-depth characterizations of Mexico's economic development in some of these periods see, *inter alia*, Solis (1981), Ramírez (1988), Buffie and Krause (1989), Bazdresch and Levy (1991), Lustig (1992), Aspe (1993) and Moreno-Brid and Ros (1994).

10 Moreno–Brid (1998a) finds econometric evidence that suggests that trade liberalization caused a lasting rise in the income elasticity and a decline in the price elasticity of Mexico's demand for imports.

19 A 'generalised' version of the balance of payments growth model: an application to neighbouring regions*

Kevin Nell

Introduction

In Thirlwall's (1979) seminal paper the idea was advanced and empirically verified that for a large group of countries the rate of growth of output is balance of payments (BP) constrained because this sets the limit to the growth of demand to which supply can adapt (Thirlwall and Hussain, 1982). The main essence of 'Thirlwall's Law' is that in an open economy, expenditure cannot grow faster than income growth without creating a current account deficit on the BP. A current account deficit cannot be sustained through an indefinite inflow of capital, because deficits above a certain percentage of Gross Domestic Product (GDP) trigger negative signals to the international community that force countries to adjust (McCombie and Thirlwall, 1997a). For a given rate of growth of exports, the brunt of the adjustment falls on a reduction in income growth to restore BP equilibrium because relative price changes do not act as an efficient BP adjustment mechanism. An open economy's real economic growth rate is therefore determined by export growth for a given income elasticity of the demand for imports. The rate of growth of exports, in turn, is mainly a function of 'world' income or 'world' demand.

The main objective of this chapter is to apply a 'generalised' version of the BP growth model by testing for long-run relationships between the output growth rates of OECD countries and two neighbouring regions; South Africa (SA) and the rest of the Southern African Development Community (RSADC).[1] In this context, the chapter attempts to make the following contributions to the existing theoretical and empirical literature.

First, Thirlwall's BP constrained growth model is a specific case involving a bilateral trade relationship between one country and the 'rest of the world'. In this chapter, the specific case is generalised into a multilateral trade relation between an individual country (SA) and blocks of countries (OECD and RSADC). One of the main findings of the chapter is that the policy implications of the 'generalised' BP growth model present a different perspective compared to the 'specific' BP model. The policy suggestions are particularly relevant to neighbouring regions

* First published in *International Review of Applied Economics*, July 2003.

that participate in a mutual economic cooperation scheme, and specifically, where one of the regions (SA) dominates the other (RSADC) in terms of economic size.[2] The 'generalised' BP growth model provides a supplement to McCombie's (1993 and Chapter 5) theoretical version in which the long-run growth rate of an advanced country (or blocks of countries) depends on the growth rate of another through the BP constraint.

Second, since all the output growth rate variables in this chapter are stationary $\{I(0)\}$, the econometric methodology employed departs from standard cointegration techniques such as the Johansen procedure which tests whether non-stationary variables $\{I(1)\}$ cointegrate to form an $I(0)$ process (see Johansen and Juselius, 1990). The methodology draws on recent advances in time-series econometric techniques such as Pesaran *et al.*'s (2001) bounds testing procedure and the autoregressive distributed lag (ARDL) approach to estimating the long-run (Pesaran and Shin, 1999). The bounds testing procedure is particularly relevant to this application as it not only provides critical values for a set of purely $I(1)$ variables but also for a set of purely $I(0)$ variables. The ARDL approach, on the other hand, yields consistent estimates of the long-run coefficients that are asymptotically normal even when all the underlying regressors are $I(0)$. As a supplement to the long-run growth rate equations, simulations based on impulse responses and forecast error variance decompositions are used to illustrate the mutual interdependence of the two neighbouring regions through the BP constraint.

The rest of the chapter is organised as follows. The second section derives the 'generalised' version of the BP model. The third section discusses the main features of the data. The fourth section presents the econometric methodology and the fifth section the empirical results. The last section concludes with policy implications.

Thirlwall's BP constrained growth model: a 'generalised' version

Following Thirlwall (1979, 1999), SA's current account of the BP, measured in its own domestic currency, may be written as:

$$P_x X = P_f ME. \tag{19.1}$$

P_x measures the average price of exports in domestic currency; X the quantity of real exports; P_f the average foreign price of imports; M the quantity of real imports; and E is the nominal exchange rate in units of domestic currency per unit of foreign currency.

By taking logarithms of equation (19.1) and expressing the result in growth rates we obtain the current account equilibrium of a *growing* economy, which starts from an initial zero current account deficit:

$$(p_x + x) = (p_f + m + e). \tag{19.2}$$

The export- and import demand functions expressed in *growth rates* are given by

$$x = \eta(p_x - p_f - e) + \theta_1 w^1 (y^{OECD}) + \theta_2 w^2 (y^{RSADC}), \tag{19.3}$$

and

$$m = \Psi(p_f + e - p_x) + \pi_1 w^3(y^{SA}) + \pi_2 w^4(y^{SA}), \tag{19.4}$$

where η is the price elasticity of the demand for exports (<0); y^{OECD} is the output growth rate of OECD which proxies a part of 'world income'; y^{RSADC} is the output growth rate of RSADC which proxies a part of 'world income'; θ_1 and θ_2 are the income elasticities of the demand for exports (>0) weighted by SA's exports to OECD and RSADC as a proportion of total exports (w^1 and w^2), respectively; Ψ is the price elasticity of the demand for imports (<0); y^{SA} is the growth rate of SA's domestic income; and π_1 and π_2 are the income elasticities of the demand for imports (>0) weighted by SA's imports from OECD and RSADC as a proportion of total imports (w^3 and w^4), respectively.

Note that the specifications of equations (19.3) and (19.4) assume that OECD and RSADC together comprise 'total world income' from the perspective of SA. This assumption is based on several propositions. First, based on 1999 figures OECD countries form a large proportion of total world income of around 84 per cent. Second, even though RSADC forms a small proportion of total world income (0.17 per cent), it may nevertheless be a significant determinant in SA's export and import equations. The inclusion of RSADC may capture important trade inter-linkages (mutual trade arrangements) between the two neighbouring regions and also shed some light on how these linkages are affected when one region (SA) dominates the other (RSADC) in terms of economic size. Third, it is assumed that income growth of the 'rest of the world' is not an independent determinant in SA's export and import equations, but rather a function of OECD growth.

Substituting (19.3) and (19.4) into (19.2) yields:

$$p_x + \eta(p_x - p_f - e) + \theta_1 w^1(y^{OECD}) + \theta_2 w^2(y^{RSADC})$$
$$= p_f + \psi(p_f + e - p_x) + \pi_1 w^3(y^{SA}) + \pi_2 w^4(y^{SA}) + e. \tag{19.5}$$

Solving for y^{SA} we obtain the growth rate of SA's domestic income consistent with current account equilibrium (y^{SA^*}):

$$y^{SA^*} = \frac{(1+\eta+\psi)(p_x - p_f - e) + \theta_1 w^1(y^{OECD}) + \theta_2 w^2(y^{RSADC})}{\pi_1 w^3 + \pi_2 w^4}. \tag{19.6}$$

If it is assumed that relative prices in international trade are constant ($p_x - p_f - e = 0$) based on the assumptions that prices are fixed in oligopolistic markets and/or that price reductions by one country can easily be matched by foreign competitors (Thirlwall, 1986), then equation (19.6) reduces to:

$$y^{SA^*} = \frac{\theta_1 w^1(y^{OECD})}{\pi_1 w^3 + \pi_2 w^4} + \frac{\theta_2 w^2(y^{RSADC})}{\pi_1 w^3 + \pi_2 w^4}. \tag{19.7}$$

Equation (19.7) can be written more compactly as:

$$y^{SA^*} = \frac{x}{\pi}.\qquad(19.8)$$

Equation (19.8) is known as 'Thirlwall's Law' and states that SA's long-run output growth rate is determined by the growth rate of exports for a given income elasticity of the demand for imports.

Similarly, by repeating the same procedure as in equations (19.1)–(19.7), the output growth rate of RSADC consistent with current account equilibrium can be written as:

$$y^{RSADC^*} = \frac{\theta_3 w^5 (y^{OECD})}{\pi_3 w^7 + \pi_4 w^8} + \frac{\theta_4 w^6 (y^{SA})}{\pi_3 w^7 + \pi_4 w^8},\qquad(19.9)$$

where θ_3 and θ_4 are the income elasticities of the demand for exports weighted by RSADC's exports to OECD and SA as a proportion of total exports (w^5 and w^6), respectively; and π_3 and π_4 are the income elasticities of the demand for imports weighted by RSADC's imports from OECD and SA as a proportion of total imports (w^7 and w^8), respectively. The underlying assumption of equation (19.9) is that OECD and SA together constitute 'total world income' from the perspective of RSADC. The propositions that underlie this assumption are exactly the same as mentioned earlier, but can now be viewed from the perspective of RSADC.

Equation (19.9) has the same interpretation as equation (19.7). The long-run output growth rate of RSADC is determined by the weighted income elasticities of the demand for exports relative to the weighted sum of the income elasticities of the demand for imports. Equations (19.7) and (19.9) have a clear policy implication: for a given weighted sum of the income elasticities of the demand for imports, non-price factors such as the structural demand characteristics of export goods will be the dominant determinants of SA and RSADC's long-run output growth rates.

Empirical applications of the BP growth model usually focus on equation (19.8).[3] This is a specific case involving a bilateral trade relationship between one country and the 'rest of the world'. In this chapter, the focus is on equations (19.7) and (19.9). These equations represent a more general case of a multilateral trade relation between an individual country and blocks of countries. The policy implications of equations (19.7) and (19.9) are particularly relevant to neighbouring regions that participate in a mutual economic cooperation scheme and may therefore present a different perspective compared to an individual economy that is BP constrained with respect to the 'rest of the world'.

Data analysis

Figure 19.1(a) plots the real GDP growth rates of OECD, SA and RSADC over the period 1981–98.[4] The output growth rates in Figure 19.1(a) display several important features. First, there is a positive relation between the output growth rates. Second, there may be several outliers with respect to SA and RSADC. SA's

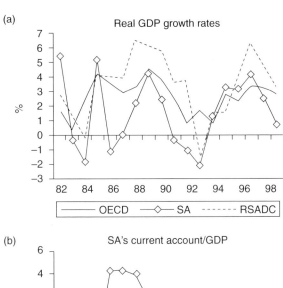

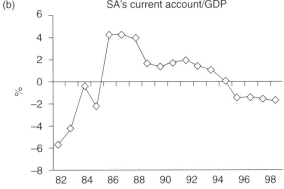

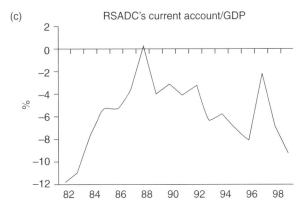

Figure 19.1 (a–c) Real GDP growth rates and current account ratios.

Table 19.1 Phillips–Perron (1988) unit root tests

Variables	Phillips–Perron tests
y^{OECD}	−3.80**
y^{SA}	−3.70**
y^{RSADC}	−3.74**

Notes
1 The 95% critical value of Dickey–Fuller (1979) is −3.08.
2 The Phillips–Perron tests contain intercepts and no trends.
3 Phillips and Perron's (1988) semi-parametric correction to the DF test is based on Bartlett weights with a truncation lag of one.
** denotes significance at the 5% level.

growth rate was visibly slower than the rest in 1983 and 1985. Slower growth over these two years may be attributed to the sharp real exchange rate depreciation in 1983 and capital outflows following the immediate repayment of foreign debt in 1985. RSADC, on the other hand, grows faster than the rest in 1987 and 1996. Third, all the output growth rates appear to be stationary in Figure 19.1(a). Phillips and Perron's (1988) semi-parametric correction to the Dickey–Fuller (DF) test in Table 19.1 confirms that all the growth rate variables are $I(0)$ at the 5 per cent significance level.

Figure 19.1(b) and (c) plot the current account balances as a percentage of GDP during 1981–98 for SA and RSADC, respectively. SA's current account ratio shows several periods of disequilibria, especially during the period 1985–93 when the current account had to be transformed into a surplus to finance capital outflows. However, since the BP model is a long-run growth rate model, it is appropriate to analyse the average for the whole period rather than year-to-year fluctuations. Over the period 1981–98 SA's current account ratio recorded a slight surplus of 0.15 per cent. By excluding the outliers in 1983 and 1985 the current account ratio is virtually zero at −0.05 per cent. When the level of the current account ratio is zero then the growth rate is zero by construction.

Figure 19.1(c) shows that the RSADC region sustained a current account deficit over the whole period with an average deficit to GDP ratio of 5.70 per cent. Although the deficit appears to be large, the result is misleading. Figure 19.1(c) depicts the *level* of the current account ratio and not the *growth rate*. A current account deficit in levels does not necessarily imply a deficit in growth rates. The growth rate of the current account deficit will average zero under the following two conditions. First, if the level of the deficit remains constant over the whole period, then the growth rate is zero. Second, if the level of the deficit displays an upward trend during a specific subperiod and a downward trend in another subperiod, the trends may offset one another so that the corresponding current account growth rate averages zero. Based on the visual evidence in Figure 19.1(c), the second condition appears to be relevant in RSADC. The level of the current account ratio trends upward until the late 1980s, but thereafter shows a decreasing trend until 1998. When the outliers in 1987 and 1996 are excluded from RSADC's average current account ratio, the average current account growth rate is close to zero at 0.47 per cent. Thirlwall and Hussein (1982) show that when the level of the current account is in a deficit, the growth rate of the current account may still be in equilibrium if the growth rate of capital inflows equals the growth rate of exports. The descriptive evidence suggests that equation (19.2), which starts from initial current account equilibrium of a *growing* economy, is a plausible assumption in the context of SA and RSADC.

Econometric methodology

To test the 'generalised' BP growth model for SA and RSADC, equations (19.7) and (19.9) are transformed into unrestricted error correction models (UECM) derived from ARDL models of order one:

$$\Delta y_t^{SA} = a_0 + \varphi_1 \Delta y_t^{OECD} + \phi_2 \Delta y_t^{RSADC} + \phi_3 D_t^{SA} + \phi_4 D_t^{RSADC}$$
$$+ \delta_1 y_{t-1}^{SA} + \delta_2 y_{t-1}^{OECD} + \delta_3 y_{t-1}^{RSADC} + \varepsilon_{t1},$$
$$\phi_1 > 0; \quad \phi_2 > 0; \quad \phi_3 < 0; \quad \phi_4 < 0; \quad \delta_1 < 0; \quad \delta_2 > 0; \quad \delta_3 > 0$$
$$(19.10)$$

$$\Delta y_t^{RSADC} = b_0 + \vartheta_1 \Delta y_t^{OECD} + \vartheta_2 \Delta y_t^{SA} + \vartheta_3 D_t^{SA} + \vartheta_4 D_t^{RSADC}$$
$$+ \lambda_1 y_{t-1}^{RSADC} + \lambda_2 y_{t-1}^{OECD} + \lambda_3 y_{t-1}^{SA} + \varepsilon_{t2},$$
$$\vartheta_1 > 0; \quad \vartheta_2 > 0; \quad \vartheta_3 > 0; \quad \vartheta_4 > 0; \quad \lambda_1 < 0; \quad \lambda_2 > 0; \quad \lambda_3 > 0$$
$$(19.11)$$

where D_t^{SA} is a short-run dummy variable that captures SA's slower growth rate relative to the others (see Figure 19.1(a)) with values of unity in 1983 and 1985 and zero otherwise; D_t^{RSADC} is a short-run dummy variable that captures the faster growth of RSADC relative to the others (see Figure 19.1(a)) with values of unity in 1987 and 1996 and zero otherwise; a_0 and b_0 are intercept terms; and ε_{t1} and ε_{t2} are unobserved error terms. Variables in differences (Δ) represent the short-run part of the models and lagged level variables the long-run part of the models.

   The long-run multipliers of equation (19.10) can be obtained by dividing δ_2 and δ_3 through by the absolute value of the error-correction coefficient (δ_1):

$$y_t^{SA} = \beta_1 y_t^{OECD} + \beta_2 y_t^{RSADC}, \qquad (19.12)$$

where

$$\beta_1 = \frac{\theta_1 w^1}{\pi_1 w^3 + \pi_2 w^4} \quad \text{and} \quad \beta_2 = \frac{\theta_2 w^2}{\pi_1 w^3 + \pi_2 w^4}.$$

The long-run multipliers of equation (19.11) can be obtained by dividing λ_2 and λ_3 through by the absolute value of the error-correction coefficient (λ_1):

$$y_t^{RSADC} = \beta_3 y_t^{OECD} + \beta_4 y_t^{SA}, \qquad (19.13)$$

where

$$\beta_3 = \frac{\theta_3 w^5}{\pi_3 w^7 + \pi_4 w^8} \quad \text{and} \quad \beta_4 = \frac{\theta_4 w^6}{\pi_3 w^7 + \pi_4 w^8}.$$

The magnitudes of the long-run coefficients in equations (19.12) and (19.13) are determined by the weighted income elasticities of the demand for exports relative to the weighted sum of the income elasticities of the demand for imports.

The choice of ARDL models, or UECM's, which are simply re-parameterizations of ARDL's, is based on several advantages. First, Pesaran *et al.*'s (2001) bounds testing procedure – which tests for long-run relations within an UECM framework – is applicable irrespective of whether the underlying regressors are purely $I(0)$, purely $I(1)$ or mutually cointegrated. The procedure is particularly relevant to this application where all the growth rate variables appear to be $I(0)$. Second, Pesaran and Shin (1999) have shown that ARDL models yield consistent estimates of the long-run coefficients that are asymptotically normal irrespective of whether the underlying regressors are $I(1)$ or $I(0)$. Similarly, Inder (1993) shows that the omission of dynamics in static equations may be detrimental to the performance of the estimator in finite samples, and alternatively proposes the UECM which includes dynamics in the estimation of the short-run and long-run coefficients. Third, Pesaran (1997) and Inder (1993) have separately shown that the inclusion of dynamics may correct for the endogeneity bias of the regressors in ARDL's and UECM's, respectively. However, for the analysis to be rigorous and methodologically consistent, we follow Inder (1993) and apply Phillips and Hansen's (1990) Fully Modified OLS estimator to all the UECM's (FUECM's). Phillips and Hansen's (1990) semi-parametric corrections have the advantages of asymptotic optimality and an asymptotic distribution free of nuisance parameters (Inder, 1993).

Empirical results

The UECM's and FUECM's are estimated over the period 1981–98 using annual observations. Wars, political instability and civil strife in several individual RSADC countries are various factors, among others, that make it difficult to obtain reliable data for all the RSADC countries before 1980. For some applications long run may imply a matter of months, for others ten years, or for some a long time span of several decades (Hakkio and Rush, 1991; Maddala and Kim, 1998). Moreover, it is well known that the power of tests for long-run relations is not improved by increasing the frequency of the data. It is the length of the time series that matters not the frequency of observations (Shiller and Perron, 1985; Campbell and Perron, 1991). In a more general context, it is worth noting that it is up to the researcher to weigh up the advantages of using a very long time series against the disadvantages of increasing the probability of introducing more unknown structural breaks. Structural breaks inadvertently affect the power of unit root and long-run tests and may also lead to the predictive failure of error-correction models (Clements and Hendry, 1997; Maddala and Kim, 1998).

Results of UECM's and FUECM's

Based on Hendry's general-to-specific methodology (Hendry, 1995), the UECM's in equations (19.10)–(19.11), and their corresponding FUECM's, are tested down to parsimonious representations. The results are reported in Table 19.2.

The semi-parametric corrections of the UECM's are based on a Bartlett lag window with a truncation lag of two. The *t*-tests for the individual significance of the redundant regressor coefficients of the UECM's and FUECM's support the model reduction process. None of the redundant regressor coefficients is significantly different from zero at the 5 per cent level, while all the retained regressor coefficients

Table 19.2 UECM's and FUECM's

Dependent variable	1(a) $\Delta y_{\text{UECM}}^{\text{SA}}$	1(b) $\Delta y_{\text{FUECM}}^{\text{SA}}$	2(a) $\Delta y_{\text{UECM}}^{\text{RSADC}}$	2(b) $\Delta y_{\text{FUECM}}^{\text{RSADC}}$	2(c) $\Delta y_{\text{REL}}^{\text{RSADC(UECM)}}$
Δy_t^{OECD}	1.34*** (18.31)	1.26*** (39.13)	—	—	—
$\Delta y_t^{\text{RSADC}}$	0.64*** (16.07)	0.66*** (45.03)	—	—	—
$\Delta(y_t^{\text{SA}} - y_t^{\text{OECD}})$	—	—	1.04*** (16.17)	1.22*** (27.21)	—
y_{t-1}^{OECD}	0.49*** (12.91)	0.43*** (11.15)	insignificant	insignificant	insignificant
y_{t-1}^{SA}	−0.64 (−16.89)	−0.61*** (−35.95)	0.74*** (10.78)	0.71*** (20.11)	0.71*** (13.45)
y_{t-1}^{RSADC}	insignificant	insignificant	−0.41*** (−10.25)	−0.25*** (−6.87)	−0.40*** (−10.51)
D_t^{SA}	−4.18*** (−16.79)	−4.17*** (−45.83)	3.63*** (9.19)	4.91*** (16.72)	3.46*** (10.69)
D_t^{RSADC}	−1.29*** (−4.77)	−1.38*** (−14.32)	2.06*** (5.94)	2.17*** (12.87)	2.13*** (6.47)
Diagnostic tests					
R^2(adjusted)	0.99		0.96		0.95
F_{ret}	$F(5, 11) = 336.46$***		$F(4, 12) = 100.05$***	$F(3, 13) = 128.50$***	
F_{red}	$F(2, 9) = 1.16$		$F(2, 10) = 2.36$	$F(2, 11) = 2.90$	
$LM^{\text{ar}} : \chi^2(1)$	0.12		0.78		0.00
$LM^{\text{arch}} : \chi^2(1)$	2.22		2.88		1.48
$RESET^{\text{ff}} : \chi^2(1)$	2.16		7.00***		0.30
$N : \chi^2(2)$	1.05		0.15		0.34
$H : \chi^2(1)$	0.00		2.65		0.00
$Forecast : \chi^2(6)$	8.22		6.08		3.77
$Chow : F(6, 5)$	1.18		0.64		0.43

Notes

1 Figures in parentheses ( ) are *t*-statistics.

2 R^2 is the coefficient of determination; F_{ret} is an F-test for the joint significance of the retained regressors; F_{red} is an F-test for the joint significance of the redundant regressors; LM^{ar} is a Lagrange Multiplier test for first order serial correlation; LM^{arch} is a Lagrange Multiplier test for autoregressive conditional heteroscedasticity; $RESET^{\text{ff}}$ is Ramsey's Reset test for functional form misspecification; N is a test for normality; H is a heteroscedasticity test statistic; *Forecast* tests whether the models suffer from predictive failure during 1993–98; and *Chow* tests whether the models are structurally stable between the subperiods 1982–92 and 1993–98.

*** denotes significance at the 1% level.

are highly significant at the 1 per cent level. The t-tests for the individual significance of the y_{t-1}^{RSADC} coefficients in columns 1(a)–(b) yielded values of 1.53 and 1.83, respectively. The results suggest that RSADC is not a significant determinant of SA's long-run growth rate. In addition, OECD does not appear to be a significant determinant of RSADC's long-run growth rate based on the insignificance of the y_{t-1}^{OECD} coefficients in columns 2(a)–(c), with t-values of 0.81, 1.32 and 1.12, respectively. The F-tests in Table 19.2 for the overall significance of the retained and redundant regressor coefficients of all the UECM's provide further support for the model reduction process.[5]

The error-correction coefficients of all the UECM's and FUECM's are highly significant and correctly signed. All the models therefore represent long-run equilibrium relationships. Suitable transformations of the variables are performed to obtain more orthogonal model specifications (Hendry, 1995). The short-run coefficients of Δy^{SA} and Δy^{OECD} in column 2(a) yielded equal magnitudes and opposite signs based on a Wald test, so the effect is captured as a differential $\{\Delta(y^{\mathrm{SA}} - y^{\mathrm{OECD}})\}$ in Table 19.2.

The magnitudes of the coefficients of the UECM's and the FUECM's in columns 1(a) and (b) of Table 19.2 are very close. By contrast, there appears to be a large difference between the magnitudes of the coefficients of the UECM in column 2(a) and the FUECM in column 2(b). The diagnostic tests show that the UECM in column 2(a) suffers from functional form misspecification. The differential effect of $\Delta(y^{\mathrm{SA}} - y^{\mathrm{OECD}})$ in columns 2(a)–(b) implies that the short-run coefficient of Δy^{SA} is positive and consistent with theory, but the coefficient of Δy^{OECD} is negative. Although the negative relation may capture a delayed growth-effect between high-income OECD countries and low-income RSADC countries, it appears to present endogeneity problems based on the diagnostic tests and the different results obtained from the UECM and FUECM.

In an attempt to correct the endogeneity bias, a Wald test showed that the coefficient of $\Delta(y^{\mathrm{SA}} - y^{\mathrm{OECD}})$ in column 2(a) is insignificantly different from unity (not reported here). A unit coefficient allows us to write (without any loss of information) the dependent variable as $\Delta y_{\mathrm{REL}}^{\mathrm{RSADC}} = \Delta y^{\mathrm{RSADC}} - [\Delta(y^{\mathrm{SA}} - y^{\mathrm{OECD}})]$. The result for the UECM is given in column 2(c). Two important results emerge. First, the magnitudes of the coefficients are very close in columns 2(a) and 2(c). Second, the UECM in column 2(c) now passes functional form specification. The results suggest that if there were any simultaneity problems in column 2(a), this is effectively addressed in column 2(c), where $\Delta(y^{\mathrm{SA}} - y^{\mathrm{OECD}})$ is endogenised.

Overall, the results in Table 19.2 suggest that all the UECM's are well determined, addresses the endogeneity problem, and passes a battery of diagnostic tests. In addition, the Chow tests for structurally stable equations between the subperiods 1982–92 and 1993–98, and the overall forecast test for the period 1993–98 in Table 19.2, show that all the UECM's are structurally stable and produce satisfactory out-of-sample forecasts. None of the tests is significant at any conventional level.

Figure 19.2(a)–(c) report the one-step ahead forecasts for all the UECM's in Table 19.2 over the period 1993–98.

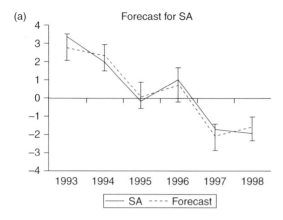

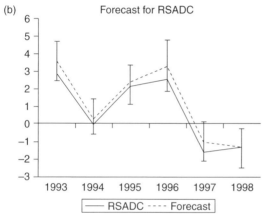

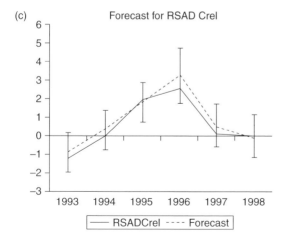

Figure 19.2 (a– c) One-step ahead forecasts, 1993–98.

All the forecasts are scaled by their 95 per cent confidence bar intervals based on Hendry (1995). Figure 19.2(a)–(c) show how well the forecasts trace the actual values of all the UECM's. Constancy is easily accepted for all the UECM's, with every actual value falling well within the 95 per cent confidence intervals of the individual forecasts. It is interesting to note that although the UECM in column 2(a) of Table 19.2 suffers from functional form misspecification, it produces satisfactory forecasts in Figure 19.2(b). The forecasts in Figure 19.2 imply that all the UECM's are constant and structurally stable.

The econometric results strongly support the notion that the simple version of the BP growth model is relevant in SA and RSADC. None of the models in columns 1 and 2(c) of Table 19.2 display signs of misspecification and forecasting failure, so relative price changes seem to be relatively unimportant in explaining output growth in SA and RSADC over the period 1981–98.

Long-run solutions of UECM's and FUECM's

The long-run solutions of the UECM's and FUECM's together with the long-run tests based on Pesaran *et al.*'s (2001) bounds testing procedure are reported in Table 19.3. The long-run test is a standard F-test for the joint significance of the long-run coefficients in equations (19.10)–(19.11). Since this statistic has a non-standard distribution, Pesaran *et al.* (2001) provide critical value bounds for a set of purely $I(0)$ variables and purely $I(1)$ variables.

Table 19.3 Long-run solutions of UECM's and FUECM's

Dependent variable	1(a) y_{UECM}^{SA}	1(b) y_{FUECM}^{SA}	2(a) y_{UECM}^{RSADC}	2(b) y_{FUECM}^{RSADC}	2(c) $y_{REL}^{RSADC(UECM)}$
y_t^{OECD}	0.76*** (15.11)	0.70*** (13.28)	insignificant	insignificant	insignificant
y_t^{SA}	—	—	1.81*** (12.51)	2.79*** (7.17)	1.76*** (13.91)
y_t^{RSADC}	insignificant	insignificant	—	—	—
Long-run tests					
Null hypothesis		$\delta_1 = \delta_2 = 0$	$\lambda_1 = \lambda_3 = 0$	$\lambda_1 = \lambda_3 = 0$	
F-test		151.43***	67.33***	92.74***	
99% CV: $I(0)$		4.81	4.81	4.81	
99% CV: $I(1)$		6.02	6.02	6.02	

Notes
1 Figures in parentheses ( ) are *t*-statistics.
2 The 99 per cent critical values (CV) in Table 19.3 are consistent with the option of no intercept and no trend and correspond to the $I(0)$ and $I(1)$ bounds in Pesaran *et al.* (2001). Although the Phillips–Perron unit root tests indicate that all the variables are $I(0)$, unit root tests are always subject to some degree of uncertainty, so the critical values are also reported for $I(1)$ variables which present a stricter test than those for purely $I(0)$ variables.
3 The long-run tests and associated critical values are only applicable to the UECM's and not the FUECM's.
*** denotes significance at the 1 per cent level.

Table 19.4 Testing the 'generalised' BP growth model, 1981–98

	Actual growth rate (y)	BP Growth rate (y*)	Difference (y − y*)	Wald test: $\chi^2 : (1)$
y^{SA}	1.88	1.76	0.12	0.10 [0.74]
y^{RSADC}	2.96	3.30	−0.34	2.33 [0.12]

The magnitudes of the long-run coefficients derived from the UECM's and FUECM's are fairly close, except for those in column 2(b) when compared to columns 2(a) and (c). Since the underlying UECM from which the long-run solution in column 2(c) was derived yielded good out-of-sample forecasts and passed all the diagnostic tests, the long-run interpretation will focus on column 2(c). The Pesaran *et al.* (2001) procedure resoundingly rejects the null hypothesis of no long-run relation in each equation based on the 99 per cent critical values for $I(0)$ and $I(1)$ variables.

The BP growth rates are obtained from the long-run models in Table 19.3 by substituting for the average growth rates of OECD and SA in columns 1(b) and 2(c).[6] For example, OECD, SA and RSADC recorded average growth rates of 2.52 per cent, 1.88 per cent and 2.96 per cent over the period 1981–98, respectively.[7] When OECD's average growth rate is substituted for in column 1(b) of Table 19.3, SA's BP constrained growth rate is 1.76 per cent (= 2.52×0.70). The BP growth rates and the actual average growth rates are reported in Table 19.4.

The results in Table 19.4 strongly support the contention that the long-run output growth rates of SA and RSADC are BP constrained. The actual growth rates and the BP growth rates are very close. The Wald tests (probability values in parentheses) show that the difference between the actual growth rates and BP growth rates is not significantly different from zero at any conventional level for SA and at the 12 per cent level for RSADC.

Simulations based on impulse responses and forecast error variance decompositions

Simulations present a useful exercise to supplement the long-run results derived from single equation UECM's. A systems approach by construction overcomes endogeneity problems and is not confined to a single long-run relation.

The simulations are based on the generalised impulse response analysis and generalised forecast error variance decomposition described by Pesaran and Shin (1998). Unlike the traditional orthogonalised versions, the generalised versions have the advantage that they are invariant to the ordering of the variables in the vector autoregressive (VAR) model.

The generalised impulse response analysis is useful to measure the response of a variable over time in reaction to shocks of other variables in the system. The generalised forecast error variance decomposition, on the other hand, measures the contribution of different shocks to the variance of the n-step ahead forecast error of a specific variable in a system. For example, the generalised forecast error variance decomposition of RSADC growth will show what proportion of the forecast error variance results from its own shock, OECD growth and SA's growth. Unlike the orthogonalised version, the generalised forecast error variance decomposition allows for contemporaneous correlations between all these shocks.

The analysis is based on a VAR model of order one that includes the output growth rates of OECD, SA and RSADC.[8] A likelihood ratio test was performed to test the joint significance of the deterministic components in the VAR (not reported). Based on the results, the deterministic components include the two dummy variables D^{SA} and D^{RSADC}. The intercept terms were jointly insignificantly different from zero and therefore excluded from the deterministic components of the VAR.

Figure 19.3(a) reports the generalised impulse responses (GIR's) with respect to a one standard error shock to OECD growth over a time horizon of ten years.

RSADC and SA's growth respond positively to a one standard error shock and also display a high degree of persistence. SA's growth rate in Figure 19.3(a) shows a large response over the first two years, but thereafter seems to stabilise at a lower level. This seems to be consistent with the results in Table 19.2 column 1(b) and Table 19.3 column 1(b). The tables show that SA's short-run elasticity of 1.26 with respect to OECD growth is much larger than the long-run elasticity of 0.70. By contrast, RSADC growth shows a large impulse response throughout the ten-year period. Two underlying reasons may be advanced to explain the different impulse responses. First, the magnitude of the impulse responses will depend on the weighted income elasticities of the demand for exports relative to the sum of the weighted income elasticities of the demand for imports. Second, SA dominates RSADC in terms of economic size. In 1999, SA's level of GDP constituted about 72 per cent of SADC's total. A positive shock to SA's growth (via OECD growth) may therefore exert a large impact on RSADC growth. The long-run growth rate equation of RSADC in Table 19.3 column 2(c) records a large elasticity of 1.76 with respect to SA's growth.

Figure 19.3(b) reports the generalised forecast error variance decomposition (GFEV) of SA's growth rate. The figure shows that SA's GFEV is dominated by OECD growth, with a small proportion allocated to RSADC growth.[9] Figure 19.3(c) shows that SA and OECD dominate the GFEV of RSADC. The high and almost equal proportions suggest that RSADC's growth rate depends on an important interrelationship between SA and OECD.

In sum, the results of the simulation exercise and the single equation UECM's are consistent and imply the following relationship:

$$y^{OECD} \Rightarrow y^{SA} \Rightarrow y^{RSADC}.$$

SA's long-run growth rate is only BP constrained with respect to OECD and RSADC's growth rate is only BP constrained with respect to SA.

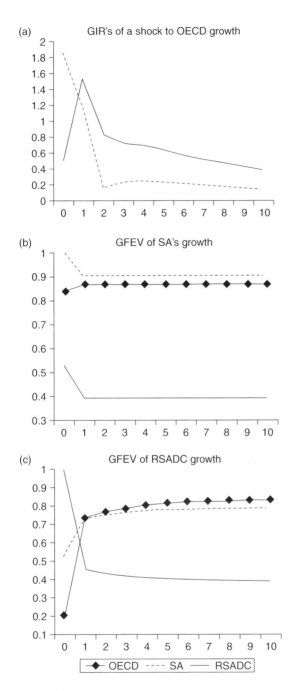

Figure 19.3 (a–c) GIR's and GFEV's.

Conclusions and policy implications

This chapter applies a 'generalised' version of Thirlwall's BP constrained growth model by testing for long-run relationships between the output growth rates of OECD countries and two neighbouring regions; SA and the rest of the RSADC over the period 1981–98. The policy implications of the 'generalised' model are particularly relevant to neighbouring regions that are engaged in mutual trade arrangements, and especially, where one of the regions (SA) dominates the other (RSADC) in terms of economic size.

The analysis provides strong support for the 'generalised' BP growth model, which stresses the mutual interdependence of the world economy where one country's (or block of countries) growth rate depends on others. Moreover, the 'generalised' BP growth model distinguishes itself from other open-economy models, which also emphasise the interdependence of the world economies. First, the empirical results should not be interpreted along a traditional open-economy Keynesian model *without BP constraints*. The descriptive and econometric analyses provide evidence that the average current account growth rates of SA and RSADC have been close to zero and that all the growth rate models represent long-run equilibrium solutions. SA and RSADC's actual long-run growth rates closely match those predicted by the BP model. Second, the 'generalised' BP model is distinctly different from open-economy models that stress relative price changes as an efficient BP adjustment mechanism. The econometric results support the simple version of the BP model. All the growth rate models are structurally stable and produce satisfactory out-of-sample forecasts without relative price changes. The brunt of the BP adjustment falls on income changes and not relative price changes. SA and RSADC cannot indefinitely grow faster or slower than the rate which is consistent with current account equilibrium. Third, McCombie and Thirlwall (1997b) argue that the BP models depicted by equations (19.7) and (19.9) should not be interpreted as a neoclassical model, where exogenous shocks to total factor productivity growth lead to increases in exports to finance planned imports. One of the main criticisms against the neoclassical interpretation is that an increase in the supply of goods is not a sufficient condition to promote faster output growth if the demand is lacking. The novelty of the BP growth model lies in the proposition that the income elasticities not only capture demand elements in the growth process, but also the supply characteristics or structural demand features of goods.

Although the policy suggestions are not mutually exclusive, they may be viewed from the different perspectives of SA and RSADC. SA is BP constrained with respect to OECD. The policy suggestion is that SA must make its goods more attractive abroad by improving the structural demand characteristics of its export goods such as quality, design, product differentiation and delivery service.

RSADC is BP constrained with respect to SA. From the viewpoint of policy makers in SA this is an important result. Growth-promoting policies in SA may have a significant and positive impact on RSADC growth. The long-run results indicate that a 1 per cent increase in SA's growth will on average lead to a 1.76 per cent increase in RSADC growth. From the perspective of

RSADC, however, policy-makers are advised to reduce their dependence on SA by improving the structural demand features of their exports to OECD countries.

Notes

1 The Southern African Development Community (SADC) is a multilateral economic cooperation scheme that includes fourteen countries from the Southern African Region: Angola, Botswana, Congo (Democratic Republic), Lesotho, Malawi, Mauritius Mozambique, Namibia, Seychelles, South Africa, Swaziland, Tanzania, Zambia and Zimbabwe.
2 Based on per capita income levels (purchasing power parity measures), SA can be classified as an upper middle-income country and RSADC as low-income countries (World Development Report, 2000/2001). The exceptions are Mauritius and Seychelles who recorded higher per capita income levels than SA. Nonetheless, SA's dominance in the SADC region is illustrated by its high level of GDP of around 72 per cent of SADC's total.
3 For extensive surveys of the empirical literature see McCombie (1997); and McCombie and Thirlwall (1997b). Recent empirical applications include those conducted by Ansari *et al.* (2000); León-Ledesma, (1999) and Moreno-Brid (1999).
4 The data source for RSADC's real GDP growth rate in Figure 19.1(a) and current account ratio in Figure 19.1(c) is World Bank Development Indicators. The data source for SA's growth rate in Figure 19.1(a) and current account ratio in Figure 19.1(b) is the South African Reserve Bank's Quarterly Bulletins (various issues).
5 Standard F-tests, diagnostic tests, structural stability tests and forecast tests are only applicable to the UECM's and not the FUECM's (see Microfit 4.0 by Pesaran and Pesaran, 1997).
6 Although the long-run coefficients of the UECM's and FUECM's are close in magnitude, there is nevertheless a difference. To correct for any endogeneity bias the FUECM in column 1(b) is used to derive the BP growth rate for SA. In column 2(c) all the variables are endogenised, so these results are used to calculate the BP growth rate for RSADC.
7 SA and RSADC's average growth rates exclude the outliers captured by the dummy variables in the previous sections.
8 Given the low frequency of the data we start with a VAR of order one. The choice of an order one VAR is strongly supported by the diagnostic tests of all the single equation VAR's. The VAR's pass diagnostic tests such as first order serial correlation, heteroscedasticity and normality. Analogous system diagnostic tests of Hendry (1995) yielded similar results. All these results are available from the author.
9 Note that the sum of the different proportions allocated to SA's GFEV will not sum to one. Recall that unlike the orthogonalised forecast error variance decomposition (OFEV), the GFEV explicitly allows for contemporaneous correlations between all the shocks (Pesaran and Pesaran, 1997). In the case of the OFEV the shocks are not contemporaneously correlated, so the different proportions allocated to the OFEV of a specific variable will sum to one.

Bibliography

Abdel-Fadil, M. (1984) 'Major Developments in the Agrarian Structure and Agrarian Relations in Egypt During the 1970s,' in M. Abdel-Fadil, M. Abdel-Hai Salah and M. Osada, (eds), *The Transition of the Egyptian Economy under the New Open-Door Policy*, Middle East Studies Series, Institute of Developing Economies, Tokyo 13.

Adams, R. H. Jr (1986) *Development and Social Change in Rural Egypt*, Syracuse, NY: Syracuse University Press.

Alexander, R. and King, A. (1998) 'Growth and the Balance-of-Payments Constraint,' *Research Paper* no. 622, Department of Economics, University of Melbourne.

Alogoskoufis, G., Pademos, L. and Portes, R. (eds) (1991) *External Constraints on Macroeconomic Policy*, Cambridge: Cambridge University Press.

Alonso, J. A. (1996) 'Enfoques Postkeynesianos sobre el Crecimiento: Una Aplicación a España,' *Información Comercial Española* 758: 103–120.

Alonso, J. A. (1999) 'Growth and the External Constraint: Lessons from the Spanish Experience', *Applied Economics* 31(2): 245–253.

Alonso, J. A. and Garcimartin, C. (1998–99) 'A New Approach to Balance-of-Payments Constraint: Some Empirical Evidence,' *Journal of Post Keynesian Economics* 21(3): 259–282, Chapter 11, this volume.

Andersen, P. S. (1990) 'Development in External and Internal Balances,' *BIS Economic Papers* 29, Chapter 10, this volume.

Andersen, P. S. (1993) 'The 45°-Rule Revisited,' *Applied Economics* 25: 1279–1284.

Ansari, M., Hashemzadeh, N. and Xi. L. (2000) 'The Chronicle of Economic Growth in Southeast Asian Countries: Does Thirlwall's Law Provide an Adequate Explanation?,' *Journal of Post Keynesian Economics* 22: 573–585, Chapter 15, this volume.

Armendáriz, B. and Armendáriz, P. (1995) 'Debt Relief, Growth and Price Stability in Mexico,' *Journal of Development Economics* 48: 135–149.

Artis, M. and Bayoumi, T. (1991) 'Global Financial Integration and Current Account Imbalances,' in G. Alogoskoufis, L. Pademos and L. Portes (eds), *External Constraints on Macroeconomic Policy*, Cambridge: Cambridge University Press.

Asensio, A. (1991) 'Compétitivité et contrainte extérieure: une comparaison internationale sur le période 1970–89 de dix pay de l'OCDE,' *Economie Appliquee* 44(1): 71–103.

Aspe, P. (1993) *The Economic Transformation: The Mexican Way*, Cambridge, MA: MIT Press.

Atesoglu, H. S. (1993) 'Balance of Payments Constrained Growth: Evidence from the United States,' *Journal of Post Keynesian Economics* 15(4): 507–514.

Atesoglu, H. S. (1993–94) 'Exports, Capital Flows, Relative Prices and Economic Growth in Canada,' *Journal of Post Keynesian Economics*, Winter 16: 289–298.

Atesoglu, H. S. (1994) 'Balance-of-Payments Determined Growth in Germany,' *Applied Economics Letters* 1: 89–91.

Atesoglu, H. S. (1995) 'An Explanation of the Slowdown in US Economic Growth,' *Applied Economics Letters* 2: 91–94.

Atesoglu, H. S. (1997) 'Balance-of-Payments-Constrained Growth Model and its Implications for the United States,' *Journal of Post Keynesian Economics* 19(3): 327–335.

Athukorala, P. and Riedel, J. (1994) 'Demand and Supply Factors in the Determination of NIE Exports: A Simultaneous Error-Correction Model for Hong Kong: A Comment,' *Economic Journal* 104: 1411–1414.

Athukorala, P. and Riedel, J. (1996) 'Modelling NIE Exports: Aggregation, Quantitative Restrictions and Choice of Econometric Methodology,' *Journal of Development Studies* 33: 81–98.

Averbug, A. and Giambiagi, F. (2000) 'A Crise Brasileira de 1998/99 – Origins e Consequencias,' *Texto para Discussädo* no.77, Banco Nacional de Desenvolvimento Economico e Social.

Bahamani-Oskooee, M. (1995) 'Is there any Long-Run Relation between the Terms of Trade and Trade Balance?,' *Journal of Policy Modeling* 17(2): 199–205.

Bairam, E. (1988) 'Balance of Payments, the Harrod Foreign Trade Multiplier and Economic Growth: The European and North American Experience, 1970–85,' *Applied Economics* 20: 1635–1642.

Bairam, E. (1990) 'The Harrod Foreign Trade Multiplier Revisited,' *Applied Economics* 22: 711–718.

Bairam, E. (1993) 'Static vs. Dynamic Specifications and the Harrod Foreign Trade Multiplier,' *Applied Economics* 25: 739–742.

Bairam, E. (1997) 'Levels of Economic Development and Appropriate Specification of the Harrod Foreign Trade Multiplier,' *Journal of Post Keynesian Economics*, Spring 19(3): 337–343.

Bairam, I. and Dempster, G. J. (1991) 'The Harrod Foreign Trade Multiplier and Economic Growth in Asian Countries,' *Applied Economics* 23: 1719–1724.

Balassa, B. (1978) 'Exports and Growth,' *Journal of Development Economics* 5(2): 181–189.

Balassa, B. (1979) 'Export Composition and Export Performance in the Industrial Countries, 1953–71,' *Review of Economics and Statistics* 61: 604–607.

Balassa, B. (1988) 'The Lessons of East Asian Development,' *Economic Development and Cultural Change* 36: 273–290.

Ball, R. J., Burns, T. and Laury, J. S. E. (1977) 'The Role of Exchange Rate Changes in Balance of Payments Adjustment – The United Kingdom Case,' *Economic Journal* 87: 1–29.

Banco de España (1995) *Las Cuentas Financieras de la Economia Española (1985–1994)*, Madrid: Banco de Espana.

Banco de México (1997) *The Mexican Economy*, Mexico.

Banco de México *Carpeta de Indicadores Económicos*, various issues, Mexico.

Barbosa-Filho, N. H. (2001) 'International Liquidity and Growth in Brazil,' *Working Paper* no. 2001. 104, Center for Economic Policy Analysis, New School University.

Bardhan, P. (1970) *Economic Growth, Development and Foreign Trade*, New York: John Wiley.

Barker, T. S. (1977) 'International Trade and Economic Growth: An Alternative to the Neoclassical Approach,' *Cambridge Journal of Economics* 1: 153–172.

Barrell, R. and Wren-Lewis, S. (1989) 'Fundamental Equilibrium Exchange Rates for the G-7,' *National Institute for Economic and Social Research, Discussion Paper* 155.

Barrett Whale, P. (1932) *International Trade*, London: Thornton Butterworth.

Barrett Whale, P. (1937) 'The Workings of the Pre-war Gold Standard', *Economica* 4(1): 18–32.

Barro, R. J. and Sala-I-Martin, X. (1995) *Economic Growth*, London: McGraw-Hill.

Bazdresch, C. and Levy, S. (1991) 'Populism and Economic Policy in Mexico: 1970–82,' in R. Dornbusch and S. Edwards (eds), *The Macroeconomics of Populism in Latin America*, Chicago: University of Chicago Press.

Beckerman, W. (1962) 'Projecting Europe's Growth,' *Economic Journal* 72: 912–925.

Ben-David, D. and Pappell, D. (1997) 'International Trade and Structural Change,' *Journal of International Economics* 43: 513–523.

Bergsten, C. F. (1991) *International Adjustment and Financing: The Lessons of 1985–1991*, Washington, DC: Institute for International Economics.

Bergsten, C. F. and Noland, M. (1993) *Reconcilable Differences? United States–Japan Economic Conflict*, Washington, DC: Institute for International Economics.

Bhaduri, A. and Marglin, S. A. (1990) 'Unemployment and the Real Wage: The Economic Basis for Contesting Political Ideologies,' *Cambridge Journal of Economics* 14(4): 375–393.

Bhargava, A. (1986) 'On the Theory of Testing for Unit Roots in Observed Time Series,' *Review of Economic Studies* 369–384.

Bianchi, C. (1994a) 'Balance of Payments Constraints in the Italian Economy,' in B. Böhm and L. F. Punzo (eds), *Economic Performance: A Look at Austria and Italy*, Heidelberg: Physica-Verlag.

Bianchi, C. (1994b) *L'economia italiana e I problemi della politica economica*, Milan: Gerini.

Blanchard, O. and Fischer, S. (1989) *Lectures on Macroeconomics*, Cambridge, MA : MIT Press.

Bleaney, M. and Mizen, P. (1996a) 'Are Real Exchange Rates Stationary? Evidence from Sterling Bilateral Rates 1973–93,' *Economic Notes* 25(3): 465–482.

Bleaney, M. and Mizen, P. (1996b) 'Nonlinearities in Exchange-Rate Dynamics: Evidence from Five Currencies, 1973–94,' *Economic Record* 72(216): 36–45.

Blecker, R. A. (1989) 'International Competition, Income Distribution and Economic Growth,' *Cambridge Journal of Economics*, December 13(4): 395–412.

Blecker, R. A. (1992) 'Structural Roots of U.S. Trade Problems: Income Elasticities, Structural Trends and Hysteresis,' *Journal of Post Keynesian Economics* 14(3): 321–346.

Blecker, R. A. (1996) 'The Trade Deficit and U.S. Competitiveness,' in R. A. Blecker (ed.), *U.S. Trade Policy and Global Growth: New Directions in the International Economy*, Armonk, NY: M.E. Sharpe, pp. 179–214.

Blecker, R. A. (1997) 'Policy Implications of the International Saving–Investment Correlation,' in R. Pollin (ed.), *The Macroeconomics of Saving, Finance and Investment*, Ann Arbor: University of Michigan Press.

Bochove, C. van (1982) *Imports and Economic Growth*, The Hague: Martinus Nijhoff.

Boggio, L. (1988) 'Export Expansion and Economic Growth. An 'Empirical Regularity' and its Explanation,' *Empirica, Austrian Economic Papers* 1: 205–226.

Boltho, A. (1985) 'Was Japan's Industrial Policy Successful?,' *Cambridge Journal of Economics* 9: 187–201.

Bonono, M. and Terra, C. (1999) 'The Political Economy of Exchange Rate Policy in Brazil: 1964–97,' *Economico* no. 341, Escola de Pós-Graduacäo em Economica, Fundacäo Getulio Vargas.

Bosworth, B. P. (1993) *Saving and Investment in a Global Economy*, Washington, DC: Brookings Institution.

Bowles, S. and Boyer, R. (1995) 'Wages, Aggregate Demand and Employment in an Open Economy: An Empirical Investigation,' in A. E. Gerald and H. M. Gintis (eds), *Macroeconomic Policy After the Conservative Era*, Cambridge: Cambridge University Press, pp. 143–171.

Buffie, E. F. and Krause, A. S. (1989) 'Mexico 1958–86: From Stabilizing Development to the Debt Crisis,' in J. D. Sachs (ed.), *Developing Country Debt and the World Economy*, Chicago: The University of Chicago Press.

Burki, S. J. and Edwards, S. (1995) *Latin America After Mexico: Quickening the Pace*, Washington: The World Bank.

Cambridge Economic Policy Group (1981) 'The European Community: Problems and Prospects,' *Cambridge Economic Policy Review* 7(2): 1–65.

Campbell, J. Y. and Perron, P. (1991) 'Pitfalls and Opportunities: What Macroeconomists should know about Unit Roots,' in O. J. Blanchard and S. Fischer (eds), *NBER Macroeconomics Annual*, Cambridge, MA: MIT Press.

Cardero, M. E. and Galindo, L. M. (1997) 'Un Modelo Econométrico de Vectores Autorregresivos y Cointegración de la Economía Mexicana, 1980–1996,' *Economía Mexicana* 6(2): 233–250.

Carlin, W. J. and Soskice, D. W. (1990) *Macroeconomics and the Wage Bargain. A Modern Approach to Employment, Inflation and the Wage Bargain*, Oxford: Oxford University Press.

Castro, C., Loría, E. and Mendoza, M. A. (1997) 'EUDOXIO: Modelo Macroeconométrico de la Economía Mexicana,' *Mexico: Fac. Economía, UNAM*.

CEPAL, *América Latina y el Caribe, 15 Años Después. De la Década Perdida a la Transformación Económica, 1980–1995*, Santiago, Chile: FCE.

Charemza, W. W. and Deadman, F. D. (1992) *New Directions in Econometric Practice*, Brookfield VT: Edward Elgar (2nd edition, 1997).

Chenery, H. and Adelman, I. (1966) 'Foreign Aid and Economic Development: the Case of Greece, *Review of Economics and Statistics* 48: 1–19.

Chenery, H. and Bruno, M. (1962) 'Development Alternatives in an Open Economy: The Case of Israel,' *Economic Journal* 72: 79–103.

Chenery, H. and Strout, A. (1966) 'Foreign Assistance and Economic Development,' *American Economic Review* 56: 679–733.

Chow, P. and Kellman, M. (1993) *Trade – The Engine of Growth in East Asia*, New York: Oxford University Press.

Cimoli, M. and Soete, L. (1992) 'A Generalised Technology Gap Trade Model,' *Economie Appliquée* 45(3): 33–54.

Clements, M. P. and Hendry, D. F. (1997) *The Marshall Lectures on Economic Forecasting*, Cambridge: Cambridge University Press.

Cline, W. R. (1989) *United States External Adjustment and the World Economy*, Washington, DC: Institute for International Economics.

Cohen, D. and Sachs, J. (1986) 'Growth and External Debt under Risk of Debt Repudiation,' *European Economic Review* 30: 529–560.

Connell, D. (1979) *The U.K.'s Performance in Export Markets – Some Evidence from International Trade Data*, London: National Economic Development Office, Discussion Paper 6.

Cooper, R. N. (1982) 'The Gold Standard: Historical Facts and Future Prospects', *Brookings Papers in Economic Activity* 1: 1–56.

Corden, M. W. (1994) *Economic Policy, Exchange Rates and the International System*, Chicago: University of Chicago Press.

Corden, W. M. (1985) 'Macroeconomic Policy Interaction under Flexible Exchange Rates: A Two-Country Model,' *Economica* 52: 9–23.

Cornwall, J. (1977) *Modern Capitalism: Its Growth and Transformation*, London: Martin Robertson.

Coutts, K., Godley, W., Rowthorn, R. and Zessa, G. (1990) *Britain's Economic Problems and Policies in the 1990s*, London: Institute for Public Policy Research, Economic Study No. 6.

Cripps, T. F. (1978) 'Causes of Growth and Recession in World Trade,' *Cambridge Economic Policy Review* 4: 37–43.

Cripps, T. F. and Godley, W. (1978) 'Control of Imports as a Means to Full Employment and the Expansion of World Trade: The U.K.'s Case,' *Cambridge Journal of Economics* 2: 327–334.

Cripps, T. F. and Tarling, R. J. (1973) *Growth in Advanced Capitalist Economies*, Cambridge: Cambridge University Press.

Cuthbertson, K. (1979) *Macroeconomic Policy: The New Cambridge Keynesian and Monetarist Controversies*, London: Macmillan.

Cuthbertson, K., Hall, S. G. and Taylor, M. P. (1992) *Applied Econometric Techniques*, Ann Arbor: University of Michigan Press.

Davidson, P. (1990–91) 'A Post Keynesian Positive Contribution to Theory,' *Journal of Post Keynesian Economics* 13: 298–303.

Davidson, P. (1991) 'What International Payments Scheme would Keynes have Suggested for the Twenty-first Century,' in P. Davidson and J. A. Kregel (eds), *Economic Problems of the 1990s: Europe, the Developing Countries and the United States*, Aldershot, UK: Edward Elgar, pp. 85–104.

Davidson, P. (1997) 'Introduction to the Minisymposium on Thirlwall's Law and Economic Growth in an Open-Economy Context,' *Journal of Post Keynesian Economics* 19: 311–312.

Denison E. (1967) *Why Growth Rates Differ: Postwar Experience in Nine Western Countries*, Washington: The Brookings Institution.

Denison, E. and Chung, W. K. (1976) *How Japan's Economy Grew so Fast: The Sources of Postwar Expansion*, Washington: The Brookings Institution.

Diaz-Alejandro, C. (1963) 'A Note on the Impact of Devaluation and the Redistribution Effect,' *Journal of Political Economy* 71: 577–580.

Dickey, D. and Fuller, W. (1979) 'Distribution of the Estimators for Autoregressive Time Series with a Unit Root,' *Journal of the American Statistical Association* 74: 427–431.

Dickey, D. and Fuller, W. (1981) 'The Likelihood Ratio Statistics for Autoregressive Time Series with a Unit Root,' *Econometrica* 49: 1057–1072.

Dickey, D., Jansen, D. W. and Thornton, D. L. (1991) 'A Primer on Cointegration with an Application to Money and Income,' *Federal Reserve Bank of St Louis Review* 73(2): 58–78.

Dixon, R. J. and Thirlwall, A. P. (1975) 'A Model of Regional Growth Rate Differences on Kaldorian Lines,' *Oxford Economic Papers* 27: 201–214.

Doornik, J. and Hendry, D. (1997) *Interactive Econometric Modelling of Dynamic Systems*, London: International Thomson.

Dornbusch, R. (1980) *Open Economy Macroeconomics*, New York: Basic Books.

Dornbusch, R. and Werner, A. (1994) 'Mexico: Stabilization, Reform, and No Growth,' *Brookings Papers on Economic Activity* 1: 253–315.

Dornbusch, R., Krugman, P. and Park, Y. C. (1989) *Meeting World Challenges: U.S. Manufacturing in the 1990s*, Rochester, NY: Eastman Kodak.

Dosi, G. and Soete, L. (1988) 'Technical Change and International Trade,' in G. Dosi, C. Freeman, R. Nelson, G. Silverberg and L. Soete (eds), *Technical Change and Economic Theory*, London: Pinter.

Dosi, G., Pavitt, K. and Soete, L. (1990) *The Economics of Technical Change and International Trade*, London: Harvester Wheatsheaf.

Dunkerley, J. (1988) *Power in the Isthmus*, New York: Verso.

Dussel, P. E. (1995) 'Recent Developments in Mexican Employment and the Impact of NAFTA,' *International Labor Studies* 5: 45–69.

Dutt, A. K. (1990) *Growth, Distribution and Uneven Development*, New York: Cambridge University Press.

Eatwell, J. (1995) 'Disguised Unemployment: The G-7 Experience,' United Nations Conference on Trade and Development, Discussion Paper 106, November.

ECLAC 'Economic Commission for Latin America and the Caribbean' (1998) *La Evolución de la Economía de México en 1997*, Mexico.

ECLAC–INEGI 'Economic Commission for Latin America and The Caribbean & Instituto Nacional De Estadística, Geografía e Informática' (1993) *Magnitud y Evolución de la Pobreza en México 1984–1992*, UNEGI, Mexico.

Economic Commission for Latin America and the Caribbean (1980–96) *Centroamérica: Nota Económica*, Mexico: ECLAC.

Economic Commission for Latin America and the Caribbean (1993) *Centroamérica: El Camino de los Noventa*, Mexico.

Economic Commission for Latin America and the Caribbean (1995) *El Regionalismo Abierto en América Latina*, Mexico: ECLAC.

Economic Commission for Latin America and the Caribbean (1997) *Series Macroeconómicas del Istmo Centroaméricano*, Mexico: ECLAC.

Edwards, S. (1995) *Crisis and Reform in Latin America: From Despair to Hope*, New York: Oxford University Press.

Eltis, W. (1976) 'The Failure of the Keynesian Conventional Wisdom,' *Lloyds Bank Review* 122: 1–17.

Engle, R. and Granger, C. (1987) 'Cointegration and Error Correction: Representation, Estimation and Testing,' *Econometrica* 55: 251–276.

Engle, R. and Yoo, S. (1987) 'Forecasting and Testing in Cointegrated Systems,' *Journal of Econometrics* 35: 143–159.

Fagerberg, J. (1988) 'International Competitiveness,' *Economic Journal* 98: 355–374.

Fagerberg, J. (1994) 'Technology and International Differences in Growth Rates,' *Journal of Economic Literature* 32: 1147–1175.

Faini, R., Clavijo, F. and Senhadji, A. (1992a) 'The Fallacy of Composition Argument: Is it Relevant for LDCs' Manufactures Exports?,' *European Economic Review* 36: 865–882.

Faini, R., Pritchett, L. and Clavijo, F. (1992b) 'Import Demand in Developing Countries,' in M. Dagenais and P.-A. Muett (eds), *International Trade Modelling*, London: Chapman and Hall, pp. 279–297.

Feinberg, R. M. (1996) 'A Simultaneous Analysis of Exchange-Rate Pass-Through into Prices of Imperfectly Substitutable Domestic and Import Goods,' *International Review of Economics and Finance* 5(4): 407–416.

Feldstein, M. and Horioka, C. (1980) 'Domestic Saving and International Capital Flows,' *Economic Journal* 90: 314–329.

Fetherston, M., Moore, B. and Rhodes, J. (1977) 'Manufacturing Export Shares and Cost Competitiveness of Advanced Industrial Countries,' *Cambridge Economic Policy Review* 3: 62–70.

Fischer, S. (1997) *Capital Account Liberalization and the Role of the IMF*, Washington: IMF.

Frankel, J. A. (1991) 'Quantifying International Capital Mobility in the 1980s,' in B. D. Bernheim and J. B. Shoven (eds), *National Saving and Economic Performance*, Chicago: University of Chicago Press.

Froot, K. A. and Rogoff, K. (1995) 'Perspectives on PPP and Long-run Real Exchange Rates,' in G. M. Grossman and K. Rogoff (eds), *Handbook of International Economics*, 3, Amsterdam: Elsevier, pp. 1647–1688.

Fuller, W. A. (1976) *Introduction to Statistical Time Series*, New York: John Wiley & Sons.

Gandolfo, G. (1981) *Qualitative Analysis and Econometric Estimation of Continuous Time Dynamic Models*, Amsterdam: North Holland.

Gandolfo, G. (1996) *Economic Dynamics*, 3rd edn, Berlin: Springer.

Garcimartin, C. (1997) 'El Papel de la Demanda en Las Teorias de Crecimiento,' PhD Dissertation, Universidad Complutense.

Glyn, A. and Sutcliffe, B. (1972) *British Capitalism, Workers and the Profit Squeeze*, London: Penguin.

Godley, W. and Milberg, W. (1994) 'U.S. Trade Deficits: The Recovery's Dark Side?' *Challenge*, November–December: 40–47.

Goldstein, M. and Khan, M. S. (1978) 'The Supply and Demand for Exports: A Simultaneous Approach,' *Review of Economics and Statistics* 60: 275–286.

Goldstein, M. and Khan, M. S. (1985) 'Income and Price Effects in Foreign Trade,' in R.W. Jones and P. B. Kenen (eds), *Handbook of International Economics* 2 Chapter 20, Amsterdam: Elsevier.

Goodwin, R. M. (1967) 'A Growth Cycle,' in C. H. Feinstein (ed.), *Socialism, Capitalism and Economic Growth*, Cambridge: Cambridge University Press, pp. 54–58.

Greenhalgh, C., Taylor, P. and Wilson, R. (1994) 'Innovation, Export Volumes and Prices – A Disaggregated Study,' *Oxford Economic Papers* 46(1): 102–134.

Grossman, G. M. and Helpman, E. (1991) *Innovation and Growth in the Global Economy*, Cambridge, MA: The MIT Press.

Hakkio, C. S. and Rush, M. (1991) 'Cointegration: How Short is the Long-run?,' *Journal of International Money and Finance* 10: 571–581.

Harrod, R. (1933) *International Economics*, Cambridge: Cambridge University Press.

Harrod, R. (1939) 'An Essay in Dynamic Theory,' *Economic Journal* 49: 14–33.

Hatsopoulos, G., Krugman, P. and Summers, L. (1988) 'U.S. Competitiveness: Beyond the Trade Deficit,' *Science* 15(241): 299–307.

Heike, H. (1997) 'Balance of Payments Constrained Growth: A Reconsideration of the Evidence for the US Economy,' *Journal of Post Keynesian Economics* 19: 313–325.

Helkie, W. L. and Hooper, P. (1988) 'An Empirical Analysis of the External Deficit,' in R. C. Bryant, G. Holtham and P. Hooper (eds), *External Deficits and the Dollar: The Pit and the Pendulum*, Washington, DC: Brookings Institution.

Hendry, D. F. (1986) 'Econometric Modeling with Co-integrated Variables: An Overview,' *Oxford Bulletin of Economics and Statistics* 48: 201–212.

Hendry, D. F. (1995) *Dynamic Econometrics*, Oxford University Press.

Hicks, J. (1950) *The Trade Cycle*, Oxford: Clarendon Press.

Himarios, D. (1989) 'Do Devaluations Improve the Trade Balance? The Evidence Revisited,' *Economic Inquiry* 27(1): 143–168.

Hirsch, M. W. and Smale, S. (1974) *Differential Equations, Dynamical Systems and Linear Algebra*, San Diego: Academic Press.

Hooper, P. L. and Mann, C. J. (1989) 'Exchange-Rate Pass-Through in the 1980s: The Case of U.S. Imports of Manufactures,' *Brookings Papers on Economic Activity* 1: 297–329.

Houthakker, H. and Magee, S. (1969) 'Income and Price Elasticities in World Trade,' *Review of Economics and Statistics* 51(2): 111–125.

Hume, D. (1752) ' "Of Money", and "Of the Balance of Trade" ' in A. Kincaid and A. Donaldson (eds), *Political Discourses*, Edingburgh.

IMF (1989) *International Capital Markets: Developments and Prospects*, Washington: International Monetary Fund.

IMF (1996) *International Financial Statistics Yearbook, 1996*, Washington, DC: IMF.

Inder, B. (1993) 'Estimating Long-run Relationships in Economics: A Comparison of Different Approaches,' *Journal of Econometrics* 57: 53–68.

INEGI 'Instituto Nacional du Estadística, Geografía e Informática,' *Sistema de Cuentas Nacionales*, Mexico, various issues.

Iwata, K. (1989) 'Comments,' *European Economic Review* 33: 1047–1049.

Johansen, S. (1988) 'Statistical Analysis of Cointegration Vector,' *Journal of Economic Dynamics and Control* 12: 231–254.

Johansen, S. and Juselius, K. (1990) 'Maximum Likelihood Estimation and Inference on Cointegration with Applications to the Demand for Money,' *Oxford Bulletin of Economics and Statistics* 52: 169–210.

Journal of Post Keynesian Economics (1997) 'Minisymposium on Thirlwall's Law and Economic Growth in an Open-Economy Context,' 19(3): 311–385.

Kahn, R. (1931) 'The Relation Between Home Investment and Unemployment', *Economic Journal*, 41: 173–198.

Kaldor, N. (1957) 'A Model of Economic Growth,' *Economic Journal* 67: 591–624.

Kaldor, N. (1970) 'The Case for Regional Policies,' *Scottish Journal of Political Economy* 18: 337–348.

Kaldor, N. (1971) 'Conflicts in National Economic Objectives,' *Economic Journal* 81: 1–16.

Kaldor, N. (1975) 'What is Wrong with Economic Theory,' *Quarterly Journal of Economics* 89(3): 347–357.

Kaldor, N. (1978a) 'Introduction,' *Further Essays on Economic Theory*, London: Duckworth.

Kaldor, N. (1978b) 'The Effect of Devaluations on Trade in Manufactures,' *Further Essays on Applied Economics*, London: Duckworth.

Kaldor, N. (1978c) *Further Essays on Applied Economics*, London: Duckworth.

Kaldor, N. (1979) 'Comment,' in F. Blackaby (ed.), *De-industrialisation*, London: Heineman.

Kennedy, C. and Thirlwall, A. P. (1979) 'Import Penetration, Export Performance and Harrod's Trade Multiplier, *Oxford Economic Papers* 31(2): 303–323.

Kennedy, C. and Thirlwall, A. P. (1983) 'Import and Export Ratios and the Dynamic Harrod Trade Multiplier. A Reply to McGregor and Swales,' *Oxford Economic Papers* 35: 125–129.

Kern, D. (1978) 'An International Comparison of Major Economic Trends 1953–76,' *National Westminster Bank Quarterly Review*, May: 38–47.

Keynes, J. M. (1936) *The General Theory of Employment, Interest and Money*, London: Macmillan.

Khan, M. (1974) 'Import and Export Demand in Developing Countries,' *IMF Staff Papers* 21: 678–693.

Kindleberger, C. P. (1967) *Europe's Postwar Growth. The Role of the Labor Supply*, Cambridge, MA: Harvard University Press.

Kravis, I. B. and Lipsey, R. E. (1971) *Price Competitiveness in World Trade*, New York: National Bureau of Economic Research.

Krueger, A. (1990) *Perspectives on Trade and Development*, Chicago: University of Chicago Press.

Krugman, P. (1989a) 'Differences in Income Elasticities and Trends in Real Exchanges Rates,' *European Economic Review* 33: 1031–1054.

Krugman, P. (1989b) *Exchange-Rate Instability*, Cambridge, MA: MIT Press.

Krugman, P. (1993) 'International Finance and Economic Development,' in A. Giovannini (ed.), *Finance and Development Issues and Experience*, Cambridge: Cambridge University Press.

Krugman, P. (1994a) 'Competitiveness: A Dangerous Obsession,' *Foreign Affairs* 73(2): 28–44.

Krugman, P. (1994b) 'Does Third World Growth Hurt First World Prosperity?,' *Harvard Business Review* 72: 113–121.

Krugman, P. and Baldwin, R. E. (1987) 'The Persistence of the U.S. Trade Deficit,' *Brookings Papers on Economic Activity* 15: 1–55.

Krugman, P. and Taylor, L. (1978) 'Contractionary Effects of Devaluation,' *Journal of International Economics* 8: 445–456.

Kugler, P. and Dridi, J. (1993) 'Growth and Exports in LDCs: A Multivariate Time Series Study,' *Rivista Internazionale di Scienze Economiche e Commerciali* 40(9): 759–767.

Kurz, H. D. and Salvadori, N. (1995) 'The "New" Growth Theory: Old Wine in New Goatskins,' in F. Coricelli, M. di Matteo and F. Hahn (eds), *New Theories in Growth and Development*, London: Macmillan, pp. 63–94.

Lafay, G. (1992) 'The Measurement of Revealed Comparative Advantage,' in M. Dagenais and P.-A. Muet (eds), *International Trade Modelling*, London: Chapman and Hall, pp. 209–234.

Larsen, F., Llewellyn, J. and Potter, S. (1983) 'International Economic Linkages,' *OECD Economic Studies* 1: 43–49.

Lawrence, R. Z. (1989) 'The International Dimension,' in R. E. Litan, R. Z. Lawrence and C. L. Schultze (eds), *American Living Standards: Threats and Challenges*, Washington, DC: Brookings Institution, pp. 23–65.

Lawrence, R. Z. (1990) 'U.S. Current Account Adjustment: An Appraisal,' *Brookings Papers on Economic Activity* 2: 343–389.

Leamer, E. and Stern, R. M. (1970) *Quantitative International Economics*, Boston: Allyn & Bacon.

Lee, J. W. (1995) 'Capital Goods Imports and Long-Run Growth,' *Journal of Development Economics* 48: 91–110.

León-Ledesma, M. A. (1999) 'An Application of Thirlwall's Law to the Spanish Economy,' *Journal of Post Keynesian Economics* 21: 55–69, Chapter 12, this volume.

León-Ledesma, M. A. and Thirlwall, A. P. (2002) 'The Endogeneity of the Natural Rate of Growth,' *Cambridge Journal of Economics* 26: 409–439.

Levine, R. and Renelt, D. (1992) 'A Sensitivity Analysis of Cross-Country Growth Regressions,' *American Economic Review* 82: 942–963.

Lindert, P. H. and Pugel, T. A. (1996) *International Economics*, 10th edn, Chicago: Richard D. Irwin.

Lomax, D. F. (1984) 'The United States Economy and Country Creditworthiness,' *National Westminster Bank International Review*: 1–19.

López, J. (1998) *La Macroeconomia de México: El Pasado Reciente y el Futuro Posible*, Mexico: Miguel Angel Porrú-UACPYP-CCH.

López, J. and Mántey, G. (1999) 'Employment Policies in an Open Semi-industrialized Economy. Reflections on the Mexican Economy,' in P. Davidson and J. Kregel (eds), *Full Employment and Price Stability in a Global Economy*, London: Edward Elgar.

Lucas, R. (1998) 'On the Mechanics of Economic Development,' *Journal of Monetary Economics* 22: 3–42.

Lustig, N. (1992) *Mexico, The Remaking of an Economy*, Washington: Brookings Institution.

McClosky, D. and Zecher, R. (1976) 'How the Gold Standard Worked: 1880–1913' in J. A. Frankel and H. G. Johnson (eds), *The Monetary Approach to the Balance of Payments*, London: Allen and Unwin.

McCombie, J. S. L. (1981) 'Are International Growth Rates Constrained by the Balance of Payments? A Comment on Professor Thirlwall,' *Banca Nazionale del Lavoro Quarterly Review* 139: 455–458.

McCombie, J. S. L. (1982) *Post-War Productivity and Output Growth in the Advanced Countries*, Doctoral Thesis, University of Cambridge.

McCombie, J. S. L. (1985a) 'Economic Growth, the Harrod Foreign Trade Multiplier and the Hicks Super-Multiplier,' *Applied Economics* 17: 55–72.

McCombie, J. S. L. (1985b) 'The Balance of Payments as a Constraint on Economic Growth,' *Research Paper No. 137*, Department of Economics, University of Melbourne.

McCombie, J. S. L. (1985–86) 'Why Cutting Real Wages Will Not Necessarily Reduce Unemployment – Keynes and the "Postulates of the Classical Economics",' *Journal of Post Keynesian Economics* 8: 233–248.

McCombie, J. S. L. (1988) 'A Synoptic View of Regional Growth and Unemployment: II – The Post-Keynesian Theory,' *Urban Studies* 25: 399–417.

McCombie, J. S. L. (1989) 'Thirlwall's Law and Balance of Payments Constrained Growth – A Comment on the Debate,' *Applied Economics* 21: 611–629.

McCombie, J. S. L. (1992) ' "Thirlwall's Law" and Balance of Payments Constrained Growth: More on the Debate,' *Applied Economics* 25: 493–512.

McCombie, J. S. L. (1993) 'Economic Growth, Trade Interlinkages and the Balance of Payments Constraint,' *Journal of Post Keynesian Economics* 15: 471–505.

McCombie, J. S. L. (1996) 'Economic Growth and the Harrod Foreign Trade Multiplier Revisited,' in G. Rampa, L. Stella and A. P. Thirlwall (eds), *Economic Dynamics, Trade and Growth: Essays on Harrodian Themes*, London: Macmillan.

McCombie, J. S. L. (1997) 'On the Empirics of Balance-of-Payments Constrained Growth,' *Journal of Post Keynesian Economics* 19(3): 345–375, Chapter 9, this volume.

McCombie, J. S. L. and Thirlwall, A. P. (1994) *Economic Growth and the Balance of Payments Constraint*, Basingstoke, UK: Macmillan.

McCombie, J. S. L. and Thirlwall, A. P. (1997a) 'Economic Growth and the Balance-of-Payments Constraint Revisited,' in P. Arestis, G. Palma and M. Sawyer (eds), *Markets, Unemployment and Economic Policy. Essays in Honour of G. Harcourt*, Vol. 2, London: Elgar, pp. 498–511.

McCombie, J. S. L. and Thirlwall, A. P. (1997b) 'The Dynamic Harrod Foreign Trade Multiplier and the Demand-Oriented Approach to Economic Growth: An Evaluation,' *International Review of Applied Economics* 11(1): 5–26.

McCombie, J. S. L., Pugno, M. and Soro, B. (eds) (2003) *Productivity Growth and Economic Performance: Essays on Verdoorn's Law*, London: Palgrave-Macmillan.

McGregor, P. G. and Swales, J. K. (1985) 'Professor Thirlwall and Balance of Payments Constrained Growth,' *Applied Economics* 17: 17–32.

McGregor, P. G. and Swales, J. K. (1986) 'Balance of Payments Constrained Growth: A Rejoinder to Professor Thirlwall,' *Applied Economics* 18: 1265–1274.

McGregor, P. G. and Swales, J. K. (1991) 'Thirlwall's Law and Balance of Payments Constrained Growth: Further Comment on the Debate,' *Applied Economics* 23: 9–20.

MacKinnon, J. (1991) 'Critical Values for Cointegration Tests,' in R. F. Engle and C. W. J. Granger (eds), *Long-Run Economic Relationships: Readings in Cointegration*, Oxford: Oxford University Press.

Maddala, G. S. and Kim, I. (1998) *Unit Roots, Cointegration, and Structural Change*, Cambridge: Cambridge University Press.

Maddison, A. (1970) *Economic Progress and Policy in Developing Countries*, London: Allen and Unwin.

Maddison, A. (1972) 'Explaining Economic Growth,' *Banca Nazionale del Lavoro Quarterly Review* 102: 211–262.

Maddison, A. (1995) *Monitoring the World Economy: 1820–1992*, Paris: OECD.

Marglin, S. A. and Bhaduri, A. (1990) 'Profit Squeeze and Keynesian Theory,' in S. A. Marglin and J. B. Schor (eds), *The Golden Age of Capitalism*, Oxford: Oxford University Press, pp. 153–186.

Marquez, J. (1985) 'Foreign Exchange Constraints and Growth Possibilities in the LDCs,' *Journal of Development Economics* 19: 39–57.

Meade, E. E. (1991) 'Computers and the Trade Deficit,' in P. Hooper and J. D. Richardson (eds), *International Economic Transactions: Issues in Measurement and Empirical Research*, Chicago: University of Chicago Press/National Bureau of Economic Research.

Medio, A. (1992) *Chaotic Dynamics. Theory and Applications to Economics*, Cambridge: Cambridge University Press.

Menon, J. (1996) *Exchange Rates and Prices: The Case of Australian Manufactured Imports*, Berlin: Springer-Verlag.

Milberg, W. S. and Arestis, P. (1993–94) 'Degree of Monopoly, Pricing and Flexible Exchange Rates,' *Journal of Post Keynesian Economics* 16(2): 167–188.

Ministerio de Economia y Hacienda (1990) *Series Historicas de la Economia Espanola*, Madrid.

Mirakhor, A. and Montiel, P. (1987) 'Import Intensity of Output Growth in Developing Countries, 1970–85,' International Monetary Fund Research Department, Staff Studies for the World Economic Outlook, August 1987, Washington, DC: International Monetary Fund.

Misselden, E. (1623) *The Centre of the Circle of Commerce*, London: J. Dawson for N. Bourne.

Mody, E. and Yilmaz, K. (1997) 'Is there Persistence in the Growth of Manufactured Exports? Evidence from Newly Industrialized Countries,' *Journal of Development Economics* 53: 447–470.

Moggridge, D. (1973) *The Collected Writings of J.M. Keynes Vol XIII: The General Theory and After: Part 1 Preparation*, London: Macmillan.

Moreno-Brid, J. C. (1998a) 'Trade Liberalization and Import Demand in Mexico,' unpublished manuscript, Cambridge, MA.

Moreno-Brid, J. C. (1998b) 'On Capital Flows and the Balance-of-Payments Constrained Growth Model,' *Journal of Post Keynesian Economics* 21: 283–289.

Moreno-Brid, J. C. (1999) 'Mexico's Economic Growth and the Balance of Payments Constraint: A Cointegration Analysis,' *International Review of Applied Economics* 13(2): 150–159.

Moreno-Brid, J. C. and Ros, J. (1994) 'Market Reform and the Changing Role of the State in Mexico: A Historical Perspective,' in A. K. Dutt, K. S. Kim and A. Singh (eds), *The State, Markets and Development*, Aldershot: Edward Elgar.

Morgan, A. (1970) 'Income and Price Elasticities in World Trade: A Comment,' *The Manchester School* 38: 303–314.

Mun, T. (1664) *England's Treasure by Foreign Trade*, reprinted (1923), Oxford: Basil Blackwell.

Murthy, N. R. V. and Phillips, J. M. (1996) 'The Relationship Between Budget Deficits and Capital Inflows: Further Econometric Evidence,' *The Quarterly Review of Economics and Finance* 36: 485–494.

Muscatelli, V. A. (1994) 'Demand and Supply Factors in the Determination of NIE Exports: A Reply,' *Economic Journal* 104: 1415–1417.

Muscatelli, V. A., Srinivason, T. G. and Vines, D. (1992) 'Demand and Supply Factors in the Determination of NIE Exports: A Simultaneous Error-Correction Model for Hong Kong,' *Economic Journal* 102: 1467–1477.

Muscatelli, V., Srinivassan, T. G. and Vines, D. (1994) 'The Empirical Modelling of NIE Exports: An Evaluation of Different Approaches,' *Journal of Development Studies* 30: 279–302.

Muscatelli, V., Stevenson, A. and Montagna, C. (1995) 'Modelling Aggregate Manufactured Exports for Some Asian Newly Industrialized Economies,' *Review of Economics and Statistics* 77: 147–155.

Myrdal, G. (1957) *Economic Theory and Underdeveloped Regions*, London: Duckworth.

Nelson, C. R. and Plosser, C. I. (1982) 'Trends and Random Walks in Macroeconomic Time Series, Some Evidence and Implications,' *Journal of Monetary Economics* 10: 139–162.

Noland, M. (1997) 'Has Asian Export Performance Been Unique?,' *Journal of International Economics* 43: 79–101.

Norman, N. R. (1996) 'A General Post Keynesian Theory of Protection,' *Journal of Post Keynesian Economics* 18(4): 509–531.

Obstfeld, M. and Rogoff, K. (1995) 'The International Approach to the Current Account' in G. Grossman and K. Rogoff (eds), *Handbook of International Economics*, Amsterdam: Elsevier Science Publishing.

OECD 'Organization for Economic Co-operation and Development (1996),' *Mexico 1997*, Paris: OECD.

OECD (1996) *Historical Statistics, 1960–1994*, Paris: OECD.

Oman, C. P. and Wignaraja, G. (1991) *The Postwar Evolution in Development Thinking*, New York: St Martin's Press.

Padoan, P. C. (1993) 'Competitivià, crescita e bilancia dei pagamenti. Considerazioni sull' equilibrio di lungo periodo,' in C. A. Bollino and P. C. Padoan (eds), *Il circolo virtuoso*, Bologna: II Mulino.

Panic, M. (1975) 'Why the UK's Propensity to Import is High,' *Lloyds Bank Review* 115: 1–12.

Perraton, J. (1990) 'The Harrod Foreign Trade Multiplier and the Developing Countries, 1970–1984: An Examination of the Thirlwall Hypothesis,' University of Nottingham (mimeo).

Perraton, J. and Turner, P. (1999) 'Estimates of Industrial Country Export and Import Demand Functions: Implications for "Thirlwall's Law",' *Applied Economics Letters* 6: 723–727.

Perron, P. (1989) 'The Great Crash, the Oil Shock, and the Unit Root Hypothesis,' *Econometrica* 57: 1361–1401.

Perron, P. (1990) 'Testing for a Unit Root in a Time Series with a Changing Mean,' *Journal of Business and Economic Statistics* 8: 153–162.

Perron, P. (1993) 'The Great Crash, the Oil Shock, and the Unit Root Hypothesis Erratum,' *Econometrica* 61: 248–249.

Perron, P. (1994) 'Trend, Unit Root, and Structural Change in Macroeconomic Time Series,' in B.B. Rao (ed.), *Cointegration for the Applied Economist*, Basingstoke: Macmillan.

Pesaran, M. H. (1997) 'The Role of Economic Theory in Modelling the Long Run,' *Economic Journal* 107: 178–191.

Pesaran, M. H. and Pesaran, B. (1997) *Working with Microfit 4.0 Interactive Econometric Analysis*, Cambridge: Camfit Data Ltd.

Pesaran, M. H. and Shin, Y. (1998) 'Generalised Impulse Response Analysis in Linear Multivariate Models,' *Economic Letters* 58: 17–29.

Pesaran, M. H and Shin, Y. (1999) 'An Autoregressive Distributed Lag Modelling Approach to Cointegration Analysis,' in S. Strom (ed.), *Econometrics and Economic Theory in the 20th Century. The Ragnar Frisch Centennial Symposium 1998*, Cambridge: Cambridge University Press.

Pesaran, M. H., Shin, Y. and Smith, R. J. (2001) 'Bounds Testing Approaches to Analysis of Level Relationships,' *Journal of Applied Econometrics* 16: 289–326.

Phillips, P. C. B. and Perron, P. (1988) 'Testing for a Unit Root in Time Series Regression,' *Biometrika* 75: 335–346.

Phillips, P. C. B. and Hansen, B. E. (1990) 'Statistical Inference in Instrumental Variables Regression with I(1) Processes,' *Review of Economic Studies* 57: 99–125.

Posner, M. V. (1961) 'International Trade and Technical Change,' *Oxford Economic Papers* 13: 323–341.

Posner, M. V. and Steer, A. (1979) 'Price Competitiveness and Performance of Manufacturing Industry,' in F. Blackaby (ed.), *De-industrialisation*, London: Heinemann.

Prebisch, R. (1950) *The Economic Development of Latin America and its Principal Problems*, New York: ECLA, UN Department of Economic Affairs.

Pugno, M. (1996) 'A Kaldorian Model of Economic Growth with Labour Shortage and Major Technical Changes,' *Structural Change and Economic Dynamics* 7(4): 429–449.

Pugno, M. (1998) 'The Stability of Thirlwall's Model of Economic Growth and the Balance-of-Payments Constraint,' *Journal of Post Keynesian Economics* 20: 559–581, Chapter 7, this volume.

Ramírez, M. (1988) *Mexico's Economic Crisis: Its Origins and Consequences*, New York: Praeger.

Ramsey, F. P. (1928) 'A Mathematical Theory of Saving,' *Economic Journal* 38: 543–559.

Riedel, J. (1988) 'The Demand for LDC Exports of Manufactures: Estimates from Hong Kong,' *Economic Journal* 98: 138–148.

Rogoff, K. (1996) 'The Purchasing Power Parity Puzzle,' *Journal of Economic Literature* 34(2): 647–668.

Romer, P. M. (1986) 'Increasing Returns and Long-Run Growth,' *Journal of Political Economy* 94: 1002–1037.

Romer, P. M. (1990) 'Endogenous Technological Change,' *Journal of Political Economy* (Supplement): S71–S102.

Ros, J. (1997) 'Employment, Structural Adjustment and Sustainable Growth in Mexico,' *Employment and Training Papers*, 6, International Labor Office, Geneva.

Sainz, P. and Calcagno, A. (1999) 'La Economia Brasilena Ante el Plan Real y su Crisis,' *Temas de Coyuntura* 4, ECLAC, United Nations.

Salazar, J. M. (1993) 'El Resurgimiento de la Integración y el Legado de Prebisch,' *Revista de la CEPAL*.

Sarantis, N. (1990–91) 'Distribution and Terms of Trade Dynamics, Inflation and Growth,' *Journal of Post Keynesian Economics* 13(2): 175–198.

Senhadji, A. (1998) 'Time-Series Estimation of Structural Import Demand Equations: A Cross-Country Analysis,' *IMF Staff Papers* 45: 236–268.

Senhadji, A. (2000) 'Sources of Economic Growth: An Extensive Growth Accounting Exercise,' *IMF Staff Papers* 17: 1.

Severn, A. K. (1968) 'Exports and Economic Growth: Comment,' *Kyklos* 21: 546–548.

Shiller, R. J. and Perron, P. (1985) 'Testing the Random Walk Hypothesis: Power versus Frequency of Observations,' *Economics Letters* 18: 381–386.

Singh, A. (1977) 'UK Industry and the World Economy: A Case of De-industrialisation?,' *Cambridge Journal of Economics* 1(2): 113–136.

Skott, P. and Auerbach, P. (1995) 'Cumulative Causation and the "New" Theories of Economic Growth,' *Journal of Post Keynesian Economics* 17(3): 381–402.

Smith, A. P. (1976) 'Demand Management and the "New School",' *Applied Economics* 8: 193–205.

Solís, L. (1981) *Economic Policy Reform in Mexico: A Case Study for Developing Countries*, New York: Pergamon Press.

Solow, R. (1956) 'A Contribution to the Theory of Economic Growth,' *Quarterly Journal of Economics* 70: 65–94.

Spanos, A. (1986) *Statistical Foundations of Econometric Modelling*, Cambridge: Cambridge University Press.

Spanos, A. and McGuirk, A. (1999) 'The Power of Unit Root Tests Revisited,' Virginia Polytechnic Institute and State University, Department of Economics.

Srinivasan, T. N. (1995) 'Long-run Growth Theories and Empirics: Anything New?,' in T. Ito and A. Krueger (eds), *Growth Theories in Light of the East Asian Experience*, Chicago: The University of Chicago Press.

Stern, R. M., Francis, J. and Schumacher, B. (1976) *Price Elasticities in International Trade*, London: Macmillan.

Stewart, M. (1983) *Controlling the Economic Future. Policy Dilemmas in a Shrinking World*, Brighton, UK: Wheatsheaf.

Stout, D. K. (1979) 'De-industrialisation and Industrial Policy,' in F. Blackaby (ed.), *Deindustrialisation*, London: Heinemann.

Taylor, L. (1983) *Structuralist Macroeconomics*, New York: Basic Books.

Taylor, L. (1988) *Varieties of Stabilization Experiences*, Oxford: Clarendon.

Taylor, L. (1991) *Inflation, Income Distribution and Growth: Lectures on Structuralist Macroeconomic Theory*, Cambridge, MA: MIT Press.

Taylor, L. (ed.) (1993) *The Rocky Road to Reform*, Cambridge, MA: MIT Press.

Taylor, L. (1996) 'Growth, the State and Development Theory,' in A. Solimano (ed.), *Road Maps to Prosperity: Essays on Growth and Development*, Ann Arbor: The University of Michigan Press.

Taylor, M. P. (1993) 'Modelling the Demand for U.K. Money, 1871–1913,' *Review of Economics and Statistics* 76: 112–117.

Terra, C. T. (1999) 'Finance and Changing Trade Patterns in Brazil,' *Ensaios Economicos* 354, Escola de Pos-Graduacao em Economia.

Thirlwall, A. P. (1979) 'The Balance of Payments Constraint as an Explanation of International Growth Rate Differences, *Banca Nazionale del Lavoro Quarterly Review* 128: 45–53.

Thirlwall, A. P. (1980) *Balance of Payments Theory and the United Kingdom Experience*, London, Macmillan Press.

Thirlwall, A. P. (1981) 'A Reply to Mr McCombie,' *Banca Nazionale del Lavoro Quarterly Review* 139: 458–459.

Thirlwall, A. P. (1982) 'The Harrod Trade Multiplier and the Importance of Export-Led Growth,' *Pakistan Journal of Applied Economics* 1: 1–21.

Thirlwall, A. P. (1983) 'Foreign Trade Elasticities in Centre Periphery Models of Growth and Development,' *Banca Nazionale del Lavoro Quarterly Review* 146: 249–261.

Thirlwall, A. P. (1986) 'Balance of Payments Constrained Growth: A Reply to McGregor and Swales,' *Applied Economics* 18: 1259–1263.

Thirlwall, A. P. (1991) 'Professor Krugman's 45-Degree Rule,' *Journal of Post Keynesian Economics*, 14(1): 23–28.

Thirlwall, A. P. (1997) 'Reflections on the Concept of Balance-of-Payments-Constrained Growth.' *Journal of Post Keynesian Economics* 19(3): 377–385.

Thirlwall, A. P. (1999) *Growth and Development with Special Reference to Developing Countries*, 6th edn, London: Macmillan.

Thirlwall, A. P. (2001) 'The Relation Between the Warranted Growth Rate, the Natural Rate and the Balance of Payments Equilibrium Growth Rate,' *Journal of Post Keynesian Economics*, 24: 81–88.

Thirlwall, A. P. (2003) 'Old Thoughts on New Growth Theory' in N. Salvadori (ed.), *Old and New Growth Theories: An Assessment*, Cheltenham: Edward Elgar.

Thirlwall, A. P. and Dixon, R. J. (1979) 'A Model of Export-led Growth with a Balance of Payments Constraint,' in J. K. Bowers (ed.), *Inflation, Development and Integration*, Leeds, UK: Leeds University Press, pp. 173–192.

Thirlwall, A. P. and Gibson, H. D. (1992) *Balance of Payments Theory and the United Kingdom Experience*, London: Macmillan Press.

Thirlwall, A. P. and Nureldin Hussain, M. (1982) 'The Balance of Payments Constraint, Capital Flows and Growth Rate Differences between Developing Countries,' *Oxford Economic Papers* 34: 498–509, Chapter 3, this volume.

Thirlwall, A. P. and Sanna, G. (1996) 'New Growth Theory and the Macro-Determinants of Growth: An Evaluation and Further Evidence,' in P. Arestis (ed.), *Employment, Economic*

Growth and the Tyranny of the Market: Essays in Honour of Paul Davidson, Vol. 2, Cheltenham: Edward Elgar.

Tinbergen, J. (1955) *On the Theory of Economic Policy*, Amsterdam: North-Holland.

Triffin, R. (1964) *The Evaluation of the International Monetary System: Historical Reappraisal and Future Perspectives*, Princeton Studies in International Finance, 18 June.

Turner, D. (1988) 'Does the U.K. Face a Balance of Payments Constraint on Growth? A Quantitative Analysis Using the LBS and NIESR Models,' ESRC Macroeconomic Modelling Bureau, University of Warwick.

Tyson, L. D. (1992) *Who's Bashing Whom? Trade Conflict in High-Technology Industries*, Washington, DC: Institute for International Economics.

US Congressional Budget Office (CBO) (1996) *The Economic and Budget Outlook: Fiscal Years 1997–2006*, Washington, DC: US Government Printing Office, May.

US Council of Economic Advisers (1997) *Economic Report of the President*, Washington, DC: Government Printing Office.

Van der Wee, H. (1987) *Prosperity and Upheaval. The World Economy, 1945–1980*, Harmondsworth, Middlesex, UK: Penguin Books.

Van Wijnbergen, S. (1990) 'Growth, External Debt and the Real Exchange Rate in Mexico,' in D. S. Brothers and A. E. Wick (eds), *Mexico's Search for a New Development Strategy*, Boulder: Westview Press.

Van Wijnbergen, S. (1991) 'The Mexican Debt Deal,' *Economic Policy* 6: 13–43.

Wacziarg, R. (2001) 'Measuring the Dynamic Gains from Trade,' *World Bank Economic Review* 15(1): 393–429.

Warming, J. (1932) 'International Difficulties Arising out of Financing of Public Works During Depression,' *Economic Journal* 41: 211–224.

Wells, J. and Imber, J. (1977) 'Home and Export Performance of UK Industries,' *Economic Trends* 286: 78–81.

Williamson, J. (1984) 'Is there an External Constraint?,' *National Institute Economic Review* 109: 73–77.

Wilson, T. (1976) 'Effective Devaluation and Inflation,' *Oxford Economic Papers* 28(1): 1–24.

World Bank (1987) *World Development Report 1987*, Oxford: Oxford University Press.

World Bank (1993) *The Asian Miracle*, Oxford: Oxford University Press.

World Bank (1995) *El Salvador: Meeting the Challenge of Globalization*, Washington, DC: World Bank Document 2.

World Development Report (2000/2001) 'Attacking Poverty,' *World Bank*, New York: Oxford University Press.

Young, A. (1994) 'Lessons from East Asian NICs: A Contrarian View,' *European Economic Review* 38: 964–973.

Young, A. (1995) 'The Tyranny of Numbers: Confronting the Statistical Realities of the East Asian Growth Experience,' *Quarterly Journal of Economics* 110: 641–680.

Ziesemer, T. (1995) 'Growth with Imported Capital Goods, Limited Export Demand and Foreign Debt,' *Journal of Macroeconomics* 17: 31–53.

Index